*Hope Fulfilled for
At-Risk and
Violent Youth*

The book provides an excellent review of the school dropout crisis and discusses how so many youth have failed in our schools. It presents an array of effective interventions and programs at all school levels for youth in at-risk situations that all schools and communities should have as part of their comprehensive education program.

The book captures dozens of ideas about how to restructure and improve public schools and includes many proven practices and strategies for school leaders. It is a wonderful guide for school and community leaders to use as tool to redesign their prevention and intervention programs for youth in at-risk situations.

For those school leaders who have the will to address the unique needs of youth in at-risk situations, this book is a must-read because it presents research-based strategies to build successful school programs that will increase the graduation rate.

Jay Smink
Executive Director
National Dropout Prevention Center/Network
Clemson University, Clemson, South Carolina

Do you want to make a difference with challenging youngsters? This book will help—a lot. It's compelling, practical, specific and hopeful. The authors go beyond rhetoric. They use research and experience to show that committed, knowledgeable educators can make a huge difference.

Joe Nathan, Director
Center for School Change, University of Minnesota

If you're concerned about helping at risk kids at the secondary level, you should read and implement the suggestions of this book. They work.

Jerry Hartsock
Recipient of the 1993 Milken Family Foundation
National Educator Award (at the time, principal,
Austin E. Lathrop High School, Fairbanks, AK)
Principal, Walled Lake Middle School
Walled Lake, Michigan

Hope Fulfilled for At-Risk and Violent Youth

K–12 Programs That Work

Second Edition

Robert D. Barr

William H. Parrett

Boise State University

Allyn and Bacon

Boston • London • Toronto • Sydney • Tokyo • Singapore

Senior editor: Virginia Lanigan
Series editorial assistant: Jennifer Connors
Manufacturing buyer: Suzanne Lareau
Marketing manager: Stephen Smith

Between the time website information is gathered and then published, it is not unusual
for some sites to have closed. Also, the transcription of URLs can result in unintended
typographical errors. The publisher would appreciate notification where these
occur so that they may be corrected in subsequent editions. Thank you.

Library of Congress Cataloging-in-Publication Data

Barr, Robert D.
    Hope fulfilled for at-risk and violent youth : K–12 programs that work / Robert D. Barr,
William H. Parrett.—2nd ed.
      p. cm.
    Rev. ed. of: Hope at last for at-risk youth. c1995.
    Includes bibliographical references and index.
    ISBN 0-205-30886-4
    1. Problem children—Education—United States.   2. Problem youth—Education—
United States.   3. Socially handicapped children—Education—United States.   4. Socially
handicapped youth—Education—United States.   I. Parrett, William.   II. Barr, Robert D.
Hope at last for at-risk youth.   III. Title.

LC4802 .B37 2001
371.93—dc21
                                                    00-042137

Printed in the United States of America
10 9 8 7 6 5 4 3 2 1   04 03 02 01 00

Contents

Preface and Acknowledgments

During the early hours of a misty February morning, a policeman spotted a suspicious looking car parked in the shadows at the side of the street. After pulling over, the young policeman tugged down his bulletproof vest, climbed out of his patrol car, and walked back to take a look. As he bent down to talk to the driver, he was shot at least three times in the face and fell dead. What makes this event so chilling is that the scene was not played out in Los Angeles or South Chicago, Detroit or Dallas, and the accused murderer was not a gang member or some drug-crazed addict. The policeman was gunned down in the small rural town of New Plymouth, Idaho, surrounded by the rich, fertile farmlands of the irrigated high desert just outside of the state capital, Boise. The person arrested for the murder was a 14-year-old boy out for a joyride in a stolen car with two of his pals. The newspaper quoted his single mother as saying, "I just couldn't do anything with him." Even though juvenile authorities had received a tip that the youth was carrying a weapon, they were far too busy to check out just another anonymous phone call. School officials explained that the boy almost never came to school. "We really didn't know him," they said.

Similar tragedies are turning up everywhere these days. Savage acts of school violence have swept the country, and what has been so shocking is that this violence has not been occurring in the desolate inner cities of the nation, but turning up in suburbs and quiet rural communities. At Columbine High School in Littleton, Colorado, Thurston High School in Springfield, Oregon, as well as the small communities of Jonesboro, Arkansas; Paducah, Kentucky; and Pearl, Mississippi, the teenage murderers appear to be just like the kid next door. Suddenly every parent and grandparent has been confronted with the very real possibility that such violence can happen anywhere: it can happen in their town, in their community, and in their schools. Suddenly adults everywhere are worrying about the safety of their kids. But school violence is just the sensational tip of a large and disturbing iceberg of risky and dangerous youth behavior. News stories have reported that the number of prison cells in state after state have doubled in recent years. During an 18-month period, youth gangs all but overwhelmed schools in Salt Lake City, Utah. There were television stories about a rash of teen suicides in Plano, Texas, and in another Texas community, an entire squad of high-school cheerleaders became pregnant. A national magazine reported that 20 percent of the first graders in a small town outside Columbus, Ohio, had been held back a grade because they could not read. And during the last decade, as the National Center for Disease Control has systematically charted the troubling increases in risky and dangerous behaviors of our nation's adolescents. It is increasingly evident that life in the United States has changed and a grim future is suddenly upon us.

Choose almost any community in the nation. Walk into one of the local schools, sit down and talk to the teachers. The story these days is almost always the same: too many kids arriving at school unprepared to learn; too many failing their courses; too many dropping out of school; overwhelming numbers of students living in poverty or in dysfunctional homes; growing numbers of students who rarely come to school, and when they do, disrupt the orderly learning of the others. Too many students are increasingly violent; too many carry weapons each day; too many are becoming pregnant; too many are influenced by drugs and alcohol.

Teachers throughout the United States tell the same stories. Their classrooms include more and more children and youth who are dangerously at risk of not gaining an adequate education and who are doomed to live out their lives underemployed, unemployed, or unemployable. Technology, international competition, and the information age have quietly closed the door of opportunity on all of these tragic youth. These at-risk kids confront public schools with some of the most difficult and complex problems our educational system has ever faced. Dealing with these problems poses for schools and communities a complex array of moral, ethical, and educational dilemmas.

In addressing these problems, schools often turn to special education for help, and as a result there has been a huge increase in the number of students identified as learning disabled, hyperactive, suffering from attention deficit disorder, attachment disorders, or a host of other disabilities. Some schools simply cannot tolerate these youth and have segregated them into slow learning tracks or expelled them. The vast majority of schools, lacking any other strategy, simply retain them in hopes that a second time through will prove more successful than the first. Part of the problem is the pulling apart of our society. In the middle of the greatest economic boom in the history of our country, a large percentage of our working citizens have seen a decline in their annual buying power. A dramatic pulling apart is occurring as the middle class and rich grow ever richer, while the lower middle class and those living at poverty level descend further and further into economic depression. For many, this economic decline is accompanied by the barrage of problems that are associated with poverty: child abuse; drug and alcohol abuse; teenage pregnancies; disruptive and often violent and criminal behavior; and school failure. With the opportunities for the American dream of the good economic life depending more and more on high-quality education and technical skills, it is increasingly essential that all children and youth learn effectively and achieve high academic standards.

Education is the single door of opportunity to success in our technical world. Yet, too many children born into poverty arrive at school unprepared to learn, confronting schools with the difficult challenges associated with their lives, and unfortunately failing to succeed or thrive in our public schools.

This book offers a dramatic, essential message to schools and communities: help is finally available for addressing the difficult, complex issues associated with children and youth at risk. At last we know what to do and how to do it. This book represents a major effort to find, describe, and integrate what we know about effective programs for at-risk youth. It represents a careful effort to provide schools and communities with specific, practical, down-to-earth information about what works and what does not. This book will prove useful to schools and communities in their quest to teach at-risk students at every level. It should help teachers and administrators to decide what to do today, next Monday, and next year. It includes suggestions for parents, descriptions of specific programs that teach all children to read, where to go for help, and the best we know about combatting youth violence. The book also provides specific directions for reforming the educational process to ensure success for at-risk youth.

Guaranteeing Success

This book provides, perhaps for the first time, a comprehensive review of evidence regarding effective programs for at-risk youth that makes it finally possible to speak with authority and assurance that effective programs can indeed be developed. Now, all children can be guaranteed success in school, even those who have been considered to be severely at risk. This guarantee has only recently become possible as an emerging body of evidence documents in the most forceful way that our educational structure does indeed possess the resources to promise school success for all children.

Others have offered a guarantee. Robert Slavin states that with the exception of severely mentally impaired youth, schools can now teach all children to read. He further argues that it is the entitlement of every child in the United States to learn to read. Slavin and his colleagues at Johns Hopkins University have documented that the Success for All Schools approach is, in fact, effectively teaching severely at-risk youth to read, youth who for decades have been considered unable to learn. The Reading Recovery program represents yet another approach which has demonstrated that we do possess the knowledge and programs to teach all youth to read, most within a 16-week period. Add to these successes the fact that some schools, like the Hawthorne Elementary School in Seattle, an inner-city elementary school serving primarily African American children, do promise to parents that their children will learn to read. They even guarantee it.

Perhaps most important, in the late 1990s, over a dozen reports were published that systematically analyzed a wide variety of school reform efforts, instructional approaches, and curriculum materials on the basis of how well each approach improved student achievement. The focus on student achievement is likely to become the basis for decision making in schools and to provide greater confidence in predicting educational outcomes.

Stop at any bookstore selling current educational materials and you will notice a number of publications that document and declare that we now possess the ability to teach all students. Recent titles such as *Every Child Can Learn, Every Child Can Succeed, What Works, Schools That Work,* and *Public Schools That Work* represent a growing number of books, articles, and reports identifying schools and programs throughout the United States where all children and youth are succeeding. During the past 25 years, thousands of alternative public schools, magnet schools, experimental schools, and other non-traditional programs have been developed and documented to be effective in teaching reluctant learners.

The 1993 Louisiana School Effectiveness Study, a 10-year qualitative and quantitative research effort involving schools in all types of communities, went even further. The study reported that certain schools, even local elementary schools, were effectively teaching all types of children and documented that these schools were successful regardless of the home situation or the socioeconomic status of the family. In another major study by the Education Trust in 1999, hundreds of public schools were identified throughout the United States that were previously low performing schools in poor communities, and which had been transformed into high performing schools. Similar results have been reported from in-depth, long-term case studies of junior-high, high-school, and K-12 alternative and magnet schools. Such definitive evidence provides the foundation for ensuring, guaranteeing if you will, the success of all children, particularly those who have been considered at risk. If some schools can be successful with all children and youth and if we identify and understand the program characteristics that are essential to that success, then it is finally possible that other schools can do the same. This recent development indeed presents a landmark opportunity and challenge to public education throughout the United States.

There is a "catch" to all this optimism. None of this is easy. To be successful with all children and youth demands that schools must start as early as possible, work extensively with parents and the larger community, provide long-term comprehensive support, and significantly change the teaching and learning process that has traditionally been used in public schools. To ensure success, schools and communities must relentlessly pursue excellence in their programs. A review of the material found in this book is also quite clear regarding school reform. To be successful with at-risk youth, schools must be significantly restructured at every school level. Public schools, as they have been traditionally organized and structured, not only do not work for at-risk youth, they often contribute to many of the problems at-risk students encounter. Schools must eliminate programs and practices that discriminate against at-risk youth, and they must redesign and restructure the traditional teaching and learning approach that has been used for so long in public education. To do less is unacceptable.

Why Read This Book

Hope Fulfilled for At-Risk and Violent Youth delivers an unprecedented synthesis of the research efforts of others, evaluations of effective school programs and practices from throughout the country, descriptions of promising practices that have yet to be fully evaluated, and a collection of the authors' personal anecdotes and experiences with teachers and at-risk students in schools and communities throughout the nation.

This book started as a highly focused effort to collect, analyze, synthesize, and interpret the research on at-risk children and youth. While the authors were at times overwhelmed by the sheer volume of research, reports, publications, scholarly papers, and monographs on the topic, much of what was found proved to be far too narrow or esoteric to be of great value to the real, complex world of schools, teachers, and students. As the authors began to spread out before them what could be gleaned from this rich array of research about at-risk youth, it was evident that huge pieces to the puzzle were missing. There were still as many questions as there were answers.

To fill these gaping holes and try to find specific answers to the hard questions facing schools or even indicators that could guide decisions, the authors turned to school and program evaluations, student assessment data, and program descriptions that seemed to hold promise for at-risk youth. It was out of this composite blend of data and insight that comprehensive patterns began to emerge. Out of the confusion regarding at-risk youth, a gestalt of order began to fall into place. As each new piece to the puzzle was added, as programs at each school level were identified and analyzed, we began to think of our work as a comprehensive, detailed, fine-lined structure of an educational blueprint. It was finally possible to begin to plan with confidence, to predict results.

The book begins with a review of the crisis which has resulted from so many youth who have failed in school. The first two chapters analyze the crisis in terms of the larger context of national and international developments in technology, changes in the economic marketplace, and social changes in the family that have created an escalating set of complex problems for schools everywhere. Criteria are presented to help schools and communities identify and anticipate at-risk students and their needs. Chapter 3 reviews the world of violent and violence-prone youth and represents a comprehensive review of what is known about the dramatic challenges confronting public schools—and what effective interventions are available. Chapter 4 reviews efforts toward improving and reforming public schools and specifically documents how traditional school programs, even those with the best of intentions, have failed the very students that they were attempting to help.

Chapter 5 provides a synthesis of what we know about children and youth at risk and includes a detailed description of the essential components of effective programs for at-risk youth. Descriptions of effective programs and conceptual models for kindergarten, elementary, middle/junior high, and high schools are presented in Chapters 6, 7 and 8. This review offers the most comprehensive effort available to date, in identifying effective programs at each of the school levels.

Chapter 9 offers distinctly new ideas about how to restructure and improve public schools, and Chapter 10 presents urgent imperatives critical to the future of public education. Appendix A provides a resource guide to technical assistance and university research centers, and foundations that have established at-risk youth as a funding priority. The book concludes with self-evaluation checklists for K-12 educators, parents, and community members designed to assist school improvement efforts to help students at risk.

Hope Fulfilled for At-Risk and Violent Youth presents a precise, step-by-step set of descriptions and options that should guide schools toward the development of successful programs for at-risk youth. This book represents the first comprehensive effort to synthesize an era of study, experimentation, and practice toward improving educational opportunities for at-risk youth. The result presents a landmark opportunity for schools and communities to finally develop schools that effectively teach all youth.

During the past five years, since the first edition of this book was published, a preponderance of educational research has continued to inform the field of at-risk and violent youth. Also during this time, thousands of public schools in every section of the country have conclusively demonstrated and documented that all children can learn, even the most seriously at risk. Research and evaluation have provided detailed identification and explanation of why these schools are so successful and how other schools can replicate their remarkable successes. This ever growing body of research, evaluation, and practice has taken the nation's public schools far beyond "hope" for at-risk youth; it has documented that the hope has been "fulfilled." We now know beyond a shadow of doubt that all children can learn, that effective schools can overcome the debilitating effects of poverty and dysfunctional families, and we know exactly what schools must do to accomplish this reality. What remains is the collective will to act. The great question that confronts our society at the beginning of the twenty-first century is whether or not schools and communities have the strength and commitment to aggressively step forward to restructure their schools and address the needs of at-risk and violent children and youth.

Acknowledgments

There is an old Texas "poor boy" depression-day story that we have all heard dozens of times. Most recently the story appeared in the periodical, *Texas Monthly,* as told by the senior United States senator from the state, Phil Gramm. The Senator from Texas explains that he had already failed the third, seventh, and ninth grades. The story always begins with a student who is doing poorly in school. Somewhere along the line the school calls the parents in for a meeting and explains that their child will never be a doctor or an engineer and should, in fact, be transferred to some type of vocational training or trade school program. "Your child," the school official says, "lacks the ability to ever graduate from high school." At this point, the mother leans across the table and in a voice quivering with anger, explains to the teacher or administrator in no uncertain terms, "In our family, I'll have you know, we don't believe in ability!" Mrs. Gramm, like so many parents, knew that determination was far more important than some educator's opinion about a child's ability.

This book is dedicated to all of those at-risk students, both past and present, who were believed to not have the ability to succeed in school but did. The authors have known and taught many of these students. A number of these students are anonymously described in this book. They include the youth who have graduated from Meridian Academy in Idaho, the St. Paul Open School, Portland's Vocational Village and Metropolitan Learning Center, Pan Terra, the schools in the Louisiana School Effectiveness Study, the Alternative Schools in East Harlem, and other programs throughout the United States. This is their story.

The authors have many people to thank for their help in researching and writing this book. The first edition of this book was researched and written in several distinct stages. The project was started at Oregon State University in 1987 when Ron and Sonya Darling walked into the office of Robert Barr, then dean of the College of Education, and donated $50,000 to fund efforts to address the problems of at-risk youth. With this generous gift and an additional matching grant from Oregon State University and the Oregon State System of Higher Education, the At-Risk Youth Technical Assistance Center was created. William Parrett helped to launch the center.

The first edition provided a comprehensive review of research and evaluation and on-site interviews in more than 200 schools throughout the country. Since the publication of the first edition, the authors have served as advisors to states, school districts, schools, legislators, and educational policy makers throughout the United States. They have worked with schools in more than 30 states and have been part of safe school efforts in Connecticut, South Carolina, and Kentucky. Bob Barr was appointed by the governor of Idaho to chair the 1999 Idaho Task Force on Safe Schools. The authors have been invited and have recently shared their work with the National School Board Association, the American Association of School Administrators, the American Education Research Association, the Association of Supervision and Curriculum Development, the National Conference on At-Risk Youth, the National Boundary-Breaking Schools Conferences, the International Alternative Schools Annual Conferences, and at state conferences on reading, and alternative education, and at-risk youth over the past three years.

The second edition of this book was researched and written at Boise State University's Center for School Improvement. A number of people were vital to the completion of this work. Sarita Whitmire, our lead research assistant, coordinated the massive amount of material reviewed. Other research and editorial assistants included Carrie Nielson, Diana Esbensen, Carol Peterson, Myrna Avila, Roxane Bennett, Ann Winslow, Julie Hutchinson, Anabel Navarro, and Shelli Rambo. Rose Crabtree, the word processor extraordinaire, compiled the manuscript.

A number of other colleagues and peers from throughout the country helped us think through problems and provided opportunities to consider various issues. They included: Idaho—Governor Dirk Kempthorne, Scott Willison, Monty Styles, Roger Stewart, Phil Kelly, Glenn Potter, Marilyn Reynolds, Bob Taylor, Fred Tilman, Darrel Burbank, Sam Byrd, Carolyn Thorsen, Sue B. Wade, Sharron Jarvis, Sally Anderson,

Jack Rucker, Craig Moore, Tom and Pam Rybus; Oregon—Rick Stiggins, Mike Harris, Paul Erickson, Chet Edwards, Paula Kinney; Iowa—Clemmye Jackson, Ray Morley, Fenwick English, Betty Steffy, Scott Gill; Kentucky—Bill Scott, Jo O'Brien, Dan Orman, Robert Cole, Melissa Abernathy; Michigan—Dan Diedrich, Jerry Hartsock, Carole Evans; Indiana—Bill Barton, Scott Williams, Bruce Ottenweller, Jeff Jones; Oklahoma—Sylvia Olsen, Richard Palazzo; Arizona—Karen Butterfield, Jana Kooi, Angela Palmer; Minnesota—Joe Nathan, Wayne Jennings, Bill Zimniewitz; Louisiana—Felicia Rapp, Alice Somler; Florida—Al Narverez, Stephen Stark; Connecticut—Jane Carlin, Cheryl Saloom, Cate Boone; South Carolina—Jennifer Kahn, Jay Smink, Catherine Samulski, Rayburn Barton; New Mexico—Virginia Trujillo, Elizabeth Orteca, Dusty Huckabee; Georgia—Jeff Chandler, Sybil Fickle, Dan Rea, Robert Warkentin; Wisconsin—Sandra Shavlik; Alaska—Steve Jackstadt, Bill McDiarmid, Ernie Manzie; Washington—Gloria Pumphrey, Dick Sagor, Gary Sotomish, Jim Parsley, Jerry Conrath; Hawaii—Mary Ann Raywid, Jan Zulich; Texas—Leo Barrera, Anna Moczygemba; California—John Hall, William Chiment, Yvonne Chan, Lee Jenkins; Colorado—Arnie Langberg, Jim Griffin, Peter Toleson; New York—Greg Farrell; Japan—Katsuhiko Yamashita, Kazuyuki Tanimoto, Shinichi Yasutomo, Kazuyuki Tamai, and, in Toronto, Michael Fullan of the Ontario Institute for studies in education.

The production staff of Allyn and Bacon, particularly our senior editor, Virginia Lanigan, and her editorial assistant, Jennifer Connors, provided valuable support throughout this project for which we are most appreciative.

The heroes of this book are of course the many scholars, policy makers, teachers, and administrators whose work we have attempted to collect, understand, and interpret. These pioneers of school improvement include James Comer, Robert Slavin and his colleagues at Johns Hopkins University, Hank Levin and his associates at Stanford, Gary Wehlage and Fred Newman and their associates at the University of Wisconsin in Madison's Center on Organization and Restructuring Schools, and, Joe Nathan of the Hubert Humphrey Center at the University of Minnesota. We also drew heavily on the works of Lisbeth Schorr, who speaks and writes so eloquently and with such hope for at-risk youth.

The authors are deeply appreciative of the understanding and encouragement provided by our families. Finally and most important of all were Beryl Barr and Ann Dehner, who encouraged and supported us through yet "another" book project, and our children, Bonny, Brady, Jerry, Mei Lin, Sam, Sadie, Mia, and Jonathan.

Chapter 1

The Crisis of At-Risk Children and Youth

I just don't know what I'm going to do. Every year, my first grade class has more and more of these kids. They don't seem to care about right or wrong, they don't care about adult approval, they are disruptive, they can't read and they arrive at school absolutely unprepared to learn. Who are these kids? Where do they come from? Why are there more and more of them? I used to think that I was a good teacher. I really prided myself on doing an outstanding job. But I find I'm working harder and harder, and being less and less effective. A good teacher? Today I really don't know. I do know that my classroom is being overwhelmed by society's problems and I don't understand it. What's happening to our schools? What's happening to society? I don't understand all of this and I sure don't know what we're going to do about it.
—*ELEMENTARY TEACHER, ATLANTA, GEORGIA*

Y2K arrived in the United States amid a continuing technological revolution and a time of unmatched economic prosperity. The new millennium also ushered in a growing national crisis that threatens the nation's future. Not a foreign war or an impending invasion, this crisis originates from within; it originates from our own neglect. The crisis centers on the role of education in the contemporary world, those who have it, and the cruel consequences to those who do not. Education has been transformed from one of the avenues to economic success to an exclusive door of opportunity for achieving the good life. Those who have education may access the incredible richness of economic opportunity in the United States; those without

1

it are doomed to a life of economic servitude or even worse. Because of this, our nation is being pulled apart, with a growing chasm between the economically upwardly mobile and a growing underclass of Americans who live out their lives trapped in a tragic ghetto of ignorance and economic want. This social and economic division that is occurring in our country grows out of our unwillingness to educate all our children. It is a crisis that places our nation at risk.

There is a renewed hope and vision for the solution of this crisis as the spotlight of national attention increasingly focuses on those youth who have not been successful in public education. Many times our nation has attempted to address this problem. Thirty years ago, it was part of the "war on poverty"; more recently, it has been part of the war on drugs. It might be better defined as a battle for survival in the international marketplace. Yet today, researchers have finally determined solutions that can address the problems of the at-risk and violent youth effectively and immediately. By the mid-1990s there was sufficient evidence to conclude that there was at last hope for our at-risk children and youth. Thousands of schools have been identified in every section of the nation where hope has been *fulfilled,* where hope has given way to proven performance. "All children learning effectively" is no longer an educational theory; it has become a proven fact of life. "Hope" for at-risk students is no longer sufficient; effective learning by all students is now expected.

Twenty years ago, the problem centered on poor and minority youth, but social and economic changes in the world have greatly expanded that target group. At first these youth were referred to as socially and culturally "deprived"; later on, as racial consciousness raised, the terminology changed to that of "disadvantaged." More recently, these students are described as the "disengaged" or "disconnected" youth of the United States.

Even more disturbing, there has been a growing realization that it is not just the poor or minority student who is of concern. Today, we recognize that any young person may become at risk. At various times in the life of all youth, there are episodes of disappointment and sometimes depression; there are encounters and pressures relating to alcohol, drugs, and the possibility of teenage parenthood. With the occurrence of widespread sexually transmitted disease and a startling increase in teenage suicide, the risks now facing our youths have become a matter of life and death. It is now clear that students who are at risk are not limited to any single group. They cut across all social classes and occur in every ethnic group. And while many at-risk youth can be identified, often with frightening accuracy, a vast number of youth, in contrast to all the predictive research, may frequently be endangered by their own behavior by placing themselves in the "risky business" of sex, drugs, and alcohol or by reacting negatively to upheavals in their home and family.

Yet to recognize that all youth can, at one time or another, become at risk cannot cause educators to overlook the fact that we can identify with high predictability a large group of students who arrive at school each year with little or no hope of success in school or productivity in later life. It is this growing group that we can no longer afford to ignore.

The term *at risk,* originally coined almost two decades ago, has found its way into the national vocabulary. But regardless of what others might call them, teachers have always known these kids. They have known them as disinterested and disruptive, as those students who refused to learn, and as those who they thought could not learn. And they have known these students as those who, by their presence, have made teaching and learning so difficult for all the rest.

Over the past two decades the nation's perspective toward and understanding of these youth have begun to change. In the 1960s, responsibility for failure in school seemed to be assigned to the student and his or her tragic social situation. Everyone knew that "something was wrong with them"; they were deprived, disadvantaged, or just plain "dumb." If these students did not learn in school, it was their fault, not the fault of the schools. We now know that we were wrong, and we know how destructive this attitude has been.

Regardless of what the in-vogue terminology happens to be, we now know far better who these youth are and the extent of their worsening problems. It is not just that some students may be illiterate or disruptive or pregnant or in danger of dropping out or have already left school. Now, we are beginning to understand that the problems associated with these youth threaten to overwhelm our schools, diminish our economy, and potentially paralyze our society. Evidence of the crisis is visible in many of the inner-city schools and communities in our nation's urban areas. Inside these schools, absenteeism and failure rates overwhelm successes; in the communities outside the school, unemployment, crime, drugs, and despair have all but destroyed the social fabric. Too many adults continue to believe that these problems are occurring only to tragic youth in Milwaukee or Miami or Los Angeles. Increasingly, we recognize that they are happening in all communities and may in fact include that kid stretched out in our own front room watching MTV.

Why Be Concerned about At-Risk Youth?

> *I asked the seventh-grade boy how he was doing. He shrugged his shoulders and mumbled, "Okay, I guess." "I understand that your mom is a single parent," I said, "and that she works as a waitress every night." He shrugged again and nodded his head. "That must be kind of tough?" I said. "Well, not really," he said. "I get my little brother to bed around 9:30 or 10:00 and then I can kick back, have a smoke, and catch a little tube. It's not so bad."*
> —*MIDDLE SCHOOL STUDENT, BOISE, IDAHO*

The problem is not simply that some students are doing poorly in school. The problems relate to all youth who are in danger of not just failing and dropping out of school, but of entering adulthood illiterate, dependent upon drugs and alcohol, unemployed or underemployed, as a teenage parent, dependent on public support, or adjudicated by the criminal justice system. Fred Newman, director of The Center on Organization and Restructuring of Schools at the University of Wisconsin, Madison, has argued for years that these students "are being 'disconnected' from the functions of society, not just from economic productivity, but from the functions of citizens in a democracy" (Newman, 1987, p. 3). The essential knowledge and skills needed to participate adequately in contemporary life have expanded far beyond the grasp of a large number of young Americans.

There exists an expanding underclass of youth who will live their lives in the United States and never work. Many of them will fill our prisons, others will demand growing health, welfare, and social services. We will support them and their children in a widening generational cycle of despair. Teenage parents tend to have a second child, and when that occurs, they tend to need public assistance for a minimum of 10 years. Over 80 percent of the inmates of America's prisons are high-school dropouts and more than 50 percent are illiterate. During the last decade the number of prison cells has doubled in many states such as New York, where prison spending tripled between the years of 1982 and 1991. During the same period, drug-related crime grew by 350 percent while public school expenditures grew by only 80 percent (State of New York Executive Budget, 1993–94).

It is now apparent that, throughout our country, we are building prisons rather than schools. Surveys of state legislatures as early as 1993 documented a significant shift of resources from education to the escalating cost of health, welfare, and corrections, and the shift continues (State Policy Research, 1993). This shift from educational support to the increasing cost of social programs vividly portrays the cost of not dealing with at-risk youth during the school years. Clearly the age-old adage is correct: *either we pay now or we pay later.* Either communities invest in educational prevention and intervention at the preschool, elementary, and secondary years, or they must confront the escalating cost of dealing with the lifelong needs and problems of these individuals through health, public assistance, police, and prison interventions.

The shift away from increases in educational funding also reflects the growing taxpayer revolt over the funding of public schools. The revolt started in California more than two decades ago with the enactment of Proposition 13. The resistance to taxes continues to gather momentum to this very day, as evidenced by the property tax limitation (Measure 5) passed in the State of Oregon in 1990 and legislative action in Michigan toward abolishing state property tax as a means of funding public education.

In the fall of 1992 California voted down a statewide voucher plan that would have allowed parents to "invest their vouchers" in either the public or private education of their children. Even though all are being tested in the courts, the states of Wisconsin, Florida, and Ohio had all passed voucher legislation, initiating a landmark trend of allocating public funds to private schools. These developments reflect a continuing citizen concern regarding the rising costs of funding public schools— the same schools where the majority of our at-risk children are enrolled.

While challenges mount and controversy continues over the funding of public education, the number of at-risk youth is increasing dramatically in our nation's schools and communities. Educators no longer talk about the one or two percent of their students who are troublemakers. Discussion has shifted to the 15 to 30 percent of the school population who are dropping out. Many educators have argued that the schools are really serving only those American youth who will someday graduate from college. The late Albert Shanker of the American Federation of Teachers stressed that the American public schools have never "really educated more than 15 to 20 percent of the kids of this country" (Miller, 1988, p. 48). Most would agree that school curriculum and graduation requirements continue to be focused primarily on the needs of those students who will someday go off to college. For the rest of the school student body, which Dale Parnell, former president of the American Community College Association, calls the "neglected majority," the school curriculum may be virtually unrelated to their needs and the needs of the marketplace (Parnell, 1982). We now are beginning to understand that those who are at risk are all youth who are unable to function effectively in the modern world, even many who have graduated from high school. The proportion of these youth continues to increase as a result of what some critics have referred to as a "plague of ignorance" (Bell & Elmquist, 1991, p. 1).

Growing Diversity

Each year our classrooms contain increased numbers of poor, non-English speaking, mainstream handicapped, culturally different, and single-parent children. Five states will soon have minority majorities (California, Arizona, New Mexico, Texas, and Florida) and in over 30 of the largest school districts in the United States, Caucasian students have become the minority (U.S. Department of Commerce, 1999; Hodgkinson, 1985).

Public education as a viable option for many has vanished. Increasing numbers of the parents who can afford it or who can obtain vouchers are leaving public education and enrolling their children in private and parochial schools; others have resorted to home schooling. Middle-class parents are having fewer children and the trend of many upwardly mobile couples having no children continues. The vast majority of parents of school-age children work, resulting in more and more children who return home at the end of the day to an empty home or apartment.

Shifting Demographics

A review of demographic data concerning U.S. society documents an incredible new world that is emerging in our midst:

- For the first time people over 65 years of age now outnumber teenagers.
- The median age of the U.S. population is 30 years today, in a decade it will be 35, and in less than three decades it is estimated that it will be 40.
- Fewer than half of all married couples have children.

- The fastest growing category of households is the childless one.
- Almost half of all households in the United States since 1980 consist of a single person living alone.
- After World War II, up to 70 percent of the adult population had children in school; today only 28 percent have children. Sixty-four percent of all households have no children at all.
- It is estimated that as of the year 2000, 42 percent of the students enrolled in public schools will be black or Hispanic.
- As of the year 2000, approximately 47 percent of the U.S. workforce were women.
- As of the year 2000, African Americans and Hispanics will make up one-third of the new entrants into the workforce.
- The number of adults incarcerated in federal prisons or in local jails has risen dramatically in recent decades. In 1980 there were 500,000 men and women in prisons or jails; in 1990 the number was 1,146,401; in 1999, 1,800,000. On a per capita basis, this means one out of every 150 people in the United States is incarcerated, second only to the former USSR.

These data depict a new society of haves and have-nots, a society growing older and older, with fewer people having a direct vested interest in supporting schools with adequate taxes to upgrade equipment and facilities, and provide necessary school programs and services.

The result of these shifts in our nation's demography is that today's public school classrooms are characterized by diminished parental involvement and support. Classrooms are filled with a growing percentage of students who are at risk of failing, dropping out of school, and disconnecting from society. Public schools continually report alarming incidences of violence, alcohol and drug abuse, and problems of discipline and disruption. Nearly every major city in America has begun to experience the type of youth gangs previously known only in Los Angeles. Drive-by shootings and carjackings have become common in more and more communities. Children are carrying guns and killing each other as well as adults. Violence in schools has catapulted into the nation's consciousness as the number-one concern in schools. Metal detectors are becoming commonplace even in elementary schools. Never before have so many youth contemplated and attempted suicide; never have so many been so tragically successful.

There may have been a time, a generation or so ago, when dropping out of school posed no great problem and carried little or no stigma. At the beginning of the twentieth century, over 90 percent of school-age youth dropped out of school but found almost unlimited opportunities to work in the forests, fields, and factories of America. As recently as the 1950s, when the national dropout rate hovered at 50 percent, there were still good jobs available for those leaving school early. Unfortunately, those opportunities are rapidly disappearing, and today they exist only for a very small percentage of our youth. The jobs that are available for our undereducated youth pay minimum wage with few benefits and are insufficient for supporting a family or household.

Demands of the Changing Marketplace

Technological advances in today's marketplace demand more sophisticated skills and abilities. In 1960 there were no industrial robots; today there are more than 20 million. In 1980 there were no cellular telephones in the United States; today there are more than 15 million. Since 1970 computers have gone from the size of a two-story building weighing the equivalent of 16 tractor-trailer trucks to the size of a dime that can be enclosed in a greeting card and then tossed away. The World Wide Web is the dominating medium of the world and increasingly drives the economic marketplace. Suddenly in the late 1990s there were on-line internet courses for public schools as well as colleges, new on-line high schools, university graduate and undergraduate degree programs, and even an emerging "virtual university."

Technology has transformed all agricultural work, replacing almost all field-workers with machines to plant and harvest oranges, cherries, apples, potatoes, onions . . . and on and on. Technology has largely replaced humans with robots on the production line of everything from the manufacturing of laser printers, to automobiles, and even to premanufactured homes. The jobs that are available demand increasingly sophisticated skills in monitoring and maintaining the machines, robots, and computers that do our work.

Technology is demanding more sophisticated skills and abilities at an accelerating rate. There are dramatically diminishing opportunities for U.S. workers in the production of steel, automobiles, agriculture, wood products, and petroleum—once the backbone of the U.S. economy and of the middle class. Increasingly, the jobs available to those with little sophisticated education and training are service-oriented minimum-wage jobs with little or no opportunity for advancement, health care, or retirement benefits. Even the U.S. military, which traditionally offered career opportunities and job training for many dropouts, will no longer accept applicants, even if they possess the general equivalency diploma. Like business and industry, the U.S. armed forces wants only the best and brightest.

The military does not want at-risk youth, and the same is true of business and industry. In the past, the federal government has discovered that employers cannot be paid to take these youth as employees. No one wants to employ these youth. So often, even special school programs do not want these youth. Even public school vocational education programs, originally created to serve the noncollege bound student, currently enroll an unusually small percentage of at-risk youth.

Sudden changes in the marketplace have attracted the interest of business and industry in relation to the at-risk youth of our society. Many of the nation's CEOs now argue that, "the American work force is running out of qualified people. If current demographic trends continue, American business will have to hire a million new workers a year who cannot read, write or count. To train these workers will cost more than 25 billion dollars a year" (Miller, 1988, p. 48). By the year 2000, the economic boom in the United States had exacerbated the problem of shortages of skilled workers and led to growing pressure to relax immigration laws to increase the number of technology workers in targeted areas.

Vanishing Opportunities for Unskilled Workers

To a very real extent our nation was built by a mass of people who dropped out of school and through hard manual labor and little or no formal education earned a decent wage, served in the armed forces, bought their family a home, owned a car, a truck, and sometimes an RV and boat, and one day sent their kids off to college. This is the stuff of the American dream, and it has disappeared. The optimism of the past is being replaced by declining opportunities for uneducated workers. Today, high school graduates earn less in real dollars than high school dropouts of two decades ago. The promise of America to the high school dropout is no longer the comforts of the middle class; it is a life without the opportunities for meaningful work and advancement. Too often it is a life of despair and discontent.

In the past, it has mattered little how many U.S. youth dropped out of school. It has not mattered that 23 million adults and almost 20 percent of all 17-year-old youth were functionally illiterate. It has not mattered that a large percentage of youth could not interpret a bus schedule, could not compute the cost of a meal in a restaurant or find the Pacific Ocean on a map. In the past, none of this has really mattered, for U.S. industry has always been able to generate a sufficient number of jobs for nearly everyone willing to work. For the future, it is now certain that this will not be true.

It is now clear that the solution to the crisis of at-risk youth, or for that matter at-risk adults, is education. Regardless of whether the at-risk person is a malnourished and abused kindergarten student, a third-grader far below grade level in reading and math, a disruptive, illiterate middle-school kid, a "Goth," a preppie, a skater, a punk-rock dropout drowning in a sea of drugs, or a 50-year-old displaced, middle-class petroleum worker, the only solution is education. We can even be more specific. The solution is not just the traditional high-school education. It is an education that enables employment, that accesses a meaningful job. It is education that creates literacy. It is education that leads to productive participation in our society.

Unfortunately, many high-school graduates lack these basic skills. The education that is demanded today requires more than reading Silas Marner, memorizing lines from Julius Caesar, and learning the causes of World War II; it may be more than wood shop and earning graduation credit in physical education. Schools must provide students, regardless of their age and their background, with the essential basic skills necessary to accommodate additional learning and an education that leads to jobs and opportunity for social participation. Our communities must meet this challenge. It is for just this reason that there is an urgent need for schools to develop programs that will be effective for *all* children and youth.

An Apartheid of Ignorance

Dramatic changes in society during the last twenty years have redefined almost everything we once thought we knew about life. As the technological revolution has swept across the world, virtually every aspect of life—social, political, and economic—has been impacted and transformed. Until very recently North Americans believed that through hard work and perseverance, anyone could achieve the good life and access the American dream of economic opportunity. We really believed that anyone could start at the bottom and through hard work make their way to the top. People believed these American dreams because they watched the previous generation achieve them. That world has disappeared. In the world today there is only one door of opportunity left to access the "good life" of the America dream . . . and that door is education. Those who have a formal education can obtain the economic opportunities that surround them and can access the continuing education that is needed to keep pace with the ever changing technological world. Without education, the door is slammed shut. We have left the "world of work," where people could build the good life with their hands, and entered the "age of the mind," where economic opportunity comes only through increasingly sophisticated training and education. Today when children arrive at school unprepared to learn, or finish the third grade without learning how to read, or drop out of school—we know without a shadow of a doubt that they are doomed to a world of economic despair. We also know that the despair leads too often to drug and alcohol abuse, criminal behavior, and for many . . . prison.

The result of all of this has been the creation of an "apartheid of ignorance"; a tragic separation in our society between those who are educated and those who are not. The wealthy have soared to unparalleled levels of economic prosperity while the "other America" has suffered a falling or flatline economic life. People with jobs paying the minimum wage can barely live above the poverty level; if they have children, it is impossible. It is not unusual today to find a single mom living in a homeless shelter while working as many as three different minimum-wage jobs, earning only enough to hold body and soul together, and unable to pay for a place to live.

Education has become the dividing line; the sharp sword in the sand that divides our nation. Those who have education and enjoy the good life live in an ever-expanding economic world. They build larger and larger homes, with three and four garages in which to park their cars, trucks, SUVs, RVs, off-road vehicles, boats, snowmobiles, jet skis, and riding lawn mowers. They live in controlled-access, gated communities, they attend the best schools—often private and parochial—and they rarely come in contact with the growing underclass of Americans who live in poverty, those people who may never find a job, who may never have health benefits, and who will never access the American dream of economic opportunity and well-being.

The tragedy of the apartheid of ignorance is that educational research has documented and demonstrated that everyone can learn effectively, especially if the efforts start early and if schools and communities have the *will* to make it happen. The following chapters provide a bold formula for success that is transforming the lives of children throughout America and holds the promise of teaching every child effectively. At hand today is the necessary knowledge to end this tragic apartheid of ignorance and open the door of opportunity to all American youth.

Chapter 2

Who Are the At Risk and Why?

The principal laughed and shook his head. "Do you remember the good old days when we had parent conferences? Well, let me tell you, the world has changed. Last week I asked the secretary to schedule a meeting with this really screwed up 15-year-old kid and everyone who had some type of responsibility for him. When I walked into the conference room I nearly fell over because the room was packed. There was the kid, his probation officer, his mother, his grandmother, his foster parents, his attorney, his case worker from Health and Welfare, and God knows who else. There must have been a dozen people in the room. Let me tell you, so many of these kids are just a mess. When you really find out what's going on in their life, the really remarkable thing is not that they drop out of school, but that they ever bother to come to school at all.
—SUPERINTENDENT, LINCOLN COUNTY SCHOOLS, NEWPORT, OREGON

During the 1980s and 1990s, as the United States experienced a dramatic period of prosperity and economic growth, many wondered out loud and in print whether or not there was anyone out there who was still at risk. There was in fact ample cause for optimism: Not only was the stock market smashing through record level after level, but consumer confidence was at an all-time high; drug use appeared to be leveling or even declining; the national dropout rate began to show a slight decrease; crime was down, particularly in the nation's cities; and the number of teenage pregnancies, after quadrupling in recent decades, had declined. There was news about a few low-performing schools around the country that had "turned things around" and were documenting that their poor students were knocking down achievement test scores that equaled or surpassed those of their middle-class peers. There was also news about the revolution in brain research and how parents could actually increase the intelligence of their children during the first three years of life. And there was good news about college graduation rates. The percentage of high school graduates ages 25–29 who had completed a bachelor's degree had risen from 22 percent in 1971 to 31 percent in 1996 (Federal Interagency Forum on Child & Family Statistics, 1997).

This "good" news, however, does not characterize education for the majority of America's youth. Through the late 1990s more and more parents abandoned public education for charter schools, vouchers, and home schooling. Youth violence shocked the nation again and again in accelerating acts of school murder. And while the 1980s and 1990s were a time of massive economic prosperity, tax records confirmed that while the rich and middle class did indeed get richer, the poor struggled along in an ever-deepening poverty.

Since 1977 the average income for the bottom 20 percent of Americans has fallen 10 percent. For the middle fifth of the population it has risen only 8 percent. However, the top 1 percent of the population has averaged an income increase of 115 percent, according to the Center for Budget and Policy Priorities (Ivins, 1999). The bottom four-fifths of the people in the United States own 16 percent of the country's wealth; the top fifth owns 84 percent of the wealth.

Unfortunately the at-risk, high-risk, violent, and violence-prone children and youth have not disappeared. Based on recent studies a greater number of children and youth are regularly involved in more unusually risky behavior than ever previously suspected. And unfortunately adults seem to share an increasingly negative view of kids today. In a 1997 "mood of America" poll, a new tragic view of adults' attitudes toward youth emerged. While previous generations had always assumed that their children would have a better life than they did, this 1997 survey found that adults were very pessimistic about youth today and in the future. The survey reported that adults felt that children today have homes that are less stable and streets that are less safe. They felt children were less respectful of their elders and more materialistic. Adults believed youth today have worse schools, worse role models, and were significantly less happy than their own generation (Raash, 1997). Recent research has not only documented the demographics of the at-risk terrain, it has also provided a growing reliability of predictive data regarding the likely outcomes of high risk conditions and behaviors. Educators are now confronted with chilling, long-term predictions about infants, young children, and teenagers. A new "science of learning" has emerged in the field of education, and this new science provides new understanding of the challenges as well as the solutions facing educators throughout the nation.

The Conditions of At-Risk Youth

For years groups like the Children's Defense Fund and the National Center for Educational Statistics have been annually documenting the conditions of children in the United States. This documentation has provided a vivid longitudinal portrait of an underclass of children who are critically at risk in the United States (see Table 2-1).

TABLE 2-1   Conditions of Children in the United States

- One in five children live in poverty—almost 14.5 million in 1996 (Children's Defense Fund, 1998).
- The number of children living in poverty has remained virtually unchanged at 20 percent for the past 20 years, even during the recent period of astonishing economic growth and prosperity (Federal Interagency Forum on Child & Family Statistics, 1997).
- In 1996, 69 percent of poor children lived in families where someone worked. But even when a parent worked, with the average wage being $6.85 per hour, in 1990, working families could still be living in poverty. Even after the 1997 increase of the minimum wage, earnings from a full-time year-round job were insufficient to elevate a family of three out of poverty (Children's Defense Fund, 1998).
- An average of 14 children die each day from gunfire in the United States—approximately one every 100 minutes (Children's Defense Fund, 1998).
- In 1996, 3.1 million children were reported abused or neglected (Children's Defense Fund, 1998).
- In 1996, 2.14 million children lived in households headed by a relative with no parent present; a majority (1.43 million) were being raised by their grandparents (Children's Defense Fund, 1998).
- During 1997, 26.9 million children received free or subsidized lunches at schools and 7 million received a daily breakfast (Children's Defense Fund, 1998).
- Two-thirds of the mothers of small children work outside the home and spend between $4,000 and $10,000 per year on child care.
- The number of teenagers 16–19 years old who are neither in school nor work has remained at 10 percent for most of the 1990s (Federal Interagency Forum on Child & Family Statistics, 1997).
- While the overall dropout rate has actually remained relatively stable at 15 percent since 1980, the dropout rate for Caucasians (15 percent) and African Americans (20 percent) has declined slightly. The dropout rate for Hispanic youth has increased in recent years.
- Since 1995 teenage births have declined, yet they remain four times the number occurring three decades ago. In 1998 eighty-four percent of all births to teenagers were to unmarried mothers.
- Every day 13 million children, including 6 million infants and toddlers, are in child care (Children's Defense Fund, 1998).
- Between 1992 and 1996, the daily use of cigarettes increased for 8th, 10th, and 12th graders, and the percent of students in each grade level who reported elicit drug use increased substantially (Federal Interagency Forum on Child & Family Statistics, 1997).
- In 1995 researchers developed a profile of a typical first-grade class in the United States. The profile dramatizes the diversity of today's public school classrooms and lays out the challenges facing teachers:

Typical First-Grade Class

Of the 28 students who compose the average 1st grade classroom in the United States:

8 are in Chapter 1 (3 of which will test as learning disabled)

1 is on a reading individual education plan

1 is an English as a second language student

3 are receiving assistance for speech problems

3 are receiving in-school counseling

2 are receiving out-of-school counseling

1 has a history of physical abuse

3 are from homes with a history of domestic violence

2 have been sexually abused

1 lives in a shelter home

1 is in fourth school since kindergarten; several others in their third

2 have been evicted from their apartments for setting fire to them

(Jones & Jones, 1995)

The factors that place children and youth at risk can be divided into two primary areas: those related to the individual, family, and community and those related to school. While it is difficult to expect immediate change or improvement in the home and community, it is not only possible, but realistic, to believe that schools can immediately eliminate many of their practices that contribute to placing children at risk. Over 20 years of research and study have provided a compelling body of data that can assist schools and communities in their quest to identify and serve youth at risk. To begin to address the dilemma, schools and communities must initially understand and identify the contributing factors which place youth at risk.

Lisbeth Schorr and Daniel Schorr, in their classic work *Within Our Reach,* argue that we currently know enough about risk factors associated with leaving school and the number of students imperiled by this crisis that we have ample reason to formulate new social policies attending to this national concern. They present the following analogy to make their case.

The seventeenth-century maritime insurers knew that the risk factors of a winter sailing presaged a more likely loss, just as today's life insurance companies know that a high cholesterol level and little exercise raise the risk of premature death. In the same way, we know that a child with school problems in the third grade is at risk of dropping out of high school and becoming a teenage parent. The experts may not be able to forecast which of seven youngsters is most likely to commit a heinous crime on being released from detention and which will henceforth lead a life of virtue. Great strides have been made in identifying factors that place whole categories of children at risk of disastrous outcomes and in determining which of these factors are most amenable to intervention. We now have proof that disastrous outcomes are much more likely when several risk factors interact. (Schorr & Schorr, 1989, p. 24)

Determining the Causes

The Charles Stewart Mott Foundation funded a study in the late 1980s entitled "Who's Looking Out For At-Risk Youth?" The executive summary of this work, entitled *America's Shame, America's Hope: Twelve Million Youth At Risk,* speaks to the urgency of the problem.

> *A crisis exists in the back rows of America's public school classrooms. It has so far eluded the full attention of the much bruited educational reform movement of the 1980's. Yet its threat to our economic future, and to the lives of millions of American youth, is present, grave, and sure to become more costly to meet, the longer we delay in meeting it. (Smith & Lincoln, 1988, p. 2)*

The crisis is the undereducation of a segment of our students presently constituting one out of three students in today's classrooms. Dominant in this group are the children of poverty—those impacted by economic and cultural disadvantage. They have come to be called youth "at risk" because they are at risk of emerging from school underprepared for further education or the kinds of jobs available. Often they are only ready for lives of alienation and dependency. The Mott study continues:

> *They are said to be failing in school, and yet it is clear that it is we who are failing to educate them. The danger this failure of education poses to these youth and to all of us grows apace. It is best described first in terms of the realities of today's and tomorrow's job market and then in terms of the young Americans who will be expected to fill those jobs. (Smith & Lincoln, 1988, p. 2)*

It is estimated that approximately one million youth per year leave school without completing their basic educational requirements. The majority of these students leave without essential literacy skills and other basic abilities, which renders them virtually unemployable. In addition, it is estimated that 700,000 students graduate yearly with skills as deficient as those of students who do not complete their schooling. Others have estimated that over 80 percent of our graduating seniors depart school with inadequate writing skills, with less than 50 percent of them being able to carry out moderately complex tasks (Davis & McCaul, 1990).

Scholars who have studied issues related to at-risk youth generally agree on the fundamental focus of the at-risk crisis. These include:

> *Those who are likely to leave school at any age without academic, social, and/or vocational skills necessary to lead a productive and fulfilled life. (Institute for At-Risk Infants, Children and Youth and Their Families, 1991, p. 8).*

While others may argue semantic variation, the crisis of our nation's at-risk youth focuses on school-age youth leaving school without adequate skills.

Risk Factors

Two decades of research have conclusively identified the range of factors that characterize youth at risk. Some of the factors are associated with individual personality;
others relate to the home, community, and school. Slavin and Madden identify low
achievement, retention in grade, behavioral problems, poor attendance, low socioeconomic status, and attendance at schools with large numbers of poor students.
They conclude, "each of these factors is closely associated with the drop-out-rate; by
the time students are in the third grade we can use these factors to predict with
remarkable accuracy which students will drop out of school and which will stay to
complete their education" (Slavin & Madden, 1989, p. 4).

The Vocational Studies Center of the School of Education at the University of
Wisconsin-Madison attempted a far-reaching analysis and description of risk factors.
The analysis presents families, students, family-related issues, cultural differences,
and gender issues as the organizing principles around which individual factors of
at-risk youth aggregate (Nash, 1990). Davis and McCaul of the Institute for the Study of
At-Risk Students at the University of Maine have taken a slightly different approach.
They subdivide risk factors around more general issues of society, students, and
school environment and teacher-student interactions (Davis & McCaul, 1990).

Stressing the existence and evidence of the interrelation of risk factors, Pallas,
Natriello, and McDill list five key indicators: (a) minority, racial, or ethnic group
identity; (b) living in a poverty household; (c) living in a single-parent family; (d)
having a poorly educated mother; and (e) having a non-English language background (1989, p. 4).

At least one study has identified student mobility, i.e., moving from school to
school and from community to community, as a major cause for dropping out. This
study tracked a group of eighth graders until a year after they would have graduated
from high school, had they graduated on schedule. Of the 615 students that they
were able to follow, only 83 had attended a single elementary school, a single middle
school, and a single high school. The graduation rate for these nonmovers was 95
percent. For those who had moved once, the graduation rate was 68 percent; for
those who had moved three times, only 30 percent. The effects of moving were
strongest between grade 7 and grade 9. Of those who did not move during those
years, 72 percent graduated (Bracey, 1989).

Virtually all scholars who have investigated risk factors for dropping out of
schools agree that an interaction of these factors is almost always present when a
youth decides to leave the formal education process.

The interaction of the various factors involved in dropping out are far from
simple. Dale Mann describes the range of circumstances for dropping out of school
as "impressive, even daunting." He states further:

> *Most students quit because of the compounded impact of, for example, being
> poor, growing up in a broken home, being held back in the fourth grade, and
> finally having slugged 'Mr. Fairlee,' the school's legendary vice principal for
> enforcement. These young people need a range of things, just as any system's*

at-risk population will need services to fit their hurts. If the problem is complex, so will be the solutions. (1986, p. 307)

Mann uses the phrase "a collision of factors" to characterize what generally precedes an unfortunate decision by students to drop out.

The nation's most comprehensive study focusing on risk factors associated with youth at risk established even wider parameters. Directing the work of Phi Delta Kappa's national study of at-risk youth, Frymier and Gansneder (1989) developed a matrix of 45 at-risk factors and ranked them from most serious to least serious (see Table 2-2).

TABLE 2-2   Factors That Place Students At Risk

- Attempted suicide during the past year
- Used drugs or engaged in substance abuse
- Has been a drug "pusher" during the past year
- Sense of self esteem is negative
- Was involved in a pregnancy during the past year
- Was expelled from school during the past year
- Consumes alcohol regularly
- Was arrested for illegal activity
- Parents have negative attitudes toward education
- Has several brothers or sisters who dropped out
- Was sexually or physically abused last year
- Failed two courses last school year
- Was suspended from school twice last year
- Student was absent more than 20 days last year
- Parent drinks excessively and is an alcoholic
- Was retained in grade (i.e., "held back")
- One parent attempted suicide last year
- Scored below 20th percentile on standardized test
- Other family members used drugs during past year
- Attended three or more schools during past five years
- Average grades were below "C" last school year
- Was arrested for driving while intoxicated
- Has an IQ score below 90
- Parents divorced or separated last year
- Father is unskilled laborer who is unemployed
- Mother is unskilled laborer who is unemployed
- Father or mother died during the past year
- Diagnosed as needing special education
- English is not language
- Lives in an inner city, urban area
- The mother is only parent living in the home
- Is year older than other students in same grade
- Mother did not graduate from high school
- Father lost his job during the past year
- Was dropped from athletic team during past year
- Experienced a serious illness or accident

(Frymier, Barber, Denton, Johnson-Lewis, & Robertson, 1992)

Risky Behaviors

A major effort to identify and monitor the risky behaviors of United States teenagers is conducted biannually by the National Centers for Disease Control and Prevention. The goal of this effort is to focus the attention of the nation on behaviors among the young causing the most significant health problems. The survey monitors the use of alcohol, tobacco, drugs, as well as sexual activity, safety, and nutrition. The 1997 study sampled 16,626, 9th–12th grade, randomly selected students (Kahn, L. et al, 1998). Results of the 1997 survey dramatized not only the many risky behaviors of teenagers today, but reported an alarming percentage of youth involved in these behaviors (see Table 2-3). This biennial data has demonstrated the existence of a continuing crisis in adolescent health caused by risky behaviors.

TABLE 2-3   Risky Behaviors of American Youth

Alcohol
- 50 percent drank alcohol on one or more days during the preceding month
- 17 percent drove a vehicle after drinking alcohol
- 37 percent rode with a driver who had been drinking in the preceding month
- 32 percent drank three or more alcoholic drinks on at least one occasion in the preceding month

Drugs
- 16 percent have sniffed or inhaled intoxicating substances (glue, contents of aerosol spray cans, or paint sprays)
- 26 percent used marijuana in the preceding month
- 9 percent used marijuana on school property in the preceding month
- 2 percent had injected an illegal drug

Sex
- 43 percent of sexually active students used a condom during most recent intercourse
- 48 percent of the students have had sexual intercourse
- 38 percent were sexually active within the preceding three months
- 18 percent have had four or more sex partners
- 17 percent were on birth control during their most recent sexual intercourse
- 6.5 percent had been pregnant or had caused a pregnancy
- 92 percent learned about HIV in school

Suicide
- 21 percent thought about committing suicide in the preceding year
- 8 percent attempted suicide in the preceding year

Safety
- 37 percent were in a physical fight in the preceding month
- 15 percent were in a physical fight on school property in the preceding year
- 18 percent carried a weapon (gun or knife) at least once in the preceding month
- 10 percent carried a weapon on school property in the preceding month
- 4 percent missed more than one day of school in the preceding month because they felt unsafe at school or when traveling to and from school
- 78 percent wore a safety belt when riding in the car when someone else was driving

(continued)

TABLE 2-3   *Continued*

Tobacco
- 36 percent of high school students smoked cigarettes in the preceding month
- 9 percent chewed tobacco in the preceding month

Nutrition
- 71 percent ate fewer than five servings of fruits and vegetables the day before
- 61 percent were enrolled in a physical education class (mostly ninth and tenth graders)
- 40 percent were attempting to lose weight
- 27 percent thought they were overweight

The Power of Prediction

Research now provides a succinct framework for educators to use in making long-term predictions about children and youth. The predictive probability of this work offers educators challenging new insights into the nature and importance of their work with students.

Predicting Dropouts by the End of Third Grade

Using only a few factors, schools can predict with better than 90 percent accuracy students in the third grade who will later drop out of school. Researchers maintain

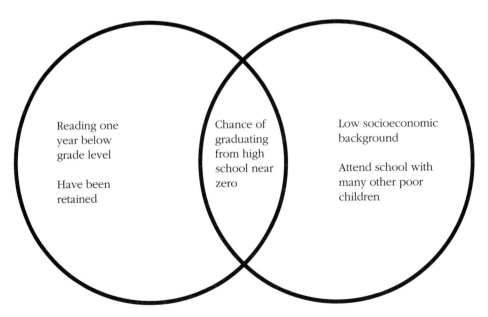

Reading one year below grade level

Have been retained

Chance of graduating from high school near zero

Low socioeconomic background

Attend school with many other poor children

FIGURE 2-1   Research on 3rd-Grade Students

(McPartland & Slavin, 1990, p. 7)

that if a poor child attends a school composed largely of other poor children, is reading a year behind by the third grade, and has been retained a grade, the chances of this child ever graduating from high school are near zero (McPartland & Slavin, 1990) (see Figure 2-1). At least one state, Indiana, has planned future prison cell needs based on projections that are developed by studying second graders ("Mark of Cain," 1990). Unfortunately, such scientific accuracy does not provide hope or any real peace of mind, for it now confronts schools with knowledge that can no longer be ignored.

Long-Term Predictions Based on the Failure to Read

It is now apparent that reading is the single most important foundational skill for learning. If children do not learn to read well, usually by the end of the third grade, what they learn is that they are "dumb." They cannot do their schoolwork or homework and their failure escalates. They will usually suffer from low self-confidence and self-concept and often exhibit disruptive behavior. Ultimately, the vast majority will drop out of school and experience no more success outside of school than they did in school. In studies of the unemployed, those who receive welfare or other public support, juvenile delinquents, and men and women in prison, it is all too obvious what can occur to these students after they drop out. They will live out their lives unemployed, underemployed, or worse, unemployable. They also tend to abuse drugs and alcohol, and many become pregnant while still teenagers. Many will end up in jail or prison (Karoly et al., 1998) (see Table 2-4).

TABLE 2-4   IMPACT OF ILLITERACY

- Low levels of literacy are powerful predictors of welfare dependency and prison incarceration—and their high cost.
- More than half of the adult prison population has literacy levels below those required by the labor market.
- Nearly 40 percent of adjudicated juvenile delinquents in the United States have reading problems and/or have treatable learning disabilities that were overlooked or went untreated by school (Karoly et al., 1998).

Predicting Poverty and Middle-Class Status

There are three powerful predictors of the socioeconomic level people will achieve during their lives. If people achieve each of the three factors, there is better than 90 percent probability that they will achieve middle-class economic status. If people fail to do all three, it is a 79 percent probability that they will live their lives in poverty. The three crucial factors are:

- Graduating from high school
- Not having a child before age twenty
- Not having a child outside of marriage (Wilson, 1997).

TABLE 2-5   Average Income Based on Education

	Dropouts	Four Years of High School	Some College	Four Years of College or more
Males	$13,961	$20,870	$23,435	$32,708
Females	$ 7,674	$13,075	$17,157	$26,043

(*Trends in the Well-being of American Youth,* 1996).

TABLE 2-6   Absent Fathers

- Boys with fathers at home are half as likely to be incarcerated, regardless of parents' income or educational level.
- 87 percent of youth in prison are from fatherless families.
- Children living without their fathers are five times more likely to be poor, and ten times more likely to be extremely poor.
- Children with fathers at home are twice as likely to stay in school and graduate.
- Children with "involved" fathers are less susceptible to peer pressure, are more competent, more self-protective, more self-reliant, and more ambitious (Ridenour, 1999).
- Children who grow up without "involved" fathers are significantly more likely to experience negative social trends including high rates of juvenile crime, teen pregnancy, and low academic achievement (Colorado Foundation for Families and Children, 1999).
- 40 percent of children from divorced families have not seen their fathers during the last year.
- In 1999, 36 percent of children in the United States did not live with their biological fathers, compared to 9 percent in 1960.
- In 1996, 2.14 million children lived in households headed by a relative with no parent present (the majority with grandparents) (Children's Defense Fund, 1998; Ridenour, 1999). ·

TABLE 2-7   Teenage Mothers

- There is a higher probability that a teenage mother will drop out of school, be unemployed, become dependent on the mother's family, and need public assistance for extended periods of her life (Children's Defense Fund, 1998).
- Almost 10 percent of all teenage mothers have babies with low birth weights—which relates to learning problems, lung problems, respiratory distress syndrome, bleeding in the brain, and birth defects. Low-weight babies are 40 percent more likely to die during the first month of life than normal weight babies.
- Compared with children of mothers 21 years of age or older, children of teenage mothers have more school difficulties, poorer health, and they too are more likely to drop out of school, be unemployed, and need public assistance.
- Sons of teenage mothers are three times more likely to end up in prison than other men.
- Girls who drop out of school are far more likely than other youth to get pregnant.

(Ventura et al., 1999)

Predicting Income Based on Educational Success

For decades, economic and sociological studies have demonstrated the dollar value of educational attainment. The information in Table 2-5 is representative of such work.

Predicting Higher Education Success

Achieving higher educational experience and degrees is strongly associated with parents' educational level. Only 30 percent of 18–24-year-olds attended college when their parents did not graduate from high school, versus 85 percent when at least one parent had a bachelor's degree.

Predictions about Fatherless Families

The absence of fathers in families appears to have a crushing effect on children, especially boys (see Table 2-6); the opposite is also true. Children with fathers at home are considerably advantaged in school and in later life.

Predictions about Teenage Mothers

Few other events in the lives of youth are so traumatic and potentially disastrous as becoming pregnant and having a child during the teenage years. Having a baby while a teenager has a tragic negative effect on both the mother and her baby. Thus, teenage births tend to create a continuing cycle of defeat, despair, and social problems (see Table 2-7).

Predictions Based on Parents' Behavior/Attitudes

Research has accumulated a growing body of data related to the influence of parents, both positive and negative, on teenage behavior in the United States (see Table 2-8, page 22).

Predictions Based on Teachers' Relationships with Students

Similar to the impact of parents, teachers can have an enormous impact on teenagers—both positively and negatively. Research has documented how important it is for teenagers to have positive connections with teachers:

- Positive relationships with teachers have been found to be significant in protecting teenagers from risky behavior.
- Positive relations between teachers and teenagers can have powerful positive effects and are more important and more influential than class size or teacher training (Resnick et al., September 10, 1997).

TABLE 2-8   Teenagers and Parents

- Teenagers who have strong emotional attachments to their parents are much less likely to use drugs and alcohol, attempt suicide, engage in violence, or become sexually active at an early age.
- Feeling loved, understood, and "paid attention to" by parents helps teenagers avoid high-risk activities, regardless of whether a child comes from a one- or two-parent household.
- While the amount of time teenagers spend with parents has a positive effect on reducing stress, feeling "connected" to parents is five times more powerful. This "emotional bond" between parents and teenagers is six times more important than the amount of activity teenagers do with their parents.
- While less significant, teenagers reported that having parents present at key times during the day was important to reducing risky behavior: after school, at dinner, at bedtime (National Longitudinal Study of Adolescent Health, American Medical Association, 1997).
- Unfortunately, one in four parents were found to be basically passive, preoccupied, or negligent regarding their children, especially after elementary school. Many parents feel that the responsibility for their children shifts to the school after the elementary years.
- In one study, only one child in three reported having daily conversations with their parents; half of the parents studied reported that they did not know their children's friends, did not know what they did after school or where they went at night.
- One-third of students report that their parents had no idea how they were doing in school.
- The most critical influences in most teenagers' lives were found not to be their parents, but their peers. Unfortunately, peer influences are largely negative regarding attitudes toward academic achievement and school in general.

(Steinberg, 1996)

Predictions Based on the Impact of a Good School

Research has provided critical evidence that a good school can overcome the negative effects of poverty and dysfunctional families and ensure that all children, regardless of their background, can learn effectively and obtain high standards of achievement. Equally as important, research has gained new understanding regarding why and how schools have been able to demonstrate such remarkable success with at-risk children and youth. Research has also been able to sort out the essential components necessary for schools to effectively teach high-risk youth (see Chapter 5). These recent research conclusions completely overturn previous beliefs that schools could not be effective with poor children, children of dysfunctional families, and other at-risk youth. Furthermore, these conclusions stand in marked contrast to the disturbing predictions we have outlined regarding at-risk and violent youth. A good school can teach all children to read, ground them in the basics, improve their self-concept and attitudes, and assist them in obtaining high academic achievement. Research on effective schools has shattered a previous generation of predictions and offers hope at last for at-risk youth (Teddlie & Stringfield, 1993; The Education Trust, 1999; The U.S. Department of Education, 1998b).

Predicting Youth Behavior Based on Developmental Assets

The more "developmental assets" of support that teens or preteens experience in their homes, communities, and schools, the less likely they are to engage in a wide range of risky behaviors, and in fact, the far more likely they are to engage in positive behaviors (Benson et al., 1998) (see Table 2-9). In addition, twenty personal internal assets have been identified (including commitment to learning, positive values, social competence, and positive identity).

TABLE 2-9   Developmental Assets

The Search Institute has identified 40 developmental assets that are directly related to youth behavior.

Supportive Assets:	Boundaries and Expectations Assets:
Family support	Family boundaries
Positive family communication	School boundaries
Other adult relationships	Neighborhood boundaries
Caring neighborhood	Adult role models
Caring school climate	Positive peer influence
Parental involvement in schooling	High expectations
Empowerment Assets:	Constructive Use of Time:
Community values youth	Creative activities
Youth as resources	Youth programs
Service to others	Religious community
Safety	Time at home

Beginning in 1989 and through the 1990 school year, over 250,000 students in 600 communities in 33 states participated in a national survey to try and identify the essential developmental assets that youth need to live healthy lifestyles. In 1996 the survey was revised and during the 1996–1997 school year, the revised survey was administered to 100,000 students (grades 6–12) in 213 communities in 25 states. Upon analyzing the data, it became evident that there was a direct relationship between the developmental assets students experience and their behavior (see Figure 2-2, page 24).

Cities and towns throughout the United States are now using the Developmental Asset Survey to obtain an indication of the degree of support that is occurring with students in their communities and mobilizing to increase and enrich the developmental assets available to students. The Search Institute has also identified over 500 strategies for building community and developmental assets (Benson et al., 1998).

Protecting Youth from High-Risk Behaviors

Assets have tremendous power to protect youth from many different harmful or unhealthy choices. To illustrate, these charts show that youth with the most assets are least likely to engage in four different patterns of high-risk behavior.

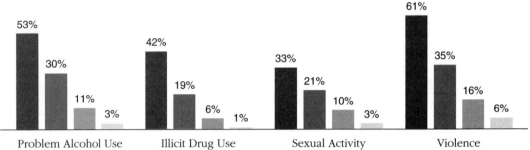

The same kind of impact is evident with many other problem behaviors, including tobacco use, depression and attempted suicide, antisocial behavior, school problems, driving and alcohol, and gambling.

Promoting Positive Attitudes and Behaviors

In addition to protecting youth from negative behavior, having more assets increases the chances that young people will have positive attitudes and behaviors, as these charts show.

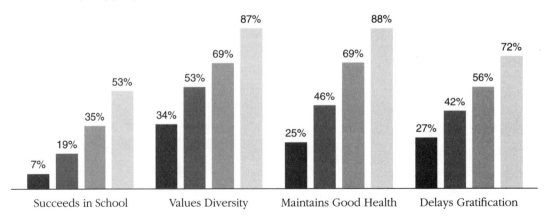

FIGURE 2-2 Protecting Youth from High-Risk Behaviors

Long-Term Predictions Based on Quality Child Care

A number of longitudinal research projects have provided conclusive documentation that high-quality child care during the early years of a child's life leads to better school performance, higher salaries as an adult, and fewer felony convictions (see Chapter 6 for a complete discussion).

Predictions Based on Childhood Bullying

Research has documented that childhood bullying has a negative effect on both the "bully" and the victim of the bullying. Bullying behaviors can be identified at as early as two years of age and, if not corrected, lead to disruptive school behavior and an increased probability of criminal behaviors and felony convictions in teenagers and adults. Research has shown that by age thirty, 25 percent of the adults who had been bullies during childhood had criminal records (Beane & Espeland, 1999). (See Chapter 3 for a complete discussion.)

Additional Issues to Consider

Any Child May Become At-Risk

Research has helped educators to understand that virtually any student may begin to perform marginally or poorly, regardless of factors related to economics, gender, ethnicity, or family structure (Sinclair & Ghory, 1987). These researchers further caution against the use of set indicators to identify at-risk youth, urging instead that schools begin addressing overall school structural characteristics and practices that negatively impact marginal youth.

Given the attention to the analysis and identification of prevailing conditions and factors related to a young person becoming at risk, it is of paramount importance that schools and teachers recognize the existence of these youth and initiate assistance. Regardless of differences and debates concerning ratings and definitions of at-risk factors, it is imperative that schools be alert to sudden changes in student behavior. Teachers and school counselors must be careful in identifying students whose grades begin to fall, who begin to miss school, and who exhibit dramatic or even subtle changes in their behavior. Often divorce, teenage pregnancy, violence and abuse in the home or community, death, drugs and alcohol, or even the breakup of a teenage romance can intrude into the life of children and youth and suddenly imperil their success in school. The tragic increase in teenage suicide has caused educators to become more attentive to the impact of disruptions in a teenage life and has helped schools to develop programs that anticipate problems.

Resilient Children and Youth

Research at the Johns Hopkins University Center for the Study of Disadvantaged Youth and elsewhere has focused on identifying the characteristics of children and youth who seem to succeed in school and life in spite of having all the characteristics of being at risk. These protective factors or characteristics of resiliency seem to enable many young people to succeed despite severe situations in their home and community. The Northwest Regional Educational Lab has synthesized research on these factors of resiliency and has urged that schools should attempt to reinforce and cultivate the personal factors that strengthen these protective factors in individuals, families, schools, and communities (Benard, 1991). The resilient child has been identified as having the following attributes:

Social Competency

Resilient children tend to have qualities of "responsiveness, flexibility, empathy and caring, communication skills, a sense of humor and other prosocial behavior" (Benard, 1991, p. 3, Krovetz, 1999). Resilient children tend to be more responsive, more active, and more flexible (Werner & Smith, 1982; Demos, 1989). Because of their flexibility and interpersonal skills, especially a sense of humor, the resilient child seems to develop more positive relationships and stronger friendships (Berndt & Ladd, 1989; Werner & Smith, 1982, Krovetz, 1999).

Problem-Solving Skills

Resilient children tend to have skills that include the ability to think abstractly, reflectively, and flexibly and to look for and attempt creative, alternate solutions to both cognitive and life problems. Such characteristics have been identified in street children who are able to survive in the midst of extremely difficult life situations.

Autonomy

Resilient children tend to be far more independent, have a greater sense of personal power, and have a stronger self-esteem.

Sense of Purpose and Future

Resilient children tend to have realistic, healthy, goal-directed, and optimistic expectations regarding the future.

Research supports the conclusion that the characteristics common to resilient children could well be developed and cultivated. The Northwest Regional Educational Lab has developed programs for the home and school that will focus on these characteristics as desirable educational outcomes (Benard, 1991).

Resistant Learners

Herbert Kohl, in his provocative book *I Won't Learn From You* (1991), explores the lives of a number of students who decide, for a variety of reasons, that they will not learn. Sometimes the student may feel that his or her self-respect, self-esteem, or racial identity may demand that he or she will not learn; other times, it may be a point of personal honor among peers that causes a student not to learn. Teachers should read this small book and be alert to the reality that some students who are failing may indeed be quite capable. Kohl suggests that these students may be effectively taught if a teacher develops a closer relationship which permits a deeper understanding of the students' reasons for not learning.

Why Have the Needs of At-Risk Youth Not Been Addressed?

Despite an enormous amount of credible research that has focused on identifying the students and remedying the many problems confronting at-risk youth, it is surprising that schools have not moved with vigor to better serve the needs of these tragic students. Three reasons appear to explain this lack of response. First, schools lack the will to act to ensure that all students receive a quality education; second, schools have proven to be unusually resistant to change, and third, communities are increasingly unwilling to adequately fund public education.

The Will to Act

Many educators have referred to the needs of serving at-risk students as similar to the services of hospital emergency rooms that provide intensive care. Research is quite clear that students possessing combinations of factors that lead at some point in their lives to a disassociation with school are in need of immediate and comprehensive diagnosis, assistance, and support if they are to have any opportunity for reentry into or success in our public school system. Toward this end, early prevention programs have been judged to be far more effective than intervention programs for older children. This concurrence of research and scholarly analysis compels immediate national attention and action toward intervention. Yet, as in many instances where a chasm between research and practice exists, developing appropriate interventions and taking immediate action appear beyond the grasp of our educational structure. Anthony Alvarado, former New York Superintendent of Schools, in testimony to the Senate Children's Caucus, stressed that our schools must start their dropout intervention effort far earlier than we presently do. "It's strange," he stated, "we know what to do. We just don't do it" (Schorr & Schorr, 1989, p. xxvi). As many scholars argue, it is clear that we now understand the significance of this crisis and furthermore are quite aware of effective interventions that can positively address detrimental factors. The problem of inaction, as discussed by Superintendent Alvarado and others, is central to our nation's current crisis. We know who the at risk are. We know what has caused their personal crisis. We know what must be done to affect their current crisis. The question remains, will we act? (Hillard, 1991)

The Difficulty of School Reform

Unfortunately, the problem of addressing the needs of at-risk youth involves more than a will to act and the financial ability to act. It must also involve knowing how to act. In Chapter 5, a detailed description of effective responses to at-risk youth will be explored. The problem, however, is complicated because schools have proven to be unusually difficult to change. Even modest improvement projects have proven extremely difficult to achieve. More profound, comprehensive efforts at reform and restructuring to address the needs of at-risk youth have proven all but impossible using traditional efforts at school reform. Compounding this problem is the unacceptable divergence which exists between research and practice. Noted curriculum authority Bruce Joyce concluded that the time required for a proven, research-based educational practice to move from theory to accepted practice in our nation's schools is 30 years (Joyce, 1986). The inability of public schools to adapt to changing societal needs continues to frustrate parents, legislators, policy makers, and educators.

School Funding

Increasingly, public education's response to at-risk children and youth has been directly related to funding. In state after state and in community after community there has been a growing reluctance to provide increased funding for public education. Far too few communities have been willing to support public education at little more than the basic minimum level. Originating from changing demographics, extended life expectancy and fewer adults having school-aged children, the resistance to school funding has focused on such basics as teachers' salaries, buildings and equipment, administrative costs, and special programs designed to serve at-risk youth.

Some communities have eliminated special funding for at-risk programs. In Vista, California, religious conservatives gained a majority on the local school board. In one of its initial actions the group made it clear that it wanted to limit support programs for disadvantaged students by rejecting a $400,000 state grant to provide health counseling to low-income kids and their parents (McGuillie, 1993).

The inequity in school funding that reflects the local tax base of rich communities and poor communities continues to penalize and punish the children of the most impoverished neighborhoods (Howe, 1991). While there are many inexpensive programs that can have a positive long-lasting impact on the at-risk student, no one can deny that many programs for these students inevitably cost more.

The combination of these three factors—how to create the will to act, the difficulty of actually changing and how to adequately fund public education—continues to frustrate public education's ability to meet the needs of all kids, particularly the at risk. The good news is that there is indeed hope at last for at-risk youth. In the coming chapters, schools and communities will be provided with the detailed components of a comprehensive blueprint for making schools effective for all youth.

The next chapter will address the escalating national crisis of school violence, violent youth, and bullying behavior.

$$C\ h\ a\ p\ t\ e\ r\quad 3$$

Violent and Violence-Prone Students: A National Crisis Escalates

After the Columbine violence, we had five bomb threats in a two-week period. Each time we cleared the building and our local police spent two hours checking everything out. When the sixth bomb threat was called in, we took a deep breath and kept the school open. My stomach is in knots and I haven't slept in a week . . . but we decided that we will not be held hostage to these threats.
—SUPERINTENDENT, OREGON

They have become road signs on a tragic journey to sadness, fear, frustration, and death: Columbine High School, Littleton, Colorado; Thurston High School, Springfield, Oregon; and the now infamous towns of Jonesboro, Arkansas; Paducah, Kentucky; and Pearl, Mississippi. And this of course is only the short list, the high profile media events in which youths and sometimes children as young as first graders have turned schools into killing grounds. Since 1997 there have been a dozen occurrences of youth violence in or around schools where youths killed other youths . . . and often teachers as well. Sometimes parents were also murdered, and more recently, bombs and booby traps were used. Youth violence has suddenly become front page news in journals and newspapers and the focus on television again and again. Scenes of body bags, teenagers covered with bloody clothing, and what an earlier generation of combat veterans called the "shocked-out" look of a "1,000-yard stare" have rocked the nation.

Over and over again, we have watched parents and children hugging one another and crying, and everyone from the media, to state and federal legislators, to ministers, to school officials, to the parents down the street has begun to wonder: How could this be? During a time of such peace and prosperity, how could this happen? What has gone wrong with our country? What has gone wrong with our kids?

Most blame each other for the violence. Parents blame lax gun laws and ineffective school officials. Students blame peer pressure and the lack of adult interest in their lives. School officials blame the media, and some explain the violence as simply "evil, unexplained" (Evans, 1999).

Many terrified parents did not wait for answers. Those who could, quickly withdrew their children from public schools (many on the same afternoon that the violence at Columbine High School occurred), resulting in a national rush to home and private schools. Like a domestic "Pearl Harbor," parents and grandparents everywhere were stunned by this cultural "sneak attack" on our society, and fear and frustration seized the country. Parents were startled by the realization that violence could happen in their schools, in their communities, and it could happen to their kids. Alarm, sometimes bordering on hysteria, swept through state legislatures and the U.S. Congress, as politicians came forward pushing and elbowing for air time and sound bites.

The U.S. Senate (Spring 1999) passed a moderate gun-control measure with the Vice President breaking a tie vote, only to be followed by a proposed gun-control measure in the House of Representatives with an amendment that required schools and classrooms in the nation to post the Ten Commandments. Some U.S. Representatives reported that they believed that it was the godless, liberal teachers of the nation pushing on their students the idolatry of "scientific evolution" that was the cause of the youth violence. The majority of the House promptly voted the measure down . . . which signaled the end of gun-control legislative action for 1999. But in state after state, gun-control measures were enacted, and a number of state legislatures reversed ground and passed laws that permitted cities to bring class-action suits against gun manufacturers and gun dealers, a move that opened the door to legal actions modeled after those involving tobacco manufacturers. Terrified parents prompted states to discuss a range of possible laws restricting everything from body piercing to tattoos to hair color—and if the legislators could not prevent the defaming of the "temple of the body," they at least tried for legislation requiring waiting periods and parental approval. The state of Louisiana even passed a law requiring public school students to respond to their teachers with "yes, ma'am," and "no, sir."

In a nation with over 200 million firearms in its homes—one for almost every man, woman, and child, coupled with research verifying a direct relationship between access to firearms and youth violence—the national legislators focused their efforts on the teaching of evolution, the Ten Commandments, traditional greetings of respect, and body art, rather than background checks at gun shows and required trigger locks.

Yet in the middle of this killing zone of youth crime and the accompanying hysteria that swept the nation, a recent study found that most teachers and students reported that they thought violence in schools was declining. Indeed, when compared to the rest of the country, schools do in fact seem to be a rather "safe place for kids to be," at least statistically speaking (Coles, 1999).

Unfortunately, while there have been marked reductions nationally in teenage pregnancies, drug use, and inner city gang warfare, teenage violence has more than doubled in the past ten years. And in that typical teenage approach, each murderous act seemed determined to be more vicious, more flamboyant than all those previous. There is a growing eerie feeling of the next impending "copy cat" act. After each high-profile media event of teen violence, an epidemic of other shootings, suicides, threats, bomb threats, siege plans, bomb explosions, and teenage arrests sweeps the country (Gegax & Bai, 1999). For too many of our troubled youth, violence has become a way of life.

Violence: A Way of Life in the United States?

> *I'll tell you that it just breaks your heart. This school violence touches everybody. A little girl in my third grade class raised her hand and said, "I am afraid with our classroom door open. Can we close and lock the door?"*
> —*TEACHER, TEXAS*

Unfortunately, high-visibility school violence is only the tip of the iceberg. For each one of the dramatic school shootings, there are thousands of other teenage murders or negligent homicides. Each year between 2,500 and 3,000 teenagers are arrested and charged in the deaths of other teenagers and adults. Between 1985 and 1994 the arrests of 10 to 17-year-old children and youth for homicide, rape, robbery, and assault increased by 70 percent (Walsh, 1997). Based on surveys of students aged 12 to 19, violent crimes at school were reported by 42 percent of the students in 1995, up 23.5 percent from six years earlier (Kathryn A. Chandler, as quoted in the *Idaho Statesman,* 13 April 1998, p. A4). In 1997 one-half of all black males 18 to 35 years of age in Washington, D.C., were either in prison, on probation, or under the jurisdiction of the court. In a single month, one in nine of the nation's high school students brought a weapon to school (Burke, 1998), and during the next decade, the numbers of teenagers in the United States will increase by more than 20 percent, the majority of whom will be poor, minority, and residents of inner-city ghettos.

Like a serial killer who leaves an accumulating amount of evidence, each act of teenage violence has provided psychologists, criminologists, sociologists, and educators with added data for a growing knowledge base that is providing understanding of the tragic phenomena of youth violence. This knowledge has articulated highly specific, predictive profiles and led to higher confidence levels in the probability statistics used to forecast violence among youth. Research on troubled youth and adults has provided a growing understanding of the causes and possible prevention of youth violence. Unfortunately, in the most recent acts of violence, it appears that violence has mutated into a new, more sophisticated, even more sinister form of teenage murder.

As research efforts accumulate more and more data on youth violence, a growing understanding of its causes, better insights into warning signs, and the documented success of programs for addressing the needs of these violent young people has emerged.

Causes of Youth Violence

I just hate this. We first had metal detectors in all of the high schools. Then we added them at all the junior highs. Now, we have them in our elementary schools. Our school used to be a real part of the community, now we are "locked down." It is very discouraging for anyone to try and come into our school.
—TEACHER, INDIANAPOLIS

With a growing research base from a variety of scientific points of view, a growing universal agreement regarding the underlying causes of youth violence is developing.

The Role of Media

Research has substantiated the impact of media on impressionable children, pre-teens, and teenagers. Youth today are surrounded, often even immersed in an ever more sophisticated virtual world created by the media. By the time children start school, they will have seen over 8,000 murders on television and over 100,000 violent acts. By the time they graduate from high school these numbers double (American Academy of Child and Adolescents Psychiatry, 1995). And, unlike in earlier generations, today's media reaches every home and hamlet, no matter how remote or isolated. Cable TV, satellite dishes, and the internet have brought the media world into almost every home. Video stores, arcades, and paint-ball game fields are now in many neighborhoods. And in ways never before realized, rather than reflecting reality, the media seems to generate and define reality, especially for impressionable children and youth. Too often youth learn how to act, behave, dress, and talk through watching TV and videos.

With media maintaining its violent tone, children and youth are saturated by murder, violence, aggression, and vicious, disturbing images. The lyrics of Marshall Mathers, better known as Eminem, talk about sticking nails through eyelids and slitting parents' throats. Youth today have access to Eminem, Marilyn Manson, gangsta rap, and frightening video games like *Doom* (the video game played extensively by the Littleton, Colorado, teenage shooters), *Diablo,* and the even more violent game, *Kingpin,* which advertises "multiplayer gang bang death" and "see the damage done including exit wounds." All of these games are referred to as "first person shooter" (FPS) and portray graphic wounds, blood, and yes, even exit wounds. As Hill Walker of the Institute on Violence and Destructive Behavior at the University of Oregon has said, the combined media creates "a virtual reality" outside the world of adults (The Secret Life of Teens, 1999). With youth listening to their music on headphones, watching TV in their bedrooms, playing video games at the arcade in the mall, and working the Internet in front of their computers, adults have little ability to monitor the media that students choose.

Studies have discovered that a growing percentage of youth today have a telephone, a television, and a computer in their bedrooms at home. Gone forever is the family gathered in the living room or family room watching TV together. In fact, the trend in new home construction is to downsize the living room/family room and expand the bedroom areas. And, since this generation of youth are more affluent then ever before, with few household chores, jobs, or other responsibilities, and with most adults away from the home working, teenagers have the time alone, the resources, and the isolation to slip away into the world of the media "massage." Researchers who have studied the relationships between media and youth violence conclude:

Media has led to increased desensitization to violence and victims of violence

If students have witnessed thousands of simulated murders and acts of aggression on TV and in music prior to starting school and as they grow up and play increasingly graphic and violent video games, they come to see violence as rather painless, like the ever dying little Kenny on the TV show *South Park*. As a 1993 study conducted by the American Psychological Association concluded, "viewing violence increases desensitization of violence, resulting in a calloused attitude toward violence." (American Psychological Association, 1993). Hundreds of studies on children and teenagers have concluded that children may "become immune to the horror of violence" or accept violence as a way to solve problems (American Academy of Child and Adolescent Psychiatry, 1995, p. 4; American Psychological Association, 1996).

Increased aggressiveness and antisocial behavior

The power of television has recently been documented in an unusually graphic manner. After a lifetime of isolation, satellite television has recently gone to the Pacific Island of Fiji, where the culture has traditionally valued heavy people. Obesity was considered beautiful, and the comment "slimming down" was considered a negative statement, or worse, a cause for alarm. Within months of TV's arrival in Fiji, with *Melrose Place, Beverly Hills 90210,* and *Baywatch,* teenage girls on the island began to develop anorexia and demonstrate bulimic behaviors as they tried to "slim down" and emulate the TV actors and actresses.

The teenage world is defined by the media

When a movie featured teenagers lying on the median line on a busy highway, filmmakers soon edited out the episode, after teenagers around the country died attempting the same stunt. When another film showed teenagers pouring gasoline into a subway ticket booth and igniting it, similar acts immediately occurred in New

York subways. Studies have been done in which preschoolers watched violent acts on video and immediately became more violent in their play. Psychologists who researched the topic have agreed, "There is absolutely no doubt that high levels of viewing violence on television are correlated with increased acceptance of aggressive attitude and increased aggressive behavior" (American Psychological Association, 1993; Josephson, 1996).

Increased fear of becoming a victim
The more violence and the more vivid violence viewed by young children and teenagers, the more youth view the world and their community as dangerous. The more violence that is viewed, the more the fear of becoming a victim and the more mistrust felt for others (American Psychological Association, 1993; American Academy of Child & Adolescent Psychiatry, 1995).

Increased appetite for more violence
The more children and youth view violence, the more their ability to tolerate violence increases. Violence and aggression that once would have shocked and frightened them are now viewed in a blasé manner (Fager & Boss, 1998; American Academy of Child and Adolescent Psychiatry, 1995).

The Role of the Family

Almost every violent youth comes from a family situation that contributes to the aggressive violent behavior. The traditional profile of troubled youth relates directly to abusive, dysfunctional families where young children were hurt both physically and emotionally or lived in an almost constant state of stress. Often abusive family situations cause children to fail to bond with an adult, and this failure to bond leads directly to sociopathic, often vicious behavior. And while research has documented the powerful, positive opportunity for enhancing the intellect and learning of children from birth to age three, there is a dark side to this critical time period. Abuse, neglect, and terror seem to cause an incessant flood of stress-related chemicals to build up and remain in the young body, leading to unfortunate changes in the brain (Perry, as quoted in *Newsweek,* 3 May 1999, pp. 32–33). Abused children grow up impulsive, aggressive, antisocial, and lacking in empathy and sensitivity to the people in the world around them.

But even in homes where there is no evidence of abuse and no apparent dysfunction, family situations may still contribute to youth aggression and violence. Over half of today's teenagers have lived through their parents' divorce and reside with a single parent or divide their time between two households in which they often feel like outsiders. Sixty-three percent of teenagers live in households where both parents work outside the home, and most teens come home to empty homes at the end of the day. This solitude often extends well into the evening. Many teenagers must look after their younger brothers or sisters, and too often, family meals are built around random visits to the microwave. Among all the issues that adolescents rank at the top of their concerns, the number one issue is loneliness

(Stevenson & Schneider, 1999). In one study of seven thousand teenagers, over a period of five years, the teens were found to spend 3½ hours alone every day (Stevenson & Schneider, 1999). Almost all teenagers who have been interviewed by researchers have pointed out that they wished they had more adult contact in their lives, especially with their parents.

Contributing Factors in Schools

Most now recognize that the large, junior/middle and high schools, which are the norm in the United States, contribute to the lonely isolation and alienation of teenagers. While these large schools have long been described as complex, clique-filled stratas of the various youth cultures, and the last real socioeconomic melting pot, recent acts of teen violence have confronted society with a new concern: that these large schools may in fact be generating violent acts. With media-immersed teenagers divided into athletes, preppies, punks, Goths, skaters, druggies, and on and on, it only takes an added element of intolerance, racism, or social-class antago-nisms to lead to a wide variety of aggression and violence. Almost everyone agrees: Middle schools and high schools are far too big (National Association for Secondary School Principals, 1996), too impersonal, and for too many of the nation's brightest students, boring. Too many schools have responded to youth violence with an emphasis on security measures. Unfortunately, ". . . there is little evidence for the efficacy of such prevention approaches as the use of metal detectors, increased police presence in schools, searches of students and lockers, the use of student and staff identification cards and so on" (Hyman & Snook, March 2000). Such approaches as these focus on students rather than the conditions of schools that prompt violence and may have a variety of unintended negative consequences.

Feelings of Alienation, Hopelessness, and Rage

Most violent youth, regardless of their family situations, tend to feel isolated, hope-less, and disengaged. Violent youth feel like they are outsiders, that no one cares for them, that no one cares about them. Too often schools contribute to this feeling. These youth often experience an overwhelming loneliness and hopelessness. Media only tends to heighten their isolation and lure them into the virtual world. Many of the violent youth of today are reported to have had suicidal thoughts and some have ended their violent episodes with suicide, or at least considered it (Josephson, 1996). "In survey after survey, many kids—even those on the honor roll—say they feel increasingly alone and alienated, unable to connect with their parents, teachers, and sometimes even classmates" (Kantrowitz & Wingert, 1999, p. 36). These teen-agers seem desperate for guidance, and when they do not find it at home or at school, they cling to cliques of other isolated outsiders and, of course, immerse themselves in the brutal world of TV, movies, and computer games. Too often, the feeling of being slighted, ignored, bullied, and victimized leads to a growing internal rage. The most recent national study of youth violence conducted by Washington State Attor-ney General Christine Gregóire identified two major causes of youth violence: home life and peer harrassment (2000). The youth interviewed called for adults—both parents and teachers—to set boundaries and provide guidance and caring.

Profiles of Violent, Violence-Prone, and Nonviolent Youth

> *I can't get it out of my mind. Every time I see a news*
> *bulletin on television of another school shooting, I am*
> *terrified because I know that it could be my child next time.*
> *How can we live like this? What is wrong with our world?*
> *—PARENT, COLORADO*

Until recently, researchers had been able to document with chilling accuracy the profile of violent and violence-prone youth. As Shawn A. Johnston, a forensic pathologist in San Francisco who has interviewed thousands of violent children, including many who are killers, has concluded: "This is an evolving body of research that very clearly suggests that by the third grade [authorities] were able to identify kids who are at risk of going on to engage in antisocial behavior" (O'Neill, 1998). And as the child grows up and goes to school, the ability to identify significant warning signs becomes increasingly more effective.

Traditional Violence Profile: The Abused Youth

The traditional profile of abused youth has powerful predictability. And while recent acts of school violence suggest a new and emerging type of violent youth, the traditional profile continues to serve to identify a subculture of violent youth:

- Poverty
- Dysfunctional families, often raised by grandparents or foster families
- Childhood abuse
- Failure to bond with adults or to develop positive relationships with adults
- Exposure to media violence
- School failure and school problems

Add to this profile, the following additional characteristics and the likelihood of violence is increased dramatically:

- Racial intolerance
- Access to guns
- A family with a history of criminal violence
- Abusing drugs/alcohol
- Belonging to a gang

And the likelihood of violence is increased even further if the following characteristics are present:

- Has used a weapon in the past
- Has been arrested
- Has neurological problems

New Emerging Profile: The Teenage Suicidal Terrorist

In recent acts of violence, a new type of violent teenager seems to have emerged though little research has yet been conducted. First, violence that had been primarily focused on urban areas, most typically inner cities, has spread to suburbs and rural areas. And the newer acts of violence simply do not fit the traditional profile. As Barry Krisberg, president of the National Council on Crime and Delinquency, has said, "These (new) murderers are against the stereotype. . . . they had nothing to do with drugs or gangs. Some were from affluent communities and intact families" (Taylor, 1998). Like any other major epidemic, the "disease" of youth violence has spread, mutated, and changed. Of the last eight school shootings, the majority of the shooters were advanced-placement or honor students.

The new profile that is emerging seems closer to that associated with teenage suicides than with the traditional characteristics of violent teenagers.

- Middle/upper middle-class family
- Intelligent
- Success in school
- Bored, isolated, angry, and disappointed
- Escalating history of violence and aggressive acts
- Feelings of alienation and loneliness
- Access to guns and the internet

Increasingly, researchers are focusing on some of the brightest and most intelligent youth. This group is usually bored with school, and 26.5 percent of these youth have considered suicide (compared with only 8.3 percent in the rest of the population). These youth may be considered weird by most of their peers and may tend to isolate themselves in their own world of computer games, music, and the Internet (Rogien, 1999).

Profile of Nonviolent Youth

In addition to the established and emerging profiles of violent and violence-prone children and youth, there is a significant body of research that defines the better adjusted, nonviolent student:

- Positive role models; exposure to a greater number of positive rather than negative behaviors
- Development of self-esteem and self-efficacy
- Supportive relationships, including those with teachers and friends

- A sense of hope about the future
- Belief in oneself
- Strong social skills
- Good peer relationships
- A close, trusting bond with a nurturing adult outside the family
- Empathy and support from the mother or mother figure
- The ability to find refuge and a sense of self-esteem in hobbies and creative pursuits, useful work, and assigned chores
- The sense that one is in control of one's life and can cope with whatever happens (American Psychological Association, 1996).

This profile of the more well-adjusted, nonviolent children and youth becomes the goal for all students in public education. The overarching goal is to help all students achieve this positive, nonviolent profile. There are also a growing number of educational programs specifically designed to help students improve their resiliency and develop stronger character traits.

Warning Signs: Child and Youth Behavior

> *I never thought I would see this day. But after 20 years of teaching, I have purchased insurance coverage that includes assault recovery benefits—as well as victim assistance. The sad part of this is that I am adding this coverage to protect me not from hardened criminals on the street, but from the students in my school and classroom.*
> *—TEACHER, NEW JERSEY*

In addition to these predictive, research-based profiles, researchers affiliated with the American Psychological Association have carefully detailed and defined "warning signs" that seem to predict violent behaviors (American Psychological Association, 1996):

Warning Signs in the Toddler and Preschool Child

- Has many temper tantrums in a single day, or several lasting more than 15 minutes, and often cannot be calmed by parents, family members, or other caregivers
- Has many aggressive outbursts, often for no reason
- Is extremely active, impulsive, and fearless
- Consistently refuses to follow directions and listen to adults
- Does not seem attached to parents
- Frequently watches violence on television, engages in play that has violent themes, or is cruel toward other children

Warning Signs in the Elementary Child

- Has trouble paying attention and concentrating
- Often disrupts classroom activities
- Does poorly in school
- Frequently gets into fights with other children in school
- Reacts to disappointments, criticism, or teasing with extreme and intense anger, blame, or revenge
- Watches many violent television shows and movies or plays a lot of violent video games
- Has few friends and is often rejected by other children because of behavior
- Makes friends with other children known to be unruly or aggressive
- Consistently does not listen to adults
- Is not sensitive to the feelings of others
- Is cruel or violent toward pets or other animals

Warning Signs in the Preteen and Adolescent

- Consistently does not listen to authority figures
- Pays no attention to the feelings or rights of others
- Mistreats people and seems to rely on physical violence or threats of violence to solve problems
- Often expresses the feeling that life has treated him or her unfairly
- Does poorly in school and often skips classes
- Misses school frequently for unidentifiable reason
- Gets suspended from or drops out of school
- Joins a gang, gets involved in fighting, stealing, or destroying property
- Drinks alcohol and/or uses inhalants or drugs

Early Warning Signs

In addition to these age-level behavior indicators, there are a general set of characteristics that experts have assembled that serve as additional "early warning signs." Psychologists agree that when these warning signs appear, especially in combinations, schools should respond quickly to analyze a student's situation and behavior and determine appropriate action (U.S. Department of Education, 1998b).

Social withdrawal
In some situations, gradual and eventually complete withdrawal from social contacts can be an important indicator of a troubled child. The withdrawal often stems from feelings of depression, rejection, persecution, unworthiness, and lack of confidence.

Excessive feelings of isolation and being alone
Research has shown that most children who are isolated and appear to be friendless are not violent. In fact, these feelings are sometimes characteristic of children and

youth who may be troubled, withdrawn, or have internal issues that hinder development of social affiliations. However, research also has shown that in some cases feelings of isolation and not having friends are associated with children who behave aggressively and violently.

Excessive feelings of rejection

In the process of growing up, and in the course of adolescent development, many young people experience emotionally painful rejection. Children who are troubled are often isolated from their mentally healthy peers. Their responses to rejection will depend on many background factors. Without support, they may be at risk of expressing their emotional distress in negative ways—including violence. Some aggressive children who are rejected by nonaggressive peers seek out aggressive friends who, in turn, reinforce these violent tendencies.

Being a victim of violence

Children who are victims of violence—including physical or sexual abuse—in the community, at school, or at home, are sometimes at risk themselves of becoming violent toward themselves or others.

Feelings of being picked on and persecuted

The youth who feels constantly picked on, teased, bullied, singled out for ridicule, and humiliated at home or at school may initially withdraw socially. If not given adequate support in addressing these feelings, some children may vent them in inappropriate ways—including possible aggression or violence.

Low school interest and poor academic performance

Poor school achievement can be the result of many factors. It is important to consider whether there is a drastic change in performance and/or poor performance becomes a chronic condition that limits the child's capacity to learn. In some situations—such as when the low achiever feels frustrated, unworthy, chastised, and denigrated—acting out and aggressive behaviors may occur. It is important to assess the emotional and cognitive reasons for the academic performance change so as to determine the true nature of the problem.

Expression of violence in writings and drawings

Children and youth often express their thoughts, feelings, desires, and intentions in their drawings, and in stories, poetry, and other written forms. Many children produce work about violent themes that for the most part is harmless when taken in context. However, an overrepresentation of violence in writings and drawings that is directed at specific individuals (family members, peers, other adults) consistently over time may signal emotional problems and the potential for violence. Because there is a real danger in misdiagnosing such a sign, it is important to seek the guidance of a qualified professional—such as a school psychologist, counselor, or other mental health specialist—to determine its meaning.

Uncontrolled anger

Everyone gets angry; anger is a natural emotion. However, anger that is expressed frequently and intensely in response to minor irritants may signal potential violent behavior toward self or others.

Patterns of impulsive and chronic hitting, intimidating, and bullying behaviors

Children often engage in acts of shoving and mild aggression. However, some mildly aggressive behaviors such as constant hitting and bullying of others that occur early in children's lives, if left unattended, might later escalate into more serious behaviors.

History of discipline problems

Chronic behavior and disciplinary problems both in school and at home may suggest that underlying emotional needs are not being met. These unmet needs may be manifested in acting out and aggressive behaviors. These problems may set the stage for the child to violate norms and rules, defy authority, disengage from school, and engage in aggressive behaviors toward other children and adults.

Past history of violent and aggressive behavior

Unless provided with support and counseling, a youth who has a history of aggressive or violent behavior is likely to repeat these behaviors. Aggressive and violent acts may be directed toward other individuals, be expressed in cruelty to animals, or include fire setting. Youth who show an early pattern of antisocial behavior frequently and across multiple settings are particularly at risk for future aggressive and antisocial behavior. Similarly, youth who engage in overt behaviors such as bullying, generalized aggression, and defiance, and covert behaviors such as stealing, vandalism, lying, cheating, and fire setting also are at risk for more serious aggressive behavior. Research suggests that age of onset may be a key factor in interpreting early warning signs. For example, children who engage in aggression and drug abuse at an early age (before age twelve) are more likely to show violence later on than are children who begin such behavior at an older age. In the presence of such signs it is important to review the child's history with behavioral experts and seek parents' observations and insights.

Intolerance for differences and prejudicial attitudes

All children have likes and dislikes. However, an intense prejudice toward others based on race, ethnicity, religion, language, gender, sexual orientation, ability, and physical appearance—when coupled with other factors—may lead to violent assaults against those who are perceived to be different. Membership in hate groups or the willingness to victimize individuals with disabilities or health problems should also be treated as early warning signs.

Drug use and alcohol use

Apart from being unhealthy behaviors, drug use and alcohol use reduce self-control and expose children and youth to violence, as perpetrators, victims, or both.

Affiliation with gangs

Gangs that support antisocial values and behaviors—including extortion, intimidation, and acts of violence toward other students—cause fear and stress among other students. Youth who are influenced by these groups—those who emulate and copy their behavior, as well as those who become affiliated with them—may adopt these values and act in violent or aggressive ways in certain situations. Gang-related violence and turf battles are common occurrences tied to the use of drugs, and they often result in injury and/or death.

Inappropriate access to, possession of, and use of firearms

Children and youth who inappropriately possess or have access to firearms can have an increased risk for violence. Research shows that such youngsters also have a higher probability of becoming victims. Families can reduce inappropriate access and use by restricting, monitoring, and supervising children's access to firearms and other weapons. Children who have a history of aggression, impulsiveness, or other emotional problems should not have access to firearms and other weapons.

Serious threats of violence

Idle threats are a common response to frustration; however, one of the most reliable indicators that a youth is likely to commit a dangerous act toward self or others is a detailed and specific threat to use violence. Recent incidents across the country clearly indicate that threats to commit violence against oneself or others should be taken very seriously. Steps must be taken to understand the nature of these threats and to prevent them from being carried out.

TABLE 3-1   Early Warning Behaviors

- Has a history of tantrums and uncontrollable angry outbursts
- Characteristically resorts to name calling, cursing, or abusive language
- Habitually makes violent threats when angry
- Has previously brought a weapon to school
- Has a background of serious disciplinary problems at school and in the community
- Has a background of drug, alcohol, or other substance abuse or dependency
- Is on the fringe of his/her peer group with few or no close friends
- Is preoccupied with weapons, explosives, or other incendiary devices
- Has previously been truant, suspended, or expelled from school
- Displays cruelty to animals
- Has little or no supervision and support from parents or a caring adult
- Has witnessed or been a victim of abuse or neglect in the home
- Has been bullied and/or bullies or intimidates peers or younger children
- Tends to blame others for difficulties and problems caused her- or himself
- Consistently prefers TV shows, movies, or music expressing violent themes and acts
- Prefers reading materials dealing with violent themes, rituals, and abuse
- Reflects anger, frustration, and the dark side of life in school essays or writing projects
- Is involved with a gang or an antisocial group on the fringe
- Is often depressed and/or has significant mood swings
- Has threatened or attempted suicide

(National School Safety Center, 1999).

In addition to these early warning signs, the National School Safety Center has been studying and tracking youth who have caused school-associated violent death and has compiled a checklist of behaviors that can signal a violent youth (see Table 3.1).

Identifying Young Bullies

As described in an earlier chapter, if a child is a bully, there is a strong possibility that the child will end up serving time in jail or prison. Research has shown that by age thirty, 25 percent of the adults who had been bullies during childhood will have criminal records. Even more disturbing, bullying behaviors can often be identified at as early as two years of age. There is also the sad indication that both the bully and the victim are vulnerable to long-term social and emotional problems (Beane & Espeland, 1999).

Recent research suggests that more students than had been imagined are involved in bullying. One study (Parents Resource Institute on Drug Education, PRIDE) reported that 40 percent of the students in grades six through twelve threatened to hurt another student at school. And other researchers estimate that as many as 75 percent of adolescents have been bullied at some time in school. As many as 10 to 15 percent of the students are bullied on a regular basis (Banks, 1997). In a recent study at a Midwest middle school by scholars at the University of Illinois, Champaign, 80 percent of the 558 students interviewed reported bullying someone during the 30 days prior to the interview. The study identified bullying as "teasing, name-calling, ridiculing, threatening, and pushing and shoving." Research has also identified another unfortunate finding. Bullying is not limited solely to boys. In one study in Philadelphia, 65 percent of the middle-school girls engaged in some sort of bullying.

As in other forms of youth violence, "early warning behaviors" have been identified for students who are bullies (Marano, 1998):

- Pushes, shoves, hits, kicks, and/or makes fun of other kids, says mean things or calls them names
- Manipulates relationships
- Starts acting aggressively as early as preschool
- Believes aggression is an acceptable way to solve conflicts
- Is quick to react with hostility to neutral events
- Gets into fights but blames others for starting them
- Lacks empathy
- Breaks rules aggressively
- Needs to dominate others
- Has two or three friends who are aggressive
- Feels no anxiety
- Generally feels well liked
- Does not feel lonely
- Hangs out with increasingly younger children

Preventive measures have also been identified for victims of bullying:

- If you think your child is being bullied, ask him. Kids are embarrassed. Parents need to take the initiative. Take notes.
- Believe your child if he says he is being bullied.
- Don't confront the bully or the bully's parents. This probably won't help and might make things worse.
- Don't tell your child to get in there and fight. Bullies are always stronger and more powerful than their victims.
- Don't blame your child.
- Don't promise to keep it a secret. Explain to your child you will help and ask the teacher to help.
- Contact the teacher as soon as possible. Request a private meeting when other students won't see you.
- Seek the teacher's perspective. Stay patient. Ask what will be done and get specifics. Ask to be kept informed.
- Help your child develop bully-resistant skills. Enroll him in a class on assertiveness skills, friendship skills, or self-defense. Build his social skills by having him join clubs.
- Consider whether your child does something that encourages bullies to pick on him. Is there a behavior that needs to change? Ask the teacher for insights.
- Get involved with your child's school, and volunteer in the classroom (Beane & Espeland, 1999).

Legal/Ethical Issues: A Word of Caution

Just as schools across the United States began mobilizing to identify violent, at-risk, and violence-prone children and youth and to be more vigilant regarding early warning signs, there was a caution from legal educators, the American Civil Liberties Union, and others regarding the potential dangerous and disruptive side effects to the children and youth being identified. Because predicting human behavior is far from an exact science and because many students who exhibit certain aspects of the violence-prone profile, are, in fact, highly resilient and never become violent, school officials must move very carefully in the identification and possible actions regarding students who display the various warning signs. All educators must realize that there is a real danger that early warning signs will be misinterpreted. To avoid doing harm, the U.S. Department of Education and the U.S. Department of Justice have provided a number of principles for schools to follow:

- Do No Harm: The primary caution in early identification is never to stigmatize children and youth and compound the problems students already face. The intent must be to provide help for youth as early as possible; it must not be to exclude, isolate, and punish students. Every effort must be made to safeguard students from mislabeling or stereotyping each other.

- Evaluation by Qualified Professionals: Even though a student may exhibit a number of the behaviors identified by psychologists as important early warning indicators, referrals for evaluation of a student must be conducted by a trained professional.
- Confidentiality/Parent Involvement: With the exception of suspected child abuse, parents must be thoroughly involved and informed, and strict confidentiality maintained.
- Understand Violence/Aggressive Behavior within a Context: Many students may react behaviorally to temporary periods of stress and emotional upheavals in the home, community, and school. Educators must recognize that certain environments or situations can "set-off" violent or aggressive behavior.
- Avoiding Stereotypes: Stereotypes can interfere with and even harm the school's ability to identify and help children. School officials need to be extremely cautious about students from low socioeconomic backgrounds, students from other racial and ethnic backgrounds, students who are low achievers, and even students with "differences" in physical appearance.
- View Warning Signs within a Developmental Context: Since children and youth have different social and emotional conflicts at different levels, school officials need to understand what is "developmentally typical" behavior so the behavior is not misinterpreted.
- Watch for Multiple Warning Signs: Educators need to recognize that most children and youth who are troubled and at risk of aggressive or violent behavior exhibit more than one warning sign, exhibit the warning signs repeatedly, usually with increasing intensity over time. Educators need to recognize that the behavior that reflects a single warning sign may only reflect the student's reaction to a particular context or situation (U.S. Department of Education, 1998b).

The recent high-profile acts of school violence have prompted a swift national response. In addition to new state legislation, the governors of a growing number of states, including Connecticut, Kentucky, and Idaho, have convened task forces or commissions to investigate youth violence and propose recommendations to improve the safety of schools. A number of states created Safe School Technical Assistance Centers; a few have established anonymous, toll-free telephone hotlines for students and adults to report threats or information about planned violence. And a growing number of centers and institutes have been created throughout the United States to collect, conduct, and disseminate research on youth violence and safe schools. A detailed discussion of the effective responses to youth violence is included in Chapters 6, 7, and 8.

As the extent and depth of the problems created by at-risk and violent children and youth has been more carefully documented, there is a parallel body of research that has documented school policies and practices that exacerbate the problems of these troubled youths, and in fact, actually place students at risk. In addition to family situations and the risky behaviors of children and youth, schools too often compound and complicate the pressures and problems of at-risk students. Chapter 4 explores this tragic situation by examining how schools fail at-risk youth.

How Schools Fail
At-Risk Youth

"Well, I just couldn't believe it. In fact," the U.S. history teacher said, "I am embarrassed to say, I never even thought about it. This kid in my third-period history class came by after school and asked if he could talk to me. And look, the kid was doing okay in my class. Not great, but believe me he was more than passing the course . . . he had a C average, and it was late November. He told me that he didn't know how to read. Of course I thought he was teasing. He was serious. Well, you know, I didn't know what to say. Here I am with an 11th grade student with a C average and he is confiding in me that he doesn't know how to read? Like, think about it; what would you do? I was at a total loss. Finally, I told the kid I would see what help was available. I immediately went to see the school counselor and asked about a reading program. The counselor gave me a blank look and said to me, "Why would we have a reading program? This is high school."
—HIGH SCHOOL TEACHER, HARTFORD, CONNECTICUT

While there is a growing sophistication in the identification of factors that contribute to students becoming at risk, most of these factors are rooted in the home, the community, and the culture of poverty. Yet almost every study of the complicated problems associated with at-risk children and youth has also identified educational factors that exacerbate the problems of those who are at risk and often drive them from school (Kirst, 1993; Hodgkinson, 1993). These school-related factors cut across the entire school spectrum and are deeply imbedded in the culture of U.S. public schools. The popular, contemporary intervention practices of expulsion, tracking, retention, pull-out programs, and special education have yet to be proven effective, yet remain common. However, the problem of how to educate at-risk youth is far more ominous than a particular set of ineffective school practices. The critical problem is one of teacher attitudes toward at-risk youth. Unfortunately, even though most teachers would deny it, too many believe that some children cannot learn. This problem is fueled by a reluctance of schools to address the problems of certain students, whether they are pregnant, malnourished, abused, lack adequate English skills or the ability to read.

Studies have found that many classroom teachers do not work hard to teach at-risk youth; they do not question them, they do not call on them in class or demand quality work. Researchers have also documented that the public school curriculum is overwhelmingly dominated by an emphasis on college preparation, even though only approximately 20 percent of Americans ever graduate from college. Too many schools do not teach financial planning, consumer economics, or computer skills beyond simple word processing. Many schools continue to offer courses in wood and metal shop and auto mechanics that reflect a world that no longer exists. Most vocational programs lack the advanced technology and skilled instructors to teach or even introduce the student to the technical demands and requirements of today's workplace.

School counselors continue to function in a guidance role, assisting high-school students in meeting college requirements and selecting an appropriate college. School counselors have almost no responsibility for ensuring that public school students gain the technical, vocational, and professional skills that would enable them to find jobs after high-school graduation or after dropping out. Articulation between public schools and colleges represents a sophisticated, complex set of agreements, aptitude and achievement testing programs, and career advising related to college. The vast majority of public schools have few, if any, support programs to assist the majority of public school students to make a successful transition into the world of work.

All of these programs and practices reflect a comprehensive, institutional bias against the at-risk child that is equally as disturbing as the sociocultural factors outside the school. At-risk youth arrive at school far from ready to learn, and public school programs tend to isolate them, stigmatize them, and place them in programs that widen the academic gap between them and their better achieving peers. Part of the explanation for school policies and practices that intellectually and psychologically brutalize students who are already at risk is rooted in an educational mythology that has endured for decades in spite of conclusive evidence to the contrary. While many of these policies and practices may originate from prejudice, intellectual elitism, or even racism, others seem to be motivated by legitimate though misguided concerns for at-risk youth. And, while research has decisively challenged the underlying assumption of much of public education's response to at-risk youth, a number of ineffective, and in some cases damaging policies and practices, have persevered so long that they have taken on the characteristics of mythology.

A Mythology of Ineffective Practices

Far too many educators continue to use instructional approaches based on a number of mythological assumptions that negatively impact children and youth. To effectively teach at-risk youth, all schools need to examine their programs and rid them of the following mythology:

Myth #1: At-Risk Youth Need Slow Learning

The idea that at-risk children and youth need slow learning cannot be further from the truth. Over the past 20 years, research has documented again and again the disastrous effects of this slow learning myth. We now know that at-risk children and youth benefit from being academically challenged in an environment of high expectation. They need accelerated, not slow, learning if they are ever to catch up and function effectively in public education and in adult life.

Myth #2: At-Risk Youth Should Be Retained during the Early Grades until They Are Ready to Move Forward

While retention seems so logical and is usually employed out of concern for the needs of at-risk youth, research has documented the disastrous effects of this practice. One study found that students ranked retention in the same category as "going blind" or losing a parent to death. Many agree that retention can have some positive benefits during the earliest grades, if approached properly, yet from the middle primary years on, retention poses an overwhelming obstacle to graduation (Roderick, 1995; Kelly, 1999).

Research has clearly documented that for at-risk youth, retention of one grade increases the student's likelihood of school failure, and if the child is retained twice, the chance of graduation from high school is near zero (see Table 2-2, Chapter 2). Rather than repeating a grade, at-risk youth need intense, accelerated, nongraded elementary classrooms that provide for the application of mastery learning and attention to their specific needs.

In the late 1990s a number of states implemented "barrier testing" that strictly prohibited the social promotion of any student who failed these "high stakes" tests. However, when large percentages of students failed the tests, many school districts, like Waco, Texas, and Los Angeles, California, implemented crash programs designed to accelerate student achievement to a level at which they could pass the test and move up to the next grade level (Texas school ties promotion solely to test scores, 1998).

Myth #3: At-Risk Youth Can Be Educated with the Same Expenditures As Other Students

While many effective programs may indeed be initiated with existing resources, they often require additional funds. Still there are large numbers of public-school students who have such severe problems that they need immediate, long-term, intensive educational care, and this care is often very expensive. Just as the health professions provide individualized intensive care that is expensive but essential in certain situations, schools too need to address the growing problems of at-risk children and youth in a similar manner. The needs of young children often demand additional resources during preschool and the early grades to ensure that they learn to read and communicate effectively before the end of the third grade. Students who are struggling to keep up as well as those who have fallen far behind need intensive, accelerated approaches if schools are to succeed at significantly reducing dropout rates.

The good news is that long-term cost analyses of public education show that providing early, intensive educational prevention and intervention is the most cost-effective means of confronting the massive problems at-risk children and youth face. The success of early prevention and intervention programs has a direct effect on reducing later costs of remedial reading, special education, school counseling, and other interventive programs and can provide for potentially dramatic reductions in the long-term cost of social services. While the long-term balance sheet will benefit from establishing proven intervention programs, the additional costs necessary will require additional reallocation of existing funds and often, new funding sources.

Myth #4: Classroom Teachers Can Adequately Address the Needs of At-Risk Youth

The problems of at-risk youth are often so complicated, so pervasive and so long-term, so rooted in the home, community, culture, and socioeconomic conditions that it is all but impossible for a classroom teacher alone to significantly address the needs of at-risk youth. The problems of at-risk students in most cases have developed and intensified over a period of years prior to entry into a particular classroom. A single teacher simply does not have the capacity to address complex problems of abuse, nutrition, home supervision and support, family disruptions, drugs, crime, gangs, violence, and other negative factors that so often impact at-risk youth. More accurate is the African saying, "it takes an entire village to raise a child." Schools must be transformed to increase student access to community services through coordinating school and social agency resources. In a very real sense a classroom teacher can only address the tip of the iceberg of their students' problems.

Myth #5: Some Students Can't Learn

In spite of the fact that almost every school in America has signs and slogans hanging in its halls, classrooms, and offices regarding the assumption that all students can learn, there is a huge amount of evidence that suggests that many teachers and school administrators not only doubt that fact but seem motivated to ensure that these "dumb kids" don't interrupt or interfere with those students who indeed can learn. Nowhere is this more evident than in the fact that elementary schools continue to fail to teach all children to read. We now know that all children can learn to read; we even know how to ensure that they do. Yet few schools can demonstrate that all children are reading at grade level by the end of the third grade.

Myth #6: The Most Effective Way to Improve Instruction for At-Risk Youth Is to Reduce Classroom Size

One of the most widely held beliefs regarding teaching effectiveness centers on classroom size. Following teachers' salaries, it is often the second issue to be considered in teacher contract negotiations. And given the growing diversity of the nation's classrooms, it would appear logical that reduced pupil-teacher ratio would be an essential goal. In the past intense lobbying has led legislatures and school boards in Tennessee, New York, Ontario, and Indiana to reduce class size by almost half. And while there is little question that reductions in class size might in some cases contribute to alleviating some of the daily stress and strain of classroom teachers, there is unfortunately little or no evidence that this practice *alone* provides for increased achievement of at-risk youth. A number of studies and program follow-up evaluations have found little improved student achievement to occur from simply reducing pupil-teacher ratios. Preschool and early public school prevention programs and supplementary, after-school one-to-one tutoring have been evaluated to be more effective in teaching reading to at-risk youth than reducing regular classroom size.

Yet, politically, smaller class size continues to be an attractive, though usually costly educational reform. California has recently invested significantly to lower the size of elementary classes to a maximum of twenty students. The State of California has also reported research that indicates that smaller classes can in fact have some beneficial effects (Illig, 1997).

Myth #7: Students Who Are Having Learning Difficulties Probably Need Special Education

With few other options available to teachers, there is a tendency to identify students having learning difficulties as needing special education. As special education has become more sophisticated, teachers now have a complex range of identified programs to use in diagnosing students. The largest special education designation is learning disabled (LD) which includes Attention Deficit Disorder (ADD) and Attention Deficit with Hyperactivity Disorder (ADHD). If a student is not learning or is misbehaving, there is a strong tendency to refer the child for evaluation (Coles, 1999). Providing service for these types of "disorders" represents a very expensive additional burden to districts. While research has documented that effective education in the lower elementary grades can dramatically reduce special education referrals, school policy and practice that ignores this promising evidence not only fails to adequately address the needs of at-risk youth, but often contributes to the growing numbers of students leaving school early.

Inequity in School Funding

For decades data have been collected that documents the profound inequity that exists in public-school funding. Jonathan Kozol's book, *Savage Inequalities,* vividly depicted the tragic and devastating impact of the inequitable funding between districts. While school funding in the United States is primarily based on local property taxes, there exists substantial variation between school funding levels from state to state and from school district to school district. Inevitably, the wealthy school districts support their schools unusually well while the poor districts lack the resources to support schools even at minimal levels. Tremendous variation occurs between affluent and poor communities, between teacher salaries, per-pupil expenditures, facilities, supply and equipment budgets, and virtually every other area. The property tax model for school funding often penalizes the very students who are most at risk and who are most in need of help. In the early 1990s the supreme court of the State of Texas declared that the state's property-tax-based school funding system was in violation of the state constitution. The court found many disparities in funding including one example of a $17,000 difference in per-pupil spending between one of the wealthiest and one of the poorest districts.

This chilling inequity originated from a $13.9 million differential in assessed property values between two adjoining districts (Kozol, 1991). Many states have enacted legislation or court rulings that require state formulas for the funding of public education to abandon the "property tax approach." Yet still today, most states continue to use property taxes as the basis for the funding of public education.

In spite of decades of civil rights litigation and legislation that has fought segregated schools and even concluded that "separate but equal" was not in fact equal, property tax funding and local control of schools have combined to stratify U.S. public education into the haves and have-nots. It is clearly recognized that poor children who attend school with other poor children have an enormous challenge to overcome if they are to succeed in school. The existence of poverty in the home and community is too often matched by poverty in the school setting, which directly contributes to the failure of so many at-risk youth. Too often the students who are so in need of enriched, accelerated education are subjected to the schools with the worst financial support, the most poorly paid teachers, the most dilapidated buildings, the worst equipment, textbooks and instructional materials, and they respond accordingly by failing, leaving, or giving up.

Programs That Isolate and Stigmatize At-Risk Children and Youth

There is a consistent record of research over the past 20 years which documents the negative, often disastrous effects of a number of school policies and programs specifically designed to address the needs of at-risk youth and the problems that at-risk youth create for schools. Unfortunately, many of these school programs and practices, including expulsion, retention, tracking, special education, and remedial pull-out programs, have in actuality proven to be harmful to at-risk youth. Research has documented that a number of these school programs have led to poor student achievement and to dropping out of school. Most unfortunate is the fact that almost all schools use these programs and continue to use them in spite of overwhelming negative evidence regarding their effectiveness. The following is a summary of research findings regarding school programs that do not work or at the very best have very limited positive results.

Expulsion

Too often, youth react to schools with inappropriate or disruptive behavior. Because of this, state legislatures, communities, and educators have recognized that it may be necessary to isolate or exclude some students in order to provide others with a more effective climate for learning. While much of the disruptive behavior often originates from antisocial tendencies rooted deep within the home and society, research indicates that often a student's negative behavior may well be precipitated by a number of school practices: inappropriate curriculum, ineffective teacher-student relations, lack of sensitivity to diversity, school failure, and insufficient support services. It is now clear that students often react to their failures in school, to teachers' negative perceptions, and to a curriculum that seems irrelevant to their needs by not attending school, or, if they come, by waging war against the teachers and schools that they perceive to be so antagonistic toward them.

Although most schools throughout the United States have developed more effective discipline policies and procedures, schools continue to use expulsion as a primary punitive reaction to absenteeism or to inappropriate or disruptive behavior. In fact, the increase in dramatic violent incidents in public schools during the 1990s led to the enactment of "zero tolerance" policies and laws nationwide. Unfortunately, as "zero tolerance" policies have been implemented and evaluated, they have been proven to generate disturbing new problems for schools and communities. The single best research on the effects of "zero tolerance" policies was a statewide study in Colorado. This study of the approximately 1,500 students expelled in the state in one year discovered that once students are out of school, they are unsupervised in the home and community, and a large percentage of these youths quickly find themselves in trouble with police. Large numbers are in jail within a year after expulsion (Colorado Foundation for Families & Children, 1995). And the effects on students from the practice of school expulsion have been carefully studied and have proved to be extremely negative. Expelled students typically fall further behind, experience increased social difficulties, and seldom return to complete school.

Frymier and Gansneder, primary authors of the nation's most comprehensive study of the factors that place youth at risk, concluded that expulsion was one of the top six factors that lead to dropping out (1989). Other studies indicate that expulsion only serves to isolate youth from school and to encourage a variety of debilitating activities such as dropping out, teenage pregnancy, drug and alcohol abuse, and crime. Nationally, 44 percent of African-American dropouts, 31 percent of Hispanic dropouts and 26 percent of Caucasian dropouts were found to have been suspended or put on probation at least once prior to leaving school (Wheelock, 1986).

Learning can seldom occur in a disruptive environment. However, schools can create orderly, safe environments by means other than suspension and expulsion. Districts and schools can contribute to their students' academic achievement by establishing, communicating, and enforcing fair and consistent discipline policies

(U.S. Department of Education, 1987b). There is strong new evidence that expulsion can be almost totally eliminated by involving students, parents, teachers, and administrators in establishing rules and by developing a careful due process procedure that protects the individual's rights (Gathercoal, 1990). A growing number of school districts and states require that students must be provided with alternatives to expulsion or for those students who are expelled from the regular school, the opportunity to attend some type of alternative education program.

Retention

The concept of retention is a simple idea and is probably as old as formal schooling. Simply put, retention is a process of requiring students who have not demonstrated minimal academic achievement to repeat a year of school. Use of retention has been encouraged by a negative reaction to the use of social promotions in public schools. Many believe that social promotion is a major contributing cause to the poor overall academic achievement of U.S. youth. Critics of public education have repeatedly cited social promotion as one of the primary reasons that many students graduate from high school unemployable and illiterate.

More recently, two major syntheses of research have once again substantiated the negative effects of retention on children and youth. "A substantial body of research has demonstrated that grade retention does not help student learning, in fact, has a harmful effect, while it also increases drop-out rates substantially . . . retaining students not only fails to help them catch up with other peers, it actually contributes to academic failure and behavioral difficulties" (Darling-Hammond & Falk, 1996). "Repeating a grade provides few remediational benefits and may in the long run, place students at risk of dropping out of school" (Roderick, 1995). Unfortunately the practice continues. In 1992, over 30 percent of 14-year-olds were behind grade level and the overall number of average students was up 40 percent over the previous two decades (Roderick, 1995).

In the late 1990s an increasing number of states began identifying the essential knowledge and skills that all students were accountable for achieving. These new, statewide standards attempted to significantly "raise the bar" of student learning expectations and were accompanied by "barrier tests" that prevented students from being promoted to the next grade level or from graduation from high school unless the established passing scores were achieved (Heubert & Hauser, 1999). Some states, like Texas and California, specifically prohibited "social promotion." When these "barrier tests" were first formally used in the late 1990s, many state and school districts discovered that huge percentages of students failed the test and were retained at their current grade level.

The practice of requiring underachieving students to repeat a grade in school is also a natural outgrowth of state and national assessment of standards-based learning. An increasing number of states are requiring the testing of minimal competency which prevents students from proceeding further in the curriculum until they have achieved required levels on academic achievement tests. This approach has and will contribute to the increase in the number of students being retained (Wheelock, 1998).

Public schools have long used retention as a major strategy for addressing the needs of at-risk youth. A Phi Delta Kappa Study reported that over 26 percent of principals and 48 percent of teachers support the use of retention (Frymier & Gansneder, 1989). Another study found that many urban schools retain 15 to 20 percent of their students at each grade level, and by grade 10, up to 60 percent of the students have been retained at least once (Gottfredson, 1988).

In spite of the fact that over 700,000 U.S. youth are retained each year, research and evaluation of retention practices have shown few, if any, academic or social benefits (Shepard & Smith, 1989). Careful study has consistently identified this practice as one of the most significant factors in increasing the risk that students will drop out of high school before graduation (Natriello, 1988). Dropouts are five times more likely to have repeated a grade than high-school graduates. If they repeat two grades, students face close to a 100 percent probability of dropping out (Frymier & Gansneder, 1989). Few students who enter high school at age 16 or 17 will stay until 20 or 21 to graduate. Schools that continue to retain students do so despite the 20-plus years of cumulative research which does not support the practice (Glickman, 1991).

Martin Haberman and Vicky Dill eloquently summarize the practice of retention:

Hundreds of studies exist examining the effects of retention. What is so exceptional about the body of literature is not the number of studies, the scope, size, or longevity of the data, but rather the uniform conclusion: retained students are negatively affected academically, socially, and emotionally. As a strategy, retention FAILS. (1993, p. 355)

A wide variety of research suggests that a number of policies and practices offer far more promise than retention. The most effective approach appears to be a combination of interventive programs at the early childhood, preschool, and early grade levels designed to provide students with a strong foundation for learning. These programs provide enrichment and support that allow students to catch up, both academically and socially, with their achieving peers through accelerated learning. Programs such as Head Start, Great Start, Even Start, Follow Through, Accelerated Learning, and all-day kindergarten have demonstrated strong positive successes (Holmes, 1990). Such enriched "front loading" of the educational process appears to be a sound and effective educational strategy and deserves widespread support.

Other programs have demonstrated effective alternatives to retention. They include multigraded and looped elementary classrooms that permit students to proceed at their own pace through developmentally appropriate learning practices; individualized continuous progress schools at the secondary level, and schools like the K-12 St. Paul Open School, which possess a long record of success using competency-based performance measures rather than graduation requirements (McPartland & Slavin, 1990).

To effectively address the needs of at-risk youth, schools must design programs that accelerate learning opportunities that enable students to catch up with their peers. Holding at-risk students back through retention has been clearly demonstrated as ineffective and harmful to at-risk youth.

Tracking

> *In 1931, A. H. Turney summarized writings on ability grouping in the 1920s and earlier. From these writings he derived a list of advantages and disadvantages of ability grouping. They are adapted as follows:*
>   *Advantages:*
>
> 1. *It permits pupils to make progress commensurate with their abilities.*
> 2. *It makes possible an adaptation of the technique of instruction to the needs of the group.*
> 3. *It reduces failures.*
> 4. *It helps to maintain interest and incentive, because bright students are not bored by the participation of the dull.*
> 5. *Slower pupils participate more when not eclipsed by those much brighter.*
> 6. *It makes teaching easier.*
> 7. *It makes possible individual instruction to small slow groups.*
>
>   *Disadvantages:*
>
> 1. *Slow pupils need the presence of the able students to stimulate them and encourage them.*
> 2. *A stigma is attached to low sections, operating to discourage the pupils in these sections.*
> 3. *Teachers are unable, or do not have time, to differentiate the work for different levels of ability.*
>
> *Turney's list is remarkably current. In any academic discussion or PTA meeting on ability grouping the same arguments are likely to be advanced on both sides. (Slavin, 1993, p. 13)*

Tracking continues to be used in over 95 percent of U.S. high schools and is increasingly being employed at the middle-school and elementary levels. Tracking is a highly popular school strategy for dealing with diverse student abilities and achievement. Within each grade level, schools utilize a student's previous grades, scores on standardized tests, and teacher evaluations to group students according to ability (Braddock, 1990). At the elementary level, this often occurs through ability grouping within self-contained classes, especially for instruction in reading and math. At the secondary level, tracks are clearly established in the vast majority of schools as distinctive educational programs with differentiated curriculum and differentiated learning expectations. Today, most high schools provide distinct programs in college preparation, general education, and vocational education, with students often being segregated by ability even further into separate classes within each of these three tracks (McPartland & Slavin, 1990).

In theory, tracking is used to accommodate curriculum and instruction to the diverse needs, interests, and abilities of students found in most schools. It is believed that teachers can focus their attention on student needs and develop curricula that relate directly to student educational levels and abilities. Such homogeneous grouping is almost universally supported by teachers who believe it makes teaching and learning more efficient and more effective. However, the effect on minority students is not likely to be positive. Kuykendall in her book *From Rage To Hope* stressed:

> *Tracking and ability grouping are likely to send subliminal messages to Black and Hispanic youth that White and middle class students are going to have opportunities to a greater range of knowledge and, therefore, opportunities for more lifelong success. (Kuykendall, 1992, p. 41)*

Unfortunately, except in special comprehensive programs, research and evaluation on tracking is overwhelmingly negative (McPartland & Slavin, 1990). There is some evidence that grouped instruction in reading during the early elementary grades can be successful when used in a comprehensive school program with specially trained teachers and tutors who have high educational expectations for the students (Madden, Slavin, Karweit, Dolan, & Wasik, 1991).

Research has identified three major reasons why tracking has not been successful, at least for the students placed into the lower tracks. First, there is evidence that slower tracks receive less resources from the school. Often these classes are large, housed in inadequate facilities, and limited by antiquated methods and equipment. Second, since teachers find these classes more demanding both behaviorally and instructionally, the slower track typically does not attract the most experienced, effective teachers. Many teachers will explain that during their early years of teaching, "I did my time in the slow tracks . . . now let someone else do it." Third, and even more disturbing, teachers tend to have significantly lower expectations for student learning in the slower tracks than for the students in the faster tracks. Frequently students and teachers feel stigmatized by being in the slower tracks and both share expectations of low achievement. The consequences of these factors for the lower-track students unfortunately include a less challenging curriculum, a slower instructional pace, test and homework assignments that are not challenging, and fewer demands for higher-order thinking skills (Oakes, 1993).

The cumulative effects of tracking during a student's educational career can be devastating. Rather than helping students to accelerate and catch up, it has been demonstrated that tracking actually widens the achievement gap between the slower and more advanced students (Goodlad, 1984). Rather than alleviating the problems of students with significant educational needs, tracking often further exacerbates the problem.

Even more alarming, tracking has been shown to resegregate schools that have been racially desegregated. In racially mixed schools, often achieved through complex desegregation programs including bussing and redrawing school district boundaries, students from the poorer socioeconomic backgrounds usually are grouped together and too often are resegregated into white and non-white educational tracks within a single school (Epstein, 1985).

Students tend to be tracked more by their socioeconomic status than by their academic ability. The higher-level academic track tends to be middle-class youth from educated families and the slower track tends to be minority, poor, and from homes with limited educational backgrounds. Unfortunately, once a child is assigned to the slow track, there is little hope of ever moving up to the advanced track (Glickman, 1991). For students who are most at risk, tracking only serves to isolate, handicap, stigmatize, and actually prevent effective learning. For almost three decades, it has been known that if students were not slow learners when they were assigned to the slow track, they soon became so.

Special Education

During the past decade and a half, the number of children classified as learning disabled for placement in special education has doubled, "even though the numbers of students in special education with physical disabilities or mental retardation have not substantially changed" (McPartland & Slavin, 1990, p. 6). Too often schools have had few if any other alternatives (except tracking and retention) to address the needs of youth who are most in need of educational programs other than regular classes or special education. Most students who are typically designated by schools as learning disabled are in fact "the lowest of the low achievers in the school" (McPartland & Slavin, 1990, p. 6), but may not have any of the usual expected mental or physical handicaps associated with special education (Deshler, Schumaker, Alley, Warner, & Clark, 1982). Schools also tend to classify students they have difficulty dealing with as learning disabled, emotionally disturbed, or as having an attention (ADD) or hyperactivity disorder (ADHD).

Standing in marked contrast to the practices of retention, expulsion, and tracking, special education programs usually do provide enriched resources and highly trained, specialized teachers to serve their students. Yet the use of special education to serve low-achieving students with no other handicap is an extremely expensive option given the paucity of research to support the continued use of this practice. There is also the unfortunate stigmatization that seems to occur when slow learners are assigned to special education (Leinhardt & Pallas, 1982). Once students are designated for special education, they tend to maintain that status throughout the school years, which severely limits the educational and occupational opportunities that are available to these students after their school years. Thus the decision to refer low-achieving students to special education may negatively affect these students for their entire lifetime.

A related problem has emerged as special education programs have dramatically increased the number of learning disabled students. As school districts continue to serve the special education students with special teachers, small classes, and highly individualized learning programs, resources for the rest of the school population will often decrease proportionately.

Remedial Pullout Programs

Some of the most controversial school programs designed for at-risk youth are those that pull out students from regular classes for special, enriched, or remedial instruction. These federally-funded programs like Chapter 1, special education, and bilingual education have been in operation for decades. In addition to these formal, externally funded programs, many schools have established resource rooms, tutorial programs, remedial programs, and special education programs that regularly pull students out of their regular classrooms for enriched instruction, especially in reading and math, and for bilingual students to participate in English as a Second Language programs.

Many of these federally-funded programs are controversial. Research interpretations, especially regarding Chapter 1 and bilingual education, have been highly politicized, with opponents often emphasizing only research and evaluation that support their partisan points of view. The former director of Chapter 1, Mary Jean LeTendre, states:

> *Chapter 1 has made a significant impact on American education. It has helped to equalize American educational opportunity for our neediest children at the local level and it has been a catalyst for improving instruction in basic skills, for improving the training of teachers and for increasing the involvement of parents in the education of their children. (LeTendre, 1991, p. 577)*

However, an extensive review of the literature on effective practices for students at risk concluded that "the effectiveness of most widely used supplemental/remedial programs, diagnostic prescriptive pullout programs provided under Chapter 1 or special education funding show little evidence of effectiveness" (Slavin & Madden, 1989). Yet, later, the authors of that study concluded that Chapter 1 programs did make important contributions to the education of low-achieving disadvantaged youth. Both conclusions may be correct. While Chapter 1 students do in fact learn more than the other disadvantaged children in a particular school, they do not seem to bridge the substantial gap that separates them from the more advanced students. There is also evidence that Chapter 1 programs may provide an indirect contribution in reducing the achievement gap among African American, Hispanic, and Caucasian students (Slavin, 1991a).

Although there is evidence that Chapter 1 and special education are successful in increasing student learning, research and program evaluation are beginning to lead to significant changes in these programs, causing program directors and others to reconsider the pullout option. Increasingly, educators are concerned with what students are missing from their regular classroom during the pullout enrichment. There is a trend toward inclusion-type alternatives to pullout programs, such as increased use of mainstreaming, after-school programs, or schoolwide programs. Guidelines for Title I (formerly Chapter I) now enable schools serving large numbers of disadvantaged students (75 percent of the school population) to use funds for schoolwide services. Unfortunately, in most cases, Title 1 continues as a pullout program serving individual students in remedial programs.

Research indicates that schools could be more effective by employing prevention, early intervention, and whole school strategies, rather than using pullout remediations. There is no substitute for early educational success, especially in reading. Children who are taught to read successfully the first time they are taught will rarely need remedial help. Bilingual education, possibly the most controversial federally-funded program, has received criticism that pullout programs in English as a second language are less effective than total English immersion classes or cross-cultural classes that teach bilingual youth English. In 1998 the state of California abandoned bilingual education in favor of mainstreamed classrooms. This development could portend major changes for the rest of the nation.

While few schools will be willing to deprive students and teachers of the federal funds that are available for these enrichment programs, educators should work to ensure that these programs do not detract or lessen the importance of high-quality classroom instruction.

Reconstitution of Low-Performance Schools

The most dramatic new approach to addressing the poor performance of at-risk youth is to completely "reconstitute" the instructional and service staff (everyone from principals and teachers to custodians) of low-achieving schools through termination or transfer and replacement with an entirely new staff. And while some of these reconstructed schools have reported major successes in transforming low student achievement with high achievement, the approach is still too new to adequately evaluate. By 1999 most educators seemed to agree that there were a number of equally successful and less disruptive approaches to school reform (Hardy, 1999). Too often, reconstitution stigmatizes the very students the reform effort was attempting to assist. Often, students attending a reconstituted school become known as the "dummy students from the dummy school" (Christensen, 1998).

Frequent Mistakes in the Development of Programs for At-Risk Youth

Well, it was my worst nightmare come true. I had never had anything happen like this in 26 years of teaching. Talk about good intentions gone to hell! See, last year we started this program for at-risk youth. We identified 13 of the school's most difficult students and scheduled them into my classroom for two hours each day. In addition to teaching them my specialty course, Applied Mathematics, I taught them study skills, helped them with their homework, discussed their problems and worked with their other teachers to be as supportive as possible. Well, everything was great. The kids started coming to school, doing their homework, their grades went up, and they began to really try. This year we transitioned those kids back into their regular classes and then scheduled a dozen new students into my two periods. The heartbreak of this story is that nine of last year's students had already dropped out of school by November and the rest are failing most of their classes. I can't believe it. What did we do wrong?
—SCHOOL ADMINISTRATOR, MADRAS, OREGON

In recent years, as greater attention has been focused on the problems of at-risk youth, school districts throughout the country have increasingly developed new programs to serve these students. Unfortunately, as is so often the case in public education, little attention has been given to research on program effectiveness. The results have ranged from disappointing to tragically unfortunate. Even the best of intentions have often created programs that have not only failed to help at-risk youth but have also compounded their problems. One could conclude that many of these programs have been developed not so much to provide significant assistance to at-risk youth but to get these unfortunate youth out of regular classrooms where they make teaching and learning so hard for teachers and the other, better achieving students. The following represents a number of design errors that fatally flaw the potential effectiveness of programs designed to specifically serve at-risk youth.

Intervention Rather than Prevention

The vast majority of programs designed for at-risk youth are implemented as intervention programs at the high-school level. On a common-sense level, this is probably understandable, since teachers and principals at the secondary level are confronted by students who are dropping out or by underachieving students who are increasingly disruptive and who often wreak havoc with the school and the classrooms. Unfortunately, most intervention programs are expensive and demand longer, more intensive efforts if they are to be successful. On this issue the researchers offer clear recommendations for prevention rather than intervention. Starting as early as possible is the most cost-effective approach and holds the most promise of long-term success.

Starting Too Small

A second tendency for schools is to start at-risk programs on a very small scale. Not only are most at-risk programs initiated at the secondary level, too many start with only one or two teachers for one or two periods a day and are focused on the most severely at-risk youth in a particular school. Teachers tend to burn out quickly in programs such as these, and in turn provide little impact toward truly addressing the needs of at-risk youth. Research consistently indicates that schools need comprehensive programs to help at-risk youth and that these programs involve as much of the school day as possible.

Transition Programs

School districts will often start short-term programs for at-risk youth with a goal of quickly correcting their problems and transitioning them as soon as possible back into the regular school program. Some of these programs last only a semester; others last only a year. Research has documented that there is no quick fix for at-risk youth, whether at the primary, middle, or high-school level. At-risk students tend to have far-reaching problems. It has taken years for many of these students to develop the problems that have placed them so at risk, and it is highly unlikely that these problems can be corrected quickly. Even the students who find themselves suddenly at risk because of family disruptions, depression, substance abuse, or other reasons have problems that can only be addressed effectively with long-term support.

School-Based Programs

Typically, schools focus only on their own environment when addressing the needs of at-risk youth and tend to create in-school programs. And while school-based programs can be designed to provide lasting benefits for at-risk youth, research indicates that these programs can be greatly strengthened by incorporating out-of-school learning experiences, community support, and the coordination of community agencies.

Furthermore, virtually all programs report the critical importance of autonomy to creating and maintaining an effective program. School-based programs have far more difficulty attaining this autonomy than do programs located separately from the host school.

Mandatory Assignments and Placements

Schools often attempt to develop effective programs for at-risk youth but then err by assigning both teachers and students to the programs. This practice diminishes the effectiveness of even a good program by including the negative effects that research has documented regarding traditional tracking programs. For maximum success, at-risk programs should be developed and made available both to teachers and students who have the opportunity to choose to participate. For at-risk youth, the element of choice affords considerable power toward stimulating their desire to be in school and, once there, the willingness to learn.

Schools that move to address the needs of at-risk children and youth must be careful that their good intentions do not serve to complicate their students' difficulties. A careful review of research clearly indicates that many school attempts to help at-risk students too often backfire and become contributing factors toward forcing students out of school.

In spite of this rather depressing survey of efforts at school reform and the disappointing effects of many of the traditional approaches to the problems of at-risk youth, there remains cause for optimism. Research and practice during the last thirty years have provided a substantial and expanding foundation for confidence that schools and communities can be improved and restructured, and that programs do exist that have a proven track record of success with at-risk youth. Today, there is significant cause for optimism regarding the opportunity for public school educators to effectively address the needs of at-risk youth. The next chapters will survey the characteristics of effective programs and provide specific recommendations for schools to follow in addressing the difficult challenge of successfully teaching all children and youth.

Chapter *5*

What We Know about Effective Programs

The ninth-grade student was certainly a show stopper. Half of her head was shaved, and the other half was freaked out in a wild explosion of hair, bells, and ribbons. She had three gold studs in her nose and was wearing at least a dozen earrings that jingled like wind chimes when she moved. In her own distinctive way she was a beautiful young girl. I asked her why she had left her former high school to travel across town to a small alternative program. She thought for a moment and then explained, "At my other school everyone treated me like a geek; everybody thought I was kind of weird." "Is it different here in the alternative school?" I asked. She cocked her head to the side and flashed a smile. "Over here I just disappeared." She wagged her head from side to side, setting her earrings chiming. "It's like, I just disappeared into this really happy family."
—HIGH SCHOOL STUDENT, METROPOLITAN LEARNING CENTER, PORTLAND, OREGON

Amid the depressing crises facing so many youth, there is cause for optimism. During the past 15 years, there has been an avalanche of research on teaching, learning, and effective schools that is leading toward a new science of learning. Many now maintain that much of what was known prior to 1985 has been rendered inadequate or incorrect by dramatic, compelling conclusions. This new research trend is providing a basis for transforming teaching, learning, and schools. This growing data base originates from a number of distinctly different, independent efforts that intersect to form a nexus of common conclusions.

Together, these studies have documented that schools can be effective with at-risk youth; why they are effective; why some schools are ineffective; why certain approaches to school improvement work so well . . . and why others create or exacerbate dysfunction. Taken as a group, these research and evaluation studies form a foundation for significantly improving the education of youth at risk.

Research on Teaching, Learning, and Effective Schools: What We Know

Schools make a difference. In almost every state, schools have been identified that have succeeded in helping at-risk youth perform up to the levels of their more affluent peers. These schools and programs can be found at the elementary-, middle-, and high-school levels and have been studied over the past 20 years through in-depth, long-term, quantitative, and qualitative studies. Even more significant, many argue that this research represents only the "first wave" of new insights into teaching and learning. This research has documented the factors associated with the remarkable successes of educating at-risk youth. There is now general agreement among researchers regarding why certain schools are so effective with at-risk and violent youth, and the essential components and practices that make up these schools. As a result, effective schools for at-risk and violent youth can and should be created, replicated, and improved. The research that has helped to identify these essential components comes from a wide variety of diverse venues.

Neuroscience Research

Research of the last two decades in the field of developmental psychology and the developing field of neuroscience have reconceptualized what educators understand about teaching and learning, learning disabilities, violent behavior, schizophrenia, Tourette's syndrome, and other learning disorders. These advances in knowledge are also paving the way to an understanding of the causes of Parkinson's and Alzheimer's diseases. It is challenging for educators to grasp the implications of this research, which represents the transformation of the "soft" field of education methodology into a science of learning (Bransford et al., 1999). In 1969 there were only 500 neuroscientists registered in the International Society of Neuroscience; today there are over 300,000. Recent discoveries have revealed truly "astonishing insights about the brain and learning" and have laid the foundations for distinctly new and effective approaches to teaching and learning (Jenson, 1998, p. 2). Scholars caution, "anything you learned two years ago is already old information" (Kotulak, 1996), and "neuroscience is rapidly moving the education of young children away from recommendations to prescriptions" (Ramey & Ramey, 1999).

Essential to this work has been the development of interactive technology (e.g., Magnetic Resonance Imaging [MRI] and Positron Emission Tomography [PET]), which has for the first time provided researchers with the ability to intimately view the brain and study its relationship to teaching and learning. This capability has dramatically advanced the knowledge base of at-risk and violent children and adults with learning disabilities. Findings are now providing parents with the ability to positively influence the intelligence and personalities of their young children and helping to explain why some children and youths become violent.

Research on Learning Disabilities

In addition to impressive advances toward understanding the nature of learning disabilities that have continued to emerge from neuroscience research and clinical studies, longitudinal research has helped to provide a new and expanded insight into the definition, causes, and effective approaches to learning disabilities (Spear-Swerling & Sternberg, 1998). Researchers at Yale have studied a group of children with learning disabilities for more than 20 years, and their study has documented the effects of learning disabilities into adolescence and adulthood (Shaywitz & Shaywitz, 1990).

Research on Early Childhood Development, Child Care, and Preschool Education

Research in the fields of developmental psychology, child care, and preschool programs has also made remarkable progress. Dramatic insights have been gained into the growth and development of infants and young children and provided the foundation for effective parent education (Shore, 1997). Child-development studies provide parents with the critical knowledge of how to stimulate the brain of very young children and actually enhance their intelligence. It also provides essential new understanding regarding the human bonding of infants with adults and the tragic effects of failing to bond. Research has documented the power of high-quality child care and the essential components of effective programs for young children. While a recent national research study is following 1,364 children ages six to seven years old (NICHD Exhibit, 1999), and another is following 700 three-year-olds (McCartney, 1999), the most significant study continues to be a longitudinal study of two groups of 191 youngsters from poor families currently in its 30th year. This study has been conducted by Lawrence Schweinhart of the High/Scope Educational Research Foundation in Ypsilanti, Michigan. After more than two decades of following these children to adulthood, Schweinhart concluded, "children exposed to good preschools that encourage creativity and active learning are more likely to stay in school longer, are less likely to be arrested for felonies, and they earn more as adults" (Barnett, 1996; Schweinhart et al., 1993). A 1998 RAND Corporation study drew a similar conclusion. It found that intervention programs can benefit disadvantaged children and, in the long run, significantly save on the cost of welfare, criminal justice, and special education (Karoly et al., 1998; National Center for Early Development & Learning, 1999). Preschool programs have also been documented extensively. No federally funded program has ever been studied so carefully over time, and with such positive results, as Head Start (Schorr & Schorr, 1989).

Research on Resilient Youth

During the late 1980s and 1990s, as some researchers were able to conclusively identify the underlying risk factors associated with such problems as alcohol and drug abuse, teen pregnancy, delinquency, gangs, and dropping out, others began to focus on identifying "protective factors" that seem to facilitate the development of youth who would not or did not get involved in severe, life-compromising problems (Benard, 1991). The result was the identification of resilient children who seemed to succeed against all odds. For the past ten years, the goal of this research has been to translate negative risk factors into positive action that would develop or strengthen the resiliency of youth (Krovetz, 1999). And while some continue to argue that "there is too little research" on how some students succeed against the odds, advances in achievement motivation theory have provided a conceptual framework for the continued study of this important issue (Bempechat, 1999). Today the search for positive action strategies have emerged into sets of strategies for strengthening resiliency in the home, school, and community (Krovetz, 1999).

Research on Violent Youth

As the nation's attention has increasingly focused on youth violence, researchers from diverse fields have been working to try and identify why some youth become violent, what are the characteristics that identify violent youth, and what to do about the growing problem. Research has helped educators to understand that violence is a learned behavior and that it can also be unlearned. It also is becoming evident that positive early interventions are the most productive approach to addressing violent and violence-prone children. Research from the American Psychological Association and the American Academy of Pediatrics has specified early indicators of violence and warning signs among toddlers and preschoolers, school-age children, and preteens and adolescents. Profiles have also been developed to help identify and predict the potential for violence (Fager & Boss, 1998). More recently, research has focused on the impact of media violence—movies, television, video games, and music—on impressionable children and youth. The recent rash of school violence, perpetuated by teenagers who did not fit the traditional profile of coming from poor, abused, dysfunctional families, has prompted scholars to focus on youth from two-parent, affluent families, on gifted and talented teenagers, and on teenagers who have attempted and committed suicides (see Chapter 4).

Research on Schools Where At-Risk and Violent Youth Are Learning Effectively

Perhaps the single most important research at the school and classroom level is a growing collection of efforts that focuses on schools in which all youths are achieving, even those at high risk of failure. What makes this growing collection of studies so important is its focus on real schools and real students. The more there is research and evaluation on these effective schools, the more evident it becomes that there is a set of educational components underlying their remarkable success. The primary areas of this research include:

School Effectiveness

The Louisiana School Effectiveness Study involved hundreds of separate research projects conducted over a ten-year period, all focused on understanding why students in some of the state's poorest communities were achieving up to and beyond students in more affluent communities. This long-term collection of studies, conducted by Louisiana State University, identified a set of school characteristics that were associated with success in educating high-risk youth:

1. Clear academic mission
2. Orderly environment
3. Focus on academics
4. Frequent monitoring of student profiles
5. Caring and demanding teachers
6. Dynamic leadership (Teddlie & Stringfield, 1993, p. 3)

The Louisiana Effectiveness Study concluded that these less affluent, successful schools had principals who motivated teachers who, in turn, motivated students. The ability to instill in students a belief that they can learn is critical in effective, low-socioeconomic-status schools. Apparently, students in effective, middle-socioeconomic-status schools had this belief instilled at home and reinforced at school (Teddlie & Stringfield, 1993, p. 34). The study documented beyond a shadow of a doubt that all children, even poor, at-risk students, can learn effectively.

Alternative Public Schools

Originally created to serve children and youth who were not succeeding in existing public schools, alternative public schools have been extensively studied during the past 30 years. At-risk students have been studied prior to arriving at and after attending alternative schools. Students in alternative schools have been compared with students in traditional neighborhood schools. Researchers have studied the alternative-school students' performance with pre- and post-achievement performance measures. Follow-up studies have been conducted for years after students graduated from alternative schools, as have in-depth case studies of individual alternative schools and studies of large numbers of certain types of similar alternative schools located in different cities and states.

Taken together, this body of research and evaluation of alternative schools serving at-risk and violent youth has been remarkably positive. Despite the challenging needs of high-risk students, participation in alternative schools has demonstrated improved student attendance, reduced dropout rates, improved attitudes, and has led to significant increases in academic achievement. This body of research has also helped to identify why these "customized" schools of choice continue to be so successful. More important, it was this research that helped demonstrate that the success of alternative schools was not solely related to the specific components of the program, but rather a complex set of factors combined to create a "surrogate" family atmosphere. Researchers at the University of Wisconsin at Madison concluded after in-depth case studies of alternative schools: "The key finding of our research is that effective schools provide at-risk students with a community of support" (Wehlage et al., 1989). For at-risk youth, this community of support or "surrogate family" atmosphere, appears to be the single most important factor in assuring an at-risk student's academic success (Barr & Parrett, 1997a).

Career-Theme Magnet Schools

In a study of 24,000 students in grades 8 through 12, researchers were surprised to discover that students in alternative career-theme magnet schools showed higher achievement scores than their counterparts in conventional high schools and in Catholic high schools. Even more impressive was the fact that these magnet schools enrolled a larger percentage of poor and minority students (Gamoran, 1996). In another study of 300 career academies (both stand-alone alternative schools as well as schools-within-schools), similar positive results regarding student achievement were documented (West, 1996). These studies conclude that when students choose to participate in magnet programs with a relevant, high-interest curriculum, they become highly motivated; students seem to be unusually interested in learning when academic programs and real-life experiences outside of school are integrated.

Comprehensive Reform Models

During the 1990s, a number of national reform efforts began assembling data to evaluate the effectiveness of comprehensive school-reform models such as Success for All, Accelerated Schools, the Coalition of Essential Schools, the School Development Program, Core Knowledge, Expeditionary Learning, and the Modern Day School House (Herman, 1999; Slavin & Fashola, 1998; and Northwest Regional Educational Laboratory, 1998). Each of the studies documented the essential characteristics of the programs and indicated student achievement gains ranging from significant gain to promising trends to little or no relevant data. In 1999 a number of groups, including the American Institute of Research, the Kentucky Department of Education, the Northwest Regional Educational Laboratory, the Education Commission of the States, National Staff Development Council, the Federal Office of Educational Research and Improvement, as well as numerous independent researchers, began to study the data from the evaluations of these comprehensive reform models as well as a number of more targeted reform efforts focusing on teaching specific skills and content. Each of these reform efforts have assembled evidence of positive effects on student behavior, achievement, and school climate. What is encouraging about the data from these programs is the remarkable similarity of design characteristics that relate to success in enhancing student achievement: comprehensive design, small size, choice of participation, extensive staff development, shared philosophy and decision making, widespread parent and community involvement, high expectations for students, relevant thematic curriculum, and the ongoing evaluation of progress (Herman, 1999).

Turnaround Schools

As more states (e.g., Virginia, Washington, Florida, Kentucky, Texas) establish educational standards and require "high stakes" student achievement exams, a graphic picture has emerged regarding the success of schools. Each of the states' achievement-test results began to appear in annual reports and usually provided data on socioeconomics, demographics, and funding. Some states also rated each school from high to low performing. Texas rates each school on the basis of the scores of the required assessment exams as low performing, acceptable, recognized, or exemplary. Since 1995, the number of Texas schools rated as low performing has fallen from 257 or 4.3 percent to 57 or .09 percent, even though the academic achievement "bar" has been raised incrementally each year and the percentage of students taking the test has gone up. Student achievement in Texas schools has risen substantially across the board and for all subgroups. The number of minority children who passed the state test doubled since 1998 (Education Commission of the States, 1998b). A similar situation occurred in Kentucky, where eight of the elementary schools in the top 20 most successful schools had a majority of children who qualified for free or reduced-price lunch programs. The same was true for 13 of the top 20 schools in math achievement. A similar pattern was also found at the middle- and high-school levels (White, Education Week 18(34), 1999).

In the nation's capital, the *Washington Post* ("The Achievers," 1998, p. D4) published a lead story entitled "The Achievers," about five low-performing Maryland schools that had made startling gains on the state-mandated achievement test in only four years. And while each elementary school was different, successes were attributed to energetic leadership, ownership, parental and community involvement, high expectations, rigorous attention to basic skills, and the fear of a state takeover of the low-performing schools.

In another study of 366 successful schools in poor communities in 21 states conducted by the Education Trust and the Chief State School Officers, six common characteristics were identified that explained their success.

- The schools draw heavily on state and local standards to design their curriculum, test students, and evaluate teachers.
- The schools build in increased instruction time for reading and math.
- The schools invest heavily in teacher development. (Successful schools spend about 10 percent of their extra federal dollars on professional development, compared with about 3 percent in less successful schools.)

- The schools use comprehensive tests to monitor the progress of each child and identify children who fall behind.
- The schools succeed in involving the parents.
- The schools are in states or districts that demand accountability for the principals and teachers. (The Education Trust, 1999)

The U.S. Department of Education has identified a similar set of characteristics that are essential for schools to be successful with at-risk youth.

- Set high expectations for students.
- Hold schools accountable for performance.
- Provide a safe learning environment.
- Create leaders at school and district levels.
- Let leaders lead.
- Recruit and retain the best teachers.
- Train teachers in instruction and curriculum.
- Support students with extra help and time.
- Involve the community in schooling.
- Create smaller schools.
- Close or reconstitute bad schools. (U.S. Department of Education, 1998b)

The findings of this research provide critical new insight into the understanding of why some schools are successful with all students, how to ensure that all students learn effectively, and how to replicate these practices to ensure improved schools.

Compelling Conclusions

Research during the past 15 years has provided the foundation for eight compelling conclusions, which provide the critical energy and driving force for all efforts at school reform. Taken as a group, these conclusions offer a structural blueprint for educating all students.

All Children Can Learn

A growing chorus of educators and researchers continue to ask: how many effective schools would you have to see to be persuaded that all children can learn? As Ron Edmonds, noted education researcher, stressed, how many effective schools would you have to see to be persuaded of the educability of all children? If your answer is more than one, then you have reasons of your own for preferring to believe that pupil performance derives from family background instead of school response to family background (Herndon, 1990). Today we know with absolute certainty that all children can learn. In fact, today there are thousands of teachers throughout the United States with poor, minority, and heterogeneous student groups who have year after year of objective student achievement data documenting that all children and youth are learning effectively and achieving high academic standards. Teachers, principals, and communities can no longer take refuge in the false concept that some students are simply too dumb, too deprived, or too disadvantaged to learn. With patient and carefully prescribed instructional programs, even profoundly mentally impaired children and adults can learn. The same is equally true for at-risk youth. The question, of course, remains whether or not communities have the determination and the will to direct the resources necessary toward addressing the needs of all children and youth.

No One Best Way to Learn

We know that students learn best in very different ways and in very different educational settings. We also know that different teachers teach in very different ways. Not all students can learn effectively in a typical school classroom with 25 to 35 students and organized into 50-minute class periods. We now know that students who fail to learn in such conventional classrooms can learn effectively in other types of learning environments when different instructional approaches are used. Whenever schools have developed learning environments that have addressed the specific needs and learning characteristics of those youth, remarkably positive outcomes have occurred.

The Necessity of Early Intervention

Research in human development and learning continues to provide an understanding of the significance of a child's early years. Increasing numbers of U.S. babies are born without adequate health, shelter, and nutrition, and at least one out of 20 of these babies enter the world with the drug addiction of their mothers. One in four can expect to be physically or sexually abused during childhood and adolescence. We also know that abused children are 50 percent more likely to be convicted of a juvenile crime and 40 percent more likely to end up in prison as adults. Childhood illiteracy has also been identified as a major predictor for dropping out of school and incarceration.

We now know that if an infant fails to bond with a caring adult, a lifetime of educational and social services may be unable to overcome this tragic beginning. Failure to bond is directly related to a lack of conscience, sensitivity to issues of right and wrong, and sociopathic behavior. It is not surprising that over 70 percent of the men and women in prison today were the sons and daughters of teenage parents. We know that early intervention not only means special programs for children from early childhood through the elementary years, but also includes educating expectant teenagers and adults about prenatal health, nutrition, parenting skills, and family planning.

Research has documented the importance of parent education. As the child's first teachers, parents must learn the importance of utilizing rather simple opportunities in stimulating the brains of infants and young children and help prepare them for reading and school success.

Educating At-Risk Youth Is Not Only a School Challenge

It is obvious that the problems of at-risk youth start in infancy and do not end when the student leaves school at the end of each day. The needs of at-risk youth often arise from social, family, and community problems. The most effective programs currently serving at-risk youth integrate components and services from both inside and outside the school. All successful programs depend on school and community collaboration and partnership to coordinate their efforts toward educating at-risk youth.

Schools Make a Difference

During the 1960s, James Coleman of the University of Chicago published his landmark research that concluded that school had little or no effect on poor children; that school could not overcome the conditions of poor homes, families, and communities. And, in spite of a barrage of criticism, conflict, and discussions, the emerging education literature, primarily the work of Christopher Jencks and his colleagues, tended to support Coleman's conclusion that school did not matter. It was not until the early 1980s that Edmonds was able to offer evidence which documented that certain "effective schools" did in fact have substantial positive influences on at-risk children and youth. More recently, research by a growing list of researchers during the late 1990s has built on earlier effective school research and provided a new, definitive set of conclusions regarding the fact that schools do make a difference. We now know that an effective school can overcome the debilitating effects of poverty and dysfunctional families. Research has also identified significant factors in schools (i.e., behaviors of principals, teachers, students, and parents) that they found to be more powerful than factors relating to socioeconomic level and racial data. Equally important, the research has documented that the significant factors in effective schools could be altered, replicated, and improved (Teddlie & Stringfield, 1993).

The conclusions are clear. Schools make a difference to at-risk students, and schools can be improved to ensure a substantial positive impact on these kids.

The Power of Teacher Perception

We know that our self-perceptions are based to a large degree on how others see us. Students seem to live up to or down to the expectations of their teachers. If teachers believe that all students can learn, develop realistic expectations, and plan appropriate learning experiences, all youth can and will learn. Unfortunately, the opposite is also true. It remains all but impossible for a student to overcome negative perceptions held by teachers.

School Programs Can Effectively Teach At-Risk Youth

Over the past 25 years a plethora of school programs have emerged and demonstrated through rigorous evaluation and research that public education can address the needs of those who are at risk. Examples include a variety of alternative schools and programs such as dropout prevention programs, continuation schools, vocational training programs, counseling programs, drug and alcohol programs, teen parent programs, magnet schools, learning centers, and in some cases the comprehensive school when its programs effectively focus on the needs of all youth.

Schools Must Be Restructured

We know that in our current educational structure an individual teacher, whether an 11th-grade biology teacher or a 3rd-grade elementary school teacher, cannot adequately address the needs of at-risk youth. Teachers, charged with teaching academic knowledge and skills to large numbers of students, are simply not able to provide the attention necessary to counter the complex noneducational problems that affect so many students. In order to adequately address the problems of at-risk youth, schools must be dramatically changed. Restructuring school curriculum, reconceiving the school calendar and daily schedule, better integrating school and community services, providing teachers with adequate planning and problem-solving time, and enhancing the climate of the school to provide for equitable inclusion and learning opportunities for every child represent critical challenges our schools must address. Many successful schools that have been significantly restructured around these and other issues and are succeeding in their attempts to address the problems of at-risk youth.

These capsulized conclusions address critical areas and issues related to learning and schooling for at-risk youth. Research, school evaluations, outcome assessments, case studies, and other forms of inquiry have conclusively identified schools that are effectively teaching at-risk youth through restructuring their schools. A review of these school and program evaluations has identified the key characteristics that make these programs so successful.

Essential Components of Effective Programs

While research has documented the irrefutable conclusion that all students can learn and obtain high standards of achievement, the task of accomplishing this outcome is far from easy. Successful intervention demands that a complex array of conditions in schools and communities be carefully integrated before an educational program can be successful with these challenging and often difficult students.

Research from the past 25 years has documented a number of components that are essential to school programs where all children and youth, particularly those at risk, are learning effectively. When a school incorporates these components into its educational program, success with at-risk students can be virtually guaranteed. The unique interaction between school size, voluntary participation, customized curriculum, caring and demanding teachers, shared vision, and the other identified components become building blocks of an effective school (see Table 5.1).

TABLE 5.1   Essential Components of Effective Programs

Positive School Climate
- Choice, commitment, and voluntary participation
- Small, safe, supportive learning environment
- Shared vision, cooperative governance, and local autonomy
- Flexible organization
- Community partnerships and coordination of services

Customized Curriculum and Instructional Program
- Caring, demanding, and well-prepared teachers
- Comprehensive and continuing programs
- Challenging and relevant curricula
- High academic standards and continuing assessment of student progress
- Individualized instruction: personal, diverse, accelerated, and flexible
- Successful transitions

Personal, Social, and Emotional Growth
- Promoting personal growth and responsibility
- Developing personal resiliency
- Developing emotional maturity through service
- Promoting emotional growth
- Promoting social growth

Creating a Surrogate Family Atmosphere

The implementation of these essential components combines to create a "surrogate family atmosphere," where students feel safe, supported, cared for, and challenged (Barr & Parrett, 1997a). As a result of this atmosphere, at-risk youth become actively engaged in learning and the school environment. For at-risk and violent children and youth, such a supportive atmosphere has an overwhelmingly positive effect that has the potential to transform their lives, improve their attitudes, and teach them effectively. For at-risk children and youth who may not have had or do not have a supportive, caring family, or who have had school experiences that may have been brutally negative, the "surrogate family atmosphere" can have an immediate positive impact. Effective schools and programs for at-risk youth often create an "all for one, one for all" community of camaraderie among teachers, parents, and students similar to that found in "crack" military organizations, superior athletic teams, cohesive private schools, and successful companies. Students in such programs become committed to their school and peers, creating an environment of positive pressure to succeed. Because students find the "surrogate family atmosphere" of an effective school so supportive, school attendance improves, academic achievement increases, and student attitudes become more positive (Barr & Parrett, 1997a).

The school as a community of support is a broad concept in which school membership and educational engagement are central. School membership is concerned with a sense of belonging and social bonding to the school and its members. Educational engagement is defined as involvement in school activities, but especially traditional classroom and academic work.

In order to develop a surrogate family atmosphere, teachers are needed who have a "moral commitment" to educating at-risk youth and sufficient autonomy and resources to develop effective programs for these students (Wehlage et al., 1989, p. 223).

Such a positive school climate fills a void in many students' lives and is central to the mission and purpose of effective schools for at-risk youth. The goal of every school must be to create just such a "caring community of respect, support, and challenge." When this community of support has developed, all students have the chance to succeed.

Over two decades of collaborative research have served to identify and distill the essential components necessary to build this community of support. These characteristics can be organized into three areas: a positive school climate; a customized curriculum and instructional plan; and a program supportive of personal, social, and emotional growth.

Positive School Climate

For at-risk youth, a positive, supportive school climate is absolutely essential as a prerequisite for learning. For these students, learning cannot and will not take place until students feel safe, secure, and supported, and begin to trust the adults of the school. Without a supportive school climate, learning will be difficult, if not impossible for at-risk youth. A positive school climate is created in the following ways:

Choice, Commitment, and Voluntary Participation

> *I don't think that I'm asking for a lot. No one assigns me and my family to a particular doctor, and I believe that my child's education is just as important as her health. And just as with health issues, I know I need a lot of information about education. I know that I need the advice of my daughter's teachers. I want to know what my options are, the potential of one approach over another. But in the end, I want to be a participant. I want to be a part of the decisions about my daughter's education, my daughter's future. I am certainly not an educator anymore than I am a medical doctor, but I believe that I would approach decisions about my daughter's school much more carefully and with a good deal more caring than some administrator sitting in an office drawing attendance boundaries for a child he has never met.*
> *—PARENT, SEATTLE, WASHINGTON*

One of the most powerful aspects of effective programs for at-risk youth occurs when students, parents, and teachers voluntarily choose to be a part of a program. Voluntary participation turns public education inside out: no more captive audiences, no more mandatory school assignments, no more school placements based on where you live, no more selective tracking systems, and no more assigned teachers, curricula, methods of instruction, or schools. The entire system of mandatory teacher and student assignments is replaced by a consumer-driven process based on educational service and satisfaction. If one alternative model does not fit a student's needs, the parent and student may find another that does. And while some find this idea very unsettling in the arena of public schooling, it is exactly the system that is used in community colleges, universities, and other forms of higher education. Following high school, students choose a college or university, select a major and often minor course of study, and their individual courses, even teachers. Public schools have been traditionally unwilling to operate in this manner.

The value of educational choice lies in more than just a commitment to democracy, political correctness, and educational accountability. Voluntary participation seems to evoke a powerful personal commitment. Students and teachers who choose to participate in an educational alternative become personally invested in the program and protective of their environment. In the same way that the school serves the parents, students, and teachers, the participants bond to serve the school. Voluntary choice encourages teachers and students to try harder to succeed. The school becomes theirs, and they endeavor to make it successful.

The power of choice and voluntary participation has been supported in the work of the noted psychologist, William Glasser (1998; 1975), and from decades of research on alternative school programs (Raywid, 1994; Barr & Parrett, 1997a; Viteritti, 2000). Voluntary choice is also essential for teachers. Only teachers who understand, care for, and want to work with at-risk children and youth should work with these students. Few things render an educational program for at-risk youth so ineffective as the involuntary assignment of teachers to a program that they do not want to be a part of. In the absence of choice, existing neighborhood schools must focus on consensus building, developing a shared vision for the school, and working for extensive community involvement, a process that usually takes several years to be successful. Where public schools have consistently failed to educate children, especially poor and minority children, a growing demand has emerged for charter schools or even voucher programs that would enable families to escape from these ineffective schools and pursue education in a school of their choice.

Choice may be difficult if not impossible to attain for violent youth or students with highly disruptive behavior. For these students, federal, state, and school-district "zero tolerance" policies often require schools to suspend, expel, or somehow exclude them. Research has documented the dangerous futility of expelling disruptive or violent youth into the community where they are unsupervised and disengaged from an educational program. Thus, wherever and whenever possible, districts must provide opportunities for these students preferably by voluntary choice to participate in programs specially designed to meet their needs, long before they get in trouble. For violent, disruptive students, assignment to highly secure educational programs is preferable to expelling these students unsupervised into the community.

Leadership

Conclusions regarding the nature of leadership have been substantially rewritten during the last fifteen years. The earlier concept of the flamboyant, charismatic, change-agent principal as the essential requirement in school reform has given way to a new type of school leader. Today, effective leadership is recognized as one of facilitation, team building, shared decision making and governance, and requires a dynamic effort to lead a school and community toward a common vision. Today's school leaders must have a strong vision about education for at-risk youth; be able to convene students, parents, and teachers and together develop and support a shared mission; facilitate shared decision making; and provide governance. Today's leaders must be relentless advocates for at-risk youth and their parents; model effective educational practices; select, hire, and support dedicated teachers and provide them with necessary staff development and resources; and constantly encourage the school and community to achieve high standards of academic excellence (Combs et al., 1999; Fager, 1998; Lambert, 1998; Gross, 1998).

Small, Safe, and Supportive Learning Environment

In a very real sense, effective at-risk programs must personalize learning and help to insulate students from the negative factors and influences of traditional schools; they must serve to incubate student learning and growth. Research on small schools, rural schools, middle schools, and alternative education programs emphasizes the importance of small, personalized learning environments. The average enrollment in individual alternative schools in the United States is approximately 175 students. This means that a relatively small group of students works closely with a cadre of caring and demanding teachers. These small educational environments can be viewed as "communities of support" or as educational "intensive care units" serving the needs of at-risk youth (Gregory, 1993; Muncey & McQuillan, 1993; Office of Educational Research and Improvement, 1987; Wehlage et al., 1989; Barr & Parrett, 1997a; Nathan, 1996; Raywid, 1999). And while research over the years has consistently documented the power and importance of small schools, recent findings have helped educators to understand the crucial relationship of small school size to effective learning. This is particularly true for at-risk and violent youth.

School size is a tremendously important factor and one that is often overlooked. A key reason that so many students drop out of school or fail academically is that they simply are lost in large, impersonal, and confusing secondary schools. Studies have identified "isolates" who are always present in large schools—students who have few friends or who feel that no one cares for or about them. Large comprehensive schools provide a very difficult environment for these isolated students. The 1999 violence at Columbine High School in Littleton, Colorado, dramatized how the student organizations, athletics, music programs, and social cliques of the 1,800 students engaged many students, but "locked out" others, causing them to feel isolated, victimized, and angry. Over a decade ago, the Carnegie Council on Adolescent Development (1989) recommended that large, impersonal junior high schools be divided into a number of small, interdisciplinary groups of teachers and students. More recently, the National Association of Secondary School Principals National Report, *Breaking Ranks: Changing an American Institution,* recommended that no secondary school should enroll more than six hundred students (1996).

In New York, several urban districts have launched a massive effort to transform larger inner-city schools into networks of "minischools." Other districts across the nation are joining the Coalition of Essential Schools, which recommends significantly smaller schools and encourages a personalization of learning "to the maximum feasible extent" (Cushman, 1999). School districts across the nation are attempting to make large comprehensive high schools smaller, while in other states, voters have rejected school bonds proposed to build more large schools. Schools with significantly smaller enrollments provide a dramatically different educational environment. Everyone knows one another, and this familiarity tends to foster mutual respect and higher achievement, and it virtually eliminates violence. Small size alone often encourages a more personal, humanistic educational program that is violence free.

A safe educational environment is also essential. In national polls of parental attitudes toward public schools, the single most important issue that has been identified is a safe school (Phi Delta Kappa International, 1998). This attitude clearly reflects the growing anxiety among parents about the violence that has been occurring in schools. The recent wave of sensational acts of teenage murder have seemed to galvanize public attitudes. The demand for safe schools led to zero tolerance laws and policies at the national, state, and school-district levels. By the late 1990s, a safe learning environment had come to mean both the school and the community. This expanded concept of "safe learning environment" led schools to design and implement special programs for violent or expelled youth. Some of the programs, designed as paramilitary "boot camp" schools, outdoor wilderness adventure programs, and "soft jails" provide safety through rigorous routine and regimens. Many programs for violent youth are operated in cooperation with juvenile corrections authorities.

It is important to recognize that the most successful approaches to avoiding school violence involve small, supportive learning environments where every student is engaged in learning and feels cared for and supported. Small schools foster safe educational environments (Fager & Boss, 1998; Barr & Parrett, 1997b).

Shared Vision, Cooperative Governance, and Local Autonomy

> *It took us a long time and a lot of work . . . but now we all share a vision. . . . We all know where we are going and we are pulling together to get there.*
> —*ACCELERATED SCHOOL TEACHER, CALIFORNIA*

> *People often think that I'm being very presumptuous when I talk about this as being "my school," but that's exactly how I feel. In my entire life I have never felt that way about any school until now. It is my school. In most schools, parents are simply tolerated; but that's not true here. We spent a year discussing, disagreeing, and developing our vision for the school. But it didn't stop there. We continued to work together to set objectives for our goals, and each semester we evaluated how well we've achieved what we set out to do. I've never been involved in anything like this as a parent in a school. To work with teachers, administrators, students, and other parents to govern the school, build curriculum, evaluate staff, set new policy—it's just an incredible experience. This really is our school!*
> —*PARENT AT AN ALTERNATIVE SCHOOL, PORTLAND, OREGON*

In recent years, research on improving schools has documented the importance of parents and teachers working to develop a shared vision. In conventional public schools, with enrollment and parental participation typically defined by the home address, the development of a shared vision may require more than seven years of hard work (Levin, 1989). Where choice is available, the development of consensus can occur much faster, because teachers, students, and parents with similar goals and philosophies choose to participate and work in a school together. Often it is a shared vision or philosophy that brings people together to form a new school.

Regardless of the time necessary to develop a shared vision for a school, the value of this effort appears to be worth the investment. In the absence of choice, consensus building is absolutely essential. An exciting factor in developing a shared vision for a school is that this process often becomes self-fulfilling. When all participants agree on what they expect to achieve, and work diligently to monitor progress, they almost always achieve their goals (Barr & Parrett, 1997a).

The staff and community of Gardendale Elementary Magnet School in Merritt Island, Florida, spent more than a year creating a vision and strategic plans to guide the improvement of their school. Four years into the completion of their work, the school staff, parents, and business partners praised the dramatic transformation of their school. Yet they still acknowledged the critical importance of reevaluation and adjustment in driving their vision toward the school's agreed-upon goals (Narvaez, 1995). Accelerated schools likewise invest the first years of their school-improvement effort in a consensus-building "visioning" process to create their mission and philosophy.

There is substantial evidence that community participation, parent involvement, and student commitment tends to increase when an authentic atmosphere of school "ownership" is present. This can sometimes occur if school districts transfer authority and autonomy for school governance from the district office to the neighborhood school. Providing neighborhood groups of parents, teachers, and students with the opportunity to participate meaningfully in budgetary, curricular, and instructional decisions can dramatically increase parent and student engagement in school. The more authority transferred to the local school, the more creative the educational approach can become and the more positive the educational outcomes.

Local autonomy is essential in developing effective school programs for at-risk youth. Without local autonomy and shared governance, schools are confined by state and local regulations that often paralyze improvement. Most important, the lack of local budget autonomy will often prevent the bold innovations necessary to ensure that all students, particularly those at risk, are learning effectively.

Flexible Organization

To be effective with at-risk children and youth, a flexible organization of the school is essential. An effective program for at-risk and/or violent students must respond to the needs of those students. Since at-risk youth often have short attention spans, many successful at-risk schools organize the academic day into blocks, and the year into five-to-nine-week minisemesters. For latchkey children, schools often provide before-, after-school, and summer programs. Since many youths have jobs, later afternoon, evening, Saturday, and year-round programs are often made available.

Since homeless students and students from dysfunctional families have difficulty completing homework in the evening, some programs extend classtime so that students can complete both in-class work and homework at school. Since at-risk youth are often far behind, or arrive in the middle of the week or the middle of a semester, a personalized, flexible academic program is often designed to accommodate these students and accelerate their learning (Barr & Parrett, 1997a).

Effective schools and programs for at-risk youth must also be flexibly organized to accommodate student participation in field trips, service learning, community practica, and internships. The school must also make it possible for students to meet with teachers and peers, to attend counseling and support group sessions, to participate in school governance, and—for teenage mothers and fathers—to have time with their babies.

Community Partnerships and the Coordination of Services

The problems confronting at-risk and violent youth are not just school problems. For that reason the school alone cannot adequately address the many needs of students who are poor, homeless, abused, dysfunctional, emotionally ill, or violent. Nowhere else does the adage, "it takes an entire village to raise a child" take on such poignant and realistic meaning. But to involve the community in an effective manner is far from easy. It demands time, effort, and patience. For at-risk and violent youth it is essential to seek help, support, services, and resources from community groups, churches, local businesses, social service agencies, and even the police and juvenile justice authorities. People in these groups can help provide after-school support and serve as school volunteers, student tutors, mentors, and resources for teachers. Often schools even appoint a volunteer to coordinate the other volunteers. Schools also work to develop community ownership of the school, to serve on management teams and advisory boards, and to become an integral part in developing and sharing the school mission and vision (Combs et al., 1999). Schools need the support that comes from partnerships with businesses or "adopt a school" programs, for at-risk students typically attend school in the poorest communities with the worst facilities and the most inadequate instructional materials (Northwest Regional Education Laboratory, 1998; Kozol, 1991).

In addition, school-community partnerships provide an invaluable service by establishing a network for career exploration and transition to the workplace (Smith, 1993). The realization that the most fundamental problems associated with at-risk youth are often far outside the direct influence of the school has led to concerted efforts to coordinate a wide variety of services from community agencies. At-risk children and youth often come from dysfunctional families that may need comprehensive, immediate assistance. Outside the school, there exists a bewildering array of community and social agencies that provide child care, health services, counseling, food stamps, welfare payments, housing, transportation, and assistance in job training and employment searches. Increasingly, effective at-risk programs have become "full service" schools by helping students and their parents gain information and access to these services and often providing space for the providers to move directly into the school (Davis, 1995). To accomplish this task, many schools have established coordinators of community services, created youth service teams, and implemented a case-management approach to work with difficult students to develop individualized plans to access the school and community services they so desperately need. Some schools have created community councils composed of representatives of participating agencies and organizations.

To be most effective with at-risk youth, schools must help all students obtain the community services they need and must facilitate access to the assistance provided by the various organizations and agencies (Hobbs, 1993; Schorr, 1992). In addition, school-community partnerships provide an invaluable service by establishing a network for career exploration and transition to the workplace (Smith, 1993).

Customized Instructional Programs

While creating a safe and supportive school climate is essential for addressing the needs of at-risk youth and their families, care and support only provides the atmosphere for effective learning. A positive school climate must be complemented by a customized instructional program characterized by carefully stated and agreed-upon standards, high expectations, and comprehensive assessment of student progress.

Caring, Demanding, and Well-Prepared Teachers
There is an abundance of research that emphasizes how important it is for teachers to care deeply for at-risk youth; to believe that these students can achieve, and then to hold high expectations for them as learners. No matter how well an education program is planned, without such teachers, the program's effectiveness is jeopardized. This may well be the most critical component in effective programs for at-risk youth (Northwest Regional Educational Laboratory, 1990; Office of Educational Research and Improvement, 1987; Parrett, 1979; Teddlie & Stringfield, 1993; Barr & Parrett, 1997a). Programs that assemble a staff of caring, demanding teachers who share a vision and philosophy exponentially increase the school's potential. Most teachers cherish the opportunity to teach with colleagues who share their educational philosophy. This combination of caring and demanding teachers and shared vision and philosophy is the reason why at-risk students in these schools and programs will outperform their previous efforts.

In a recent study of expelled students in Colorado, researchers asked the students if they could name one or more teachers during their elementary years who cared about them and worked hard to help them learn. Almost every student queried could recall teachers from their elementary school experiences. When asked the same question about teachers at the secondary levels, not a single expelled student could identify one teacher (Colorado Foundation for Families and Children, 1995). This study offers a dramatic insight into the importance of caring adults in the lives of students. For students who are at risk of violent behavior, a positive connection with a caring adult may reduce harm, even save lives. Since many students do not have such a relationship at home, the school environment is even more important.

While caring and demanding teachers are of the utmost importance in ensuring that all students learn effectively, their effectiveness can be significantly increased if they are provided with highly focused preparation and staff development regarding best practices in working with at-risk youth. When working with at-risk youth, teachers must be thoroughly prepared to use new and evolving technology, be able to align their curriculum and instruction to high standards, and be able to assess students' learning as they progress toward those standards. Increasingly, teachers are not only being charged with teaching all students, they are being evaluated on their success in fostering positive student achievement and on their preparation related directly to improved student achievement (*What Matters Most: Teaching for America's Future*, 1996).

Comprehensive and Continuing Programs

While some ancillary programs have demonstrated success by working with at-risk youth for a relatively short time each day, and for a few short weeks or months, these successes are rarely maintained over time. High risk youth need programs that address their individual needs and provide consistency and continuity in approach. It is evident that the more comprehensive a program, the better the chance of effecting lasting, positive change in student behavior and achievement. Too many school districts make the mistake of creating programs for at-risk youth that operate for a period or two each day and only allow students to remain for a semester. With few exceptions, this approach represents a fundamental mistake in the initial efforts of many school districts toward addressing the needs of at-risk students. Such programs tend to offer too little, occur far too late, and cannot overcome the years of negative impact on the child of home, school, and society. If students have experienced years of negative interaction with schools, it is unrealistic to believe that a part-time program can hope to adequately address their problems. Even the benefits gained by successful programs like Head Start diminish rapidly without continuing enrichment and support. Programs for at-risk youth must start as early as possible, be as comprehensive as possible (including academic, social, economic, and health components), and continue as long as the student is in need.

If a school district is serious about serving at-risk youth, it needs to conceptualize a program that addresses the comprehensive needs of at-risk students. The goal must not be to provide a quick fix and rapid transition back into a traditional classroom. The goal must be to help students to develop strong self-concepts, master basic skills, develop realistic plans, and then achieve academic goals. Only rarely will a student successfully transition back to the traditional program and then it usually occurs when the student chooses to return. A comprehensive and continuing program will serve as a bridge to graduation, employment, and/or continuing education (Wehlage et al., 1989; Office of Educational Research and Improvement, 1987; Barr & Parrett, 1997a).

Challenging and Relevant Curriculum

A school's curriculum must be carefully aligned with state and school district standards and required assessment. Yet for at-risk children and youth, this is often not enough. To be successful with these educationally demanding students, a curriculum must be carefully customized to address the specific needs and interests of these youth. If the students reading is deficient, the school must provide an instructional program in this basic skill. For minority youth, schools may choose to provide additional cultural and ethnic awareness offerings; for young mothers, offerings in pre- and post-natal care. If students are abusing drugs or alcohol, have difficulty controlling their anger, have trouble interacting with adult authority, other targeted curricula may be necessary.

While the concept of the full-service school has only recently received serious consideration in America's school districts, many schools have long sought to incorporate awareness, service, and intervention programs into the school curriculum (Dryfoos, 1998). Such topics as substance abuse, sexually transmitted diseases, suicide prevention, conflict resolution, parenting, pre- and post-natal care, nutrition, gangs and violence, racism and hate behaviors, and others may be proactively addressed through counseling, peer groups, organized interventions, and out-of-school learning projects. Many schools have embraced a comprehensive approach to integrating programs that promote healthful living through informed decision making. Effective schools educate the "whole" student and thus do not exclude the realities of life from school.

- Academic Rigor. For at-risk children and youth, the most pressing problems are often deficiencies in basic skills. But in an age of increasingly rigorous standards, the school must help students progress from the basic skills to very sophisticated levels of learning. Every school should conduct an initial assessment of the needs of each student and create, if necessary, a plan for the student. The curriculum must address basic skills and the means for accelerating learning to catch up with their peers. Where states require barrier testing, students must be prepared to satisfactorily pass examinations. More and more districts and schools have developed the motto, "whatever it takes" (many have backed up this motto with policy and resources), to ensure that all students obtain the high levels of achievement required for passing the state assessments so as to graduate and succeed in our increasingly sophisticated world.

  It was once considered sufficient for schools for at-risk youth to serve almost as "rescue missions"—to get students off the streets and back into school, to provide them with a stabilized learning environment, to provide them with a basic skill training, and then to assist them in completing a graduate equivalency diploma. Today, such minimal education expectations are simply not enough. State legislators, state boards of education, and local school boards are now establishing high educational standards for all students and expect even the most at-risk students to achieve these standards. Policy makers throughout the United States are increasingly demonstrating their commitment to the belief that "all children can and will learn."

- Relevance. For at-risk youth, the relevance of their education is a critical factor. Unlike their more academically successful peers who will accept learning simply because "you may need it someday to get into college," at-risk youth demand relevance in their learning. For young children this may mean field trips and community projects. For older students it maybe applied rather than theoretical courses, career exploration, career internships, and apprenticeships. One of the most effective means of increasing curriculum relevance is to integrate out-of-school learning experiences that allow students to leave the school on a regular basis for experiences in banks, businesses, industry, and community agencies. For secondary students, school-to-work programs may incorporate many of these components and can be highly effective. In addition to applied courses and out-of-school learning experiences it is essential that the curriculum also include an emphasis on technology.

- Career-Theme Schools. Research during the 1990s documented the power of career theme schools that combined career interests with academic excellence (Gamoran, 1996). These schools are typically organized as alternative public or magnet schools and focus their programs on a career theme such as the health professions, law-legal professions, broadcast journalism, business, science and technology, performing arts, and others. Such schools permit students to voluntarily choose a career area of interest to them, enroll in special-emphasis academic courses that relate to the career theme, and participate in on-site internships two or three afternoons per week. Research has demonstrated the significant effectiveness of programs such as these to motivate and engage the students, eliminate behavioral problems, and produce high academic achievement.

- High School Majors. Participation in career theme schools at the high school level is very similar to college students choosing an academic major. Student mean grades and achievement during the freshman and sophomore years at postsecondary institutions are lower than during later years. Often, only after college students select an academic major do they become engaged and motivated and demonstrate higher achievement. Career theme schools at the junior and senior high school levels appear to affect public school students in exactly the same manner. Some school districts like those in Vancouver, Washington, are developing programs so that every student can "declare" a high school academic major and choose to participate in a career professional theme program (see Chapter 8). For at-risk youth who are so often bored with academic learning in the middle and high schools, such an approach promises significant results and dramatizes the concept of a customized curriculum for each public school student.

High Academic Standards and Continuing Assessment of Student Progress

During the mid-1990s a new approach to school reform swept the country, with many states establishing educational standards, identifying the knowledge required for students to achieve those standards, aligning curricula to consistently focus instruction on the standards, and establishing "high-stakes" assessments, usually at grades five, eight, and eleven. By the year 2000, more than 30 states had established standards and most others were working toward the goal. Some states established these assessments as "barrier tests" and prohibited students who failed the tests from being promoted. In 1998 ten states had established policies that ended social promotion (U.S. Department of Education, 1999). Each of these states, using mandated standards and assessments, reported the results of the test for each school in the state and often developed a variety of incentives, punishments, and recognitions based on performance. In some states and school districts, low-performing schools that have been unable to improve their student achievement performance have been closed or "reconstituted" with an entirely new professional staff. The state of Texas rates every school in the state on the basis of student achievement and encourages the students to improve their individual performance. These new state standards reflect a determination that *all* students can and will demonstrate high levels of achievement.

While educators had long recognized the importance of clearly stated goals and objectives, statewide accountability efforts have suddenly provided substantial evidence to verify the positive effects that high standards and the careful monitoring of student progress has on student achievement. While there is continuing concern over using standardized tests as the sole method of assessment and a backlash seems to be occurring against school reconstitution, by and large, schools in these states are demonstrating significant improvement in student achievement.

Establishing rigorous educational standards and goals that are supported by the school and community, ensuring that the curriculum is effectively aligned with these standards, and consistently monitoring students' progress toward these learning goals appears to lead to significant improvement (Education Commission of the States, 1998). What is working at the state level and school-district level can also work at the local school level with at-risk children and youth. Even better, far more authentic assessments at the local school level can be developed and employed. Many alternative schools and other programs for at-risk youth have replaced course graduation requirements with highly specific graduation competencies (St. Paul Open School, 1993; Coalition of Essential Schools, 1999; Darling-Hammond et al., 1995).

Individualized Instruction: Personal, Diverse, Accelerated, and Flexible

> *High school dropouts leading fourth-graders on environmental field studies along the river? Without teachers? I wouldn't have believed this could work, and certainly wouldn't have enrolled my nine-year-old before seeing it. These high school kids know so much about every aspect of this river and its biology. Obviously, having them teach classes of elementary students is certainly good for my child and must really help the high school kids. My fourth-grader is now asking me if she'll get to do this in middle school.*
> *—ELEMENTARY-SCHOOL PARENT, IDAHO*

Students who fail in traditional classrooms have often been found to be very successful in instructional programs that allow them to work at their own pace, focus on their own instructional needs and learning styles, use incentives for learning, and use teachers as facilitators. Such individualized, personalized learning has long been designed and available for special education students, and it is now recognized as essential for at-risk youth (Barr, Parrett, & Colston, 1977; Wehlage et al., 1989; Young, 1990, Barr & Parrett, 1997a).

The overriding goal of a redesigned school instructional program for the at-risk student is to ensure that students acquire basic skills and begin demonstrating academic success and achievement. Once this occurs, students will develop more posi- tive attitudes toward self, school, and learning and then have the opportunity to achieve high academic standards.

How instruction is delivered often becomes the deciding factor in a student's success in the learning process. Central to this concept is the commitment on the part of the school staff to providing a menu of instructional opportunities. Small schools, with low pupil-teacher ratios, voluntary enrollment of students, and a focus on addressing individual needs, create a framework for delivering a personalized, flexible, and relevant course of study—a course of study that offers many students their first opportunity to connect with educators in a serious learning partnership. The following approaches characterize instructional delivery in effective alternative schools:

- Focus on individual needs. All students possess a complex array of needs and academic abilities. Effective schools for at-risk students begin the learning part- nership through a careful assessment of these needs and abilities and prescribe an initial schedule of goals and participation that addresses the students' basic needs and connects the students with the instructional opportunities of the school.

  If the students are abusing drugs and alcohol, support groups may be needed. Violent students may need instruction in anger management or conflict resolu- tion. Teenage mothers need instruction in child care, health, and nutrition, and most students need instruction in basic life skills.

- Opportunities to accelerate learning/catch-up. Through the development of a menu of formal and informal opportunities, students structure a program of study that allows them to learn as fast as they can. Opportunities might include intensive tutoring in reading to reach grade level; an internship with an accoun- tant to apply advanced mathematical skills and investigate a career; an interdis- ciplinary course in U.S. literature and government that meets two graduation requirements; the opportunity to study independently six to ten hours a day to catch up in physical science; and the chance to focus complete attention on preparing for a GED, ACT, SAT, or state-mandated assessment exam.

- Creative use of time. For many alternative schools, the doors open at 7:00 A.M. and close between 7:00 P.M. and 10:00 P.M. (Community Learning Centers in Min- nesota are working to be open 24 hours a day). Throughout the day, students are provided with a learning environment that accommodates work, child care, transportation, and sleeping schedules. Credit is earned by demonstration of academic achievement and competency, rather than seat time, as students take increased responsibility for meeting their educational goals. Flexible use of time and schedules also provides for individual staff/student contact, as well as staff planning and professional development. The school sets the educational "clock" based on student needs and the realities of their lives.

- Diverse instructional practices. While every school is unique, a commitment to choice, active learning, and diversity in instructional practice characterizes all effective programs for at-risk youth. Again, from a needs-based perspective, the practices range from traditional forms of direct instruction to independent, community-based learning.

Individual and group projects, small cooperative learning groups, learning contracts, internships, on-line courses, apprenticeships, and individual tutoring are all often needed. Teachers teach in different ways and diverse students often learn best in different ways. The most effective schools for at-risk youth incorporate instructional programs in which teaching styles and learning styles are matched through a diverse menu of educational offerings.

For at-risk youth, who often have a low regard for their abilities, cooperative learning has proven to be far more effective than the traditional competitive classroom. In cooperative learning activities, students focus less on "how smart" they are and more on how to accomplish a task. In this type of instruction, students come to see mistakes and failures as opportunities to learn, regardless of how they view their own abilities (Nichols, 1990; Bempechat, 1999).

Successful Transitions

Family mobility and the accompanying school transitions have been documented as powerful determinants of dropping out. Recent research has documented the importance of these educational transitions: from the home to kindergarten, to the first grade, to middle school, to high school, to postsecondary education, to training or work, and from one school and/or school district to another. For the at-risk student, these transitions are emotionally charged and stressful. In recent years a new type of "migrant" student has emerged in public education. These new migrants are not the seasonal farmworkers of an earlier generation; rather they are poor families that tend to move and relocate when they are unable to pay their bills. In poor communities, the percent of turnover is significant. One of the great challenges of public education today is to assist these unfortunate children during their lonely migration through school after school.

Children's long-term success can be made more certain or be placed in jeopardy by how they negotiate school transitions (Alexander & Entwistle, 1999). While research has documented the significance of educational transitions and the negative impact of the transitions on at-risk youth, not enough is yet known about how to ease the impact of these transitions. The importance of the transition to the first grade is well documented. Some researchers have argued that the first hours in the first grade can be compared to the imprinting that occurs during the first twenty-four hours of a duckling's life. Yet a recent study found that few teachers do anything to help children and their families adjust to school before the critical first day (Viadero, 1999). For far too many at-risk children, the first days in the first grade mean a first encounter with failure. Recent studies have found that more students are currently being retained during the first grade than ever before.

The transition to the junior high–middle school is especially difficult, even more so for at-risk youth. From an educational program involving basically the same classmates for years, with primarily one teacher each year, students find themselves in large, complex schools being taught by as many as seven or more teachers each day and with a different group of peers each period. In this situation, students feel anonymous and unknown. It is easy for students to slack off in their academic work and make bad choices, because they feel no one will notice, no one will care.

The transition from junior high–middle school to high school is also difficult because high schools are rarely effective in assisting with transitions, or in remediating student deficiencies. Increasingly, schools and programs for high-risk students employ full-time transition counselors and specialists to coordinate efforts, as many seasoned teachers of at-risk youth believe the facilitation of successful transitions to be their most important work. The transition from high school to the world of work or postsecondary education is also perilous for the at-risk youth. Many programs require high school students to develop carefully thought-out plans for their high school years and their lives after graduation. Often these post graduation plans are incorporated into high school graduation requirements.

Experts agree that regardless of the grade level, successful transitions are critical to the at-risk student. Yet, as more schools and districts have begun to develop transition or bridge programs designed to help students prepare and make these difficult transitions, studies report that most programs are established in middle-class and suburban schools, leaving large numbers of America's inner-city and rural at-risk youth without support at this critical time.

Personal, Social, and Emotional Growth

During the mid-1990s acts of violence in and around public schools shocked the nation and focused attention, not only on why these violent acts were occurring, but on how to avoid them. In addition to these dramatic acts of violence even larger but related problems were identified. Every day teachers are confronted with accelerating degrees of abusive language, student disrespect, racial prejudice, schoolyard bullying and abuse, threats and actual acts of physical violence. As we enter the new millennium, the world of children and youth has been fundamentally altered.

Because of the disintegration of the family unit, because of television, movies, and video games surrounding youth with violent images, and because many children grow up with negative attitudes and even worse behaviors, there is little surprise that today's youth have turned violent in the most brutal and shocking manner. The question, of course, is what can and must schools do.

The answers, it seems, are complex. Many lobby to lock down the schools by installing high external fences, metal detectors, surveillance cameras, and police in the hallways, by eliminating student lockers, and requiring that backpacks have see-through netting; some have even called for arming our teachers. Fortunately, there is a growing momentum for a much more positive and effective approach (Hyman & Snook, 2000).

Some call for character development, citizenship education, or values education; others suggest "resiliency training" or "the other curriculum." The Association for Supervision and Curriculum and Development recommends attention to a child's "social and emotional learning" (O'Neil & Willis, 1998). Everyone seems to have their own way of defining the issues and identifying a remedy. Despite these various points of view there is growing agreement, increasingly supported by research, that this area represents a "missing piece" of public education today. And while this emerging arena of curriculum is still rather ill-defined, there is universal agreement that for at-risk youth, especially violent youth, this "missing piece" of the curriculum is absolutely essential. Many predict that through addressing these needs, schools will graduate adults who are tolerant and responsible and possess a strong degree of personal honor and integrity.

The goal of this "other curriculum" is to help students develop the "attitudes, behaviors, and cognitions, to become 'healthy and confident' overall—[including] socially, emotionally, academically and physically" (Elias et al., 1997). In Alexandria, Virginia, the Character Development partnership has established "the long-term goal of good character, i.e., knowing, caring about, and acting upon core ethical values such as fairness, honesty, compassion, responsibility, and respect for self and others" (Elias et al., 1997). The National Secondary Principals Association has endorsed character education in all schools. In addition, a new mandate for character education has been established in the states of Florida and Louisiana. Yet some of the political responses to the need for character education seem almost laughable, if not irresponsible. A Louisiana law seems to do little more than require students to refer to adults with, "Yes, ma'am" and "No, sir," and the U.S. House of Representatives recently voted down "gun control" legislation that would have required that the Ten Commandments be posted in every school and classroom in the country. While such efforts have been largely ridiculed, the underlying need to instill character traits in students continues to grow.

The goal of this area of curriculum is to "teach our students to be good citizens with positive values and to interact effectively and behave constructively." The challenge for educators and scientists is to clarify the set of educational methods that most successfully contributes to these outcomes (Elias et al., 1997) (something educators have been attempting to do since the Seven Cardinal Principles of education were proposed at the turn of the last millennium). Today, there exists a growing research base that supports a number of new approaches.

Promoting Personal Growth and Responsibility

There are a number of approaches to the development of personal growth and responsibility that can help schools develop the self-concepts and self-worth of students. Helping students develop self-motivation, make intelligent decisions, and become more independent, autonomous, and responsible will directly contribute to their success in school and more importantly, to their success as an adult (Bernard, 1991; Elias, 1999).

Specific approaches are supported by a substantial research base and will be described in later chapters (elementary, middle, and high schools). They include a variety of offerings and programs designed to help students make healthy choices about their lives.

Developing Personal Resiliency

The development of personal resiliency is related directly to students' perceptions of self, which is often defined in large measure by those around them. For this reason, the "surrogate family" atmosphere of a supportive, caring school is crucial. Likewise, the power of teacher perception is highly influential. When teachers believe in students, care for them, support them, and hold high expectations for their personal achievement, students will learn that they are worthy and valued and try to live up to their teachers' expectations (Krovetz, 1999).

Developing Emotional Maturity through Service

The development of emotional maturity appears to be much more simple. A particularly effective means of developing personal responsibility is to provide students with opportunities to be responsible and held accountable for their actions. When students work in retirement centers or hospitals, participate in "Paint the Town" projects or "Habitat for Humanity" projects, they learn responsibility, which transfers over to their personal lives. Through tutoring younger children, serving on school governance boards and committees, being involved in the cooperative development of rules and regulations for their school, participating in youth courses, and mediating student conflicts, they also learn and grow. And since so many of the high-risk students have had few, if any, positive adult role models, adult mentoring programs can provide students with an ongoing experience in working with caring and supportive adults, and the results can be impressive (Ernst & Amis, 1999). Learning experiences such as these place students in real world situations where they must act responsibly and contribute. The subsequent personal learning that occurs is often quite remarkable.

Promoting Emotional Growth

One of the greatest challenges in working with at-risk and violent youth is the fact that their lives are often built on a wide variety of nonproductive and disrespectful behaviors. But since human behavior is learned, including violent behavior, it can also be unlearned. Alternative public school or other successful programs for at-risk youth have developed structured efforts to help abused, dysfunctional, and angry children and youth deal with their frustrations and emotions. To promote emotional growth, students can learn anger management, conflict resolution, and peer mediation (Rogers, 1994). Programs such as these all involve carefully developed, established curricula in which students learn more effective ways and skills for dealing with their frustration and anger. And, once again, like all other significant learning, the earlier students are involved in structured approaches that promote emotional growth, the more effective the results will be (Goleman, 1995, 1996).

Promoting Social Growth

To be successful in their personal, academic, and later adult professional lives, students must grow up with an increasingly effective set of social skills. For at-risk and violent youth, this is a particularly difficult area of growth, for too often, it is these students who have not had great success in establishing friendships, and who often feel ostracized, disengaged, victimized and alone. Yet success in school and in later life depends in large part on the ability to get along with others, establish friendships, work cooperatively in projects, and become more skilled at social efficacy. To be successful, students must learn how to deal with a complicated social world and with authority, and how to avoid the negative effects of social intolerance.

During child care, preschool, and the early elementary grades, every effort should be made to involve children in community-building activity so that students learn to respect and appreciate one another, learn to be tolerant, and learn how to deal effectively with social conflicts and problems. In the earlier grade levels students can learn cooperative learning skills, such as sharing and working together on projects, they can learn about bigotry, bias, and stereotyping, and once again they can learn the skills necessary to get along with others. Social growth comes through social experience. The goal of every public school in the United States is citizenship. Promoting social and emotional growth works to further this goal through cognitive learning, participation in group activity, and joining others in establishing group goals and making intelligent personal decisions.

Programs That Work: Early Childhood and Elementary Schools

I hate to admit it . . . but I have surrendered. I have just given up. I know that I used to be a great teacher, but that is simply no longer true. In fact, I think if other teachers were honest, they would say exactly the same. Teaching has become impossible. Our classrooms are being overwhelmed with kids who won't learn and kids who are so far behind that I wonder how they could ever catch up. Do you have any idea how many little kids are taking Ritalin and how many of the really bright kids have left for private or home schools? It's so sad. . . . I feel like the army has simply pulled out and deserted, and here I am alone in the frontline trenches with this sad group of needy kids. I don't know what else to do. I have sent up the white flag. I surrender.
—HIGH SCHOOL TEACHER, MICHIGAN

While visiting a small elementary school, I was walking down the halls with two teachers on our way to lunch. While passing an open classroom door, one of my friends stopped and called out to a fellow teacher, "Come and join us for lunch." The teacher left a small group of students sitting around her desk and walked over to the door and replied, "I really can't. I've got a group of kids here who are having real problems with their reading, and I've been working with them over part of their lunch period all year." Knowing the type of students who generally attended this school I responded, "Isn't it sad how tragic so many of these poor kids' lives are?" The teacher turned and gave me a surprised look and said, "You know, I don't care who these kids are or where they're from or what their problems are. Before they leave my classroom I'm going to teach them to read. I can't do much about their home lives, but I can definitely teach them to read."
—TEACHER, SUNRISE ELEMENTARY SCHOOL, ALBANY, OREGON

Many schools and communities begin to develop intervention programs for at-risk students during the late middle- and high-school years when the problems confronting youth often become most visible and dramatic. However, prevention programs for very young children are the most cost-effective and have the greatest potential for lasting success. The period from conception and infancy through third grade encompasses the most critical stage in the development of children. In terms of the potential for personal development and learning, these are indeed the wonder years. For at-risk children this period is even more critical. Without early success in school, at-risk children's hope of successfully completing school diminishes with each passing year. By the end of the elementary-school years, only intensive, comprehensive, and costly intervention programs offer the potential for transforming the lives of these youth.

The period from conception through elementary school is also a time of grave danger for children and youth. Because of prenatal problems and premature births, increasing numbers of infants are born emotionally and/or learning disabled. If children are battered or sexually abused, they will carry these emotional and psychological scars with them throughout their lives. If children do not receive adequate love and care during infancy, they may fail to bond with an adult and then live out their lives with antisocial behavior. If young children are not talked to, read to, and provided cultural and educational stimulation, their young minds will atrophy rather than grow and develop, and they will arrive at school far from ready to learn. It is these children who will be retained, be tracked into slow learning groups and slow reading groups, and often be assigned to special education. The complex problems of these children, left unattended, will only be overcome after the third or fourth grade with intensive effort.

The problems associated with at-risk youth often originate long before schools ever see the child. When they do arrive at school, too often they are isolated, stigmatized, and overwhelmed with the large, impersonal approach that is the norm in too many of our schools. Middle and high school becomes a time to drop out, turn to drugs, alcohol, or gangs, and enter adulthood with little or no hope of building a successful life.

The opposite of all this is equally true. If children are born healthy and are cared for, supported, and stimulated, they develop security and self-esteem and their minds grow and expand. These students arrive at school with enthusiasm, equipped with an arsenal of skills and attitudes that all but ensure success at school. And if young children learn to read and experience academic success during their early elementary grades, they build a solid foundation for success in school and later life.

None of this is any longer speculation. We now know how to provide for the healthy development of all young children and how to improve the IQ of children and ensure that every child learns to read during the early grades. But solutions to the problems of the nation's youth at risk remain daunting. Like the very problems they address, the solutions are interrelated, costly, long-term, and involve the home, the community, social agencies, and child-care providers as well as the school. Yet there are schools and communities throughout the country that have demonstrated and documented that they can teach all children to read, that they can help all children to learn and experience academic success, and that they can keep almost all children in school until they graduate. These programs have been successful in both rural and urban areas and in wealthy and poor communities. These schools and school programs have been studied and analyzed sufficiently to provide educators with the essential components necessary for success and replication.

The previous chapter provided the theoretical framework and models that are the building blocks of successful programs for at-risk youth. This chapter will focus on a more specific, practical level. If the essential components described in the last chapters provide the beams and braces for building the internal structures of successful programs, this chapter provides the nuts and bolts, the fine line drawing that focuses on the practical, day-to-day realities of schools and communities. It deals with what to do on Monday, what to teach the parents, and how to help children learn to read and master the other basics. This chapter will provide descriptions of successful programs that can be replicated from early childhood through the elementary-school years. Subsequent chapters will focus on the middle and the high-school years. Taken together, these three chapters provide a blueprint for action and success for schools and communities.

In the following pages, brief descriptions are provided of a number of specific approaches and programs that have been employed in public schools and communities and have been judged through research and evaluation to be highly effective with youth who are at risk. Yet a word of caution is necessary. While each of these interventions can be successful in improving the learning of participating at-risk children and youth, no single program or practice can effectively meet the needs of such a diverse group of students. Schools must integrate a number of successful approaches into an overall, comprehensive program of intervention.

Family Planning and Health Services

Building a foundation for educational success or failure begins during infancy and possibly during pregnancy. Although there are few issues in the United States so controversial and explosive as family planning, strong evidence exists that children of unwanted pregnancies tend to be less educated, less healthy, and significantly more dependent on public assistance than other children. Unwanted pregnancies often coincide with drug and alcohol abuse, and this in turn has led to a dramatic increase in the incidence of "drug" babies, children who at birth carry the mother's drug or alcohol dependency. Many cities report that 20 percent of all babies are born with illicit drugs in their systems. Long before many children come in contact with schools, substandard nutrition, sexual abuse, physical abuse, and lack of medical treatment have taken a heavy toll. Schools face a grave challenge to reverse this negative beginning, but schools have demonstrated that it can be accomplished. For schools and communities to be successful with at-risk children and youth, they must provide family planning and health services to all pregnant women and infants (Schorr & Schorr, 1989).

Developing the Brain in Infants and Young Children

Brain research during the past 15 years has profoundly altered our understanding of how infants and young children grow and develop. It was once believed, and even supported by the available research of the day, that children were born either "smart" or "dumb" and little could be done to alter this. We now know that nothing could be further from the truth. Recent neurological research has yielded a new and essential set of conclusions about infant and child development:

IQ Is Not Fixed at Birth

There is solid evidence to support the conclusion that an intervention program for impoverished children can prevent low IQs as well as certain levels of mental retardation (Wolf & Brandt, 1998). Well-designed programs for disadvantaged children have been able to boost IQ by as many as eight points on the average and significantly higher for some children. Unfortunately, without well-designed follow-up support, these benefits may be difficult to sustain (Shore, 1997).

Environmental Influences

The environment in which a child lives determines to a large degree how well the brain will function (Wolf & Brandt, 1998). Throughout the entire process of development, beginning even before birth, the brain is affected both for good or bad, by environmental conditions. Impacted by prenatal use of tobacco, alcohol and cocaine, poor nutrition, infant care, surroundings and stimulation, a developing fetus/child faces dramatic environmental consequences. This environmental influence actually affects how the "intricate circuitry of the brain is wired" (Shore, 1997). The degree to which nutrition, surroundings, care, stimulation, and teaching is either provided or withheld has a long-term crucial impact on the development of all children.

Early Child Care

Early child care has a decisive and long-lasting impact on how people develop, their ability to learn, and their capacity to regulate their emotions: It is now recognized that a strong, secure personal attachment to a nurturing caregiver, either the parent or some other caring adult(s), has a powerful, protective function in helping children withstand and learn from the stresses of daily life (Shore, 1997; Wolf & Brandt, 1998).

Windows of Opportunity

There are windows of opportunity that maximize the development of the brain. The human brain has a remarkable capacity to change, but timing appears to be crucial. Research has documented that the human brain can be significantly altered, or helped to compensate for problems, with timely, intensive intervention. These critical periods include the first decade of life, especially the first few years of life (Shore, 1997).

Negative Influences

There are times when negative experiences or the absence of appropriate stimulation are more likely to have serious and sustained effect. A number of researchers have focused their attention on experiences/circumstances that interfere with effective caregiving and have long-term, negative effects on children. These negative influences include maternal depression; early exposure to nicotine, alcohol, and cocaine; and early experiences with trauma, ongoing abuse, and stress. Factors such as these can result in extreme anxiety, depression, mental illness, and the inability of young children to form healthy attachments to others; they can impair cognitive abilities. When these factors occur together, the healthy development of children is even further jeopardized. Unfortunately, many of these risk factors are also associated with poverty, and more than a quarter of all children in the United States under the age of six are growing up in poverty (Shore, 1997).

Prevention and Early Intervention

Widespread evidence collected during the last decade clearly documents the power of prevention and early intervention, as study after study has shown that intensive, well-designed, and timely interventions can significantly improve the quality of life of children who are considered at risk of cognitive, social, or emotional problems (Shore, 1997).

As a result of the growing research on the human brain and child development, educators and psychologists have been able to identify ten essential parental activities that ensure the most positive development of infants and young children:

1. Be warm, loving, and responsive. When children receive warm, responsive care, they are more likely to feel safe and secure with the adults who care for them.
2. Respond to the child's cues and clues. Recognize and respond to the sounds, movements, and expressions that your child makes. This helps to build secure attachments.
3. Talk, sing, and read to your child. All of these interactions help the brain of the child make the connections it needs for growth and later learning.
4. Establish rituals and routines. Children need to have established routines, such as singing a song and pulling the curtains, so that they come to know when it is time for bed. Daily routines and rituals associated with pleasurable feelings are reassuring for children.
5. Encourage safe exploration and play. As infants grow, they begin to explore the world beyond their caregivers. Parents should encourage this exploration. While many may think of learning as simply acquiring facts, children actually learn through playing.
6. Make television watching selective. Parents should watch television with their children and talk about what they are viewing. TV should not be used as a baby-sitter.

7. Use discipline as an opportunity to teach. In addition to consistent and loving adult supervision, children must be taught to understand limits. A child should never be hit or shaken.
8. Recognize that each child is unique. Children grow at different rates. Children's ideas and feelings about themselves reflect, in large measure, parents' and caregivers' attitudes toward them.
9. Choose quality child care and stay involved. Selection of warm, responsible caregivers is essential. Frequent visits to child care providers are important.
10. And, for parents: They should take care of themselves. (Adapted from Special Early Childhood Report, 1997)

Recent research has expanded the list of activities parents can use to stimulate the brain and enhance child development. Marian Diamond and her team of researchers at the University of California, Berkeley, believes that enriched environments unmistakably influence the brain's growth and learning. An enriched environment for children, Diamond says:

- includes a steady source of positive emotional support
- provides a nutritious diet with enough protein, vitamins, minerals, and calories
- stimulates all the senses (but not necessarily all at once!)
- has an atmosphere free of undue pressure and stress but suffused with a degree of pleasurable intensity
- presents a series of novel challenges that are neither too easy nor too difficult for the child at his or her stage of development
- allows social interaction for a significant percentage of activities
- promotes the development of a broad range of skills and interests that are mental, physical, aesthetic, social, and emotional
- gives the child an opportunity to choose many of his or her efforts and modify them
- provides an enjoyable atmosphere that promotes exploration and the fun of learning
- allows the child to be an active participant rather than a passive observer (Wolfe & Brandt, 1998; Shore, 1997)

Parent Education

Recent research has led to greater attention being focused on the early childhood years and on the role of the parent as the child's first teacher. While on a common sense level we have always recognized the importance of parents in the education of their children, research has verified such understanding and provided new insights into the influence of parenting techniques. We know that the most important factor in the education of children is not the school, the teacher, or the curriculum; it is the parent. Long before a child arrives in school, parenting practices will have created an able young learner or will have significantly retarded the child's development. We once thought that children were born with basic intelligence, that a person's I.Q. was established at birth. This conclusion could not be further from the truth. We now know that students' mental abilities can be stimulated and expanded during the early years. The reverse is unfortunately also true. Without a fertile learning environment in the home, children will often atrophy intellectually, enter the first grade far behind their classmates, and without costly intervention never catch up. We know that the optimal time for children to learn to read is from three years of age to approximately the third grade and that the most positive force in developing strong literacy skills is the simple practice of parents reading to their children.

Recognizing the essential role of the parent as the child's first teacher, a number of states and a large number of school districts throughout the United States have developed effective parent education programs. For almost two decades the state of Missouri has operated a program for parent education that is often described as a model for other states. The New Parents as Teachers Project, initiated in 1981 through a Danforth grant, has grown from a four-district, 380-parent project to 53,000 families in all 543 school districts of the state. New Parents as Teachers features "education for new parents, physical and developmental screening for children ages one through four, and parent education for parents of three- and four-year olds" (National School Boards Association, 1989, p. 37).

Another parent education program, *Success by Six,* is being used in Minneapolis, Atlanta, Charlotte, Houston, Nashville, Syracuse, and Boise. This program was first developed in Minneapolis through a collaboration between private industry, the mayor, the school superintendent, and United Way. The program identified five barriers preventing children from achieving healthy early childhood development. These barriers include:

- unrecognized crises facing children
- poverty
- inaccessible information
- cultural misunderstanding
- fragmented service delivery

To address these barriers, the Success By Six program has three major goals:

- educating people about the crises facing children
- helping parents access the help and human services they need
- building partnerships that are sensitive to peoples' diverse background and cultures (Our mission and goals, 1999).

More recently, both commercial and public television have developed programming on educating parents to be more effective teachers and parents. There is also a growing body of superb literature that has translated sophisticated research findings into easy-to-understand practices for parents to use with their children during the early childhood years. There is dramatic evidence that these rather simple practices, such as reading aloud to children and having appropriate reading materials available in the home, can be taught to parents and can have an enormous positive effect on enhancing the learning capabilities of young children (Gathercoal, 1999). Few other programs offer the promise of such lasting influence as that of improved parenting practices. Because of this, schools must recognize that parent education, combined with comprehensive preschool programs, may well be the most necessary and the most cost-effective approach to attacking the problems of at-risk youth.

There are several excellent publications and video programs that focus on a wide variety of behavior and learning outcomes that parents can influence, i.e., self-esteem, work habits, and decision making; others focus specifically on helping children learn to read. With reading problems being identified as the most common characteristic of at-risk children and youth, these publications provide a clear emphasis on those parenting practices that can help to ensure that children will learn to read.

Phi Delta Kappa and the World Book Encyclopedia company have developed a 16-minute videotape entitled *Little Things Make a Big Difference* that can be used in parent education programs. Another video entitled *Read to Me* was developed by the Idaho Literacy Project and is being distributed through the International Reading Association. The University of Illinois has developed a brief yet succinct research-based pamphlet entitled *Ten Ways to Help Your Children Become Better Readers* (Center for the Study of Reading, 1989), and the American Association of School Administrators has developed *101 Ways Parents Can Help Students Achieve* (1991).

Another superb set of brochures has been developed by the ERIC Clearinghouse on Reading and Communication Skills at Indiana University. Once again, these brochures include specific, simplified instructions for parents that are based on the best available research. The brochures include such titles as *How Can I Be Involved in My Child's Education, How Can I Improve My Child's Reading, How Important Is Homework,* and *What Do Parents Need to Know about Children's Television Viewing* (ERIC, 1993). There is also an older yet worthwhile publication developed during the Reagan administration by the Office of Education entitled *What Works,* which includes numerous activities that parents should use in helping their children learn to read and to develop learning skills (U.S. Department of Education, 1987a).

These and other publications that serve to identify effective parenting practices can have an enormous impact on small children. They are also essential to the continued success of adolescent youth. These simple practices may have a more dramatic positive effect than years of schooling. Research, especially recent brain research, recommends the following approaches for all parents to make a significant, lasting, and positive impact on their children.

Parents Can Help Their Children Learn to Read

Parents can play a key role in helping their children become literate. To ensure that children will learn to read and be successful in school, parents should read aloud to young children and infants, even before they are able to comprehend the stories being read. The process of holding, cuddling, and reading to small children is critically important. Research indicates that there are few specific practices that have such positive long-lasting influence as that of reading aloud to infants and young children. Reading aloud provides both the closeness and human warmth that are essential to early bonding; it also provides an essential foundation for school success. As children grow older, parents should encourage the child to participate in the reading by identifying words and letters and talking about the story that they have read.

Parents Should Talk to Their Children, Ask Questions, and Encourage Children to Make Decisions

Talking with children about their experiences helps them to develop new words and to understand what they mean. Talking with children, asking them questions, and encouraging them to make decisions stimulates the young mind by encouraging the skills of expression, communication, and interpretation and helping students to be independent decision makers.

Parents Should Provide a Stimulating Environment for Children

Parents should try to provide a rich variety of experiences to stimulate small children. These do not need to be expensive experiences: trips to shopping malls, grocery stores, parks, zoos, and museums all provide stimulating learning opportunities for children. These excursions provide children with a forum for asking questions, talking, and experiencing real-life events that can be related to the stories that their parents read at home.

Parents Should Encourage Responsible Television Viewing

There are many wonderful, enriching television programs that help children learn about reading and language. These programs, such as Sesame Street, Reading Rainbow, and others that can be found on public television, CNN, and the Discovery Channel, are known to have a positive impact on children's learning and development. Parents should use these programs to intellectually stimulate young children and provide yet another experience about which to talk and ask questions. Careful selection of television viewing of up to ten hours per week can have a slightly positive effect on children's achievement later in school. As the number of hours increase beyond ten, television viewing becomes a negative influence. Children who watch more than 20 hours of television per week usually do poorly in school (ERIC, 1990).

Parents Should Be Interested and Involved in Their Children's School

Research indicates that the more parents are interested and involved in children's schoolwork, the better children tend to do in school. Parents should regularly visit their child's school, become acquainted with the teacher, learn how they can help their children at home, and discuss how they can encourage the child to be more effective in school.

Parents Must Provide a Safe, Loving Environment for Young Children

Overshadowing all other practices, parents must provide young children with love, care, and security in order for them to develop secure, positive self-concepts and self-esteem. While this should go without saying, we know the opposite is unfortunately true, and child abuse, sexual abuse, and poor nutrition are a way of life for many children. In this age of rampant poverty, divorce, single and teenage parents, and latchkey children, the loving, secure environment that is so essential to children's development is too often sadly lacking. Many children are so deprived of basic love and security that they fail to bond with any adult. Others spend lonely lives in front of televisions, accompanied by brothers and sisters, and arrive at school without the stimulation, support, and self-esteem that is necessary for success in school. Parents must be helped to understand how to love, care for, and discipline their children in positive ways. And in the absence of caring parents, child care providers and school programs must attempt to provide the essential support that these children so desperately need.

The Critical Importance of Early Childhood Care and Preschool Education

Because so many children are born in poverty to single parents and often to teenage parents, significant numbers of children today are reared by adults with few effective parenting skills. This is especially true for teen parents, who are often still children themselves. Research indicates that it is essential to provide child care for children in poverty and especially for teen parents. This is true for several reasons:

- In stark contrast to previous generations, the majority of women with children under five years old work away from home.
- Though declining slightly in recent years, the number of unmarried teens with babies continues to persist at alarming levels.
- There is growing consensus that young welfare mothers must have opportunities to be in educational training programs and should be employed.
- Systematic professional child care can have dramatic long-term positive benefits. (Schorr & Schorr, 1989; Barr & Parrett, 1997a)

It is now evident that without consistent, effective child care, many children born in poverty may not bond effectively with adults, and that, without this bonding, a life of antisocial psychopathy is predictable. Caring for children under the age of three has become the fastest-growing type of child care program. It is now generally agreed that out-of-home child care, even for very young children, is possible and effective when the staff is well trained, turnover of trained staff is low, and the child-to-staff ratio is low. However, poor-quality child care for small children can be damaging. The characteristics of effective child care have been identified as follows:

- *It must go beyond custodial care to provide intellectual stimulation—with books, the spoken word, play, the interchange of ideas, a developmental orientation, and with nurturance, hugs, approval, and responsiveness.*
- *It must include health, nutrition, and social services.*
- *It must clearly and systematically involve, collaborate with, and provide support to parents.*
- *It must be provided by competent staff, with a staff-child ratio low enough that children at each developmental state get the personal attention they need in order to thrive. (Schorr & Schorr, 1989, p. 202)*

"Success in the early childhood years is a critical prerequisite for success in later schooling and ultimately in life" (McPartland & Slavin, 1990, p. 7). The inverse is unfortunately also true. Children who begin school academically behind their peers will rarely catch up, unless provided with intensive intervention programs to address their needs.

To provide for maximum success, programs for at-risk children must begin much earlier than the school years. In fact, to be most effective, the programs should focus on the health and well-being of the child's mother before birth and continue throughout infancy and child care, preschool and kindergarten programs. There is mounting evidence that when poor preschool children and elementary school children are provided enriched early education which combines high expectations with immunizations, medical checkups, hot meals, and social services, almost all children can be successfully taught to read in the early grades and thus begin their education with a strong foundation for success (Schorr & Schorr, 1989, p. 189).

The enormous importance of high-quality early childhood care and education has been documented in a number of longitudinal research projects that have followed the growth and development of young children into adulthood. As a result of this research and by studying the child care of young children, it has become possible to make long-term predictions regarding such diverse outcomes as school success, violence, and even felony convictions. It is also possible to track the long-term costs associated with child care from childhood into adulthood. And while the home environment of young children is crucial in the positive development of children, research has documented that child care outside the home is not only important, but it can even overcome many of the negative affects of impoverished and/or abusive families. So influential and pervasive is the impact of high-quality child care, that its effects can be documented more than twenty years later. Five major studies have been instrumental in identifying this phenomenon:

High/Scope Perry Preschool Study

Twenty-three years ago, Lawrence Schweinhart of the High/Scope Educational Research Foundation in Ypsilanti, Michigan, began studying the impact of high-quality preschool experience on 123 young African American children living in poverty. This longitudinal study revealed that preschools that encourage creativity and active learning appear to be the most effective. The study concluded that children exposed to these high-quality preschools are considerably more likely to stay in school, graduate from high school, have higher annual salaries as adults, and are often less likely to be convicted of felony crimes during their lifetimes. In 1999, when the Perry preschool students were compared to other poor children in the same community who were not involved in preschool, the savings during the lifetime (to date) of the Perry preschool students was over $6,000 in special education costs, over $2,900 in welfare, over $12,700 in justice system costs, and $57,500 in crime/victim costs. It was also estimated that during the Perry Preschool group's lifetime, they would pay more than $8,800 in taxes over and above comparison children not in early child care (Barnett, 1996).

Minnesota Parent-Child Study

Since 1975, a group of researchers at the University of Minnesota have been studying 267 women and their children. More than two decades later, 180 of the original children are still participating in the study. The conclusions of this study include:

- Abuse, neglect, and trauma during the early years have a long term adverse effect on children's development.
- The negative effects of poverty increase with age.
- It is possible to predict children's later school achievement by studying the early experiences of high-risk children (12 to 42 months old). The key factors in these predictions have been identified as the primary attachments of children to an adult(s) and the level of environment support. Predictions regarding school achievement were fairly strong for the first and third grades, even stronger at the sixth grade as well as at age 16.
- The factors that seem to contribute most to developing resiliency in high-risk children were identified as: emotionally responsive caregiving, early competence in children, a well-organized home environment, and well-developed intellectual and language capabilities. The single most important factor in enhancing the potential of young children is to reduce the level of stress they experience and to ensure a caring relationship with an adult. (Shore, 1997)

Society for Research in Child Development

A recent study of the long-term effects of quality child care involves 1,300 children at ten sites. Preliminary results of this study indicate that quality child care has a significant effect on school readiness and language skills. Kathleen McCartney, who directed the study, reported that 57 percent of the children in high-quality child care had above average scores on school readiness assessments compared to only 42 percent of these involved in low-quality child care. Quality child care, whether provided by teachers or parents, has more physical contact with the children, shares positive emotions with the children, and is responsive to children when they speak (Study: High quality child care pays off, 1999).

Abecedarian Project

A project similar to the Perry Preschool Project has been conducted by researchers at the University of North Carolina with even more impressive results. The Abecedarian Project, a longitudinal study of children receiving early child care began studying children at birth and has followed them until today when the subjects are in their early twenties. The results of high-quality child care with an educational focus was:

- Over time, IQ scores of the program children were raised seven to ten points.
- Student retention in elementary school was significantly reduced.
- Referrals to special education were cut in half.
- At age 15, program students tested 1.4 grades ahead of the control group in reading and math (Whitmire, 1997).

Head Start

One of the most successful federal programs for providing assistance to preschool youth is Head Start. Started in 1965 as an intensive summer program during President Lyndon Johnson's "war on poverty," the federal program continues to serve over 600,000 disadvantaged preschool youth with an allocation of over $2 billion per year (Lang, 1992). A wide variety of research has documented that the Head Start program has had strong positive effects on language development and IQ scores. Lisbeth and Daniel Schorr address this issue in their classic work, *Within Our Reach:*

> *We now know that the education, health, nutrition, social services and parent support provided by these Head Start programs have prevented or ameliorated many of the educational handicaps associated with growing up in poverty. We now know that children who have attended quality early childhood programs develop social and academic competencies that are later manifested in increased school success. They enter school healthier, better fed, and with parents who are better equipped to support their educational development. . . . When three to five-year-old children are systematically helped to think, reason, and speak clearly; when they are provided hot meals, social services, health evaluations and care; when families become partners in their children's learning experiences, are helped toward self-sufficiency, and greater confidence in themselves as parents and as contributing members of the community, the results are measurable and dramatic (1989, p. 192).*

Unfortunately, research has also documented that the early positive effects of Head Start can diminish rapidly with each subsequent year until, for the most part, they are undetectable by the end of the second or third grade. This result has led to a variety of follow-through programs that attempt to maintain and continue educational enrichment gains from preschool and early elementary years. There is also evidence from longitudinal studies that Head Start children do have long-term positive gains in high-school graduation and lack of delinquency (McPartland & Slavin, 1990). In 1999 a study conducted by the National Institute for Child Health and Development reported that the 34-year-old Head Start program was effectively preparing young children for kindergarten, though there were some areas that needed improvement. This study, conducted during the fall of 1997, followed 3,200 children in 40 Head Start programs. The study not only found Head Start children "ready to learn," but also found that graduates had made significant progress at the end of kindergarten. The study found that Head Start teachers needed to emphasize early reading skill to a greater degree in order to improve reading readiness (Study: High-quality child care pays off, 1999). Many states have developed programs to supplement the success of Head Start with names like Great Start, Even Start, and Strong Start. These programs have been developed to address the needs of children unable to participate in Head Start. These programs focus on parenting skills, literacy, and a variety of developmental opportunities.

High-Quality Child Care Programs

The importance of high-quality child care, especially for poor children during a time when welfare has been significantly reduced nationwide, has led a number of states and cities to expand support for small children in low-income families. A leader in this work is the state of Georgia. For several years, the state of Georgia has provided a free prekindergarten program for any four-year-olds in the state, regardless of income. The program has grown from 10,000 children in 1994 to over 60,000 children in 1998, as approximately 80 percent of all eligible four-year-olds attended the prekindergarten classes. In 1997 the program cost $211 million. Low-income families receive additional assistance to participate, including transportation, extended day programs, and other necessary social services (A jump-start on school, 1998).

A recent report by High/Scope Education Research Foundation and the National Association for the Education of Young Children has identified and recognized ten exemplary programs in the United States that work. These programs include:

- Bridges Family Child Care, a family child care home in Madison, Wisconsin
- Children's for Children, a corporate child care program at the nonprofit Children's Hospital Medical Center in Cincinnati, Ohio
- Day Care Services Association, a statewide child care organization that provides resource and referral services, conducts research, and runs a scholarship program for child care providers in Chapel Hill, North Carolina
- Kindergarten and Children's Aid Association Preschools of Hawaii, a nonprofit organization in Honolulu, Hawaii
- Kennewick Early Childhood Education and Assistance Program, a nonprofit, public school–based prekindergarten in Kennewick (Washington) School District 17

- Lakewood Avenue Children's School, a for-profit center in Durham, North Carolina
- Miami Valley Child Development Centers Inc., a Head Start agency in Dayton, Ohio
- River Valley Child Development Services, a nonprofit community-action agency in Huntington, West Virginia
- Sycamore Tree Preschool, a nonprofit, part-time, church-based program in Bremerton, Washington
- UCLA Child Care Services, a nonprofit, university-based center in Los Angeles, California (Jacobson, 1998)

Kindergarten

Almost everyone has come to agree on the value of kindergarten; in most states, kindergarten attendance is now required. Today, kindergarten enrollment is the fastest-growing area of public education. Research focusing on full-day kindergarten compared to half-day programs and on the available curricula have found the effects of all-day kindergarten to be similar to the effects of preschool programs: initial positive results are likely to diminish quickly without continued programmatic support. Like preschool, kindergarten is not sufficient to ensure lasting educational success, but it is an essential foundation to later success (Schorr & Schorr, 1989).

The debate continues regarding the most appropriate, most effective kindergarten curriculum. This debate centers around whether or not kindergartens should be highly academic or nonacademic or how to balance these two positions. Some feel that the first-grade curriculum should be simply moved down to the kindergarten level while others believe that too much academic pressure on young children is debilitating to their development. Many educators now support a developmentally appropriate curriculum (Charlesworth, 1989).

Increasingly, research has begun to identify those aspects of the kindergarten curriculum that are most significant. And while it is important to have extended or all-day kindergarten, how the kindergarten students spend their time appears to be equally as important as the amount of time spent in kindergarten. Early childhood curriculum experts believe that the kindergarten curriculum should offer a variety and balance of activities that are provided in the context of project work which might include investigating real objects or events (Katz and Chad, 1989). Examples of a quality kindergarten curriculum include:

- *Integrated topic studies, rather than whole-group instruction in isolated skills*
- *Opportunities for children to learn by observing and experimenting with real objects*
- *A balance of child- and teacher-initiated activities*
- *Opportunities for spontaneous play and teacher-facilitated activities*
- *Group projects in which cooperation can occur naturally*

- *A range of activities requiring the use of large and small muscles*
- *Exposure to good literature and music of the children's own culture and of other cultures represented in the class*
- *Authentic assessment of each child's developmental progress*
- *Opportunities for children with diverse backgrounds and developmental levels to participate in whole-group activities*
- *Time for individuals or small groups of children to meet with the teacher for specific help in acquiring basic reading, writing, mathematical, and other skills as needed (ERIC, 1993, p. 1)*

Elementary School Programs for At-Risk Youth

As previously indicated, there is a best time to address the needs of at-risk youth. That opportune time is as early as possible. For schools, this means that the maximum opportunity to have a positive impact on children is in kindergarten and grades one through three. Increasingly, schools are establishing child-care programs, especially for their teen parents, and expanding preschool and Head Start programs.

Early intervention programs have enormous potential for at-risk students. These programs are effective because children tend to arrive at school excited and eager to learn. Unfortunately, in some urban districts, as many as 20 percent of these new students fail the first grade and are retained (Madden, Slavin, Karweit, Dolan, & Wasik, 1991). Others begin falling behind during the first grade, and each year the gap widens between their achievement and the achievement of their peers. The longer at-risk students stay in school without intervention, the farther they tend to fall behind. By the 6th grade their achievement is two years behind grade level on average, and by the 12th grade, if they are still in school, they are four years behind.

Guaranteeing That Every Child Learns to Read

> *One morning in 1997, as I was driving to work, I heard the radio DJ announce that there were only 1,000 days left in the century. It struck me that our incoming kindergarten students would also have only 1,000 days between the time they entered Scott Lane and their "graduation" from 2nd grade in June 2000. What was the most important thing we could do for those children in that time period? Teach them to read!*
> —PRINCIPAL, SCOTT LANE ELEMENTARY SCHOOL, CALIFORNIA

The good news is that research, evaluation, and long-term student follow-up assessment have made it dramatically clear that all students, with the exception of a very small number of seriously mentally impaired, can be taught to read. Today, there are a number of programs available to schools and communities that have well-documented track records of success in teaching all children, even those seriously behind, the skills of reading.

So compelling is current research and program development in reading that it is now possible to predict success, or as a growing number of schools are doing, to guarantee parents that their children will learn to read. This remarkable development in teaching and learning represents perhaps the most important advancement in schooling since public education was made available to all children. As reported earlier, reading deficiency is the most identified problem in research on at-risk children. Now we have the means to correct this problem (Wasik & Slavin, 1993; Slavin, Karweit, & Wasik, 1992; Barr & Parrett, 1997b).

Every parent should demand that local elementary schools provide assurances that their children will learn to read and seek information regarding what they can do to assist in this process. The time has come when schools must ensure that all children learn to read. This may require that certain expectations be established between the school and the home. Parents must assist their children by reading at home and monitoring homework for a specified amount of time each day. Parents must, if at all possible, keep the children in the same school for at least the first three to four years of school. With little more than these two assurances, the school should be able to teach all children to read. In 1998, four California schools began a new "1,000 Days to Success" program that was designed to ensure that all children learn to read by the end of the second grade. One thousand days is roughly the equivalent of the number of days from kindergarten through the second grade. Each school in the "1,000 Days" program spells out its commitment to teaching all students to read on a printed reading warranty card (Wheaton & Kay, Oct. 1999).

Reading as an Entitlement

Because of the importance of reading and the positive developments that have occurred in reading instruction, there is a growing national consensus that learning to read is an entitlement for all children. As Robert Slavin, one of the nation's leading scholars on the study of at-risk youth and reading instruction, has said, "If success is seen as an entitlement, educators must have methods that produce success for all non-retarded children regardless of home background, no matter how expensive these methods may be" (Wasik & Slavin, 1993, p. 180).

Recognizing the importance of learning to read early, an increasing number of elementary schools are reallocating school resources from the upper grades (fourth, fifth, and sixth) to enrich the resources of the early grades. Public education now possesses the knowledge, methodology, and access to model programs to achieve the goal of teaching every child to read. Implementing this knowledge and methodology into comprehensive, schoolwide programs represents the critical challenge public schools must confront if all children, particularly those at risk, are to succeed in school.

Need to Redesign Grades K–3

Because of the growing understanding of the essential importance of teaching all children to read by the end of the third grade, there is a corresponding recognition of the need to restructure and redesign kindergarten through the first three grades of elementary school. This redesign must focus on teaching all children to read. This may mean allocating more of the school day to reading and it may demand that one teacher be held responsible for teaching all children to read. Because of the essential nature of teaching reading, some schools are moving instructional aides from intermediate grades and clustering them in the first three grades. Other schools are offering "looping," a practice involving the same teacher being responsible for the same group of students through the first three years of school (Rasmussen, 1998). Other school districts are providing after school, weekend, and intensive summer programs that focus on students who are reading below grade level.

Growing Concern over Medicating Elementary-Age Children

Attention Deficit/Hyperactivity Disorder (ADHD) and Attention Deficit Disorder (ADD) are the most commonly diagnosed disorders in schoolchildren in the United States. Between 3 percent and 5 percent of all schoolchildren in the United States have been diagnosed as having some type of attention deficit disorder. As a result, the use of the prescription drug Ritalin, the most common treatment for ADD, has increased 260 percent between 1992 and 1997 (Coles, 1999). Unfortunately, the National Institute of Health reminds parents and teachers that attention deficit disorder is a behavioral problem, not a learning disability. And the medical community continues to insist that there are "no specific or conclusive medical tests to identify the disorder" (Coles, 1999). Yet many prominent researchers continue to maintain that attention deficit disorder is a neurological disease and strongly endorse the use of Ritalin (Diller, 1998). In spite of this clash of viewpoints, most medical leaders, educators, and parents believe that ADHD/ADD is a reflection of a "living imbalance, rather than a chemical imbalance" (Coles, 1999), and point to poor child-rearing practices in families, communities, child care, and schools as an explanation for the growing behavioral problems of children in the United States. There is growing national concern that schools too often identify students as having ADD who are only in need of more stimulating learning experiences and more effective approaches to classroom management. The behavioral symptoms of students previously diagnosed as ADD often disappear when enrolled in effective alternative schools (Barr & Parrett, 1997a).

Some believe that in the near future 10 percent of all children in the nation may be taking Ritalin, as many as one in six boys between the ages five and twelve (Diller, 1998). And while Ritalin can bring about short-term improvements in behavior, there is a continuing concern regarding the long-term implications of the use of the drug. Many now believe that designing more effective, more responsive educational programs could significantly reduce the need for Ritalin.

Schoolwide Elementary Programs

There are a number of independent instructional components that have been documented as highly successful with at-risk children during the elementary years. These components (tutoring, extended day programs, cooperative learning, and computer-assisted instruction) will be discussed later in this section. What is most promising is that when effective components are blended into a comprehensive program, truly exceptional gains can occur with at-risk children.

Research and evaluation during the past decade has documented the impact of a number of comprehensive school-reform models and programs on the student achievement of at-risk youth. As a result, it is now possible to identify those programs that have documented evidence of improving student achievement, and those that have not. Offering the most impressive evidence of success for elementary youth at risk are the Success For All, Direct Instruction, Accelerated Schools, and the School Development Program. A number of other programs showing promising evidence of improving student achievement include: Atlas Communities, Consistency Management and Cooperative Discipline, Core Knowledge, Expeditionary Learning, Perry Preschool/High Scope, Roots and Wings, Turnaround Schools, and Alternative Elementary Schools.

Success for All

We have been a Success For All School for three years and it has been an incredible experience. We started out providing one-to-one tutoring in reading every other day, but we failed to get the results we wanted. Now, we have trained just about every adult in the school as a tutor, moved instructional aides from the upper grades down into the lower grades and are providing daily tutoring as part of our total educational program. While we believe that we must teach children to read during the first three grades and that they will then be more successful in the upper grades with fewer instructional aides and fewer resources, we still worry about reducing resources at the upper grades. But while we are still experimenting and still learning, we have been incredibly successful. All our kids are reading up to grade level and beyond by the end of the third grade. And our students come from a relatively poor, rural area.
—A SUCCESS FOR ALL SCHOOL PRINCIPAL, CANYON ELEMENTARY SCHOOL, VALLEY VIEW, IDAHO

The Success For All (SFA) project is coordinated by Robert Slavin and other leading scholars at Johns Hopkins University. The SFA school concept was started in seven schools in three of the most disadvantaged urban and rural school districts in the country. Today there are over 1500 SFA schools in forty-eight states and five other countries. The SFA program prescribes a schoolwide effort that has successfully experimented with Chapter 1 funds to enrich the entire school student body, rather than to support a separate pullout program. The SFA approach is grounded in a strong foundational knowledge base and has demonstrated exceptional success in helping at-risk youth achievement (Madden et al., 1991). Success For All is perhaps the most widely recognized and implemented model showing evidence of successfully improving student achievement for elementary youth at risk (Herman, 1999).

The SFA schools emphasize the importance of early intervention. As Slavin and his colleagues have stressed, "the most important goal in educational programming for students at risk is to try to make certain that we do not squander the greatest resource we have: the enthusiasm and positive self-expectations of young children themselves" (Madden et al., 1991, p. 594). As a result of this belief, Slavin has been instrumental in developing the SFA approach, which has four major goals:

- *Ensure that every student will perform at grade level in reading, writing and mathematics by the end of the third grade.*
- *Reduce the number of students referred to special education classes.*
- *Reduce the number of children who are held back a grade.*
- *Increase attendance.*

Research has documented that the SFA program has been successful in achieving all of these goals (Education Commission of the States, 1991, p. 21). Characteristics of the SFA schools include the following:

Reading Tutors
Chapter 1 funds are used to employ certified reading teachers who provide one-on-one reading instruction, which Slavin maintains is the "most effective form of instruction known" (Madden et al., 1991, p. 594). The program focuses on students who are having difficulty in their reading groups and consists of 20-minute daily tutoring sessions. This tutoring is not used as a pull-out program.

Cross-Age Reading Groups
Using a method of student grouping called the Joplin Plan, first-, second-, and third-grade students are cross-age grouped for 90 minutes each day, according to reading level. This enables teachers to instruct an entire classroom of students who are functioning at the same reading level.

Family Support Teams
Family support teams are organized that encourage attendance, coordinate social services, train volunteers, work for better behavior, and help parents to ensure that their children will be successful in school.

Building Advisory Committees
SFA schools establish an advisory committee composed of the principal, facilitators, teachers, and parents to help shape policy and plan the program. A key role of this committee is to assess student reading levels at eight-week intervals. The results are then used to determine who needs tutoring. A recent evaluation of the SFA schools found that their students were far out-performing matched control groups. Students in 22 first-grade, 14 second-grade and 7 third-grade cohorts in 8 SFA schools out-performed the control groups by three months at the first-grade level, five months in the second grade and almost seven months at the end of grade three (Ascher, 1993). Although not all children in the SFA schools were reading at grade level, they were

close enough to grade level that they could benefit from classroom instruction in the other subject areas (Ascher, 1993).

Perhaps most important within SFA schools, there exists a schoolwide commitment and consensus toward the belief that all children can learn. Teachers in the schools are determined that all children will learn, and classrooms exhibit high expectations and teamwork between school and community. Today, SFA schools demand that 90 percent of the teachers in a school must agree to participate in a long-range program of reform. In a continuous effort to improve, SFA schools are also using STaR, story telling and retelling, during the prekindergarten and all-day kindergarten program, and employ a variety of newly developed reading materials (Madden et al., 1991). It is encouraging to visit SFA schools in their third or fourth year and discover that all third graders are reading at grade level.

Despite early successes, teachers and administrators working in SFA schools often worry about the effects of consolidating resources and efforts for the first three grades, even though they know that this approach is enabling students to catch up during the upper elementary grades. The SFA schools provide proof of how research-based approaches can be integrated into a schoolwide approach to effectively teach at-risk youth. No other elementary-school program has so carefully researched their program; none has reported such significant evidence of success.

Direct Instruction

Created to extend the low SES student gains of the federally funded Head Start program into the early elementary school years, Direct Instruction was originally referred to as Project Follow Through. Developed by Siegfried Englemann and his colleagues at the University of Illinois, Champaign, and later at the University of Oregon, Direct Instruction was primarily employed as a basal reading intervention for remedial students and has demonstrated success as a comprehensive school-reform model (Slavin & Fashola, 1998, p. 19). The Direct Instruction program is currently involved in serving kindergarten through grade six in 150 schools and several thousand classrooms nationwide. While it was developed primarily for low-performing schools in high poverty areas, it has been used successfully with all students.

Teachers involved in Direct Instruction follow highly specific instructions regarding how to teach the prepared units as well as what units should be taught. Students begin Direct Instruction at the kindergarten or first-grade level. Students participating in the program have been evaluated positively on academic performance using both criterion-referenced and norm-referenced measures (Herman, 1999).

Accelerated Schools

The school has emerged with a clearer and more unified focus,
a greater capacity for understanding and overcoming its
challenges, and most importantly, a deep-rooted belief in the
ability of all of its children to excel if properly nurtured. (Mason
Elementary School: Helping children beat the odds, 1993, p. 4)

Growing out of a concern that the traditional elementary school model was actually inhibiting the educational progress of many youth, Hank Levin and his associates at Stanford University developed the concept of accelerated learning and in 1986 initiated the Accelerated School Project. Levin and his colleagues are now working in over 1,300 schools in forty-one states, all with large at-risk student populations. They are attempting to transform these schools into places of accelerated learning. The concept of accelerated schooling is based on a very simple set of principles. First, Levin believes that at-risk students need and deserve the same approach as gifted and talented students, mainly to accelerate their learning rather than slow it down. Second, the entire school must share a unity of purpose and teachers must be empowered to have control over schools. Third, everyone involved must have high expectations for student learning.

Accelerated schools share the following characteristics:

- *Change the entire structure of the school instead of simply grafting remedial classes onto a school with a conventional agenda*
- *Empower teachers to plan the school's educational program*
- *Require substantial parental involvement (parents are expected to sign an agreement detailing their obligations to their children)*
- *Utilize the services of businesses, college students, senior citizens, and other community resources*
- *Use an extended day program with emphasis on language and problem solving*
- *Stress acceleration rather than remediation and attempt to bring all students to grade level by the end of the sixth grade (Levin, 1989, p. 3)*

These programs exceed the traditional range of practice regarding the education of at-risk students. This is done in the following manner:

- *Instead of labeling certain children as slow learners, accelerated schools have high expectations for all students.*
- *Instead of relegating students to remedial classes without setting goals for improvement, accelerated schools set deadlines for making such children academically able.*
- *Instead of slowing down the pace of instruction for at-risk students, accelerated schools combine relevant curriculum, powerful and diverse instructional techniques, and creative school organization to accelerate the progress of all students.*
- *Instead of providing instruction based on "drill and kill" worksheets, accelerated schools offer stimulating instructional programs based on problem-solving and interesting applications. (What are accelerated schools?, 1991, p. 1)*

Equally important to the success of the accelerated schools approach is the careful change strategy the Stanford team has developed. In order for a school to be associated with the accelerated school network, a school district must make an application, send a staff member for an eight-day training program at Stanford, and attain a 90 percent participation from the teaching faculty of the school or schools (typically three schools are proposed). Applicants for training are interviewed via telephone and asked to make a three-to-five year professional commitment. The school district or the district and the university partner must commit to ongoing staff development of at least one day per week for the trainer in the school or schools, and the cost of consultants from Stanford to visit the schools several times a year. The accelerated school network staff believes that the process of change cannot be accomplished in a month, six months, or a year. A complete transformation from a traditional school to an accelerated school takes about six years (Ascher, 1993). Consistent work toward goals and the nurturing of a long-term relationship among committed, trained staff ensures a successful transition.

The accelerated school program is expanding the network of schools each year and has been funded by Chevron USA to develop satellite centers at four other universities, including Texas A&M, California State University at Los Angeles, the University of New Orleans, and San Francisco State University (What are accelerated schools? 1991). Chevron studied more than 250 projects and programs before selecting the accelerated school program as their centerpiece of educational reform. While it is too early to determine the long-term impact of accelerated schools on children at risk, progress to date of participating students is extremely encouraging (What are accelerated schools? 1991).

School Development Program

> In 1968, Dr. Comer walked into the inner-city Baldwin School in New Haven for the first time. It was a school with boarded up windows and a playground strewn with glass. A school where teachers often didn't show up for work and where students ran out of control up and down the hallways. A school where, as Dr. Comer notes, you could feel the hand of hopelessness. But through the School Development Program forged by James Comer and his colleagues, the teachers, parents and community came together in new and innovative ways to turn Baldwin and several other New Haven schools around. (Edeman, 1993, p. viii)

James P. Comer, a child psychiatrist and director of the School Development Program at Yale University's Child Study Center, has developed an approach for school improvement that has experienced remarkable success with at-risk youth. Developed during several years of collaboration with the New Haven, Connecticut, public schools and later expanded to over 541 elementary, 107 middle, and 73 high schools in 12 states, Comer's intervention model addresses the problems of poor minority youth who come from environments that often possess values which conflict with the mainstream American values found in public education. Students from poor minority homes often come from families who not only do not trust or support public education but often voice and act out in direct opposition to schools.

Concerned that educational reform typically focuses on instructional and curricular issues, Comer developed an approach that focuses on bridging the social and cultural gap between the home and the school. As Comer has stated:

*A child from a poor, marginal family is likely to enter school without ade-
quate preparation. The child may arrive without ever having learned such
social skills as negotiation and compromise. A child who is expected to read
at school may come from a home where no one reads and may never have
heard a parent read bedtime stories. The child's language skills may be
underdeveloped or non-standard. Expectations at home and at school may
be radically at odds. For example, in some families a child who does not
fight back will be punished. And yet the same behavior will get the child into
trouble at school. (Comer, 1988, p. 45)*

Comer's approach emphasized that the key to academic achievement was to
encourage the psychological development of students, to encourage bonding between students and the school. This, he found, is best accomplished through fostering positive development between parents and school staff. In each of the Comer
intervention schools, a governance and management team and a mental health team
is developed. The management team includes approximately 12 individuals led by
the principal and consists of elected parents, teachers, a mental health specialist, and
members of the nonprofessional support staff. This group is charged with making
recommendations and decisions on a broad range of issues which impact a variety of
academic and social procedural changes in the school environment. Mental health
teams often include a social worker, the school psychologist, counselor, nurse, speech
and hearing teacher, and the principal. This group uses a case management approach to ensure that every child is progressing satisfactorily in the school. Schools
where these teams work usually develop very different programs and practices. In
one school, students stay with the same teacher for two years. In another, a discovery
room was established for troubled children to develop positive relationships with an
adult and learn through play. In another school, a crisis room was created to help students cool off and calm down in a positive atmosphere. Yet in each school, the key
characteristics of the management team were having parents and teachers work
together for common goals and using a case management approach to focus the attention of specialists, parents, and teachers on particular students and their problems. The
management teams are guided by three simple but effective principles: no-fault assessment (the teams focus on problems rather than on affixing blame), the teams are truly
collaborative, and the teams work for consensus (Ascher, 1993, Comer, 1999).

The results of this approach with the New Haven schools have been most
impressive. Comer explains:

*The students had once ranked lowest in achievement among the 33 elemen-
tary schools in the city, but by 1979, without any change in the socioeconomic makeup of the schools, students in the fourth grade had caught up to
their grade level. By 1984 pupils in the fourth grade in the two schools
ranked third and fourth-highest on the Iowa Test of Basic Skills. By the early
1980s, attendance rates (at one of the schools) were either first or second in
the city. There have been no serious behavioral problems at either of the
schools in more than a decade. (Comer, 1988, p. 48)*

To achieve this record of success, Comer schools each developed a collaborative school plan with specified goals, a program to monitor and assess progress toward the goals, and ongoing staff development programs designed to provide the school and community with the skills necessary to achieve their goals.

Schoolwide Efforts Showing Promise

A number of new, emerging programs have been documented as having a positive effect on student achievement for at-risk learners. These programs include:

Atlas Communities (K–12)

Based on a collaborative design of Comer, Gardner, Sizer, and Whitla models, Atlas Communities focuses on creating active learning classrooms, teacher coaching, project-based learning, portfolios, performance assessments, student exhibitions, and successful transitions between grades and levels of K–12 schooling. Atlas is currently operating in 57 schools in 7 states (Herman, 1999).

Consistency Management and Cooperative Discipline (CMCD)

CMCD originally emphasized discipline through student sharing of responsibility in inner-city schools at all grade levels. The key components of this model are organization, cooperation, caring, community, and prevention. Substantial evidence exists that documents the positive impact of the program on student achievement, especially for students who stay in the program for at least six years. The program is currently implemented in 58 schools in 4 states and in 2 other countries (Herman, 1999).

Core Knowledge

Core Knowledge Program is based on teaching a common core of concepts, skills, and knowledge that are central to becoming educated. This model employs a set of curriculum materials and instructional strategies used to create the core curriculum. Designed by E. D. Hirsch, Core Knowledge programs are currently implemented in 950 schools in forty-six states. The program focuses on the acquisition of a classical curriculum specifically outlined in grade-level guides. Rigorous assessment precedes passage to succeeding grades (Herman, 1999).

Expeditionary Learning (K–12)

Based on the Outward Bound model of adventure-based learning, the 80-plus Expeditionary Learning schools focus on expeditions into the real world as vehicles for action learning, teamwork, personal and group challenges, and individual research. The model focuses on student projects, cooperative learning, and performance assessments components. Expeditionary Learning, one of the original New American School Design programs, is based on the concepts which have successfully driven its parent model, Outward Bound, for over 50 years (Herman, 1999).

Perry Preschool/High Scope (K–3)

Based on the Perry Preschool Curriculum, this model, found in every state, focuses on strong, enhanced connections between the school and home. Following a Piaget model, the curriculum requires active learning and student choice to guide instruction. Long-term studies demonstrate significantly positive results for participating at-risk students to date.

Roots and Wings

Roots and Wings, a comprehensive school-reform program, was developed at Johns Hopkins University as an extension of the university's highly successful Success for All program. Currently over 90 Roots and Wings programs work to expand the Success for All effort to focus on mathematics, social studies, and science. Students who have been involved in the program have demonstrated substantial growth in reading, language, writing, math, science, and social studies (Slavin & Fashola, 1998).

Turnaround Schools

As described earlier, a recent study by the Education Trust identified 360 schools in poor communities throughout the United States whose students were achieving up to and above the levels of more affluent middle-class students. In both Kentucky and Texas, a number of the top ten student-achieving schools were previously low-performing schools that "turned around" their educational programs and became high-achieving schools. Most of these remarkable success stories reflect state policies of establishing high academic standards, aligning curriculum to address those standards, monitoring student progress, and "grading" schools on the achievement level of their students. The states of Texas, California, and Washington have also established high-stakes tests at the fifth grade level and banned promotion of any students unable to pass the exams. There is increasing evidence that such statewide efforts have a powerful positive impact on schoolwide achievement (The Education Trust, 1999; see Chapter 5). Critics counter that utilization of a single test to assess student performance has led to a variety of difficulties and inappropriate testing practices at the local level (Lewis, 1999). Despite these concerns, impressive gains have been demonstrated by these schools that serve high proportions of at-risk youth.

Elementary Alternative Schools

Beginning in the late 1960s, public school districts throughout the United States, especially in urban areas, began to develop alternative schools. While many school districts continue to experiment and develop new and increasing numbers of alternatives, some of the most notable programs have been in operation for over 25 years with remarkably positive research and evaluation on student achievement and attitudes. Some of these schools represent the best, most creative examples of restructured schools found in all of U.S. public education. Some of these schools are K–12, serving entire school districts, others focus on high school or middle school only, and many exist as elementary schools especially designed to meet the needs of certain groups of students. Some elementary alternative schools have been developed as small schools within schools and more recently as charter schools. What makes these schools so distinctive is that parents, teachers, and students voluntarily choose to participate in a different approach from that typically available in the conventional elementary school.

Elementary alternative schools have been developed for four basic reasons:

- *The belief that children learn in different ways*
- *The belief that teachers teach in different ways*
- *The belief that students, parents, and teachers who have a particular learning style or philosophy ought to be able to choose to work together in a school setting*
- *As a component in school desegregation plans in order to enable children of different ethnic groups to attend school together*
- *These schools have accumulated over 30 years of research data documenting the positive effects of alternative schools on student achievement, attendance and attitude* (Barr & Parrett, 1997a).

While some alternative elementary schools offer choices for talented, high achieving youth (science and math academies and programs focusing on language immersion, environmental studies, performing arts, and others), many of these programs were designed to address the needs of at-risk youth. Supported by a growing research base and years of practical experience regarding teaching and learning styles, these schools are flourishing. A number of established elementary alternative school models are currently in use.

Multiple Intelligences Schools

Informed by the work of Harvard scholar Howard Gardner, public schools throughout the United States have developed new alternatives based on the concept of Multiple Intelligences (Campbell & Campbell, 1999). Reflecting a belief that each child has a variety of intelligences other than academic ones, schools have emphasized the development of the full child—including emphases in art, music, linguistics, interpersonal relationships, logic/mathematics, kinesthetics—utilizing multi-age groupings of students. The most widely known elementary school to implement the multiple intelligence approach is the Key School in Indianapolis, Indiana. The Key School, which some have suggested may be the best school in the country, emphasizes the development of multiple intelligences. Through a theme-based approach, the school offers an integrated curriculum, has nongraded classrooms, uses a project approach, and employs portfolio-based assessment. The curriculum focuses on enrichment instead of remediation, encourages motivation, uses technology extensively, requires a second language, has a fully integrated arts program, makes extensive use of community resources, and uses a qualitative approach to evaluate students. A second school focusing on multiple intelligences, the Renaissance Middle School, was created as an outgrowth of the original Key School. ASCD has recently recognized multiple intelligence elementary schools in Lexington, Kentucky, and St. Paul, Minnesota, which have demonstrated exemplary achievement results using this approach (Campbell & Campbell, 1999).

Montessori Schools

Based on the classic work of the Italian physician Maria Montessori, the Montessori concept has been available to parents able to afford private school tuition costs for over 100 years. During the late 1970s, Cincinnati and Indianapolis became the first school districts in America to offer Montessori schools as part of public education. This growth of Montessori schools has continued for the past 15 years as more and more public schools have incorporated the highly successful Montessori approach into their educational program. Over 90 Montessori Public Schools are in operation today nationwide (Education Commission of the States, 1991). This has meant that, for the first time, many parents of at-risk children have an opportunity to enroll their children in an educational program which focuses on developmentally appropriate learning, an approach which can be critically important in the early development of these children.

School #56, one of the public Montessori options in Indianapolis, provides a K–5 program which incorporates a full-day kindergarten into its highly individualized approach to learning. Following 12 years of successful operation, School #56 clearly demonstrates the efficacy of this approach as an option within public education.

Back-to-Basics Traditional Schools

Many public schools have developed elementary alternative programs that model private schools. One of the most popular alternative programs during the 1980s was the back-to-basics school. Often requiring dress, behavior, and homework codes, these traditional schools provide an educational program based on high expectations, solid grounding in basic subjects, and relatively few special programs.

The Jefferson County public schools in Louisville, Kentucky, established several of the first back-to-basics schools in the early 1980s. Today, this district continues to offer elementary, middle and high schools that focus on the traditional back-to-basics model. Greathouse Shyrock Traditional Elementary enrolls 592 students in its K–5 school which features a nongraded primary, strong parental involvement, strict dress codes, and a culturally and economically diverse student body. Despite continued success in Louisville and other cities during recent years, the nationwide popularity of the traditional back-to-basics model has begun to decline (Barr & Parrett, 1997a).

Nongraded, Developmentally Appropriate Schools

A considerable number of elementary alternative schools have been developed throughout the United States using a nongraded, developmentally appropriate approach to learning. These schools utilize highly individualized programs that incorporate developmentally appropriate practices in a nongraded curriculum. Many of the nation's first nongraded elementary schools were established in the Minneapolis, Minnesota, public schools over 20 years ago, including open concept, continuous progress, and Montessori programs and are available by choice to all parents and children in the community.

Open Schools

The K–12 St. Paul Open School in St. Paul, Minnesota, was developed in the early 1970s and provides the model of a U.S. open school. While the majority of open schools in the United States were designed to replicate the British infant school concept, the St. Paul Open School was based on the research and philosophy developed during the Eight-Year Study, which had been conducted three decades earlier to investigate the relationship between success in college and college entrance requirements. The St. Paul Open School was one of the first public schools in America to eliminate course requirements for graduation and to replace them with graduation competencies. The school serves the entire St. Paul school district and enrolls a widely diverse student body. Today each student who attends the school must validate an adequate performance in each of the school's competency areas.

The St. Paul Open School's elementary program incorporates the concepts of cross-age teaching and tutoring, out-of-school learning experiences, and authentic student assessment into its program of study. This school provides a proven model for restructuring public education in the U.S. today, as the St. Paul Open School may have been studied and evaluated more than any other school in the nation. When compared to students in other St. Paul schools and in follow-up studies conducted four years after graduation, the Open School students appeared to be better adjusted, possessed a better understanding of academic knowledge, and were most successful following school graduation. The St. Paul Open School has also been used as a model to establish a growing number of Community Learning Centers in Minneapolis, St. Paul, and throughout the state of Minnesota.

Magnet Schools

For over 20 years, magnet schools have been used as an effective strategy to aid in districtwide school desegregation efforts. Today, many of these schools provide rich multicultural learning opportunities for diverse urban populations. Across the nation, school districts have developed magnet schools that emphasize the visual and performing arts, environmental education, technology, world language study, economics, and others. Gardendale Elementary Magnet School (GEM), created in the early

1990s, is a redesigned neighborhood elementary school with robust parental and student enthusiasm for its success and unique approach to providing choice at the elementary level. Located on Merritt Island off the east coast of Florida, the Gardendale Elementary Magnet School serves 820 students, many of whom are low SES, and is available by choice to the entire district. GEM offers four theme-based magnet programs under one roof, which include: Performing Arts, Math and Sciences, Arts and Cultures, and Micro Society. Primary students (K–3) remain with the same teacher and home-based classroom for an entire year, but rotate through the magnet programs for a series of four nine-week sessions. Students in grades four through six then select an option to spend the final three years of their elementary experience (Narvaez, 1995). Born out of community support and the dedication of a committed staff, GEM has won numerous national awards for its achievement, design, and success.

The Hawthorne Elementary School, a (Seattle Public Schools) Magnet Program, serves as an excellent example of the magnet approach. The school is characterized by a rich academic and cultural program that is focused on African-American students and their culture. The multicultural faculty, staff, parents, and students embrace the primary goal of the school, which is to ensure that all students complete the elementary years with an adequate level of student achievement. The school is organized around two key principles:

> ### Student Warranty:
> *The school emphasizes high expectations for all students; in fact, the school is one of the few in this country that provides a warranty for students and parents. The warranty assures parents that if they will keep their children in the school for five years, the school guarantees that the students will be achieving at grade level.*

> ### Each Teacher Is Responsible for All Children:
> *Each of the teachers in the school has responsibility for all children. This means that each teacher has high expectations for all children in the school, monitors all children on the playground and in hallways, and is personally responsible for all children who are not achieving up to grade level. (Hawthorne School, 1991, pp. 1–4)*

Charter Elementary Schools

Charter public schools have become increasingly available throughout the country. Since 1991, when Minnesota became the first state to establish charter legislation, a total of 37 states have now legislatively approved the concept. Much of the rush to charter schools has occurred at the elementary level where parents have seemed eager to escape the stifling regulations of most public school districts, join teachers as full partners in shaping schools, and participate in highly customized programs that reflect common interests and needs.

Some charter schools like ANSER Charter in Boise, Idaho, which is based on the concepts of Expeditionary Learning and multiple intelligences, emphasizes a unique learning theory. Others, such as the Flagstaff Charter for Performing Arts and Academics in Arizona, emphasize a content focus. Still others, such as Options in Education Charters in Pasadena, California, focus on a special clientele such as dropouts and/or home-schooled children.

Charter schools tend to reflect a greater social/economic diversity than other public schools and must document increased student achievement to stay in business (Barr & Parrett, 1997a, Nathan 1996). As of the year 2000, charter elementary programs appear headed for continued growth as many states are moving their status from experimental to permanent. Many high-risk youth attend these schools, which are increasingly being viewed as yet another viable option for every state.

The early development of alternative and magnet schools and later, charter schools, represented the first time public schools were created specifically to attract a rich diversity of socioeconomic and ethnic backgrounds and academic abilities into a single school. Many of these alternatives accepted students who had formerly been assigned to special education yet were realizing limited success there. Each of these elementary alternative schools combined high expectations, student assessment, parental involvement, and out-of-school learning experiences to build effective programs. Research and evaluation of these schools have been extremely positive (Young, 1990; Barr & Parrett, 1997a).

Effective Elementary-School Practices for At-Risk Youth

The schools described above represent examples of elementary schools that have been unusually successful in addressing the needs of at-risk youth through comprehensive, schoolwide efforts. In addition to these schoolwide efforts, there are particular approaches at the elementary-school level that have been documented as highly successful with at-risk youth, even when they were not used in a schoolwide comprehensive approach. The research is quite clear that the best way to meet the needs of at-risk youth at the elementary level is through schoolwide programs that integrate the various approaches into a comprehensive effort. However, the demands placed on the schools by increasing numbers of at-risk children require that schools must begin implementing practices that are known to work.

One-to-One Tutoring

One-to-one tutoring is the most effective form of instruction known (Slavin et al., 1992). One-to-one tutoring offers immense potential for use in the first grade to ensure that all children without serious learning disabilities can learn to read, especially when the tutor is a trained professional. Research and evaluation of one-to-one tutoring using trained professionals have demonstrated the dramatic effectiveness of this educational approach, especially with at-risk youth (Center for Research on Effective Schooling for Disadvantaged Students, 1990). First-grade success in reading has long-term positive effects on at-risk youth, either without additional intervention or with low-cost continuing intervention. "These long-term effects include achievement in later grades, less retention, fewer referrals to special education, and reduced dropouts" (Center for Research on Effective Schooling for Disadvantaged Students, 1990, p. 1).

The primary obstacle to implementing tutoring programs typically centers around cost, since the majority of the programs that have been studied use trained, certified teachers to provide the one-to-one tutoring. However, when one considers the long-term positive influences on children who learn to read versus the long-term societal costs of not learning to read and dropping out of school, implementing tutoring programs in elementary schools makes eminent sense. The Center for Research on Effective Schooling for Disadvantaged Students has identified five programs that have demonstrated considerable success. They include Reading Recovery, Success For All, Wallach Tutorial Programs, Programmed Tutorial Reading, and Prevention of Learning Disabilities. Each of these programs has been studied extensively and each provides impressive evidence documenting the effectiveness of one-to-one tutoring programs that use professional tutors (Wasik & Slavin, 1993).

Reading Recovery

The tutoring approach that has been researched most carefully over time is Reading Recovery (Pinnell, 1990; Pinnell, Lyons, DeFord, Bryk, & Seltzer, 1994; and Clay, 1991). This early intervention approach is a unique program credited to Marie Clay, a New Zealand child psychologist. Clay designed and refined the program and conducted the early research on this intervention approach. Later, the program was expanded and studied at The Ohio State University and has emerged as a highly successful approach for teaching reading to the poorest readers in the school. Today Reading Recovery is being used in 10,000 schools in 49 states.

The program relies on the use of certified teachers who have been trained in the Reading Recovery approach (a training program that is approximately one year in length and requires an internship). The program is implemented in elementary schools and focuses on the lowest achieving students in the first grade. In addition to classroom reading instruction, these students are provided supplemental, intensive, one-to-one tutoring for 30 minutes each day for approximately 16 weeks. The Reading Recovery teacher tutors each child to become an independent reader. When the goal is attained, the tutoring is discontinued and the next lowest level reader takes his or her place in the program (Wasik & Slavin, 1993).

After nine years of study in New Zealand, research and evaluation of the Reading Recovery approach found that "regardless of sex, socioeconomic status, or social linguistic group, the lowest achieving children make accelerated progress in the program and continue to make satisfactory progress after release from the program" (Pinnell, 1990, p. 19). Fewer than 1 percent of the students in the program have needed further referral.

Through more recent comparative studies in Ohio, it was found that Reading Recovery children "achieved at higher levels than did children who received other compensatory treatments" (Wasik & Slavin, 1993, pp. 185–187). Reading Recovery children were found to read material three levels above comparison children. Ninety percent of the Reading Recovery children met or exceeded the average range in reading. An Ohio follow-up study of Reading Recovery graduates found that by the third grade, the Reading Recovery children could read material one grade level above comparison children, and 69 percent met or exceeded the average range of reading ability of their fellow students. The research clearly indicates that Reading Recovery has immediate as well as long-term positive results. Reading Recovery teaches low-achieving children to read and write and helps them to progress rapidly to the levels of success experienced by their classmates (Wasik & Slavin, 1993; Pinnell et al., 1994).

Other Successful Tutorial Programs

There are a number of other highly successful one-to-one reading tutorial programs that have accumulated solid research and evaluation data. Other successful one-to-one tutoring programs include Success For All, described earlier in this chapter, Prevention of Learning Disabilities (which uses certified teachers), Wallach Tutorial Program (paraprofessional tutors in both inner-city Chicago and rural North Carolina), and Programmed Tutorial Reading materials (once again paraprofessionals use this program in both urban and rural areas). Wasik and Slavin have conducted a detailed evaluation of the effectiveness of these one-to-one tutorial approaches and have documented each as successful. In 16 separate studies of cohorts involving the five different tutorial methods, the significant differences were substantially positive in nearly every case (Wasik & Slavin, 1993). In addition, research on these five tutorial programs led to four important conclusions:

1. *The most comprehensive models of reading, and therefore the most complete instructional interventions, have larger impacts than programs that address only a few components of the reading process. Reading Recovery and Success For All were found to be the most successful programs.*
2. *It is not enough to simply use tutors. For tutoring to be most effective, the quality of instruction must be improved. Also, better achievement occurs by increasing the amount of time, incentive, value, and appropriateness to student needs.*
3. *Tutoring by certified teachers appeared to have substantially more impact than tutoring by paraprofessionals.*
4. *The initial positive effects continued into second and third grades (Wasik & Slavin, 1993, p. 196).*

Because of the cost of one-to-one tutoring, the lasting effects of this approach are of great importance. Two of the programs, Success For All and Programmed Tutorial Reading, have documented substantial reductions in student retention. Success For All reports fewer referrals to special education during the intervention and in successive years (Wasik & Slavin, 1993).

Using Volunteers and Peers for One-to-One Tutoring

Not only is this a cost-effective approach to teaching reading, there is a growing body of literature designed to help volunteers be more effective tutors. One of the best materials available is a delightful and useful collection of strategies entitled *The Volunteer Tutor's Toolbox* (Herrmann, 1994).

One-to-one tutoring can also be extremely effective using peer tutors. There is also research demonstrating the positive effects of peer tutoring on the tutor as well as the tutee. Sam Winter, noted reading scholar, describes an example of a peer tutoring program in reading:

Reading together:

1 *Read aloud with your partner, letting her set the pace and share her book.*
2. *If your partner hesitates or makes a mistake, tell her the correct word, and make her repeat it before continuing.*

Reading alone:

3. *If your partner signals that he wants to read alone, then stop reading aloud and follow the story.*
4. *If your partner hesitates or makes a mistake while reading alone, then tell him the correct word, make him repeat it, and then read aloud with him until he next signals.*
5. *Whenever your partner reads a difficult word or sentence, corrects his own mistake, or signals he can read on his own, then praise him. (Winter, 1986, p. 103)*

In a landmark peer tutoring study, "tutees were able to read faster, make fewer errors, and where a mistake was made, it was more probably self-corrected" (Winter, 1986, p. 104). This study concluded that one-to-one peer tutoring not only taught children to read, but made them more self-confident in their reading.

The use of professional, paraprofessional, and peer tutoring to help at-risk youth overcome reading deficiency in the early grades represents a practice that works and should be available in every elementary school (Adler, 1998).

Looping and Multi-Age Classrooms

There is a growing body of research that supports two increasingly popular concepts, both rooted in the traditional, one-room schools of an earlier era. Looping keeps the same teacher with the same class of students for two to three years rather than the traditional one-year assignment. Participating teachers report substantial gains in learning due to building and maintaining a community that dramatically increases instructional time because of a greatly enhanced knowledge base and relationship between parents, teachers, and students. The concept of multi-age grouping is as old as schooling. Society and families are multi-aged so why shouldn't classrooms be? The primary motive of this concept is that since students in any age-grouped grade level will be achieving in the various subjects at a wide variety of grade levels, multi-age grouping permits for better targeted instruction. It also provides older students the opportunity to serve as role models and peer tutors for younger students (Walser, 1998).

Extended-Day Enrichment Programs

Many elementary-school programs that are especially successful with at-risk youth utilize an extended day. These programs, often referred to as latchkey programs, are often a feature of urban magnet schools which use the extended day concept to attract working parents from far distances. In Houston, Texas, the most popular magnet school is the Extended Day Program because it offers such advantages to both parents and students. For parents who leave for work before the traditional school day begins and who do not finish their work day until after school is over, these programs offer a welcome alternative to a number of undesirable options which working parents regularly encounter. In Springfield, Virginia, public schools at all levels use before and after school programs for student enrichment.

For the at-risk student, such programs provide additional time for tutoring, homework, and cultural enrichment. Extended day programs provide additional school time to help at-risk youth catch up and accelerate their learning without pulling the students out of their regular classes. Extended day programs may be staffed with teachers, aides, college or university student teachers, parents, or other volunteers. Staffing these programs with teachers can be an expensive but highly effective approach. Before and after school enrichment programs provide a wonderful means to solicit and gain community, business, and volunteer support. Many community service clubs support these programs, and many schools use these programs to mobilize school volunteers. If a college or university is nearby, before and after school programs can be largely staffed with teacher education practicum students or university volunteers. These programs can also be staffed with older students serving as cross-age tutors to help younger students.

Before and after school programs can also include supervised playtime and personal development activities, while simultaneously saving children from lonely time at home in an unsupervised situation. Many programs develop one-to-one tutoring programs for children who are having reading problems. They provide students with a supportive place to complete their homework, to get tutorial assistance from other students or from adults, and to have library and computer resources available for their work.

Research has documented the many advantages of extending the school day as well as providing a time for personalized instruction that avoids pulling students out of class. Many of these before and after school programs include free breakfast programs and health assistance. Other programs offer gymnastics, intramural sports, chess, and art and music enrichment programs in addition to academic activities. Every elementary school should seriously consider the valuable advantages of before and after school programs. Any school with a sizable at-risk student population should offer all-day kindergarten as well as extended day programs for the early elementary-school years.

Parent/Family Partnerships and Two-Way Communication

There is a clear relationship between parent involvement with teachers and schools and increased student achievement. This is even more true for at-risk children. Programs that involve parents in full partnerships with teachers and schools find "student achievement for disadvantaged children not only improves, it can reach levels that are standard for middle-class children; and the children who are furthest behind make the greatest gains" (National PTA, 1998, p. 7).

The essential foundation for effective family/school partnerships is trust and communication, which can be developed through home visits, student-led conferences, telephone/e-mail discussions, active school/classroom participation and evaluation by parents, and weekly classroom newsletters with a return comments section (National PTA, May 1998, p. 10). Virtually every successful improvement model at the elementary level includes building more positive school-community-home relationships.

Cooperative Learning

Cooperative learning is certainly no new idea, but recently it has been studied, refined, and implemented extensively throughout public education. The concept of cooperative learning encourages students to work together and helps students teach one another in highly structured small-group activities. This practice stands in rather stark contrast to the typical large-group, direct instruction model of competitive learning that traditionally characterizes most public school settings. The importance of cooperative learning has been stressed by Slavin:

> *Cooperative learning has been suggested as the solution for an astonishing array of educational problems: it is often cited as a means of emphasizing thinking skills and increasing higher-order learning; as an alternative to ability grouping, remediation or special education; as a means of improving race relations and acceptance of mainstreamed students; and as a way to prepare students for an increasingly collaborative work force. (Slavin, 1991b, p. 71)*

Research on cooperative learning is impressive. Through cooperative small groups, students work together to help one another master academic material. There are many quite different forms of cooperative learning, and the effectiveness of cooperative learning (particularly for achievement outcomes) depends on the particular approach used.

- *For enhancing student achievement, the most successful approaches have incorporated two key elements: group goals and individual accountability; that is, groups are rewarded based on the individual learning of all group members.*
- *When group goals and individual accountability are used, achievement effects of cooperative learning are consistently positive: 37 out of 44 experimental/control comparisons of at least four weeks' duration have found significantly positive effects, and none have favored traditional methods.*

- *Achievement effects of cooperative learning have been found to be about the same degree at all grade levels (2–12), in all major subjects, and in urban, rural, and suburban schools. Effects are equally positive for high, average, and low achievers.*
- *Positive effects of cooperative learning have been consistently found on such diverse outcomes as self-esteem, intergroup relations, acceptance of academically handicapped students, attitudes toward school, and ability to work cooperatively. (Slavin, 1991b, p. 71)*

While research on the effects of cooperative learning shows consistent improvement in student achievement as measured on standardized tests, there are two elements that must be included in cooperative learning if it is to be effective. First, groups must be rewarded as a group for doing well, and second, the group's success must depend on the individual learning of each team member.

For the at-risk student, cooperation rather than competition toward academic achievement provides for an inclusive environment. Many children arrive at school ill-equipped to learn and achieve through the traditional authoritative classroom structure. Cooperating with their peers and achieving academic success during the early years of school can help a child to overcome many barriers to success in school and life (Bauwens and Hourcade, 1994).

Counseling Programs

Over the past decade a growing number of elementary schools have added school counselors to their staffs. Unfortunately, in most cases this invaluable resource for at-risk youth is available only on a part-time basis to a limited population of students. Virtually any elementary counselor will dramatically describe the overwhelming needs of elementary youth and then lament the reality of the present-day critical underfunding of counseling interventions. Nonetheless, those elementary schools that have developed counseling programs provide at-risk youth with the critical assistance that may literally save lives.

James and JoAnne Wigtil have identified a lengthy list of issues which elementary counselors must be prepared to address, including substance and alcohol abuse, death, divorce, lack of parental bonding, depression, aggression and anger, negative body images, suicide, eating disorders, poverty, abuse, and poor school performance (1993). When one considers that at any time 20 percent or more of the elementary school population may be confronted by one or more of these issues, the need for trained counseling personnel and programs seems imperative.

Effective Responses to Violent and Violence-Prone Children

The most crucial period in a child's life is the time from birth to grade three. During these years it is essential that parents and families provide an environment of support.

Parents and Family Support

There is overwhelming evidence that the period from infancy through age three is the single most important time in the prevention of violence. This short time period has an enormous consequence in the life of a child—both good and bad. It is during this brief period that parental action can dramatically raise a child's IQ; it is also the time when parental actions can all but doom a child to a tragic life of behavioral problems, violence, and often, incarceration. Because of the importance of this time period, schools, hospitals, doctors, social service agencies, churches, and youth organizations should mount educational programs designed to help parents understand and employ positive child-rearing practices. Such practices must include:

- Love and nurturing of young children
- Strict avoidance of anger, angry outbursts, physical, sexual, and emotional stress and abuse
- Positive programs for reading, educational enrichment, and rich experiences outside of the home
- Careful, consistent supervision and discipline
- Responsible media utilization, doing everything possible to limit the amount of time children watch television and the types of programs that are viewed
- Family time for children to share experiences, talk and be together with others, ensuring time everyday for sharing meals and reading
- Participation in church, school, and youth organizations where values, positive support, and supervision and recreation are available

In 1997 a report was published by the National Longitudinal Study of Adolescent Health that had surveyed 90,000 students grades seven through twelve throughout the country and conducted follow-up interviews with over 20,000 teenagers in their homes. The findings of this study confirmed conclusively that teenagers who had strong emotional attachments to their parents and teachers are much less likely to use drugs and alcohol, attempt suicide, engage in violence, or become sexually active at an early age (Resnick et al., 1997). A similar finding was reported by Search, Institute, as part of their Development Assets survey of students grades six through twelve. (See Chapter 2.) Parental involvement in a child's life must not decline as the child becomes a teenager. In some ways parental involvement is even more important at this time. Teenagers who feel loved, understood, and "paid attention to" by parents are helped in avoiding negative activities—regardless of whether or not students come from one- or two-parent families.

Child Care and Preschool Education

In much the same way as research emphasizes the importance of the early life of a child, child care and preschool programs have likewise been documented as having a crucial relationship—either for the positive development of children or negative. Studies over the years of high-quality child care programs have documented the long-term, lasting effects of these programs. Strong, supportive, and educationally sound child care can affect success in school, reduce problems during the school years, reduce problems in both the school and the community, and as a result, even affect the lifetime salary and economic/social situation as well as incidence of felony arrests. In a similar situation, effective preschool programs also have the potential for aiding in the positive development of young children. Programs like Head Start or other state-supported equivalents can provide essential, positive educational experiences, provide community building experiences, consistent behavioral standards, positive discipline for behavioral problems, and essential educational enrichment. Child care and preschool programs also provide early opportunities to identify child abuse and behaviors that serve as warnings for potential violent behavior. They also encourage the seeking-out of professional help from social services and community organizations for children identified with aberrant or violent behavior. Child care and preschools should:

- be staffed with trained caregivers/child care workers, who provide consistent care over time
- have low adult/children ratios
- have high standards of behavior and positive approaches to discipline
- involve young children in "community building" activities and reinforce the positive values of respect and relationships
- have structured group play and activities
- have an effective educational enrichment program

Community Support

Ensuring that young children and youth do not develop violent or destructive behavior is an issue for the entire community. Research has validated the positive impact on young children of programs emphasizing structured recreation and play, high standards of behavior, and positive values of respect, teamwork, and community. Such programs as the YMCA, YWCA, Boys and Girls Clubs, Boy Scouts/Girl Scouts and their affiliates, career/vocational organizations like Future Farmers of America, and organized soccer/basketball/football programs have powerful, positive impacts on children and youth. Programs such as these provide structured, supervised activities for children and safe, positive experiences with other children and also serve as an opportunity for the early identification of troubled children with the potential for violent or destructive behaviors.

Communities can also provide before- and after-school programs, provide mentors and tutors for young children, participate in neighborhood watch programs, provide foster parents for troubled youth, and provide essential social services for families and children.

Elementary Schools—A Climate of Respect

In regard to violence, the goal of any school must be to create a "climate of respect," a sanctuary of safety and civility where there are no put-downs, no name-calling, and no bullying. Nowhere is such an atmosphere so important as in an elementary school. The goal is to "bully-proof" any school (Banks, 1997; Steins et al., 1996).

In the 1999 publication *Violence in American Schools,* Hawkins and his colleagues David Farrington and Richard Catalano identified five key ways schools can keep disruption, uncivility, and violence at bay:

- Fostering social bonding and academic achievement: Kids who feel bonded to their neighborhood school and succeed academically have a powerful shield against disruptive and violent behavior.
- Promoting norms of nonviolence: Formal rules of conduct are critical, but not sufficient, to fostering a peaceful school climate. Schools also must work to influence "the informal norms and expectations for behavior that exist among the students themselves."
- Teaching skills for living according to nonviolent norms: These skills are teachable. High-quality violence-prevention and conflict-resolution curricula are valuable tools for teaching students to regulate their emotions, solve problems, and manage anger.
- Eliminating firearms and other weapons: Kids have always had conflicts, but easy access to weapons has raised the stakes.
- Identify troubled kids' schools and begin "noticing when we have troubled kids and connecting those kids to the right services" (Hawkins, 1999; Northwest Regional Education Lab, 1999).

School also must include curricula that promote the development of community as well as positive, personal, emotional, and social growth (Elias et al., 1997). School programs that promote anger management and conflict resolution, and utilize peer mediation, can have powerful, positive results (Dill, 1998). To "bully-proof" a school and create a "climate of respect", the Northwest Regional Educational Lab recommends the following curricula:

- *Safe School: Safe Students: A Guide to Violence-Prevention Strategies,* Johnson Institute, Minneapolis, 1998.
- *Daniel the Dinosaur,* Johnson Institute.
- *Quit It: A Teacher's Guide on Teasing and Bullying*. National Education Association. Wellsley College's Center for Research on Women.
- *Bully Proof: A Teacher's Guide on Teasing and Bullying for Use with 4th and 5th Grade Students*. Lisa Sjostrom and Nancy Stein. Wellsley College, Center for Research on Women.

Once again, before- and after-school programs, adult mentoring and tutoring programs, early identification of abuse and aberrant behavior, and referrals are essential. Elementary schools must be involved in strong, positive parental education programs.

Technology and Learning

When IBM moved five computers into my fifth grade classroom,
I almost died. I didn't have a computer at home, didn't even
know word processing; in fact, I wasn't even sure how to turn
one on. But while I was terrified of the things, the kids just
couldn't leave them alone. Some of the students asked to see
the instruction manual and almost overnight had the
machines operating. Once the class saw those shimmering
blue screens, they really became excited. Well, it didn't take
long before the students had me seated in front of the
keyboard and patiently took me through step after tortuous
step until I could call up a program and begin experimenting
with some of the individualized, elementary software. Did you get
this? My fifth-grade students were teaching me how to use elemen-
tary level program software and they were being patient and sup-
portive in their teaching. I don't think I'll ever be the same!
—TEACHER, JEFFERSON ELEMENTARY SCHOOL, BOISE, IDAHO

Schools have lagged far behind many other aspects of life when it comes to technology. The revolution in communications, computers, and other forms of technology
networks has only recently begun to impact public schools and too often only in
demonstration situations. While some entire school districts have moved energeti-
cally into technology and into connecting classes and schools with state, national,
and international data systems and networks, the vast majority of schools still have
only a small number of microcomputers, usually housed in a small computer laboratory with limited availability to all students.

There are several reasons for the lack of current technology in schools. First, the
cost of acquiring, maintaining, and updating hardware and software is a substantial
commitment. In a time of increasing taxpayer revolts, few states or communities
have been willing to make the investment. An exception is the state of Texas, where
schools have been provided with the equivalent of $30 per student per year for tech-
nology. Computer software has been defined as instructional materials and can be
purchased with textbook funds. Second, in most school districts, the average teaching experience is approximately 15 years or more. This means that the vast majority
of teachers were trained before microcomputers were a part of classroom instruction. Even if computers were available for every classroom in the school district,
state, and nation, it has been estimated it would take 7 to 10 years before teachers
would be able to make the adjustments to a new approach to teaching and learning
and then only after extensive training. Third, even those districts that possess the
resources and commitment to implement technology find the actual process is made
more difficult due to the lack of direction and agreement in the field regarding
method and approach. Confusion over what students should learn, when, and from
whom continues to inhibit widespread adoption of technology throughout the school.

Some districts are attempting to provide computers to all classrooms at the elementary and middle-school levels. While experts maintain that what is needed is

one computer for every three children, even adding four or five computers to a classroom creates a dramatic new learning environment. To adjust to this change requires that even experienced teachers must learn to incorporate a significantly different approach to instruction. This can be a painful process for many teachers, and for some it may never be accomplished. Many districts estimated that a minimum of 20 staff development days per year may be necessary to help teachers begin to learn new skills, become comfortable with the technology, and develop new instructional materials for their classroom.

Despite the challenge of schoolwide implementation, clustering computers in elementary classrooms appears to hold great promise for at-risk youth. Since most classrooms do not possess enough computers for every child, teachers must develop learning centers and use cooperative learning techniques. The teachers can then rotate children through a number of learning experiences, including those available via the computers. Both the cooperative learning experiences and the highly individualized computer work can prove extremely effective with at-risk children. Early evaluations of schools where computers have been clustered in the classrooms report that many students often do not want to go to recess or even lunch once they participate in computer learning. Parents of at-risk youth also support using computers with elementary students.

The National Dropout Prevention Center reports considerable academic success for at-risk youth using Computer-Assisted Instruction (CAI), Integrated Learning Systems (ILS), videodisc technology, and information databases such as CD ROM (Duttweiler, 1992). However, one study of low-achieving high-school students who had been using computer-assisted instruction for four years reported that the students scored disproportionately lower on the lesson assessments than low-achieving youth in other treatment groups. The researchers concluded that using computer-assisted instruction exclusively for remediation may well have stigmatized students in the same way that ability grouping had done (Dalton, 1986).

While teachers initially rely almost exclusively on programmed software like IBM's TLC and Right to Read, once they become more secure with the technology, they tend to increase the use of the computer as a tool to develop and edit technical reports, manage classroom data, develop critical thinking assignments, and, via networks, communicate with other classes and grade levels at different schools, even schools in other countries. With regional and international networks, electronic bulletin boards, and a variety of accessible databases and services, a vast world of knowledge has become available to teachers and students (Eisenberg & Ely, 1993).

Traditional cable television and other commercial applications such as Channel 1 and a variety of satellite programming are beginning to be used extensively in public schools. And while increased programming has provided additional opportunities for student learning, the advent of fiber-optic cable will dramatically increase a school's access to specially designed educational programming. Many feel that this arena is on the verge of significant developments in terms of the instructional potential that will soon become available. Even more dramatic, a wide variety of on-line, distance, and CD-ROM courses and programs are becoming available to schools and home schoolers. These programs are being developed by instructional designers, universities, and private companies and portend a revolutionizing of education from kindergarten through the university level. Yet, the question regarding technology continues to be, does it make a difference in student, particularly at-risk student achievement? While almost everyone agrees that technology makes learning more fun and develops technological skills, evidence of improved academic performance remains spotty (Trotter, 1998). There exists a growing recognition that technology, especially the internet, is becoming as important as the telephone, yet the gap between affluent families and the families of the poor and minorities grows wider each day (Lieberman, 1999). For at-risk youth, who often possess highly visual and/or tactile learning styles, these developments serve to provide additional hands-on, visual, and highly personalized approaches to learning that will prove extremely effective.

Creating an Effective Model for Elementary-School Programs

Research has identified a significant number of school practices and programs that are so effective in helping at-risk youth learn and succeed in schools that they can be guaranteed. A number of experimental approaches, like the Success For All program, the Accelerated School Project, Comer Intervention Schools, and others, have demonstrated remarkable success with at-risk youth through employing a variety of nontraditional school and classroom practices. Successful intervention strategies and program components from these various approaches can be integrated to create a theoretical model for improving elementary school programs. Drawing from the research and the lessons learned from programs designed to teach youth at risk, the following components, coupled with the essential characteristics for program development described in the previous chapter, create an effective model for elementary schools (see Appendix B for the Self-Evaluation Checklist).

High Academic Standards and Continual Monitoring of Student Achievement

Whether or not a state or school district has established high academic standards, every elementary school in the United States should have clearly defined academic standards and specific instructional goals for each grade. Each elementary school should align its curriculum to address standards and goals and continually monitor student achievement to ensure that all children are learning effectively, especially that they are learning to read and achieving high levels of academic achievement. Every elementary school should identify those students who are performing below state or district means, and should mobilize a schoolwide/community effort to help them catch up and accelerate their learning.

School and Community Consensus Building

Successful elementary schools employ schoolwide consensus building among teachers, parents, and students. Many of the experimental programs require that teacher support reach the 80 to 90 percent level before starting a school improvement project.

Most successful programs have discovered a number of effective approaches to integrating students and parents into the planning, decision making, and governance process. For schools with culturally diverse students and parents, it is even more essential to find ways to include all participants in the school's mission.

Parent Education and Child Enrichment Programs

Effective elementary schools must create effective parent and early childhood education programs that both support parental needs and help young children learn during the critical years of transition from preschool through kindergarten and into the elementary school. Before and after school programs must then be available throughout the school years to continue this support.

Schoolwide Emphasis on Teaching All Children to Read

Successful elementary schools must focus on teaching all children to read. Schools should identify those children with reading deficiencies or problems and mobilize school and community efforts to work together to ensure that all children learn to read at grade level by the end of their third-grade year at approximately age nine. One-to-one tutoring and an expanded reading program are essential in ensuring that every child learns to read.

Enriched Instruction during the Early Elementary Years

Recognizing that the best opportunities to positively impact children's learning begin to decline by about the end of the third grade, successful elementary schools are enriching the instructional program for preschool, kindergarten, and the first three years of elementary school. This is accomplished by using state and federally-funded programs for young children, all-day kindergarten, widespread use of volunteers, school-community partnerships, the coordination of social services, and the reallocation of school resources from the upper grades into the early grades.

High Expectations and Accelerated Learning

Successful elementary schools maintain high expectations for all students. These schools use every approach available to help at-risk children accelerate their learning so that they can catch up with their higher-achieving peers. At the earliest possible time, high expectations and accelerated learning create an atmosphere of hope, challenge, and accomplishment which drives the school's mission of educating all students.

Continuous Progress Learning

Successful elementary schools use a highly individualized, continuous progress learning approach to help children learn at their own level without fear of failure or retention. This is often accomplished by cross-age grouping or through some type of nongraded elementary organization. A continuous progress approach is vital to providing opportunities for at-risk youth to accelerate their learning and catch up.

Counseling, Case Management, and Coordination of Social Services

For young children, the needs of health, clothing, security, and nutrition may far outweigh any educational program or service. If these needs are unmet, the likelihood of any approach to increase the achievement and hope of an at-risk child's academic success is severely diminished. The development of a schoolwide counseling program provides a crucial function needed in every elementary school. Trained counselors can help young children to persevere, to overcome, or in some cases to survive the horrors of abuse, violence, and neglect which characterize so many of their lives.

Schools should also employ a case management approach to review the comprehensive needs of each child and develop appropriate intervention strategies. This requires that schools be informed of services that are available from the many government and community social services and work closely with the providers. Schools often need to coordinate these services with the child's education program to ensure that the needs are met. To accommodate this approach, many schools actually provide office space for a variety of human service providers so that the majority of their time can be devoted to the parents and students in the neighborhood school and its community.

Transition Programs

The transition from elementary school represents the single greatest shock in a student's educational life. From working with a single teacher for most of the day each year and with a small group of students for five to six years, students move to junior high/middle schools where they are often assigned a different teacher for each class, sometimes as many as six or seven different teachers each day, and a different group of peers each period. All elementary schools should work with middle level schools to develop programs that moderate this transitional shock, which is particularly difficult for high-risk students.

The Need for Choice

With more than 25 percent of all students in the United States enrolled in some type of nontraditional educational choice (alternative public schools, magnet schools, and charter schools), and many others attending non–public school choices—private/parochial schools and voucher programs and home schooling—it is apparent that choice is essential in the partnership of schools with parents and families (Lieberman, 1999). Many districts have embraced the Constitutional reality of this nation, which is built on the concept of choice, to redesign their schools and program offerings so as to reflect the concept of choice (see Chapter 5).

Elementary schools, to most effectively educate youth at risk, must redesign grades K–3 to reflect the growing understanding of the human brain and to ensure that every child is provided a developmentally appropriate opportunity to learn to read and master other basic skills. This may include multi-age grouping of students, looping, and implementing intensive catch-up/acceleration programs or schoolwide improvement models. The redesign of elementary schools to effectively teach at-risk students is imperative if our nation truly believes that all children can and will learn.

The individual success of the approaches described in this chapter are compounded and enriched when combined to form a comprehensive early-childhood-through-elementary plan. They also become more effective when parents are actively involved; when parents, teachers, and administrators hold high expectations for all children; and when student performance is authentically assessed. Addressing the needs of at-risk youth during the early childhood and elementary years holds critical importance for the individual child's future as well as the opportunity for subsequent schooling to be effective.

Unfortunately, even if many of these programs, practices, and interventions are implemented in a comprehensive schoolwide effort, the student achievement gains accomplished may soon be lost as the child moves into a standard junior high or middle school. Improving early childhood and elementary schools represents an important, yet only initial, step toward guaranteeing the effective education of youth at risk.

$Chapter$ 7

Programs That Work: Middle Schools/Junior High Schools

These kids keep coming and coming. It seems with every new intervention we try, new unmet needs appear. What are we going to do next? Five years ago we transformed our traditional junior high to a middle school. You know, we went to interdisciplinary teaching, collaborative teams, longer classes and breaks, more parent contact, and student rewards. We also stopped rotating kids. All of this helped. Yet we continued to lose kids. Most recently we've added Natural Helpers, peer mediation, a crisis intervention team, and started a Students Staying Straight Program and alternatives to violence. We created an Insight Program with focus groups for concerned friends, one-on-one counseling and support for problems of divorce, smoking, and drugs. We've increased nonteaching staff contact with students and initiated an intervention program for 75 of our most troubled kids. I even personally sing to each of our 742 kids on their birthday! All of this has made a dramatic difference, but we're still losing some kids. We can't do this alone. We need help!
—PRINCIPAL, RYAN MIDDLE SCHOOL, FAIRBANKS, ALASKA

Middle-level education tends to be the forgotten segment of public education. Students at this level are not only experiencing enormous biological and social changes, but advances in health, nutrition, and social conditions have quickened the adolescents' biological clock, impacting the maturation process. It is also during these middle-level years that many students drop out of school. If these challenges were not enough to capture the attention of any concerned educator, there are other problems as well. A fundamental weakness of most middle-level schools is that teachers are rarely adequately prepared for working with this demanding age group. This lack of training is compounded by a curriculum that often fails to reflect the developmental needs associated with young adolescents and tends to lack any strong theoretical foundation of learning. Goodlad and his colleagues, in their landmark study, discovered that teaching and learning in junior high schools tend to be removed from student needs. Teaching and learning were primarily centered around teacher lectures, preparation of assignments, and teachers monitoring student work at their desks—three activities that are teacher-centered and involve students in rather passive learning experiences. In spite of the fact that repeated studies have found that 40 percent of the students in middle-level schools have not mastered reading skills, less than 3 percent of class time is devoted to improving reading (Goodlad, 1984). A decade later, the situation appears to have worsened. In 1994 only 29 percent of the 8th grade students who participated in the National Assessment of Education Progress scored at the proficient level in reading (Killion, 1999, p. 2).

Teachers who work at this level in most cases have been trained as either elementary or high-school teachers. In a 1988 study of middle schools, 61 percent of the schools surveyed reported that less than 25 percent of their teachers had been prepared to teach at this level (Alexander & McEwin, 1989, p. 28). Ten years later, the situation had not improved (Killion, 1999, p. 4). Teachers often report that they feel like educational retreads, trained for one or another specialty and then reprogrammed into middle-level education. As a result, there tends to be an unfortunate low status associated with teaching at the middle school/junior high level. In spite of decades of concern focused on the young adolescent years, there are few examples of middle-school programs that have been designed to meet the complex educational and social needs of this challenging age level. Even fewer university teacher education programs devote the time or content emphasis necessary to prepare teachers to work effectively with these youth. Unlike the elementary school level where there are a growing number of successful, schoolwide restructuring projects underway that are being carefully documented, the middle-school level has experienced little change over the past four decades.

Despite a growing interest in restructuring public education, the middle-level school continues to demonstrate a startling lack of experimentation and reform, particularly for at-risk youth. Even school districts with large numbers of intervention programs and alternative schools designed to serve at-risk youth tend to operate most of these efforts at the elementary and the high-school levels. Yet it is during this critical period of adolescence when the vast majority of students drop out of school. It is here that students first suffer the shock of leaving a self-contained classroom and a relatively small educational environment and stepping into a large, content-centered approach to education that requires them to work with a different adult and often different peers almost every period of the day. Studies have found that close to 50 percent of all seventh graders change class at least four times a day (Wells, 1991; Killion, 1999, p. 1–2). Many attend seven classes per day with seven different teachers and different groups of students. Junior high or middle school tends to be a social shock for all students. For the at-risk student, it often is an overwhelming experience. The importance of this transition from elementary to middle school is dramatic and too often negative. "Nationally, middle grade students tend to perform less well academically than they did in elementary school. Inequalities between high achieving and low achieving students deepen with detrimental consequences for those students in the low achieving track" (Killion, 1999, p. 2; Wheelock, 1998).

Middle or junior-high schools come in a bewildering array of grade organization. As many as 30 different grade configurations have been identified by the Center for Research on Elementary and Middle Schools (Wells, 1991). Yet the vast majority use a grade six-through-eight or seven-through-nine organization. Most middle-level schools continue to look far more like high schools than they do elementary schools and regularly employ the practices of tracking, grade retention, and expulsion—all known to exacerbate the problems of the at-risk student. Middle or junior high schools in lower-income neighborhoods also provide at-risk youth with fewer resources and fewer opportunities in curriculum and instruction than schools in more advantaged neighborhoods (MacIver & Epstein, 1990).

A major report on adolescent development funded by the Carnegie Corporation stressed a number of recommendations for transforming middle-level education. These included the following:

- *Create small communities for learning. . . . The key elements of these communities are schools within schools or houses, with students and teachers grouped together as teams.*
- *Teach a core academic program that results in students who are literate, including in the sciences, and who know how to think critically, lead a healthy life, behave ethically, and assume the responsibilities of citizenship in a pluralistic society.*
- *Ensure success for all students through the elimination of tracking by achievement level.*
- *Staff middle-grade schools with teachers who are expert at teaching young adolescents.*
- *Improve academic performance through the fostering of health and fitness of young adolescents.*
- *Reengage families in the education of young adolescents.*
- *Connect schools with communities—which together share responsibility for each middle-grade student's success—through identifying learning opportunities in the community. (Carnegie Corporation, 1993, pp. 2–3)*

This set of recommendations clearly applies research on young adolescents and effective middle-level education to define a basic reform model for schools at this level.

Developmental Needs

> *In a recent phone conversation with the principal of the Barret Traditional Middle School in Louisville, Kentucky, he explained that the school was trying out a very new idea. "In the three traditional elementary school alternatives including the Barret Traditional Middle School, we are handing out laptop computers to every student and forbidding them to use any pencils or pens. How's that for catapulting kids into the new world of technology? Is this great or what? What do you think will happen when these kids go on to high school or later to college? We think this is simply going to transform the world. We're sure in a few years laptops will be just like books and notebooks and every school in America will be checking out computers to all of their students. We are just a little ahead of our time. I think that we are the first.*
> —PRINCIPAL, BARRET TRADITIONAL MIDDLE SCHOOL, JEFFERSON COUNTY SCHOOLS, LOUISVILLE, KENTUCKY*

Concern for at-risk youth during young adolescence has intensified as schools struggle to seek solutions for the problems confronting these youth. In response, a growing body of research into the developmental needs and assets of this age group is emerging. Recent studies suggest that these developmental needs represent a set of characteristics and preconditions that should guide educational reform at the middle-level school, especially for at-risk youth (Wheelock, 1998) (see Table 7-1).

TABLE 7-1   Developmental Needs of Young Adolescents

- **Structure and clear limits:** Students who are going through rapid physical and social-emotional change need security in order to learn and grow. Clear, consistent rules are appropriate, but they are more likely to be accepted and valued by students who have participated in their formulation and adoption.
- **Diversity:** In early adolescence, students' cognitive abilities are grounded largely in concrete thinking while they move toward a greater capacity for abstract thinking. This, combined with the wide range of abilities and interests of the age group, demands school routines, instruction, and curriculum which balance a variety of learning activities and materials.
- **Self-exploration and self-definition:** At the core of developmental issues for many young adolescents, the question "am I normal?" reflects students' need to define for themselves their values and their relationship to their family, friends, and school. The need for self-definition also plays into students' need for reassurance that they will be accepted as individuals in their schools.
- **Competence and achievement:** Schools play a major role in providing young adolescent students with experiences of achievement which, in turn, students incorporate into their emerging definition of themselves as competent individuals. Successful academic and social experiences are essential to building confidence and self-esteem which allow for further growth in later adolescence and young adulthood.

TABLE 7-1 *Continued*

- **Meaningful participation in the school and community:** As young adolescent students grow into adult bodies, they also need opportunities to begin to try out adult roles. While still too inexperienced to take on total responsibility for themselves and their environment, their new roles and increasing ability to think abstractly are at the core of their need to expand their responsibilities into wider arenas, to reflect on their future, and to negotiate with responsible adults the norms and expectations for behavior in the school.
- **Positive social interaction with adults and peers:** As young adolescents begin to differentiate themselves from their own families and define their own individual identities, they need increased contact with adult role models who can represent a variety of potential choices for students. At the same time, students' preoccupation with acceptance by their peers reflects their need to develop confidence in interacting with a wide range of other students.
- **Physical activity:** The needs of young adolescents' growing bodies require frequent opportunities to release the physical energy present during early adolescence.

(Massachusetts Advocacy Center, 1988, p. 22; Benson et al., 1998)

These developmental needs are highly consistent with the research conclusions of other groups (Carnegie Council on Adolescent Development, 1989). They are also consistent with the Developmental Assets developed in recent years by Search Institute. (See Chapter 2 for a description of these "assets" and their relationship to youth behavior.) Using these developmental needs as a guide, a number of middle-school programs have been developed that hold great promise for middle-level at-risk youth.

Schoolwide Reform Efforts

Schoolwide efforts to improve middle/junior high schools have demonstrated significant promise toward enhancing the academic and learning gains of youth at risk. These comprehensive improvement models focus primary attention on the entire school; its staff, students, and community.

The following section will describe schoolwide efforts for reforming the middle and junior high schools that provide evidence that their approach enhances student achievement (see Appendix A for contact information).

Multiple-Intelligences Middle Schools

A recent study published by the Association for Supervision and Curriculum Development documented the positive impact on student achievement when schools utilized the concept of multiple intelligences as an operating philosophy. The study identified two middle schools that are based on the concept of multiple intelligence. And while the two schools are distinctively different, both have student achievement that outperforms other comparable schools in their local communities. The research project documented that teachers in the two schools faithfully practiced their beliefs in the multiple intelligence philosophy (Campbell & Campbell, 1999). These two schools are the Skyview Junior High in Bothell, Washington, and the Key Learning Community in Indianapolis. The Skyview school is a large, suburban junior high school of 900 students. In contrast, the Key school is an urban middle school with 165 students in grades 6 through 8. The Skyview school serves a predominantly middle class student body; almost half of the Key school's students are below the poverty level. In addition to using more authentic assessments like projects, videotapes, and portfolios, both schools have documented high student achievement in state and school-district standardized tests (Campbell & Campbell, 1999).

Expeditionary Learning

This approach (see Chapters 6 through 8) was the most highly regarded of all school-wide models in a recent study completed by the National Staff Development Council. *What Works in the Middle* (Killion, 1999) found significant academic gain in math and reading in comparative studies of program students with localized control groups. Exemplary sites include the King Middle School in Portland, Maine, Rafael Hernandez School, Roxbury, Massachusetts, and the Rocky Mountain School of Expeditionary Learning in Denver, Colorado.

Accelerated Middle Schools

As described in the previous chapter, the first accelerated schools were initiated at the elementary level. In 1989, Henry Levin and his colleagues at Stanford University extended their research effort to focus on middle schools. Beginning in 1990, the Stanford group helped initiate the accelerated school approach at the middle-school level, and it has been expanding ever since. The accelerated concept at the middle-school level builds on the strength of the elementary approach while adding a number of new components. The approach includes:

- Creating cadres of teachers, students, and parents working together to improve teaching and learning
- Involving students and parents in all aspects of school planning through "taking stock," "visioning," and in-school governance and steering committees
- A shared decision-making model for governing the middle school

Even though the accelerated school network includes more than 900 elementary and middle schools in 39 states, data on achievement gain to date is largely anecdotal. As the program takes up to five years to be fully implemented, research on accelerated schools is only beginning to document student improvement (Slavin & Fashola, 1998).

Community for Learning

The Community for Learning program focuses on improving student achievement and learning, behavior, and attitudes related to promoting independent habits of learning. Serving 25 middle schools, the program has demonstrated significant academic gains. Implementing the three year design for a school of 500 students costs approximately $264 per student (Herman, 1999) (see Chapter 8).

School Development Program

The School Development Program is a comprehensive approach to school reform at the elementary and middle school levels. Based on the work of James Comer, this program features support teams of staff, parents, counselors, and social workers who work together to improve school climate, promote parental involvement and create a comprehensive plan for improvement. The program is currently operating in more than 565 elementary and middle schools in 22 states, and is demonstrating promising results for high risk youth at the middle level (see Chapter 6).

Coalition of Essential Schools

The Coalition of Essential Schools is a network of middle and high schools engaged in a process of reform that is built on the ideas of Theodore Sizer. The reform approach in each of the Essential Schools varies rather broadly, but all emphasize an intellectual focus, a small set of goals that apply to all students, and a belief that teaching and learning should be personalized. Diplomas are awarded upon the demonstration of mastery, and teachers are expected to work with no more than eighty students. As of 1996, the Coalition was involved in more than 1,200 schools nationally.

While there is limited evidence to date from standardized tests of the positive impact of the Coalition approach on improving student achievement, a considerable amount of anecdotal data indicates positive gain in other aspects of student learning (Slavin & Fashola, 1998).

A number of more recently developed schoolwide reform models have emerged and are demonstrating significant achievement gains with middle-level at-risk students. They include the Consistency Management and Cooperative Discipline (CMCD) three of the New America's School Designs' Atlas Communities, Expeditionary Learning, and the Modern Red School House (Slavin & Fashola, 1998). (See Chapter 6.)

AVID

The AVID program (Advancement via Individual Determination) is available in over 900 middle and high schools in 26 states. The program emphasizes college preparation, improved enrollment and success of middle school students, a rigorous curriculum, and onsite team support to participating students.

Classroom Instruction Models

A number of school-improvement efforts regarding specific classroom practices exist that are demonstrating evidence in several key content areas (Slavin & Fashola, 1998).

Cooperative Learning

There is considerable evidence that a number of cooperative learning approaches have documented increased student achievement. These programs include: Cooperative Integrated Reading and Composition, grades 2–8, including a bilingual adaptation (Stevens et al., 1987).

Complex Instruction

Developed by Elizabeth Cohen (1994), the Complex Instruction Program includes three components. One of the components is an English/Spanish program, entitled Finding Out/Descubriendo La Lectura, available for grades 2–12. The other two components include Jigsaw, grades 2–12 (Slavin, 1994), and Learning Together, grades 2–12 (Johnson & Johnson, 1994).

Reading, Writing, and Language Arts

Programs that have been documented as positively effecting student achievement in reading and math at the middle grades include: Exemplary Center for Reading Instruction, grades 1–10 (Reid, 1989); Reciprocal Teaching, grades 1–8 (Palincsar & Brown, 1984); Profile Approach to Writing, grades 3–12 (Profile Approach to Writing, 1995); and Multicultural Reading and Thinking, grades 3–8 (Arkansas Department of Education, 1992; Slavin & Fashola, 1998).

Mathematics

Three programs at the middle-school level have been documented as improving student achievement in mathematics: Project SEED, grades 3–8 (Project SEED, 1995); Skills Reinforcement Project, grades 3–8 (Skills Reinforcement Project, 1992); and Maneuvers with Mathematics, grades 5–8 (Maneuvers with Mathematics, 1995; Slavin & Fashola, 1998).

Exemplary Middle Schools

A number of middle-level schools in the United States have developed practices and programs that have demonstrated impressive results related to the engagement and achievement of at-risk students. They include:

Central East Middle School

A new program, the Talent Development Model, which was developed at Johns Hopkins University, has been implemented at Central East Middle School in Philadelphia. Following concepts developed by the Talent Development Model, the school was reorganized into three small learning communities and redesigned for a major curriculum emphasis on reading. Each year, the entire student body reads the same book and then participates in schoolwide activities to enrich learning from this common experience. Two periods were collapsed to create a 90-minute block to emphasize reading, English, and language arts. Research conducted by the Center for the Education of Students Placed At-Risk found significant increases in student achievement in reading comprehension at the Philadelphia Middle School (Middle school model builds on common theme, 1997). Following the success with reading, the school plans a similar effort in mathematics.

Lincoln Middle School

The Lincoln Middle School in Passaic, New Jersey, developed a half-day summer camp to boost student self-confidence and ease the transition from the elementary grades to the 7th grade. Students participated in competitions such as opening combination locks, finding classrooms and offices in the buildings, locating books in the library, and working to develop study skills and conflict resolution skills and to improve their skills in reading and math (Camp competition builds middle school confidence, 1997).

Plainfield Middle School

The Plainfield (Indiana) Community Middle School encourages every student to be involved in sports, band, choir, cheerleading, and student council. There are no try-outs, no auditions, and everyone can participate without rejection. As a result, the 900 students, grades 6th through 8th, have 107 cheerleaders and 56 students on the wrestling team. The goal is to build the self-confidence and self-esteem of all students, making sure that every student is involved and engaged in the school and feels a sense of inclusion (Hill, 1999).

Jepson Middle School

Jepson Middle School (Vacaville, California) reorganized the school around interdisciplinary teams. The seventh grade was divided into teams of approximately 160 students, each with four or five teachers representing the major subject areas. "Early results for the experiment show the test scores have improved and the school atmosphere has been changed . . . in a positive way" (Carnegie Corporation, 1993, p. 4).

Promising Middle-School Developments

A number of developments have recently occurred that are demonstrating positive achievement results for middle-level high-risk students. They include:

Staff Development Increases Middle-School Student Achievement

The National Staff Development Council has identified 26 improvement models with exemplary staff-development support that have documented positive impact on student learning. After a two-year study of over 500 staff-development programs, the Council reports that targeted, effective staff development can improve middle-school student achievement. The twenty-six programs identified shared several common characteristics: teacher time for refinement and implementation; a reliance on training teachers; reinforcement of follow-up activities; access to experts and a variety of support materials (Killion, 1999).

High Academic Standards, Aligned Curriculum, and Student-Achievement Assessment

A growing number of states have established new academic standards for public education and required student achievement assessments at the 5th, 8th and 11th grade levels. Many of these states have also required passage of these tests for promotion to the next grades. As a result, middle schools are aligning their curriculum with these standards and implementing internal assessments to monitor student achievement. Schools have determined that they also need intensive support programs to assist the students who fail the 8th grade state assessment. Middle schools that are not governed by statewide standards and assessments should consider developing similar interventions for high-risk students. Clearly, the emerging policy imperative for all schools and school districts is that all youth are expected to learn and achieve high academic standards and that student progress be regularly assessed. In the absence of state assessments, schools and school districts are developing a more personalized set of performance assessments to enhance the authenticity of measuring students' progress.

Boston Strengthens the Middle Schools
Sixteen of Boston's 23 middle schools are being assisted by the Center for Collaborative Education to implement the principles recommended by the Carnegie Council for Adolescent Development (1989). The goal is to ensure that these schools establish flexible schedules, small groupings of students, family partnerships, and interdisciplinary learning (Middle schools reflect essential school ideas, 1999).

No Social Promotion from Middle School to High School
A number of states, including Texas and California, have eliminated social promotion from middle school to high school. These states have established high academic standards and high-stakes assessment exams in the 8th grade. Unless students pass the 8th grade exam, they are not permitted to matriculate to high school. Each of these states has established intensive programs to help students remediate so as to pass the exam as soon as possible (Johnston, 1998).

Nevada Toughens Middle-School Standards

Beginning in the 1999–2000 school year, all middle-school students will be required to earn an average grade of C for an entire year in math and English courses before they can be promoted to the high school (Nevada toughens middle school, 1998).

Middle-Level Alternative, Magnet, and Charter Schools

> *While evaluating the McKinley Alternative Junior High School in Fairbanks, Alaska, I conducted interviews with teachers, administrators, parents, and students. As I finished the last student group interview, one of the kids said to me, "Can I ask you a question?" "Sure," I said, "Let's hear it." "Well, we were wondering if you could help us." "Sure," I said, "If I can. What can I do for you?" The student leaned closer and said, "The teachers at this school are really screwed up." He turned to look at the three other students, who all nodded their heads. "They're driving us crazy." Now really curious, I reopened my note pad, turned on my tape recorder again and asked, "What do you mean, 'They're driving us crazy'?" Becoming impatient with me, he spoke louder and more rapidly, "It's just really screwed up. These teachers don't know that we're dumb. They're driving us crazy because they think we can learn. They just won't leave us alone. You've got to talk to them," he pleaded. "Tell them that we can't do this stuff. Go in there and tell them to get off our backs. Tell them that we're dumb."*
> *—JUNIOR HIGH STUDENT, MCKINLEY ALTERNATIVE JUNIOR HIGH SCHOOL, FAIRBANKS, ALASKA*

The vast majority of alternative public schools have been developed at the elementary and high-school levels, lending further support to the "forgotten school" notion which characterizes middle-level education. Fortunately, in recent years, this has begun to change as a number of effective alternative schools and schools within schools have been successfully developed at the middle level.

While alternative middle schools remain relatively rare, effective schools within schools are often found. During the late 1980s and 1990s, the Portland, Oregon, Public Schools conducted a careful assessment of their many alternative and magnet schools and concluded that the middle-school level offered very few special alternative programs or choices for students. Responding to this need, the school district created funding and solicited proposals from area middle schools. Most of the new alternatives that were developed were school-within-school programs, usually located in a wing of a building or a special section of the school that provided a group of teachers and students an opportunity to work exclusively together. Some of these programs included the Whitaker Middle School Learning Lab, the Gregory Heights Middle School Alternative Program, and the Ocklea Green Middle School

Green House. Consistent with the alternative school model, students and teachers chose to participate in the programs.

A review of most large-city school districts reveals that the majority of middle-level alternative or magnet programs have been developed for the academically proficient student. Unfortunately, far fewer middle-school alternative and magnet programs have been created for at-risk youth. Select programs that do serve at-risk youth include:

Barret Traditional Middle School, Jefferson County Schools, Louisville, Kentucky

As part of the National Alliance for Restructuring Education, the Barret Traditional Middle School encourages a high degree of parental involvement and functions as a site-based decision-making school. A council of three teachers, two parents and the principal share the decision-making responsibility for the school. The school is also part of the traditional, back-to-basics philosophy that characterizes three elementary schools, three middle schools, and two high schools in Jefferson County. The school is available to students on the basis of choice and has a dress code, a behavior code, required homework, and encourages high academic performance, patriotism, courtesy, respect, responsibility, and citizenship. The school also has a strong new emphasis on technology and provides every student with a laptop computer.

Saturn School of Tomorrow, St. Paul, Minnesota, Grades 4–8

Reflecting the best of what is known about learning and emerging learning technology, the school serves over 280 students (grades 4 to 8) with a curriculum designed to prepare them to live and work successfully in the world of tomorrow. Saturn students work individually, in small groups, and in cooperative teams using advanced learning technologies such as computers and interactive videos as part of the basic curriculum. Students attend regular classes, conduct independent and group research, participate in apprenticeship and mentorship activities in state and local government offices, businesses, and art and science museums. Students explore concepts that relate to later vocational and professional opportunities and careers. Each student has a personal growth plan (PGP) developed by the student, their parents, and teachers. Students are actively involved in establishing their own learning goals and objectives and in determining their own progress.

Center for Visual and Communication Arts, Los Angeles Unified School District, Los Angeles, California, Grades 7–9

One of the many LA magnet schools, the Center for Visual and Communication Arts (grades 7 to 9) provides interested students an opportunity to supplement and enrich the conventional middle school curriculum with special courses and internships in script writing, stage performance, dance and music, and radio and television productions.

Crispus Attucks Academic Academy, Indianapolis Public Schools, Indianapolis, Indiana

Crispus Attucks is located near the city center and provides interested students with a thematic program of study that includes math, science, English, social studies, and Spanish. Themes of the academy (grades 6 to 8) focus on developing writing, studying, and thinking skills. The school emphasizes the use of computers, state-of-the-art instructional technologies, multicultural resources, cooperative learning strategies, study skills, and career awareness activities.

Teenagers in the Middle Program (TIME)

The St. Charles Parish School District in Louisiana created the TIME program to accelerate the learning of high-risk middle-level students. Operating as a school-within-a-school, TIME serves up to 60 students and has demonstrated impressive success in both keeping these students engaged in school and accelerating their achievement in preparation for a successful transition to high school.

Crossroads Academy

The Crossroads Academy (Meridian, Idaho) was created in 1997 to enroll a maximum of 150 high-risk youth during their middle-school years (grades 7–8). Each student is provided a Netschools laptop computer, which provides the school-home connection previously missing for too many high-risk students. Classes are organized on a 90-minute schedule and offered through an individualized approach. Based on the effectiveness of Crossroads, an additional academy is being considered.

Middle-Level Charter Schools

Beginning in 1993, states began legislating the opportunity for public charters to develop and operate. While most are at the elementary or high-school level, a growing number of small middle-level K–12, K–8, 7–12 charters have opened featuring a variety of curricular and instructional innovations.

One example is the Knowledge Is Power Program (KIPP) Academy. Located in Houston, Texas, and serving poor, high-risk kids, this grades 5–8 middle-level charter school has one of the highest academic performances in the state. The school opens early and stays open as late as 10:00 P.M. to assist students with their homework. The school is open Saturdays and throughout the summer. The 300-student-body school has a waiting list of 300 students and has test scores among the highest in Texas: 100 percent of the students passed the state-mandated math test. Teachers at the school say that the secret of the school's success is high expectation and a rigorous curriculum. The school stays open long hours to provide more instructional time in math, science, and reading and gives students hours of homework each night. Teachers are on-call 24 hours a day to answer students' questions via cell phones.

Many of the middle-level charters opening today are designed to serve all students, particularly those at risk (see Chapter 9).

Research findings and examples of effective alternative programs that are currently operating at the elementary and high-school levels provide a wealth of useful information for those concerned with developing alternative programs at the middle-school level. These effective alternative schools are characterized by small, supportive learning environments, voluntary participation, caring and demanding teachers, and a curriculum that is tailored to the developmental needs of their constituents (Raywid, 1983; Barr & Parrett, 1997a). In fact, the organizational characteristics that seem to make alternative schools so successful are quite similar to the recommended components of school restructuring that research suggests are essential for all students at the middle level. Alternative schools indeed provide an effective model for revitalizing middle schools in America (Massachusetts Advocacy Center, 1988; Barr & Parrett, 1997a).

Characteristics of Effective Middle Schools

Research on effective middle schools helps to create a distinct model for restructuring schools to better serve at-risk youth. This data on effective programs also relates directly to the recommendations of the Carnegie Council on Adolescent Development described earlier. The following characteristics of effective middle schools serve as a foundation for improving educational efforts for middle-level youth.

Small Learning Communities

The most effective junior high/middle schools have developed small learning communities, teams, or schools within the larger middle-level school. Few structural accommodations seem to help young adolescents more than creating social and organizational smallness within the larger school. Creating this smallness enables every teacher to know every student by name and performance level and establishes a common set of rules, regulations, and expectations that provide the young adolescent with the educational stability that they need during these difficult years.

There is no better way to ensure that every teacher at this level is responsible for every student than the creation of organizational smallness. In some way, these small communities become an essential support group and often seem to serve as a surrogate family. This is done by creating interdisciplinary groups of teachers who take full responsibility or the majority of the responsiblity for a cohort of students. One teacher might teach both math and science to the same students; another teaches the students language arts and social studies. Teachers are also assigned as advocates and mentors for this group of students and serve as classroom counselors. This type of program takes on the characteristics of elementary schools and alternative education programs that have proven so effective for all students, especially those who are at risk (Carnegie Council on Adolescent Development, 1989).

For the at-risk youth who feels insecure and often academically and socially incapable, the shock of arriving at the large, impersonal junior high school can be stunning. For this reason, school or program size may represent the most significant aspect of guaranteeing that at-risk youth stay in school, are provided the individual attention that they need, and have the opportunity to achieve academic success in their classes. No other level of schooling seems more in need of the benefits of smallness than does the middle school. Unfortunately, as reported earlier, more than two-thirds of the middle schools surveyed in 1988 reported that they had not created any small in-school instructional teams (Alexander & McEwin, 1989).

Interdisciplinary Core

Effective middle-level schools often organize an interdisciplinary core curriculum that includes English, fine arts, foreign language, history, literature, math, science, and social studies. The goal is to develop interrelationships between ideas through critical thinking and problem solving using a team approach (Carnegie Council on Adolescent Development, 1989). Teachers also develop curriculum by organizing themes to help integrate the diverse areas of knowledge the young adolescent is trying to learn. High-interest themes such as the Old West, dinosaurs, space exploration and travel, endangered species, and the Olympics are often found in middle-school interdisciplinary curricula.

Unfortunately, a majority of middle schools (and junior highs) continue to overlook the benefits of an interdisciplinary curricular organization or flexible block scheduling. They continue to teach separate subjects scheduled in rigid time slots and to use subject-matter departmentalization in most of the upper grades. They also provide limited (if any) intervention for high-risk students.

Flexible Block Scheduling

Directly related to interdisciplinary teams, schools within schools, and other groupings that allow for personalization of the curriculum, some effective middle-level schools use block scheduling. This concept allows teachers and students time for in-depth projects, field trips, and cooperative learning. It also helps to eliminate the disruption and disorganization of the 50-minute class school day (Massachusetts Advocacy Center, 1988). This might include an extended homeroom period for classroom counseling, 90-150-minute time periods for interdisciplinary, in-depth study, shorter 45-to-60-minute blocks of time for survey courses in career education and physical education, and a 30-to-40-minute period for high-interest mini courses.

Activities, Mini Courses, and Exploration Courses

Many successful middle schools have developed a wide variety of courses and activities where students can explore, experiment, and gain new experiences. Often these courses are scheduled one period each day and provide a vast array of activities, mini courses, and survey exploration courses that focus on student interest areas. Young adolescents are extremely interested in these courses, which are formed in the majority of middle schools. These courses and activities tend to break up the school day and permit students to explore a wide range of topics, skills, and activities that expand their interests and abilities, permitting them to test themselves in new areas. Mini courses often include such activities as arts and crafts, sports statistics, pen pals, math games, etc. (Massachusetts Advocacy Center, 1988).

Intramural and interschool sports programs for both girls and boys are also extremely popular. The most popular exploratory-type courses available as either a required or elective course in middle schools by order of popularity include health, computers, sex education, creative writing, and careers (Alexander & McEwin, 1989). Each of these clubs, hobbies, competitions, participation, support groups, and specialized elective courses are extremely important for the personal and social development of the young adolescent, and they often dramatically enhance the school day for the young at-risk adolescent.

Transition Programs

Many school districts have attempted to alleviate the transition from elementary to middle school and from middle school to high school with programs that help to bridge the different school levels. These programs provide elementary students with opportunities to visit the middle school, have orientation programs, and meet with teachers. Many middle-school programs organize 6th-grade students into a self-contained "school within a school" to ease the transition from elementary school. Others offer structured programs designed to assist 8th or 9th grade high-risk youth in the transition to high school. These programs maintain contact with students to reduce the number of youth who fail to successfully transition to the middle-school level. Such programs are critical between the middle school and the high-school level, where so many students tend to drop out of school. High schools need to be extremely aggressive to ensure that all middle-school graduates successfully transition into high school.

Service Learning

One of the most promising concepts for middle-level education ties academic programs to school and community service projects and activities. Developing opportunities for the students to learn through peer teaching, cross-age tutoring, and a host of public service activities enables middle-school youth to appreciate the value of giving and responsibly participate in their community. Many schools use students to assist with clerical, custodial, technology, and media needs of the school. Out-of-school applications include community cleanup and improvement projects, service to child-care centers, senior citizen centers, museums, zoos, the Salvation Army, homeless shelters, and many others. Few school programs have proven so effective in enhancing self-esteem as participation in service learning activities (Barr & Smith, 1976; Nathan, 1989).

Cross-age Tutoring

Cross-age tutoring is especially effective for enhancing the self-esteem of young adolescents. A study of middle-school students who had profound behavioral and attendance problems as well as deficiencies in basic skills found that when the students were trained as tutors and began working with younger children, extremely promising results occurred. The tutors learned as much as the young students they were helping, and all participants, teachers and students, voiced support for the concept (Big kids teach little kids, 1987). In study after study, year after year, dropout-prone youth who become tutors experience lower dropout rates and fewer absences and behavioral problems (Massachusetts Advocacy Center, 1988).

Health and Fitness Programs

Self-esteem and academic performance can often be improved through the creation of health and fitness programs. School-based health clinics or related health services are absolutely essential for so many young adolescents today, yet these services have been slow to develop. Often described as suffering from raging hormones, young adolescents are in urgent need of effective health and hygiene instruction as well as appropriate fitness programs. In addition to instruction, schools need to provide access to health care and counseling programs, preferably through a health coordinator, a school nurse, or through on-site health clinics.

One effective approach to address the health needs of young adolescents is to coordinate school and social service agencies. In Baltimore's Canton Middle School, educators and concerned community members have organized a Primary Assessment Committee that meets weekly and focuses on individual student problems and needs through a case management approach. The committee is composed of the school nurse, the guidance counselor, a mental health therapist, a school social worker, representatives from departments of juvenile and social services, and teachers. With any particular child, the committee might assist in obtaining eyeglasses, providing dental care, arranging for counseling for emotional problems, providing medical care, family planning, or vocational training. In Brunswick, Maryland, the middle school is part of the Community Agency Social Service, an agency responsible for coordinating health, mental health, nursing, and police services. This coordinated effort attempts to address the problems of alcohol, drug use, family planning, home conflict, poverty, and homelessness for middle-level students (Carnegie Corporation, 1993).

Middle schools also need strong fitness, exercise, and intramural sports programs to complement community youth programs outside the school. Intramural sports programs are particularly effective, as almost every young boy and girl in the school can be involved.

Parental Involvement

As at every other school level, parental involvement is extremely important at the middle-level grades. Parents can have a powerful influence on keeping their children in school during the middle-school years by sharing a direct interest in schooling, especially for low socioeconomic status students. At-risk students whose parents reported regularly discussing future education plans with their eighth graders were less likely to drop out of school than students whose parents did not engage in such discussions (Office of Educational Research and Improvement, 1992).

Positive parental involvement at the middle-school level is critical, as many young adolescent boys and girls spend these years striving for independence from their parents and attempting to assert themselves as mature individuals. Unfortunately, parental involvement is often not actively encouraged at the middle-school level; for these very reasons it should be emphasized.

Nancy Berla, a leading authority on parental involvement, identified examples of effective ways parents can help their children:

- *Communicate every day with your son or daughter about what happened that day at school. Be available to listen to your child's concerns and criticisms about teachers, courses, and policies without lecturing or arguing. Be ready to offer praise and extend help. Be honest—support what you feel is good about the school, but also share your concerns if you think that the school's policies and practices are harmful to your child.*
- *Encourage your child to do his or her homework every night by suggesting an acceptable time and a quiet place and being available if and when he or she needs help. If you don't know the subject or speak the language, you can be supportive and help your child by assisting him or her in identifying the steps necessary to complete the assignment.*
- *If your middle schooler consistently and continually expresses complaints about the teachers, the courses, or school policies, be prepared to take action. Call the school and make the appointment to meet with the teacher, guidance counselor, or principal at the school. Even if scheduling is a problem, contact your school before it interferes with your child's learning and success at school (Berla, 1991, p. 16).*

Effective middle schools should develop a schoolwide plan to encourage and support parental involvement. This should include regular communication with parents, organizing parent-to-parent discussion events, pitch-in meals with guest speakers, establishing a parent room in the school, establishing a lending library for parents, requiring consistent and timely teacher-parent contact, and including all parents in school planning and governance.

Counseling, Caring, and Self-Esteem

In the midst of transforming from child to adolescent, a student needs strong personal relationships with teachers and other adults as well as effective counseling programs. Block scheduling, an interdisciplinary core, and organizational smallness all provide improved means for teachers to relate personally to their students. These approaches often lead to teacher teaming, using intensive case management approaches to address student needs, and involving all teachers in decisions related to a particular student's program. Effective middle-level schools also use peer counseling, teacher advocates, counselors serving as consultants to teachers, counselors provided by social service agencies, and drug and alcohol counselors (Massachusetts Advocacy Center, 1988). Effective middle schools often use teachers as classroom counselors and organize the school day so that much of the one-on-one and group counseling sessions can occur in a classroom setting. Many effective middle schools use an extended homeroom period to provide for this type of counseling process.

Increasingly, at-risk youth need counseling for sexual and physical abuse, dysfunctional families, gender-related issues, and drug and alcohol problems. To address these issues, the schools also need to develop peer support groups to foster and maintain healthy life decisions. All of these programs are designed to address the problems and concerns of students and lead to better academic achievement and enhanced self-esteem. Many schools have initiated curriculum and schoolwide programs designed to enhance student self-esteem.

Mentors

Children entering adolescence at a significantly younger age than ever before are making crucial decisions that can alter their entire lives. Research has helped to identify the importance of adult relationships to middle-school youth, especially violent, bullying, or violence-prone adolescents, since they relate directly to the developmental needs of the youth at this age. The establishment of a mentor relationship may not only be the best, but perhaps the only way for the young adolescent to develop a strong relationship with an adult.

Mentor programs have become an essential part of an effective middle school by providing the organization to recruit adults and providing the at-risk middle-school students with the needed adult model to talk to, to trust, and to help explore career opportunities. For further information, contact the National Dropout Prevention Center (see Appendix A).

Career and Vocational Education

While vocational education is almost universally viewed with hope and positive expectations, historically such programs have produced less than satisfactory results. Unfortunately, for middle-level schools, this has been even more true. In the past, vocational education at the middle level, where and if it has been available, has focused on such hands-on programs as automobile mechanics, wood and metal working, home economics, and in rural areas, agriculture. Often these courses are available in a one-year introductory-style survey course. One can still find home economics courses at the middle-school level where at-risk youth from dysfunctional homes are being taught how to set a formal dining table. There is little evidence that such programs keep the young adolescent in school and even less that the programs lead to job opportunities after students graduate or leave school. Even programs involving actual on-the-job work experience have proven disappointing.

"Isolated work experience will not reclaim impoverished and troubled youth" (Institute for Educational Leadership, 1986, p. 59).

For successful vocational or career education programs, the development needs of the young adolescent must be taken into consideration and used as a basis for planning (Massachusetts Advocacy Center, 1988). Programs must consider the needs of the whole child. While older students may benefit from job skill training, for the young adolescent an effective vocational program means a concern for career education, job surveys, field trips to business and industry, and career fairs.

Before- and After-School Programs

Before and after school programs are especially valuable at the middle-school level. Non-school time becomes extremely important for young adolescents, especially during times when they are unsupervised. Studies have discovered that large numbers of young adolescents have sex and often get pregnant between 3:30 and 6:30 in the afternoon, a time when the students are out of school and their parents are not home from work (Barr & Ross, 1989). This is also a time of high incidence of violence, vandalism, shoplifting, and even burglary. In many communities there are often few adults in entire neighborhoods until after 5:30 P.M.

At Intermediate School 218, in New York's Washington Heights area, an area that has become notorious for urban unrest and drug trafficking, the school has created an all-day neighborhood school. The school is open from early morning until late at night and serves the entire community. The after-school program offers students opportunities in computers, multimedia, environmental studies, drama, dance, arts and crafts, music, photography, athletics, and academic tutoring. After 6:00 P.M. older teenagers and adults are welcomed into the school for a range of opportunities, from employment workshops to citizenship classes to health and athletics programs (Carnegie Corporation, 1993, pp. 10–11). For rural schools, transportation poses a difficult problem for before- and after-school programs. It is often solved by extending the school day for all students or providing additional bus service in the afternoon.

Community Youth Programs

Out-of-school community programs are vitally important throughout early adolescence. It is during young adolescence that students are experimenting and exploring social and physical limits, taking risks, learning about sexual relationships, and trying to become more independent. For these reasons, the out-of-school time becomes a crucial experience for most adolescents. It is a time of great risk as well as great opportunity. It is during the out-of-school time that youth can become involved in crime, drugs, violence, gangs, and other antisocial behavior. For any of these reasons, after-school and weekend community programs and activities are incredibly important during the middle-school years. When young adolescents were asked what they would most like during nonschool hours, they indicated "safe parks and recreation centers; exciting science museums; libraries with all the latest books, videos, and records; chances to go camping and participate in sports; long talks with trusting and trustworthy adults who know a lot about the world and who like young people; and opportunities to learn new skills" (Carnegie Council on Adolescent Development, 1992, p. 43).

The primary way young people obtain these types of services is through community youth organizations. These organizations are second only to public schools in the number of young people they reach. These organizations include both local and national groups that serve literally millions of young adolescents. Nationally, the largest of these organizations include Boys and Girls Clubs of America, Girl Scouts, Boy Scouts, Boys and Girls Campfire, 4-H, Future Farmers, Future Homemakers, YMCA, and YWCA. Together these groups reach over 30 million young people each year and provide everything from traditional programs of recreation, sports, and camping to informal education and youth development activities. They also offer teen parent programs, drug awareness programs, and some even provide foster care, protective services, remediation and treatment programs, and juvenile justice programs.

There is substantial evidence that youth organization programs have a strong positive effect on young adolescents. Although metropolitan areas tend to have a greater variety of youth organizations, there are many youth programs available in rural areas. The Carnegie Council on Adolescent Development has summarized studies of the effects of these programs on young urban and rural adolescents:

- *A 1987 survey of alumni of 4-H and other youth groups found that, on average, alumni believed that participation in the program contributed to their personal development by giving them pride in accomplishment, self-confidence, the ability to work with others, the ability to set goals and to communicate, employment and leadership skills, and encouragement of community involvement. . . .*

- *Four annual evaluations of the Association of Junior Leagues' Teen Outreach Program, a school-based, life-skills management and community service program for middle- and high-school students, found that participants were less likely than peers who did not participate in the program to become pregnant, drop out, or be suspended from school.*

- *A multiyear evaluation of a targeted intervention developed by Girls Incorporated, called Preventing Adolescent Pregnancy, indicated that participation in all program components was associated with lower overall rates of pregnancy, and that participation in individual components led to specific pregnancy-related effects (e.g., young adolescents who took assertiveness training to learn to refuse early intercourse were only half as likely as non-participants to become sexually active).*

- *An evaluation of WAVE, Inc.'s drop-out prevention program found that those who participated showed improved school attendance, lower drop-out rates and improved scores on job readiness, mathematics, reading and self-esteem.*

- *An evaluation of Boys and Girls Clubs of America's SMART Moves (substance-abuse prevention) initiative showed substantial differences between housing projects that had clubs and those that did not. Residential areas with clubs experienced an overall reduction in alcohol and other drug use, drug trafficking and other drug-related crime. (Carnegie Council on Adolescent Development, 1992, p. 38)*

Program evaluations and related research provide a "solid rationale for strengthening and expanding the role of community-based programs in promoting healthy adolescent development" (Carnegie Council on Adolescent Development, 1992, p. 39). It is essential that schools recognize the importance of youth organizations and work to encourage youth participation and to coordinate school programs with those in the community.

Encouraging Social and Emotional Growth

Increasingly, effective middle schools throughout the United States have implemented a variety of programs to help middle-school students grow socially and emotionally. Many schools have implemented character-education programs, service learning, and mentoring programs. Such programs have enormous impact on the impressionable preteens and teenagers of the middle grades. Two such programs are:

Peaceful Settlement and Conflict Resolution
An effective interventive approach to combating school violence, vandalism, and disruption is peer conflict mediation. Not only has mediation led to the peaceful settlement of disputes and conflicts among students, but it has proven valuable in the adult world of divorce, child custody, and other legal and quasi-legal disputes. Such peer mediation programs can be extremely beneficial when students are carefully trained and supported by teachers and counselors. Peer conflict mediation can lower dropout and truancy rates and improve student behavior. In some schools, peer mediation has been cited as resulting in lowering the suspension rate by more than 50 percent (Dallea, 1987; Stichter, 1986). Peer conflict mediation can help students experience first-hand critical thinking and problem solving. It reduces violence and disruption problems and improves the self-esteem of the student mediators. In one study, three-quarters of students involved in disputes reported that they would have had a fight if they had not been referred for mediation (Stern & Van Slych, 1986; Dill, 1998).

Judicious Discipline
There is a growing body of evidence demonstrating the effectiveness of democratizing student discipline in schools. In comparative studies of authoritarian and democratic schools as well as in studies of student involvement in rule formulation, there is sufficient positive evidence to support such programs. One program, Judicious Discipline, has been developed to help schools apply a simple set of legal principles based on the Bill of Rights to involve students in rule formulation in schools and classrooms. Early studies of Judicious Discipline have yielded promising results as evidenced by a number of schools being able to eliminate expulsion and suspension by using this particular approach (Gathercoal, 1999, 1997).

Dramatic New Alternatives to Middle-Level Education: K–12 Schools

Just about everyone has heard this story. When we enrolled our first-grade son at the Metropolitan Learning Center, we were of course somewhat apprehensive. Rather than walking to a neighborhood school, he was off daily across town to this really different alternative school. From the first day, our son complained that he was not able to work the combination lock on his locker. But in a few days he excitedly reported that everything was working out all right. My son explained that Mr. Jones was helping him getting his locker open and was helping him store his belongings and then making sure that the locker was locked. Later when we visited the school we wanted to express our thanks to Mr. Jones. We discovered that there was no teacher or custodian in the building named Mr. Jones. After some discussion and exploration, we discovered the delightful news that Mr. Jones was a seventh-grade student who shared a locker next to our son's.
—PARENT OF FIRST-GRADE STUDENT, METROPOLITAN LEARNING CENTER, PORTLAND, OREGON

The most exciting and perhaps most effective example of middle-level education in America today may not be occurring in either the traditional junior high school or the innovative middle school. A number of public schools in the United States, in both urban and rural areas, have developed K–12 public schools that seem to have an unusually positive impact on young adolescents and may in fact be superior to the traditional concept of separate middle-level schools. Unfortunately, very few of these schools are in operation today. Most of the K–12 programs exist as alternative public schools in urban areas or as small rural schools. Yet the research on K–12 schools is remarkably positive. Part of the reason for this comes from the small school size that characterizes these programs and the personalized education that such smallness encourages and accommodates. Success also originates from the continuous educational transition that these schools provide for students from preschool through high school. A review of the research and evaluation on K–12 schools, both urban alternatives as well as small rural schools, documents rather well that there is a better alternative to the concept of middle-level education. That better alternative is an educational program which provides for continuous progress from kindergarten through high school in a small, personalized educational environment with highly individualized teaching and learning.

In fact, the very characteristics that scholars recommend be employed in effective, middle-level education are very similar to the characteristics of K–12 schools, except that they are not limited to a particular middle-level age group. And since K–12 schools are providing this type of education from kindergarten through graduation, the impact of these approaches seems to be magnified. This is now recognized as one of the reasons so many small, isolated rural schools are so effective at teaching all children and keeping them in school through graduation.

K–12 Alternative Schools

Over the past 25 years a number of public K–12 alternative schools have emerged and flourished throughout the United States. Two examples of this concept demonstrate the dramatic success of the approach.

Metropolitan Learning Center

One of the most widely recognized alternative public schools in the nation is the Metropolitan Learning Center, a Portland, Oregon, public school. Originating in 1968, Metropolitan Learning Center today serves approximately 450 students, makes frequent use of interage grouping, and has a schoolwide emphasis on building student responsibility at each age level. There are schoolwide goals that emphasize independence, personal decision making and responsibility, and a goal for each student to take responsibility for each other. The school works hard to encourage students to help, support, and nurture one another. Because of this, there is a remarkable caring atmosphere at the Metropolitan Learning Center. It is common to find older students working with younger students and young children dropping by high-school classes seeking information, assistance, and support.

The Metropolitan Learning Center is organized in four school teams, K–3, 4–6, 7–8, and 9–12, but simultaneously encourages cross-age grouping within and between each team. The school day is flexibly organized, including 1 1/2 hour instructional blocks for interdisciplinary courses like Urban Waterways and Wetlands, Graphic Metaphors, Creativity and Self, Nature Studies, and Racial Nationalism, plus a number of 45-minute classes like science and math projects, history, reading for pleasure, and integrated math.

Parents are almost militant in their support for this school. Many families come from far distances throughout the city to have their children attend the Metropolitan Learning Center. The parents participate in school governance and serve in a wide variety of volunteer instructional roles. More than 100 parents and other community volunteers are at work in the school at any given time. In spite of the fact that all types of students, including many at-risk youth, attend Metropolitan Learning Center, the student dropout rate is approximately 2 percent per year, compared with 30 percent for the entire school district. And by comparison of achievement test results, Metropolitan Learning Center students are among the best in the school district as well as the state.

Metropolitan Learning Center conducts large numbers of field trips, outings, and out-of-school study opportunities. They also have large numbers of schoolwide events that bring all age groups, teachers, and parents together. For the young adolescent, the difficulties of growing up seem far less stressful in this caring, multi-age environment.

St. Paul Open School

Perhaps the best known and most widely studied school in America is the St. Paul Open School in St. Paul, Minnesota. Pursuing a set of 18 specific competencies rather than course requirements for graduation, students at this K–12 school experience learning that is structured more like that of university doctoral programs than that of the usual public school. Periodically, at each grade level, students meet with educational advisors to decide which graduation competency to pursue, determine how much time to invest in the pursuit, and continuously review progress toward achieving their learning objectives. For example, students pursuing the cultural awareness competency might develop an extended reading list, interview culturally different individuals in the community, take courses at the school or at a community college, pursue foreign language study, visit or complete a short-term stay in the home of a family of another culture, etc. Learning activities often occur in small groups and with students of different age and ability levels. Students later meet with faculty committees and demonstrate their development toward achieving the competency. Students must demonstrate competency in 18 areas (see Table 7-2).

The St. Paul Open School is organized into two academic centers: the Early Learning Center (K–6) and the Older Learning Center (7–12). All Early Learning Center and Older Learning Center students are placed in cross-age continuous progress groups. Most classes have students participating from several age levels, so that ninth graders and sixth graders might be working together at their own pace. This instructional organization has proven to have a significant positive effect on the students:

> *Open School's K–12 configuration has a number of advantages over a straight elementary or secondary school. One benefit of having primary and secondary age children in the same building is the softening effect the younger children have on the older ones. It is difficult for a 15-year-old to be a "tough" guy or keep a "hard" pose when a 7-year-old asks him for help. (Young, 1990, p. 61)*

Early in the school's development, young children planned, designed, obtained external funding, and actually constructed a complex outdoor play area. Older children in the school created a consumer hotline service and provided community

TABLE 7-2   St. Paul Open School Graduation Competencies Validation Areas

• Post High-School Plans	• Coherent Communication
• Employment Seeking Skills	• Science and Technology
• Career Investigation	• Cultural Awareness (Student's)
• Learning from the Community	• Cultural Awareness (Selected Minority)
• Service to the Community	• Cultural Awareness (Student's Choice)
• Service to the School	• Information Finding
• Current Issues	• Healthy Body
• Consumer Awareness	• Group Process
• Mathematics	• High-School Summary

(St. Paul Open School, 1999)

members with a variety of services that included tracking down and correcting situations where consumers felt they had been cheated or taken advantage of.

Over two decades of research on the St. Paul Open School has consistently shown unusually positive student achievement, attitude, and behavior results. Studies of teacher satisfaction and community support have yielded equally positive data. Any educator, parent, or individual concerned with restructuring public schools would benefit from visiting the St. Paul Open School, as this long-standing program continues to serve as a model approach for effective education.

The conclusion from a review of K–12 schools is that they have demonstrated and documented the existence of a better way of approaching education, especially for at-risk youth, than dividing schools into a three-tier approach involving an elementary, middle school, and a high school. The concept of K–12 schools simply seems to be a better idea, certainly a better idea than arbitrarily dividing and organizing schools into different age groups. Surprisingly, the K–12 organizing concept does not seem to be part of the emerging or current agenda for middle-school educational reform. Yet for the fragile learning needs of at-risk children and youth, the K–12 school may well be the best approach to organizing learning for a maximum impact, especially during the difficult years of the young adolescent.

Creating an Effective Model for Middle-School Programs

Despite the lack of research available on effective programs at the middle-school level and the fact that fewer schoolwide reform efforts have been initiated at the middle/junior-high-school level than at other levels, there remains a compelling argument for conceptualizing middle-school programs that can better serve young, at-risk adolescents. The research and school evaluation data consistently suggest that middle-level schools should more closely resemble successful elementary school models as opposed to the current comprehensive high-school model. Middle schools should create smaller organizational units, develop cadres of interdisciplinary teams of teachers and students, and use block scheduling to provide time for thematic lessons that focus on critical thinking and problem solving. Middle-school youth need adult role models, opportunities outside of school to test themselves and explore their limits, and concerted efforts to develop healthy lifestyles and choices (Beane, 1997).

None of this is new. It reflects precisely the concepts and ideas that initiated the transition movement from the junior-high-school model to the middle-school model in the 1970s. Today, there is a growing body of evidence that urges a more complete transition and middle-school restructuring. The revitalized, reorganized middle school is desperately needed by all young adolescents, and for the at-risk youth it is indeed a matter of staying in school, career success, and perhaps even life and death. A review of the most promising approaches for at-risk youth at the middle-school level suggests a truly restructured junior-high school. Effective middle schools should include the following:

- Smaller components where cohorts of students and teachers work together for most of the school day.

- High academic standards that align the curriculum to content standards.
- A curriculum which focuses on the developmental needs of young adolescents and includes interdisciplinary course subjects that foster communication, critical thinking, social development, and healthy lifestyles.
- Flexible scheduling to provide blocks of time for interdisciplinary study with teams of students and shorter periods of time for career exploration and specialized studies.
- Programs that provide cooperative learning, mentoring, computer and technical education, and so on, should be employed for the middle-level student (see Chapters 6 and 8).
- Teachers that serve as classroom counselors and advisors.
- Out-of-school programs in the community. These may be more crucial at the middle level than in either the elementary or high-school years, for it is during early adolescence that students are placed most at risk during their time away from school.

While research and evaluation are far from abundant at the middle-school level, there is sufficient evidence to conclude that all students could in fact learn effectively and succeed in schools that employ the essential components described in this chapter (Wheelock, 1998).

What is so disappointing is that many school districts have simply adjusted the grade structure of the junior-high school or changed the name of the school from a junior high to a middle school, but have done little else to transform this school level to address the critical needs of the young adolescent.

Yet, there are a growing number of middle schools in almost every state that have been successfully restructured. Furthermore, a number of states, including Delaware, Indiana, Kentucky, Maryland, New Mexico, Colorado, Vermont, and Texas have developed guidelines and statewide policies for reforming middle-level education (Carnegie Corporation, 1993). Unfortunately, while some organizational improvements appear to be occurring, far too many middle level academic programs continue to resemble those of two decades ago.

Improving education at the middle level for youth at risk will profoundly influence the effectiveness of our system of public schools. We know what to do. . . . We now must act.

$$Chapter \quad 8$$

Programs That Work:
High Schools

The student was surly and it was clear he didn't feel comfortable being in a school again. He had been expelled from school and in spite of the fact that he needed only a few credits in order to graduate, he had not been in school for over two years.

Student: *I would like to get back to school and get this over with.*

Principal: *That's good; that is exactly what our program is about.*

Student: *Do I have to wait until next January to start?*

Principal: *Why would you want to do that?*

Student: *Every school that I have ever been in started courses only in September and January.*

Principal: *No, at our school you can start any time you like. Do you want to start today?*

Student: *Well, I don't know, you know. I've got a part-time job, you know, and I don't want to be in school all day.*

Principal: *That's fine, you don't have to be in school all day.*

Student: *Really? Every other school that I have ever attended made you be in school all day and they checked the roll about a thousand times a day to make sure you didn't get away.*

Principal: *Well, here you can come for one course, two courses or for a full program. You can also work all day on one course and as soon as you finish it you get credit for the course.*

Student: *You mean I don't have to wait until June to get credit?*

Principal: *That's exactly right. As soon as you complete a course you get credit for it.*

Student: *Hey, what time do you open here?*

Principal: *We open at 7:30.*

Student: *How late are you open?*

Principal: *We stay open until 7:30 in the evening.*

Student: *Now let me get this right. If I came in the morning I could start at 7:30 and work as long as I could until 7:30 in the evening and continue doing that until I finish a course.*

Principal: *That's exactly right.*

Student: *Well, that's great! In a month or so I could complete these courses and then graduate! This is incredible; why don't other schools do this? I don't understand this. What kind of school is this anyway?*
—*HIGH-SCHOOL STUDENT AND PRINCIPAL, VOCATIONAL VILLAGE, PORTLAND, OREGON*

In a very real sense, high schools are the final battleground for the lives of at-risk youth. The students have grown up and are often angry enough to cause severe problems for teachers, principals, and communities. Many of these students are filled with rage from the humiliations schools have caused them. Imagine being unable to read and sitting in class after class, year after year, where learning centers on textbook reading. Imagine being in classes where everyone is a year or more younger because you were retained during the elementary or middle-school years. Try to imagine going to school where almost everything revolves around students who are going to college and you know that for you higher education is an impossible dream. How must it feel to have spent nine or ten years in school, being retained, tracked into slow classes with other "dumb" kids, suspended on occasion, suffering through failure after failure on test after test, and then to have high-school counselors talk down to you about graduation credit, college entrance requirements, and your poor attitude?

For the at-risk high-school student, it is obvious that most schools have compounded the problems of poverty, dysfunctional families, and low self-esteem with a decade-long barrage of humiliation, despair, and defeat. It is no wonder so many at-risk youth become pregnant during middle and high school; why so many turn to drugs and alcohol; why so many carry guns to school and make violence, vandalism, and school disruption an everyday occurrence; why too many violence-prone city youth see life as valueless and why so many at-risk kids wage daily war against teachers and the school. Most remarkable is the fact that so many of these students still come to school and continue to hang on to the diminishing dream of high-school graduation. For many others, the decision to stay in school is not prompted by educational considerations but determined by the declining opportunities for jobs for the high-school dropout. Unlike other generations of youth who found remarkable opportunities for good jobs in the economic marketplace and in the armed forces, today's at-risk youth are held hostage to a no-win situation—trapped in schools that are not meeting their needs, with few choices or other places to go.

The high school is clearly the last chance for many of our at-risk youth. If they leave school or even graduate lacking the basic skills necessary for the workplace, there is little hope for a self-supporting, productive life. The encouraging news is that even at this late date in the development of these youth, programs are available in schools that can effect dramatic, positive change. Many of these programs report truly remarkable successes. We now know that a student who has been labeled as severely at risk and who is a dangerous troublemaker can often learn to read in a relatively short time and within a few months, can pass a high-school equivalency test. And as job opportunities continue to diminish for the uneducated, many dropouts are returning to public school or community colleges to complete a high-school degree or an equivalency diploma and then enroll in some type of technical program. Nearly 83 percent of 19- and 20-year-olds had completed high school or its equivalent by the year 1990 (National Center for Educational Statistics, 1991).

Research has documented that effective high-school programs can improve self-esteem, transform attitudes toward teachers and school, and salvage young lives from drug and alcohol addiction and abuse. Unfortunately, these tend to be stand-alone programs that address the needs of a relatively small number of high-school students. It is rare to find high-school at-risk programs serving more than ten percent of the total high-school population. And while there are a few projects, programs, and isolated success stories of comprehensive high schools that are effectively teaching all students, these examples are few and far between. The comprehensive high school in the United States has increasingly been recognized as the most entrenched and perhaps the most dysfunctional public institution in the United States. Public high schools continue to operate throughout the country as college prep programs with less emphasis on general and vocational education, with either formal or informal tracking programs, and few programs for at-risk youth.

Almost two decades ago, the National Commission on Excellence in Education recommended a rigorous program for *all* high school students: four years of English, three years each of math, science, and social studies, two years of a foreign language, and one-half year of computer science. Unfortunately, only 13 percent of high school graduates in the United States complete such a curriculum today and most schools in low-income areas do not come close to even offering such a curriculum. Even more disturbing, a wide variety of research has identified the single most important factor in graduating from college. It is not family income, grade-point average, test scores, or race, but the quality and intensity of the high school curriculum. In a new study by the College Board's National Task Force on Achievement released during the fall of 1999, the task force reported that a continuing disparity in achievement exists between Caucasian and Asian students in the United States and students from other minority groups (Lewis, 1999). This disparity begins before the 3rd grade and continues through graduate school. The report concludes that the reason for the racial disparity is pure and simple: prejudice. Teachers and counselors tend to ask less of underrepresented minority students, and frequently discourage them from taking demanding high-school college-prep courses.

High School Programs with Evidence of Improving Student Achievement

While it is difficult to find comprehensive high schools that have been sufficiently restructured to ensure that all students are achieving, by the year 2000 it became possible to identify a surprising and growing number of high schools that have documented remarkable success in improving the academic achievement of all students. In addition to these impressive success stories, there are thousands of public-school optional programs, alternative, magnet, and charter schools, and a growing number of supplemental/enrichment programs demonstrating impressive evidence of success with at-risk and violent youth. Examples include:

High Schools That Work Program

The High Schools That Work Program (HSTW), an initiative of the Southern Regional Educational Board in Atlanta, represents one of the largest and most successful programs in the United States in improving the academic performance of at-risk students. Starting in 1987 with 28 schools in 13 states, the program had expanded to 860 schools in 22 states by 1998. Plans were under way to add from 200 to 300 additional schools by the year 2000. The goals of the HSTW Program include:

- high expectations for student learning
- rigorous vocational courses
- more required academic courses
- learning in a real-world work environment
- collaboration among academic and vocational teachers

The overall goal of these schools is to close by one-third the gap in reading, mathematics, and science achievement between career- and college-bound students.

The research is unusually positive for HSTW. Of ten studies reporting results of the HSTW program on student achievement, four utilized sufficiently rigorous methodologies to document the effectiveness of this program. The HSTW program also documents that students in these schools, including vocational students, take more academic courses, especially math and science, than students at the same school did before the program was initiated. More important, students in the HSTW have documented improved student performance on the National Assessment of Educational Progress (NAEP) as well as a test developed by the HSTW program (Herman, 1999). The HSTW program utilizes six school and classroom practices designed to improve learning (Bottoms & Mikos, 1995, p. 5). (See Table 8.1.)

TABLE 8.1   High Schools That Work: School and Classroom Practices That Improve Student Learning

- Providing a support system for academic and vocational teachers in implementing improved school and instructional practices
- Expecting more from their students, including getting more career-bound students to complete an upgraded academic core and a career major
- Making learning meaningful by integrating academic and vocational studies
- Setting high standards and getting students to work hard to meet them, including providing a system of extra help and time
- Getting students to complete challenging and engaging classroom assignments
- Creating a guidance and advisement system that involves teachers and parents in helping students plan and pursue a challenging and focused program of study

(Bottoms & Mikos, 1995, p. 5)

National Recognition of Outstanding High Schools

After two years of research, involving over 1,000 high schools in the United States, The *U.S. News and World Report* selected a list of "Outstanding American high schools" (public, parochial, and independent) in six metropolitan areas of the United States: Atlanta, Boston, Chicago, Dallas–Fort Worth, Detroit, and New York City. The news magazine used a complex, "value added" statistical model to make their selections, which included the following criteria:

- state achievement test scores, especially math and English
- percentage of students taking the SAT or ACT
- advanced placement test taking
- persistence rate; the percentage of students grades 9–12 who complete the school year

The model also included data from public sources regarding families' socioeconomic status and dropout rates (McGraw, 1999). The schools selected as outstanding in each geographic area represented striking diversity—economically, racially, and demographically. The selected schools seem to share eight key characteristics that contributed to their success:

- high academic standards
- a strong core curriculum
- highly qualified teachers who care about their students and hold high expectations
- strong mentoring of new teachers
- partnerships between parents and schools
- administrators and teachers who know each student

- teacher mentor programs
- high attendance rates

Of the six regionally selected outstanding high schools, the following two represented inner-city schools with large numbers of poor and minority students.

Renaissance Magnet High School, Detroit Public Schools

Renaissance is a 21-year-old public magnet school that had 832 students enrolled in 1999. The Renaissance School attracts students from throughout the school district who voluntarily choose to attend. The goal of the school is highly focused: It is to prepare all students not just for college, but for outstanding colleges and universities. The school's students' achievement scores reflect this lofty goal. The school offers few electives and a rigorous curriculum. All students take four years of math, science, English, social studies, and a foreign language. New students spend four weeks at the school during the summer, prior to September, reviewing and improving their academic skills. Parents must pledge, in writing, their dedication to the school's demanding requirements, including the scheduling of students' doctor appointments outside of school hours and the reading of the syllabi of every course their children take (Viadero, 1999).

Lincoln High School and the Humanities/Communication Magnet Program, Dallas Public Schools

With a student body of slightly over 1,000 students, Lincoln High School is located five miles south of downtown Dallas, in one of the city's poorest sections. The neighborhood is populated with liquor stores and bars. Next door to the school is a cemetery and across the street is the Top & Bottom Lounge. But unlike other inner-city schools in poor communities, the students at this high school have academic achievement levels equal or better than affluent suburban schools. Approximately one-fifth of the students at Lincoln come from throughout the city to participate in the Humanities/Communication Magnet school within the school. Students in the magnet program must score above average on the state achievement tests to be admitted. But all students at Lincoln High, including the magnet school students, take the same core curriculum courses together. For safety, the school uses metal detectors, and all students wear ID badges. The school emphasizes strict discipline and is operated like a business. Lincoln High School credits its success on the implementation of two controversial strategies: first, the school stresses racial pride among its students, including school classes designed to boost self-esteem. Second, and perhaps even more controversial, Lincoln High School has adopted a very strong, public spiritualism. This spiritualism is reflected in school assemblies, teacher education, and classroom emphasis on character building.

Multiple Intelligences Schools

While more widely found at the elementary and middle-school levels, there are at least two high schools in the United States (Lincoln High School in Stockton, California, and

Mountlake Terrace High School in Mountlake Terrace, Washington) that have been using the concepts of multiple intelligences as an underlying philosophy since 1994. These schools have been able to document a positive impact on student achievement. Both schools promote "project based" learning, performance-based assessment, and the development of students' intellectual talents (Campbell & Campbell, 1999). (See Chapters 6 and 7.)

Public School Options

As impressive as the High Schools That Work and the *U.S. News* Outstanding Schools are the wide variety of public high-school programs have been specifically designed to address the problems and needs of at-risk and violent youth. These schools include alternative public schools, career-theme magnet schools, and charter schools. Over the past 30 years, these schools have quietly emerged as leaders in the nation's campaign to educate at-risk and violent youth and improve its high schools. Today, schools and communities do not have to reinvent the wheel, isolated and alone; rather they may select from a comprehensive and growing menu of successful models that have been successfully developed and evaluated. These models may be organized into distinct groups that focus on the needs of students; thematic, curricular, or career emphases; instructional approaches; or experiential learning. These characteristics, when integrated, provide the foundation for a variety of effective models.

Alternative Public Schools

Alternative public schools have an established record of success at the high-school level that is based on over 25 years of effective practice. Alternative public schools may be the most important at-risk programs at the high-school level. Some see these programs as educational "intensive care" units where students who have been battered by home, community, and school are provided with immediate responsive care and support. The reasons for success are the same as they are at other school levels. An alternative high school provides the small educational atmosphere of support that seems to function as a surrogate family for at-risk youth. It provides a place to insulate and protect these fragile, often abused and angry youth. It provides a highly individualized program designed to meet the unique needs of at-risk youth, and it provides the at-risk student with strong, positive advocates to work with juvenile authorities, parents, schools, and social services. The success of alternative schools is noted by their productive longevity and an increasing recognition of their value as environments for research and development related to improving public education.

Longevity

Many alternative public schools were started during the late 1960s and have been in operation for more than 25 years. Today, it is estimated that well over 20,000 of these schools are in operation within public education. Unlike other educational innovations, these schools have endured and even led to changes in earlier research conclusions. Research studies during the 1960s conducted by the Ford Foundation concluded that once a vigorous, reform-minded principal left a school, the innovations that he or she had helped to create would quickly cease and the school would return to earlier ways of doing business (Nachtigal, 1972). During the past 20 to 25 years, almost every alternative school in America has changed principals, sometimes many times, and most have completely changed their faculty without dramatically impacting the school and the integrity of the school programs (Young, 1990; Barr & Parrett, 1997a). This research underscores the power of programs that address the needs of specific youth, that encourage parental involvement, and that provide teachers, parents, and students with real opportunities to participate in a relevant educational process.

Environments for Research and Development

Alternative public schools have provided the nation with the richest collection of experimental programs that has ever been developed and evaluated. Through the creation and support of alternative schools, educators have experimented with such concepts as out-of-school learning, peer tutoring, cross-age grouping, challenge education, open education, schools without walls, individualized continuous progress schools, traditional back-to-basics education, authentic assessment, nongraded learning, competency-based graduation requirements, school choice, and site-based decision making. It is startling to consider the vast numbers of concepts, approaches, and programs first developed in alternative schools that now have become widely used in traditional public schools. Nearly every major public school restructuring effort of the past 15 years is based in part on effective practices and concepts previously developed, implemented, and evaluated in alternative public schools (Raywid, 1983; Young, 1990; Barr & Parrett, 1997a).

Because alternative schools have been evaluated more often and more carefully than virtually any other type of public school, their programs have constantly been refined and improved. A review of the characteristics of effective programs for at-risk youth described earlier in this book parallels closely the characteristics of alternative schools: small size, caring and demanding teachers, individualized curriculum, choice, etc. (Barr, 1981; Raywid, 1983; Wehlage et al, 1989; Young, 1990; Barr & Parrett, 1997a).

Positive Research and Evaluation

Many of the nationally recognized alternative schools have been the focus of continuous study, evaluation, and research during the past 25 years. Students have been pre- and post-tested, compared to other public school students through assessments of academic performance and behavior, and evaluated through long-term follow-up studies. Most aspects of program conception, design, funding, curriculum, staffing, and community relations have been studied and evaluated (Raywid, 1983, 1993a; Wehlage et al., 1989; Smith, Barr & Burke, 1976; Barr & Parrett, 1997a; Young, 1990). This body of research, evaluation, and student assessment forms a foundation of confidence for public schools and represents the most positive data available for addressing the needs of at-risk youth. Research-based conclusions from alternative public school practice will continue to influence significant reform and restructure of the nation's public schools. Research and evaluation has documented:

Improved Self-Esteem

Over time, students enrolled in alternative public schools develop more positive self-esteem and attitudes toward teachers and schools (Estes et al., 1990; Raywid, 1983; Young, 1990). Many who reviewed this research have concluded that the data are almost too good to be true. Yet even school dropouts, once they are away from the negative impact of traditional schools, often develop improved self-image, at least for a while. Alternative schools provide a supportive atmosphere so that these attitudes and behaviors can be enhanced.

Improved Achievement

Public school teachers and administrators are often surprised or even suspicious when their former at-risk students begin to achieve so positively, often dramatically in alternative schools (Estes et al., 1990; Raywid, 1983; Young, 1990; Barr & Parrett, 1997a). This is true for both basic as well as vocational skills. Once at-risk students leave the difficult world of traditional school classes and enter the supportive, focused programs of an alternative school, truly remarkable achievement often occurs. Many alternative educators report significant improvement that is not directly related to the curriculum or the instruction (although these most certainly make a difference). It is student attitudes that seem to make the difference. Often, at-risk students who have never tried to do well in courses or on standardized tests assert themselves for the first time in alternative schools. As a result, many alternative schools report that their students learn to read almost overnight or raise their achievement scores several years in a few months. It has become an accepted belief among teachers in alternative programs that student gains in self-esteem are absolutely necessary before significant improvements in academic achievement can occur.

Improved Student Behavior

Students in alternative schools often have returned to school after brief or extended periods of complete separation from public or private education. These students tend to stay in these schools far more frequently than in their past educational experiences. Truancy and violence diminish as overall school and class attendance increase. In one study, 81 percent of those surveyed reported improved attendance and 38 percent reported a sharp rise in attendance rates (Estes et al., 1990; Raywid, 1983; Young, 1990; Barr & Parrett, 1997a). School vandalism virtually disappears in alternative schools as the students, perhaps for the first time in their lives, develop school behaviors that reflect positive feelings toward teachers, peers, and learning.

Positive Teacher Attitudes

Staff morale is unusually high in alternative public schools. As many as 90 percent of alternative school teachers in one study reported they felt a real ownership of their program, and a similar number reported that they were willing to assume even greater responsibilities in order to continue working in the program (Raywid, 1983). The vast majority of effective alternative school teachers demonstrate real concern for the needs of youth at risk, which helps to create and maintain the positive environment that these youth need to succeed.

Meeting Student Needs
In one of the classic studies comparing alternative schools to other public schools, students were asked how well the school they attended met their needs, using Maslow's Hierarchy of Needs. The study discovered that students in alternative schools believe that their schools met a larger range of their needs and met them better than students in other public schools (Smith et al., 1981). Alternative schools often have goals and curricula focused on self-esteem and study skills, and offer support groups, personal development opportunities, and subsidized breakfast and lunch programs. Students in these schools recognize the positive influence the school has on their lives.

High Quality of School Life
A number of studies over the years have identified school size, school culture, and the general quality of school-life as the most important aspects of alternative education. In fact, alternative public schools reflect a similar set of conditions usually found only in highly successful elite private schools (Erickson, 1981; Barr & Parrett, 1997a). For many students, enrolling in an alternative school begins with a period of skeptical uncertainty, during which they evaluate the "reality" of a seemingly different type of school. After all, for many of these youth, school has never represented an environment in which they could experience success or even have fun. Over time, these students tend to develop a strong positive bonding with their schools.

Distinctive Teaching Methods
Teachers in alternative schools report that they must employ distinctive instructional approaches that relate to student needs. These include: independent study and research; peer teaching; out-of-school action learning; highly individualized self-paced instruction; tutoring; vocational training; and career exploration and computer-assisted learning. For youth at risk, a blend of diverse instructional practices that complement individual student needs, interests, and learning styles is essential.

Customized Curriculum
It is not difficult to comprehend that a program planned to meet the needs of certain youth will be more successful in teaching those youth. For the first time, many youth feel responded to, respected, and connected with a school. Meeting the needs of individual students creates an environment of trust that translates into a student developing a willingness to learn in school. For many at-risk students, the basic needs of health, safety, and emotional support must first be addressed before significant learning can be expected to take place.

Choice
Ultimately, the fact that students and parents choose to participate in alternative schools carries significant power. Students and parents feel invested in the program and respond with positive efforts. Furthermore, the professionals who choose to work in alternative schools do so out of personal concern for those youth and the

desire to work in a smaller, collaborative approach (Nathan, 1989; Young & Clinchy, 1993; Barr & Parrett, 1997a).

Alternatives That Focus on the Needs of Students

> *The blond girl in the back desk is smarter than me. The boy by the window is always angry. The messy-haired girl has sex with her father. That child is loved by both parents. This one forgot his medication, while that one "self-medicates." The sleepy-looking one watches TV all night. The young-looking girl is a perfectionist. The parents of the one looking out the window are getting a divorce. That one's father died last year. The smiling one can't learn enough and that one can't read. What can I teach these children?*
> *—TEACHER, NORTH JUNIOR HIGH, BOISE, IDAHO*

The vast majority of alternative schools in the United States are designed to address the unique needs of a particular type of student. While many of these schools also integrate career themes, their primary distinction grows out of an effort to meet the needs of the students they serve. Some schools serve teen parents and pregnant students; others serve students who are far behind academically, have already dropped out of school, or are incarcerated. Some schools address the needs of highly motivated and talented students; others are designed for students skilled in the arts. These schools provide school programs and services that ensure the success of all students. If students have drug or alcohol problems, the schools provide extensive substance-abuse education programs, support groups, and counseling services and often are affiliated with a treatment center. If students are pregnant or are parents, the instructional program will focus on pre- and post-natal care, nutrition, health and often will provide infant and child care to enable parents to attend academic classes. If students are motivated and talented in math and science, they may attend magnet or residential programs and work directly with professional engineers and scientists.

Teen Parent Schools

> *"Listen," she said, "these teen moms couldn't care less about school." Then holding her hand up, the director of the Teen Parent Program ticked off items one by one on each finger. "Most of these young women don't have a job, don't have child care, and most don't have a phone or a car, or, perhaps worse, they have a car that doesn't work. They are all on food stamps or welfare, or both; many have been kicked out of their homes and have no place to live; many of them are sick, their babies are sick, and they have no health care. And most have been abused by their father, their boyfriend, or sometimes by both; and they all have this screaming, demanding little bellion with a dirty diaper on. You think they are interested in continuing their education? Get real! Dealing with teen parents is a monster problem. If we have any hope of helping these kids and their babies, we have to do the wildest things. We have to find a safe place for them to live, seek out all types of social*

> *services for them, go pick them up and take them home and pro-*
> *vide health care and be very, very careful that we don't schedule*
> *anything during the afternoon soap operas or Oprah. That, my*
> *friend, is the heart and guts of a first-rate teen parent program. In*
> *this world, you get real, real quick or you get out of the business.*
> *—DIRECTOR, TEEN PARENT PROGRAM, SALEM, OREGON*

Serving the needs of teenage parents or pregnant teenagers may well be the most demanding job in public education. Not only do the students face the usual challenges of learning, earning credit, and graduating, they have or soon will have an infant or young child to care for. Often these students are poor and do not have access to adequate health services. They often have no child care and may not even have a home. Without carefully designed schools to address the many needs of the teen parent or pregnant teenager, these students almost always drop out of school, have more children, and rely on some form of public assistance for years, sometimes decades. And all too often, their children also grow up in poor, dysfunctional settings only to perpetuate the cycle of despair into the next generation.

Perhaps the most widely recognized teen parent program in the United States is the New Futures School in Albuquerque, New Mexico. Opening its doors in 1970, this school continues to be a model of community organization. Over the past three decades, New Futures has helped more than four thousand adolescents progress through the difficult experience of teen pregnancy and parenthood. The school features an academic program that leads to a regular diploma, or a GED course for older students, an in-school clinic that provides for mothers' health and parental needs, counseling services, a child care facility, and a career exploration/jobs program.

Dropout and Dropout-Prevention Alternatives

The oldest form of alternative school focused on the school dropout and the potential dropout. These early schools often were referred to as continuation schools and eagerly recruited students from the jailhouse steps, juvenile courts, and street corners. Today, dropout and dropout-prevention programs represent the largest number of alternative public schools in the United States. Almost every school district, regardless of how small or how isolated, will have access to some type of dropout prevention program. Many states require school districts to provide such programs, which also may serve troubled youth and expelled students. Most recently, the states of Kentucky and South Carolina have funded all school districts to establish alternative schools for at-risk youths.

These schools often have a significant positive effect on students who have not succeeded in traditional academic settings. For students who have never been academically successful, participation in a high-quality alternative school typically will lead to impressive, often astounding academic gains. Many such schools use tutoring, high-interest curricular material, self-paced learning, and high school equivalency exams to enable students who are far behind academically to catch up, accelerate their learning, and graduate from high school. These schools often operate from early morning to late evening, provide for individual contract learning, maintain small classes, and provide health services.

Today, outstanding dropout-prevention programs can be found throughout the United States. Four nationally recognized programs include:

- Vocational Village: For three decades, Vocational Village (Portland, Oregon) has been nationally recognized for its success with high-school-age dropouts through vocational intervention and skills development (Barr & Parrett, 1997a).
- Metropolitan Regional Career and Technical Center: Each of the 160 students at the MET (Providence, Rhode Island) has a customized education, and achievement is measured not by grades and achievement tests, but by real-world performance and postgraduation success. Directed by the acclaimed principal, 'Doc' Dennis Littky, the MET has gained national attention for its success with potential dropouts (Keough, 1999).
- Meridian Academy: Open for less than a decade, this 9–12 program (Meridian, Idaho) for high-risk youth has enjoyed remarkable success through integrating the essential characteristics of effective alternative programs into a comprehensive, student-centered school of 150 students (see Chapter 5).
- Westbridge Academy: Located in Grand Rapids, Michigan, Westbridge was started in the late 1960s, to provide dropouts and potential dropouts with a personalized curriculum, individual needs-based counseling, and a array of interest-based curricular offerings. Westbridge has helped thousands of Grand Rapids' adolescents to return to school, achieve, and graduate.

Expelled/Incarcerated Student Programs

With zero tolerance now established in almost every state and many districts and the increasingly aggressive efforts of police and juvenile authorities to enforce violations, more and more school-age youth have been removed from the public schools. Based in part on this reality, a growing number of states now require school districts to provide alternative programs for these youth.

School districts often create programs for expelled students to ensure that these troubled youth continue to be supervised and educated. Because some expelled youth are so violent and aggressive, some school districts have even established daytime incarceration programs so that parents of these youth can still maintain their daytime jobs without worrying about their children's actions. With substantial increases in the number of juvenile offenders, education inside the juvenile detention and prison system has also become increasingly essential.

While these programs cannot provide for voluntary choice, they are developed to address the unique needs of the student being served and often model successful dropout-prevention schools. Many of these programs emphasize drug and alcohol education, anger management, self-esteem improvement, and conflict mediation as central themes throughout the academic curriculum.

Some schools and communities, often in cooperation with law enforcement and juvenile justice authorities, have created wilderness- and adventure-based programs, boot camps, and other types of highly secure, highly organized programs for violent or expelled students. One such boot camp program, the About Face Academy, staffed with certified teachers with previous military experience, has been established in Oklahoma City.

Programs for Motivated and Talented Youth

Many students in public education report that they are at risk because they are bored and unchallenged. As a result, many of the brightest students develop behavioral problems and fail to fulfill their potential. Too many of these students contemplate, attempt, and/or actually commit suicide. Some of these students also turn to violence. By carefully designing educational programs to capitalize on the skills, abilities, and talents of these students, schools can facilitate truly remarkable learning. From elementary-school students doing geometry and calculus to high-school students taking advanced college courses, programs for these students often involve highly individualized and group research projects and provide opportunities for students to work with outstanding professionals in areas of interest to the students.

Many urban magnet programs and statewide residential alternatives enroll primarily motivated, talented, and gifted students, and an increasing number of districts now have performing arts programs for K–12 students that provide an opportunity for students to work with professional artists.

Alternatives That Focus on Thematic, Curricular, or Career Emphases

At the middle- and high-school levels, many alternative, magnet, and charter schools focus on a curricular or career theme. These schools have been extremely successful in motivating students toward enhanced academic achievement. The concept is simple. In addition to the usual requirements for high-school graduation, student learning is connected to the academic or professional world. Content coursework is integrated into a real-world interest or theme. Focus areas include radio and television broadcasting, engineering, performing arts, law, international and cultural studies, and the diverse health professions. These schools often are located in the workplace, and students usually study with professionals in their fields of interest. Research has documented that students who attend these magnet, career-theme schools are motivated, engaged, and have higher achievement than students in both comprehensive high schools and parochial schools (Gamoran, 1996).

At the elementary level, these schools may emphasize culture and language, and teach through the immersion process. Some may focus on math and science, the study of the environment, or the performing arts. Hawthorne Elementary School in Seattle focuses its curriculum on the richness of the African American culture. Utilizing this theme, the faculty, staff, parents, and students join to embrace the primary goal of the school, which is to ensure that all students complete the elementary years with a successful level of student achievement. The school offers a warranty that assures all parents that if they keep their children in school, the children will learn to read and achieve high standards of academic excellence.

Thematic, curricular, and career options at the secondary level are abundant in the Houston Independent School District in Texas, where a student may enroll in high schools for the health professions, law enforcement and criminal justice, performing and visual arts, and many others. Thousands of middle- and high-school students take advantage of a full menu of alternatives offered throughout the city.

These programs are growing rapidly because of the dramatic increase in parental interest in choice and in smaller, focused schools. They are discussed in more detail in later sections on charter and magnet schools.

Alternatives That Focus on Instructional Approaches

While many of these alternatives exist primarily at the elementary- and middle-school level (Montessori, Multiple Intelligence, and Continuous Progress), a number of K–12 and high-school programs using distinctive instructional approaches have been established. These include:

Open Schools

Based originally on the British Infant School and later on the ideas of Roland Barth, John Holt, Herb Kohl, Charles Rathbone, and other educators, a number of K–12 public schools have flourished for decades; Research and evaluation data on them is unusually positive. Open schools in the United States tend to be developed around classroom learning centers. Children and youth are encouraged to pursue their own curiosity and inquisitiveness, select learning activities, and to some extent, decide where and how long they will pursue those activities. Three of the nation's most recognized Open Schools are the K–12 St. Paul Open School; the 2–12 Metropolitan Learning Center in Portland, Oregon; and the K–12 Brown School in Louisville, Kentucky.

Traditional/Fundamental Schools

Because many parents desire increased structure and drill for their children, school districts throughout the United States have modeled private and parochial schools by developing schools that emphasize basic education. These schools often have dress codes, uniforms, daily homework, structured expectations for parents, and strict behavior expectations for children. Where these schools are available, parents who are frustrated by what they consider to be lax discipline and the "fun and games" approach to public education have been eager to enroll their children. Endorsed by the National Council for Basic Education, Traditional/Fundamental schools remain a popular choice. While these schools can be found throughout the United States, the Jefferson County School District, Louisville, Kentucky, was among the first school districts in the Midwest to develop a network of elementary and secondary Traditional/Fundamental schools.

Paideia Schools

In 1982 the renowned philosopher Mortimer Adler outlined a rigorous approach to public education. The proposal emphasized a single-track, liberal arts educational program designed to prepare students for work, citizenship, and lifelong learning.

These schools prepare all students for further postsecondary education. Paideia education is based on three "volumes" of learning—didactic teaching, Socratic questioning, and coaching (Adler, 1982). The goal is for 80 percent of learning to be student centered. In 1984 the Chattanooga (Tennessee) school district established one of the nation's first magnet programs based on the Paideia concept. Later, the district established the School for the Arts at the middle-school level and a K–4 program. In 1991 the school district created a second Paideia school, a K–8 School for the liberal arts, and later established Paideia schools as neighborhood schools (Phoenix Paideia schools) and as fine arts and performing arts magnet schools.

Alternatives That Focus on Experiential Learning

Based in part on the ideas of the educational philosopher John Dewey, many alternative schools in the United States emphasize "learning by doing." These schools place a high priority on getting students out of school and away from traditional school environments. Experiential learning programs are usually centrally located and offer the students opportunities to complete core requirements in a base school and also travel to field sites where they can learn in hospitals, radio and television stations, corporations, and a host of small-business settings. These school-without-walls programs can be found in Seattle, Grand Rapids, Chicago, New York, and many other medium to large urban areas.

The first such alternative school in the country, established in 1969, was the Parkway Program in Philadelphia. Today, Parkway students continue to attend classes in museums, hospitals, libraries, government agencies, banking institutions, and newspapers. Their teachers are curators, biologists, health professionals, librarians, and bankers. Back at their home base, the students work with teachers and staff to meet graduation requirements and discuss their out-of-school learning experiences.

These programs also feature extensive real-life practica, internships, and volunteer service projects to enhance learning. Many internship programs place students with business and government leaders so that they can gain experience with executive decision makers. Technical apprenticeships also provide invaluable training and career preparation for participating students.

Another flourishing model involves creating small businesses operated by students as entrepreneurs. These programs prepare students to learn market analysis, how to create and operate a business, and how to maintain financial accountability. From small student stores to international import and export ventures, these programs and schools teach students the essentials of entrepreneurship through real-life experience. Several national networks and organizations, including Rural Entrepreneurship through Action Learning (REAL) in Athens, Georgia, and MicroSociety Inc., in Philadelphia, support these programs and schools.

Perhaps the most well-known program involving out-of-school learning experiences is Foxfire. Originating in Rabun Gap, Georgia, in the late 1960s, students in Rabun Gap began collecting and writing about the folkways and culture of the rural mountains of eastern Georgia. What started as a student-created, mimeographed newsletter soon grew into a million-dollar business operated and managed by a group of high-risk high school students and their teachers. Today, Foxfire has established national Teacher Outreach Centers to train teachers in the Foxfire approach and has created regional Foxfire-affiliated teacher networks to support teachers throughout the United States.

Magnet Schools

Nearly every major city in the United States has developed an array of alternative schools and, in many locations, these offerings are referred to as magnet schools. While most of these programs were started initially to attract students from diverse regions and populations of a city or to provide a specific, enhanced focus, the concept quickly became the approach of choice and an integral part of court-ordered desegregation efforts. Magnet schools were evaluated during the 1970s as the most successful aspect of desegregation plans (Estes et al., 1990; Waldrip et al., 1993). The concept proved unusually successful as parents and students from ethnically diverse neighborhoods willingly chose to attend academically focused alternative schools and chose to do so without forced busing. After over 20 years of success, this desegregation by choice continues to demonstrate that parents and students from different ethnic groups are willing to attend school together, even travel long distances to do so, in order to participate in quality educational experiences. Career theme magnet schools have not only demonstrated the ability to attract a diverse student body, but have also documented that students perform at high levels of academic excellence when they choose to participate in a curriculum focus that they are interested in (Gamoran, 1996; West, 1996).

While often started by court orders, magnet schools have grown and expanded far beyond their original purpose for desegregation. Today, magnet schools have become characterized primarily by an emphasis on career, professional, and vocational programs. They have grown and thrived because of their remarkable educational success. Cities such as Houston, Dallas, Milwaukee, San Diego, Los Angeles, Boston, Louisville, St. Louis, Kansas City, Seattle, and others have developed large numbers of magnets, and many cities (like Vancouver, Washington) are currently expanding the magnet school concept. Many magnet programs have become significant components of public education. In Houston, for example, over 25 percent of all public school students attend one of the more than 60 magnet school programs available. With the motto "The Best Education That Money Can't Buy," the Houston public schools have attracted back to public education not only dropouts, but parents and students who had abandoned public education for private, parochial, and suburban schools (Barr, 1982, 1997a).

One of the nation's most successful magnet schools is the Skyline Magnet School in Dallas. First opened in 1971, the school today serves over 800 students with a comprehensive academic program including nine foreign languages, advanced placement in the arts and sciences, and extensive preparation in communications, military science, and vocational and career training. In Houston, the Health Professional Magnet is located at the Baylor Medical Center Complex and focuses on health and medicine. Popular magnet school concepts created for at-risk youth can be found in most major U.S. cities and include the following:

- Aerospace schools
- Business or management schools
- Computer technology schools
- Environmental studies/outdoor schools
- Traditional back-to-basics high schools
- Global studies and international focus schools
- Health careers schools
- Interdisciplinary educational parks
- Performing arts schools
- Science/math enrichment schools
- Multicultural schools

Complementing these schools are a number of more exotic magnet programs which include petrochemical engineering programs, media schools for radio and television, sports magnets, marketing and business schools, and teaching career magnets. Many of these schools and programs are available at both the middle-school and the high-school level and provide for conventional high-school graduation through intensive enrichment in their magnet emphasis.

Magnet schools enable students to select a career emphasis and pursue a major in a manner similar to students in community colleges or universities. The opportunity to focus high-school careers in an area that relates both to a student's interest and to later jobs and opportunities has had enormous success. A statewide study of 41 magnet schools in New York documented a compelling success story. The report concluded that magnet programs helped keep kids in school, helped them improve educational achievement, and when compared to public school students on standardized tests, 58 percent of the magnet school students performed better on reading and 65 percent better on math. Average daily attendance was also higher in 98 percent of the magnet programs (Magi Educational Services, 1985). Similar studies have been conducted with equally positive results in magnet schools in Chicago, Houston, San Diego, and St. Louis (Estes et al., 1990). More recently, scholars from the University of Wisconsin found magnet school students to outperform both traditional public high school students and their peers in Catholic high schools on standardized achievement tests (Gamoran, 1996).

Manhattan's District 4 in East Harlem is one of the nation's most celebrated magnet success stories. The district offers 23 magnet schools at the elementary, middle, and high-school level. In an economically devastated area where city dropout figures are reported at 78 percent for Hispanic youth and 72 percent for African-American, the District 4 Elementary Magnet could identify only two high-school dropouts in an eight-year period during the 1980s and reported that students' reading scores were raised from last in the city to over 62 percent reading at or above grade level (Estes et al., 1990).

There exist few high schools in the United States today, other than specifically designed alternative schools, where comprehensive schoolwide programs have been initiated at the high-school level. One school system where such a comprehensive program is being developed and implemented is the Vancouver, Washington, public schools. During the past few years, the school district has moved to develop and implement a large number of new magnet programs, to develop schoolwide instruction programs in the high schools, and to expand the school district's alternative school for at-risk youth to sites on the other high-school campuses.

The at-risk alternative program in Vancouver is the Pan Terra High School, housed in its own building and serving approximately 250 students. Students may attend a morning, afternoon, or evening block or any combination of these sessions to pursue their learning. Each student meets with parents and teachers to develop a personalized education plan that establishes learning goals, the amount of time to be invested in the learning, a plan for achieving the goals, and an outcome assessment plan. The individualized approach has proven extremely successful over the years for Pan Terra, whose program is now being expanded to the high schools as Pan Terra Satellite Centers. Plans are being explored for similar satellites at the middle-school level.

New magnet school programs have been developed at each high school. These include a performing arts magnet; a law/legal magnet; a science and technology magnet; and a health professions magnet, as well as an International High School Baccalaureate Program.

Such districtwide, comprehensive high-school magnet programs should offer great assistance for at-risk youth, providing them with the individualized, continuous progress that they need for their academic work while also assisting them in technical career and job opportunities.

While the term magnet schools became popularized during desegregation efforts and continues to be used to describe programs in many of the nation's largest cities, a number of schools have moved away from a cultural diversity theme. Today, magnet schools are often indistinguishable from other alternative public schools, and the terms magnet schools, alternative schools, optional schools, and schools of choice are often used interchangeably.

Supplemental Programs: Youth at Risk

Recently, a number of programs have emerged with the goal of reducing dropouts and assisting at-risk youth make the transition to college (Slavin & Fashola, 1998). Each of the following programs has demonstrated success and is currently in operation throughout the United States.

Coca-Cola Valued Youth Dropout Prevention Program (7–12)

A cross-age tutoring program with the goal of increasing self-esteem and school success for at-risk middle-school and high-school students. The program attempts to reduce school dropout rates by improving self-esteem and academic achievement.

Achievement for Latinos (ALAS, 7–12)

Designed for high-risk Hispanic middle- and high-school students from high poverty areas. The program focuses on students with learning disabilities and behavioral problems and works with the home, school, and community to improve student behavior and performance.

Advancement via Individual Determination (AVID)

The AVID program, developed in 1981, was designed to assist low-achieving students with good academic potential to succeed in ongoing college preparatory curriculum. Based on years of success, AVID is widely recognized as a program that teaches high-risk students to excel academically. AVID is designed for students in grades 6–12 and is currently available in 900 middle and high schools in 26 states.

Upward Bound

Upward Bound assists talented high school students who are poor and/or minority to make a successful transition to college. The program is part of the larger TRIO Program, which includes a middle-school support program, Talent Search, and the College/University Assistance Support Program (CAMP). Linked together, these three programs have demonstrated remarkable success in serving and maintaining talented students from the middle school through college. Upward Bound has been thoroughly and favorably evaluated for the past decade.

Programs Showing Promise of Improving Student Performance

Coalition of Essential Schools

The Coalition of Essential Schools (CES) is one of the most ambitious and well-funded school-reform efforts in the United States. Conceived by Ted Sizer, the Coalition is now working in more than 1,200 schools, mostly at the high school level in 39 states. Coalition schools are guided by nine common principles:

- Schools should have an intellectual focus.
- Schools' goals should be simple.
- Schools should have universal goals that apply to all students.
- Teaching and learning should be personalized.
- The governing metaphor should be student as worker, teacher as coach.
- Diplomas should be awarded upon demonstration of mastery.
- The tone of the school should stress unanxious high expectations.
- Principals and teachers should view themselves as generalists first and specialists second.
- Teacher load should be 80 or fewer students, and per-pupil cost should not exceed traditional school costs by more than 10 percent. (Cushman, 1999)

Each of the CES schools designs its own individual reform effort, which is guided by the Coalition's common principles. While there is no specific reform design for all

CES schools, in practice, Coalition members have tended to employ block scheduling, project-based learning, and student demonstrations of competency (exhibitions). Despite minimal evidence to date on standardized test scores, the Coalition has demonstrated impressive progress and inroads into improving the comprehensive high schools' efforts in a number of other areas related to better serving and preparing all students, especially those at risk.

School Development Program

The School Development Program (SDP) was initiated in 1968 by James Comer of Yale University. Based on an analysis of the research and evaluation of SDP schools, a number of groups have cited evidence of promising effects on student achievement for high-school-age youth. While the majority of this program's efforts have focused on elementary and middle schools, the concepts driving the success of the School Development Program are proving effective for high-risk high school students in high poverty areas (Comer, 1999). (See Chapter 6.)

Community for Learning

The Community for Learning Program was initiated by Margaret C. Wang of Temple University Center for Research in Human Development and Education in 1990. Based on over 30 years of research and experimentation, the Community for Learning Program "encourages the coordination of classroom instruction with community service (e.g., health, libraries, social services, and law enforcement) in an effort to improve individual student learning" (Herman, 1999, p. 43). For some years, research has documented the influence of the school, family, and community on student learning. This program, primarily found in middle schools, also shows valuable potential for improving at-risk student success at the high-school levels.

Expeditionary Learning Outward Bound

Expeditionary Learning Outward Bound is a comprehensive K–12 school improvement design to transform curriculum, instruction, assessment, school culture, and organization. A Comprehensive School Reform Design (CSRD) model, it is based on two fundamental ideas: that students learn better by doing than listening, and that the development of character, high expectations, and a sense of community are just as important as developing academic skills and knowledge. Expeditionary Learning Outward Bound includes the following core practices (Herman, 1999, p. 67):

- Learning Expeditions: long-term, multidisciplinary projects that combine academic, service, and physical education
- Reflection and Critique: includes teachers working with each other to expand their own instruction and students' worth
- School Culture: emphasizing community and collaboration, high expectations for all students, service, and cultural diversity

- School Structure: is reorganized to include shared decision making among teachers and administrators and to develop positive relationships among staff, students, parents, and the community

Established in the early 1990s, Expeditionary Learning is closely affiliated with its parent organization, Outward Bound USA. Over 80 schools throughout the country are currently using the approach and even though the program is relatively new, a significant amount of research has indicated significant gains, particularly for at-risk youth and other participating students (Herman, 1999).

Effective Programs for Addressing the Violent, Violence-Prone, and Bullying Student

High schools have an urgent need to address the needs of disruptive, violent, and violence-prone youth. Effective approaches and interventions that address violence begin with creating a climate of respect.

Other than the family, the single most powerful, positive impact on at-risk and/or violent youth is a school climate in which there is an atmosphere of caring, support, and academic challenge, a school climate that takes on the characteristics of a "surrogate family." Such an educational setting is developed by ensuring that schools employ the essential components of effective schools described in Chapter 5. In particular, high schools should work toward developing the following:

Small School Size

Research has documented that there is a direct relationship between violence and school size. While violent acts have taken place in schools in almost every locale—cities, suburbs, and rural areas—most had one thing in common: they nearly all occurred in schools with close to or over 1,000 students. In numerous studies since the mid-1970s, the relationship between violence and school size has been demonstrated (Another take on school violence, 1999). The single most effective approach to reducing school violence is to simply downsize the large clique-filled comprehensive high schools into more personalized schools-within-schools, or teacher-student teams. The goal of large comprehensive high schools must be to ensure that every student feels cared for by teachers and is engaged in significant learning (see Chapter 5).

Alternative Schools

A school climate of caring, support, and respect is most easily created in alternative schools and programs (Safe Schools and Communities Coalition, 1998). Research has documented in a number of major reports over the years that there is almost a total lack of violence in alternative schools—even those who serve high-risk, previously disruptive or violent youth (Barr & Parrett, 1997a). Alternative schools that are specially designed to help teenage students who are doing poorly, failing, or have dropped out of schools may be the single best approach to preventing violence. These programs include continuation schools, dropout programs, and teenage parent programs.

Positive Relationship with One or More Teachers

Having a positive relationship with a teacher can have a powerful, positive influence on student decisions and behavior. Students who are "connected" with one or more teachers are less likely to be violent, engage in risky behaviors, or pursue destructive impulses (see Chapter 2).

Positive Relationship with a Caring Adult

Because so many violent, violence-prone, and bullying students have come from abusive, stressful, or disinterested homes, mentoring programs are especially important for students during their teenage years. Research has documented how important it is for every teenager to have a strong, positive relationship with an adult. A number of groups throughout the country provide mentor programs that have proven highly successful (see Chapter 2).

Alternatives to Expulsion

Research has offered conclusive evidence that the single most critical issue regarding teenagers who engage in violent, disruptive, and criminal behavior is lack of adult supervision. Review of the demographic data of teenagers incarcerated in juvenile-justice detention centers has found that incarcerated juveniles are between 15 and 16 years old, have been out of school for at least a year, and are so lacking in basic skills that finding a fulfilling job is all but impossible. As a result, a growing number of states, including Oregon, Kentucky, Connecticut, and Colorado, have required schools to provide high-security educational programs outside mainstream schools so that violent youth can continue their education and work to address their problems with anger and frustration. Two approaches that are now being used include:

- Educational Boot Camps: For teenage students already involved in disruptive, aberrant, or violent behavior, and who may have already been expelled from regular school programs on the basis of zero tolerance, a new type of educational program has been developed. Sometimes these programs are operated in cooperation with juvenile justice or corrections officials, sometimes they are available in youth detention centers or jails. Some school districts have developed "daytime incarceration" programs where attendance is mandatory between specified hours. Other school districts have developed programs modeled after military boot camps. Often these programs, like the "About Face" Academy Program in Oklahoma City, use retired military professionals as teachers, have students dress in camo-fatigues, and utilize a paramilitary structure of order and obedience.

- Wilderness- and Adventure-Based Programs: Another kind of program that has been developed for troubled, often violent youth is the comprehensive residential experience, which uses a wilderness setting as part of the rehabilitative process. For example, in the "wilderness" setting at Camp E-HUN-TEE in Exeter, Rhode Island, small groups replicate family living. The development of positive peer-group bonding is integral in helping young people make the changes and learn the skills they need in order to be more successful when they return to their home communities. Counselors, teachers, clinicians, and support staff work closely with groups of "campers" as well as with individuals. To achieve positive change, the Wilderness Educational Program integrates key principles and activities, including highly structured activities, experiential education, adventure-based counseling, resiliency theory, close group work and peer counseling, and self-responsibility. For some troubled youth the Wilderness Educational Program is the last resort. A second type of program is the outdoor adventure-based experience that has long been available through the U.S. Outward Bound Program. Believing that youth, especially troubled or violent youth, react negatively to most school and other institutional settings, Outward Bound has long provided educational extremes in the more neutral setting of the outdoors—where youths have little or no previous frame of reference. Activities include major challenges like rock climbing, rapelling, rafting and canoeing, and backpacking into wilderness areas. Often, students learn the skills necessary to perform these tasks and then serve as leaders to teach other students these skills. Few programs have documented such remarkable success in transforming student attitudes, building self-concepts and even furthering academic achievement as Outward Bound, and Outward Bound has documented its accomplishments for more than two decades.

After-School Programs

After-school programs have a powerful and positive effect on keeping middle-level and high-school at-risk students out of trouble. Fifty percent of all youth crime occurs after school, when teenagers are unsupervised by adults. This is also when most teenagers get pregnant. High schools should work closely with Boys and Girls Clubs, YMCA/YWCA, and recreational leagues to provide supervised after-school programs for teenagers.

Promoting Personal, Social, and Emotional Growth

For teenagers, especially at-risk and violent students, it is absolutely essential that they learn productive approaches for dealing with frustration, conflict, anger, and rage. Effective programs include anger management, conflict management, and peer mediation. So many school youth have learned only one approach to frustration and anger—a disruptive or violent response. Students must learn more effective approaches for dealing with their own emotions. Schools can assist students through service learning in the community, an integrated program of character education, student courts, attendance courts, cross-age tutoring of younger children, and working with adult role-model mentors.

Identification, Intervention, and Treatment

Violent, violence-prone, and bullying students must be identified at the earliest possible level, but often elementary- and middle-school teachers, counselors, and administrators have failed to do so. Schools must identify these troubled youths and provide them assistance. As a quick fix is rarely helpful, schools must provide for continual intervention and support to help these youth.

Community Mobilization

School behavior is only the tip of the iceberg regarding children and youth, and the world outside the school is important in their healthy development. Developmental assets (see Chapter 2) are essential in helping children and youth adopt healthy behaviors and lifestyles. Communitywide campaigns regarding drugs and drinking are also important. The Community Assets Surveys and campaigns can likewise help to focus a community's attention on problems and mobilize action. The Assets Survey, if conducted on an ongoing basis, perhaps every two or three years, also provides a way to monitor the degree of success of the community in developing youth support.

The Comprehensive High School: A Need for Dramatic Transformation

While recent years have witnessed a growing interest in transforming comprehensive high schools in the United States, it was the murderous attack at Columbine High School in Littleton, Colorado, in 1999 that seemed to catapult high school reform to the top of the educational reform agenda. Almost immediately following Columbine, U.S. Secretary of Education Richard Riley and a number of state governors and superintendents came forward with proposals not only to ensure the safety of high school students, but to transform the comprehensive high school into a structure that would be more capable of serving all students, particularly those at risk. The violence at Columbine graphically dramatized many of the problems with large comprehensive schools that educators and reformers had been talking about for years: the relationship between school size and violence; the clique-plagued youth culture of the high school; the lack of engaged learning of so many high school students; the educational vacuum of the senior year; the inability of teachers and school administrators to personalize learning; and a host of other problems and social issues that seem to confront students. Suddenly high-school reform became urgent and focused.

A few months following the Columbine High School incident, Riley stated in his annual 1999 back-to-school address that it was time to rethink high schools and called for a national dialogue to address the problems associated with the nation's comprehensive schools. He explained that high schools "seem to be caught in a time warp from long ago. We still seem to be using America's high schools as a 'sorting machine,' tagging and labeling young people as successful, run of the mill or low achievers" (Riley, 1999).

As early as 1973, the National Association for Secondary School Principals (NASSP) shocked the educational establishment by recommending radical reform of the nation's high schools. More recently, Breaking Ranks, a blue-ribbon, commissioned study of the NASSP, recommended a comprehensive high-school reform agenda that included downsizing comprehensive high schools into educational programs of no more than six hundred students (1996). In 1968 Mark Tucker and Judy Codding, both of the Washington-based National Center on Education, also called for doing away with a "central, yet outdated institution," the comprehensive high school. In their book, *Standards for Our Schools: How to Set Them, Measure Them, and Track Them,* Tucker and Codding argued that high schools should be about academic and applied academic schooling. They argued that students should attend K–8 schools, followed by two years of high school. Tucker and Codding called for requiring students to pass a statewide assessment test after the first two years of high school. High schools would have two goals: to educate students sufficiently to pass the assessment examination and to provide additional preparation for students who pass the competency assessment to prepare them for college entrance exams. Students wanting vocational, technical, or professional programs would go directly to community colleges or technical centers after two years of high school (an approach similar to that legislated in Oregon in 1991). And while the secretary of education helped to focus attention on high school reform, events were occurring in states and school districts across the country that seemed to suggest that a significant restructuring of the comprehensive high school might have been under way, at least in a growing number of communities. Responsible in part, if not primarily, for the continued concern over the efficiency of the comprehensive high school is the model's consistent failure to effectively educate high-risk youth.

An Emerging Reform Agenda

By the beginning of the twenty-first century, a clear reform agenda for high schools had emerged in the United States. And like a huge educational pendulum, the earlier effort to consolidate small, isolated community schools into large, uniform comprehensive high schools began to give way to downsizing large schools, diversifying educational programs, providing students with a range of opportunities to select appropriate educational programs and to seek highly specialized studies. But while the pendulum of change seems to be gathering momentum, the speed of change is agonizingly slow. High-school reform will not be easy; in fact, it represents the single most difficult area of public-school restructuring. Until the late 1990s, it was almost impossible to find high schools in the United States that had been successfully restructured. High schools in the United States appear to be the single most entrenched, intransigent institution in the country. The emerging reform agenda for United States high schools focuses on downsizing, providing choices, personalizing programs, blending opportunities with postsecondary education, enhancing relevance, providing for student needs, scheduling enhancements, the demonstration of competency at graduation, successful transitions, opportunities to accelerate, and the promotion of social and emotional growth.

Downsizing the Comprehensive High School

With support from the NASSP, Secretary Riley, influential governors like James Hunt of North Carolina, and a substantial research base documenting the relationship between violence and school size, there is a growing agreement that large junior/senior high schools must be reorganized and restructured into small educational programs with no more than 600 students. This can be accomplished in three ways: creating small "teams" or "families" of teachers and students who work exclusively together throughout most of the school day; the creation of small schools within schools with special themes; and the development of a number of alternative public schools or magnet schools designed to serve the needs and interests of focused groups of students. Examples of these efforts at reform are becoming increasingly more prominent:

- The New York Public Schools have restructured a number of large comprehensive high schools and replaced them with more than 50 minischools that are smaller and offer more personalized education. The goal of the project, starting in 1994, has been to "humanize high school education and transform large inner-city schools into successful learning environments for all students."
- The Coalition of Essential Schools has encouraged its member schools, especially large junior/senior high schools, to consider ways in which they can become "smaller, more personalized learning communities." This is often achieved by limiting enrollment in Coalition programs, or employing a school within school strategy, at least as the first step in full schoolwide implementation of its ideas (Herman, 1999, p. 39).
- Central Park East, one of the nation's most well-known and highly celebrated public schools, subdivided itself into three distinct schools in a single building. The school is small to begin with (450 students grades 7–12), but the school is downsized further by the creation of three subdivisions—Divisions I and II and the Senior Institute. Even further, Divisions I and II programs are divided into two "houses" of 80 students and 4 teachers (Raywid, 1999). Former director of the school Deborah Meier maintains that size alone does not guarantee success, but large schools can render school effectiveness impossible. Meier recommends a twenty-by-twenty school: Class size would be limited to 20 students and the school would have no fewer than 20 teachers (Raywid, 1999).

- The Chicago Public Schools, in the mid-1990s, began restructuring comprehensive high schools into small, redesigned learning communities. By 1999 over 130 "small by design" elementary and secondary schools had been created. And while many of these high school programs are schools within schools, others have been established at off-campus sites, and many today are charter public schools (Klonsky & Klonsky, 1999).

Creating a System of Optional Schools and Programs

Recognizing that no simple, uniform curriculum can meet the diverse needs of the complex high-school student body of today, many school districts in the United States have begun to supplement comprehensive high schools with an array of optional, alternative, and magnet school programs for the voluntarily participation of students and their parents. Each of these optional school programs utilizes individualized themes that enable students to specialize in areas of study that reflect their own personal needs and interests. Each of the options meets all graduation requirements but also includes specialized courses, internships in real-life settings, and service learning. Research has documented that students in these programs represent considerable diversity, and that they are more enthusiastic and motivated and their academic achievement increases. Examples of this approach include:

- The Jefferson County Public Schools, Louisville, Kentucky: The Jefferson County School District (JCSD) is a recognized leader in school restructuring and educational reform. As one of the country's 25 largest school districts, JCSD serves 97,000 students (infants through adults) at 150 locations. JCSD offers a large amount of choices at the elementary-, middle-, and high-school levels. Each year, more than 9,000 students apply for positions in the district's eighty-seven alternative schools and programs. In an effort to achieve an appropriate mix of students at each site, a common set of criteria for selection of students includes consideration of race, gender, and geographic location based on postal zip codes. These "managed" choices are dependent on space availability and transportation.

    At the middle- and high-school levels optional programs are available that emphasize self-directed learning in programs with an engineering focus, communications and media arts, mathematics, science and technology, visual arts and acting, dance, instrumental music, theater, and vocal music. The school district also provides magnet programs and career academies that focus on medicine and allied health, business management, entrepreneurship, banking, finance and accounting, technology, legal/government services, child care, and small optional neighborhood programs as schools within schools (Barr & Parrett, 1997a).
- Similar clusters of alternative schools, magnet schools, and optional programs can be found in Boston, Houston, Los Angeles, Seattle, and many other urban school districts in the United States. Many of these school districts report as many as 20 percent of their students attending some type of alternative public school program (Barr & Parrett, 1997a).

- In a 1999 study, researchers at the Policy Analysis for California Education at the University of California–Berkeley, reported a significant increase in the numbers of school-age children enrolled in school-choice options (both public and private) outside their neighborhood. The number has grown from one out of five students in 1993 to approximately 25 percent in 1999. The number grew by 1.4 million students between 1993 and 1996—from 5.3 million to 6.7 million. This was an increase of 11 to 13 percent in only three years. During the same time, private school enrollment grew by 800,000—from 4.4 million to 5.2 million, from 9 to 10 percent, and these figures do not include students being home schooled. This trend of students participating in public-school options was projected to increase to 15 percent by 1999 (Schnaiberg, 1999).

Personalizing Education

As more and more school districts develop systems of optional schools and programs, many are attempting to offer all high school students the opportunity to personalize and individualize their learning. They are doing this by designing "academic career majors" similar to the academic majors used in higher education. The goal is not only to serve students in specific magnet programs, but to serve all students by developing academic majors. Each major combines required academic core courses, electives, independent study/research with job shadowing, mentoring, internships, and service learning. In addition, a growing number of schools require all high school students to develop a personal four-to-six-year plan to guide their high school studies and then aid them in their transition into college or the world of work.

- After the Vancouver (Washington) public school system created four new magnet programs and implemented the International High School Baccalaureate Program, all of the programs quickly filled and had large waiting lists. In order to serve the many students who could not participate in optional programs, the school district immediately began developing a complex variety of academic/career majors for all high school students.
- The highly successful High Schools That Work Program in the southeastern United States arranges meetings with parents, students, and school officials at the ninth-grade level to develop personalized six-year plans for each student that are reviewed and revised each year.
- The National Association of Secondary School Principals has recommended that high schools help students develop a personal progress plan and continually review the plan to ensure that every student is progressing satisfactorily toward established goals (1996).
- The St. Paul Open School and other effective alternative public-school programs have established post high-school plans as a graduation requirement for all students.

Blending High School with College

> *There were about a dozen representatives from area public schools and universities, discussing programming for on-line courses, compressed video courses, and courses broadcast via public television or satellite. Almost all of the small, rural schools that were represented expressed a need for advanced mathematics courses, especially calculus, since rural schools rarely have many students interested in taking calculus and few qualified teachers to offer such a course. As the discussion continued, a university math professor asked a question that simply turned everything around. He said, "Do you want to offer a high school calculus course or a university calculus course?" For a few minutes, everyone sat around with these really dumb looks on their faces until one high school principal looked around and asked, "Wait a minute . . . isn't calculus, calculus?" And everyone quickly agreed that what was needed was a first-rate calculus course that would provide students with both high school credit and university credit. Before the group could finish congratulating them- selves on such a "brilliant idea," someone else interrupted and asked, "Well, isn't history, history?" And it seemed like a whole new world just opened up before us.*
> *—SCHOOL SUPERINTENDENT, WASHINGTON STATE*

A growing number of states have developed programs that not only allow, but encourage students to leave high school and begin taking college courses (New initiatives can help students prepare for college early, 1999). The state of Washington initiated Running Start to encourage students to attend college during their high school years. Other states allow college courses to serve as equivalents to high school requirements so that students will eventually graduate from high school while pursuing their college degrees. High schools throughout the United States have also developed 2 + 2 high school/college programs that articulate the last two years of high school with two years of community college, technical courses, tech prep programs, extensive school-to-work programs, and a wide variety of applied academic courses. Many communities have developed regional technology training centers, as well as cooperative programs with area community colleges and higher education. For students who drop out of school, the U.S. Job Corps offers a power- ful array of technical courses designed to help students complete their high school education and gain job training.

In the 1990s, the state of Oregon began implementing a new K–12 public- education plan that called for ending academic studies at the end of the tenth grade with a comprehensive examination called a Certificate of Initial Mastery, followed by two years of technical preparation at technical centers, community colleges, or higher education. By the beginning of the year 2000, this plan was well underway.

Enriching High School with Real-World Experiences

Research has helped emphasize how important out-of-school learning can be for all students, especially those who are at risk. Even more important, research has helped identify wide varieties of legitimate out-of-school learning experiences in both rural and urban areas and has also identified the elements of effective internships and service-learning programs (Waterman, 1997). In addition to providing real-world, hands-on experiences, these programs, especially service learning, also lead to social and emotional growth, particularly in the areas of responsibility and respect. Examples of real-world-experience programs include:

Service Learning
Both high schools and colleges have embraced service learning in the community. These programs include students providing service in retirement centers, health centers, hospitals, and a wide variety of community clean-up, paint-up, and fix-up projects. Such service learning activities build positive attitudes and help students learn the important lesson of responsibility.

Entrepreneurism
There is growing movement throughout the country to assist students in becoming business owners. Originally started as part of vocational education and Junior Achievement, the concept of student-operated and -managed businesses has greatly expanded during recent years. Students have started small companies to sell school supplies, hardware, crafts, and jewelry. They fix small engines, run bakeries, and operate import/export businesses. One group in Minnesota runs a consumer-protection group. One of the nations' most famous entrepreneurial efforts has been Foxfire Incorporated, a multi-million-dollar student-owned business selling books and newsletters documenting Appalachian and American folklore.

Collecting Folklore
While national interest in students collecting regional or cultural folklore started with Foxfire, the concept has expanded throughout the country to include a wide variety of rural and urban ethnic experiences. Foxfire was established in a poor, rural, southern area where many students traditionally dropped out of school and went to work in the region's textile mills. Based on the rather simple idea of collecting and publishing the folklore of their region, students traveled throughout the countryside interviewing parents, grandparents, and mountain people about subjects ranging from how to make homemade soap, to dowsing for water, to building log cabins (Barr & Parrett, 1997a).

School-to-Work
Fueled with resources from the federal grant, students throughout the country are now participating in a variety of real-world learning experiences in business and industry. These experiences range from short-term orientations, career fairs, and internships, to summer employment.

Schools Without Walls

Ever since the Philadelphia Parkway School was created as a school without walls, many cities have created programs to move learning experiences out of school buildings and into museums, aquariums, government offices, banks, and businesses. Students attend classes in a number of venues and are taught by professionals in a wide variety of occupations.

Career Theme Magnet Programs

During the past 20 years, there has been a huge increase in career-theme magnet programs where students voluntarily choose to participate in areas where they have a strong personal interest. Examples of magnet schools include such focal areas as performing art, law/legal professions, science and technology, and health professions. Participating students are dramatically influenced by the opportunity to learn in the real world from participating professionals. The result is high academic performance.

Scheduling Enhancements

While opportunities for internships, practica, apprenticeships, and service learning have helped to transform the high-school schedule, two other developments have had an equal impact. Increasingly, high schools in the United States are replacing the 6-, 7-, or 8-period day with 4×4 block schedules and other options that enable teachers and students to participate in longer, more in-depth studies. Many schools have developed "flex" schedules so that teachers and students start their school day at different times (Fager, 1997). Technology has fueled this need for more appropriate scheduling due to the growing availability of on-line high schools, courses, and "virtual" university programs that provide an ever expanding range of state-of-the-art course work available to students in their homes. Florida has created an on-line high school where students can earn a diploma (Lehman, Mar. 31, 2000). These web-based and CD-ROM courses developed by universities, private companies, and regional public school consortiums are available worldwide. Other examples of flexible scheduling include:

- A new comprehensive high school in Vancouver, Washington, was developed and built to accommodate only one-third of the students at any one time in classroom learning. The school was also designed to accommodate one-third of the students in small group study and projects, and one-third of the students in independent on-line research.
- The state of Florida has established the nation's first on-line high school available to students throughout the state 24 hours a day.
- A growing number of schools provide laptops and/or computer access to every student with the expectation of out-of-school usage.

Full-Service High Schools

The more that is known about at-risk and violence-prone children and youth, the more it is recognized that schools deal with only one part of the problem. It is now known how significant a student's family situation, socioeconomic level, and a wide variety of risky student behaviors, including tobacco, drug, alcohol abuse; community violence; and personal depression can all but overcome even the best efforts of high school programs (Dryfoos, 1998; Tomlinson, 1999). Every day, of the 40 million children and youth who arrive at school, one in four, fully 10 million elementary and secondary students, are at high risk of school failure. In many communities, almost all of the students have serious social, emotional, and health handicaps. Some have described these school/community situations as being like an "under-developed country," isolated and abandoned by the mainstream society (Dryfoos, 1998). In order to ensure that schools can be successful with all students, schools today must: "feed children; provide psychological support services; offer health services; offer health screening; establish referral networks related to substance abuse, child welfare, and sexual abuse; cooperate with the local police and probation officers; add curricula for prevention of substance abuse, teen pregnancies, suicide, and violence . . . and actively promote social skills, good nutrition, safety, and general health" (Dryfoos, 1998, p. 5). All this, and still provide for high-quality education. Recent incidents of school violence have further increased the pressures on schools to supplement academic programs with the widest range of services. The results of these pressures have led to an almost universal call for "one-stop," "seamless," unfragmented health and social services. Districts from throughout the United States are heeding this call by creating full-service high-school programs.

Increasingly, high schools and a few middle-level and elementary schools have established school-based health centers. While almost always controversial, these clinics build on a long tradition of having a school nurse in the building and relate directly to some of the major health-related dangers to healthy teenage development: pregnancy, venereal disease, AIDS, and drug and alcohol abuse. In some schools, up to 40 percent of the student body takes advantage of health services when they are available, since many of these students have no other form of health care. There is also data to support the fact that clinics reduce the number of teenage pregnancies in the school (the role of the clinic in planning and preventing pregnancies is one of the greatest controversies). The goals of most programs are to provide for comprehensive, ongoing health care and health education as opposed to an episodic, crisis intervention approach (Northwest Regional Educational Laboratory, 1993c). Clinics are often operated by community-based social service agencies and hospitals who work together to move services closer to the needs of, and to make these services more accessible to, adolescents.

School health clinics are increasingly important because of the scarcity of health care facilities for adolescents. Unfortunately, the Center for Population Options reported in 1991 that there were only 327 such centers in 33 states and Puerto Rico (Heckinger, 1992). More than half of the users of these clinics report they have no other health care. While 51 percent of the centers serve high schools, centers serve middle schools and elementary schools as well. In 1988 there were fewer than 100 school-based health centers. By 1998 there were more than 1,000 (37 percent based at high schools) (Tomlinson, May 1999). In addition to traditional health services, school health clinics provide physical examinations, treatment, screening, pregnancy tests, and psychological services.

While it is too early to draw any firm conclusion about the effectiveness of the centers on more positive teen behavior, several reports are very encouraging. In New York City, students who use the clinic miss fewer days of school. In Kansas City, the clinics reported a significant decline in the number of adolescents who used alcohol or drugs or smoked tobacco. Similar findings are expected as more data becomes available (Heckinger, 1992).

Demonstration of Competency at Graduation

There is growing momentum for establishing high-school-proficiency exit exams. This concept of high-school exit exams is already policy in more than 20 states and is supported by the secretary of education and the National Secondary School Principals Association. There is also considerable interest in a new international exam for high school students (Kennedy Manzo, 1999). Yet controversy continues to rage about whether or not a standardized test can adequately asses the complex learning that occurs during the K–12 public school years. A number of districts, schools, and patrons, including the more than 1,000 schools participating in the Coalition of Essential Schools (CES), object to standardized testing. In a recent response to standardized testing, representatives from the coalition reported that they are withstanding pressures from legislatures and communities to use standardized tests to assess student achievement (Tucker, 1999). The CES and many other schools and districts have attempted to establish a more balanced approach to assessment. Principle number six of CES states, "The diploma should be awarded upon demonstration of mastery of the central skills and knowledge of the school program" (Cushman, 1999). In CES, high schools are encouraged to establish promotion and graduation requirements that use demonstration of mastery rather than time spent in class as criteria for promotion or graduation (Darling-Hammond et al., 1995).

Decades ago, America's alternative schools pioneered the concept of graduation competencies. During the late 1960s, one of the nation's first alternative schools, the St. Paul Open School, replaced high school graduation requirements with a set of a dozen graduation competencies. Rather than earning credit by spending a year in a course with a passing grade, the Open School developed a process by which students, teachers, and parents developed individualized plans for students to pursue each of the graduation competencies. Each year, students meet with school officials to determine whether satisfactory progress is being made toward the competencies, and plans are made to continue their work until they have satisfactorily achieved the competencies. This approach, developed over 25 years ago, continues today, and the competencies now total 18. Students continue to demonstrate, through a critical review process using parents and teachers, their achievement of the required competencies (see Table 7.2 in Chapter 7, p. 161).

Successful Transitions

With growing research on the danger points in adolescent development, greater attention is focusing on the transition from elementary schools to the middle school, the transition to high school, and the transition from high school to the world of work or college. Increasing numbers of high schools are creating 9th grade acade-mies, using the school-within-a-school concept or "teaming" to help 9th grade stu-dents make a successful transition. Many students, like those in High Schools That Work programs, start their freshman year with parents, students, and school officials meeting together to plan a six-year personalized plan for each student.

The Freshman Academy at Walled Lake Central High School in Michigan, has dramatically reduced 9th grade failure through providing a focused, comprehensive support network to every 9th grade student.

Acceleration Opportunities

Many at-risk youth arrive at the high school so far behind in graduation credits that without some method of accelerating their credit production, these students often become despondent and drop out of school. Many alternative schools provide stu-dents with opportunities to earn extra credit through independent study, evening school, Saturday school, summer school, and flexible scheduling. In recent years, summer-school programs have received increasing interest as state after state has established "barrier tests" and eliminated social promotion and high school graduation unless these exams are passed. Intensive summer-school programs are increasingly the most effective approach for quickly getting student achievement up to required levels (Abercrombie, 1999). Almost all effective high schools provide some type of high-school-equivalency exam process.

Programs to Promote Social and Emotional Growth

As described elsewhere, high schools must address the nonacademic side of educa-tion, including personal, social, and emotional development. The more high schools treat teenagers as young adults and provide them with opportunities for real respon-sibility, the more teenagers tend to develop positive attitudes, self-concepts, and behaviors.

While the agenda for high-school reform has emerged in a forceful way and is sup-ported by the U.S. secretary of education, influential governors, and national profes-sional organizations, the comprehensive high school continues to be the most change-resistant institution in our country. Institutional culture of the high school seems frozen in time. Yet, the high school years represent the final opportunity for public education to transform the lives of at-risk and violent youth. Only time will tell whether or not reform efforts will succeed in changing the American high school.

Chapter 9

Restructuring Public Education for At-Risk Youth: Three Approaches That Work

> *To those who would dismiss the idea that the solution to the problems of high school lies in the development of very small schools because they are too expensive, I recommend the following exercise. Imagine a school district modeled not on the practices of General Motors but on those of a cottage industry. The average per-pupil expenditure in this country is about $5,260 a year. Envision a small, highly autonomous school, given that funding level. If the school has 200 kids in it, its annual operating budget is over $1,050,000. Return 20 percent of it—$210,000—to a trimmed-down central administration for its reduced services and for bus transportation. Imagine a low student/teacher ratio, say 20:1. Pay your 10 teachers well, say an average of $45,000 a year (including fringe benefits). Hire a head teacher and pay him or her $60,000. Find an appropriate building for your program in your community and rent it at $7,000 a month plus another $3,000 for utilities. Hire a secretary, a custodian, and a cleaning person at $20,000 each. Budget $1,000 a year for supplies for each of your teachers and $3,000 for the central office. Put aside $10,000 to buy books each year and $20,000 for computers and A-V equipment. If the idea of trips is appealing, lease three vans, each at $5,000 dollars a year. That's probably enough to cover maintenance of them, but include another $3,000 just to be sure. Put $12,000 into a mileage budget. Now comes the fun: figuring out what to do with the $70,000 that has yet to be spent.*
> —GREGORY, p. 244

A significant change occurred during the last half of the 1990s in school reform and restructuring. Prior to this time, the focus on school reform and restructuring was on upgrading and improving public schools and then monitoring the test scores of students on the ACT, SAT, NAEP, and a variety of international achievement tests to determine the effects. As a result, the emphasis on school reform during the last three decades focused on developing new, more reliable curriculum materials; improving teacher education programs; integrating technology into school classrooms; restructuring the school day through block and modular scheduling and phase electives; and implementing new instructional approaches such as cooperative learning and team teaching. State legislators and Boards of Education attempted school reform through increasing the number of credits needed for high school graduation and expanding the requirements for teacher certification. Private foundations, such as Carnegie, Ford, Kettering, and Mott, provided massive funding to develop a variety of innovative programs. Unfortunately, most of these reform efforts have come and gone.

Few of these efforts were even partially successful in changing or significantly restructuring the public schools of the country. For more than thirty years, the institutional culture of public education and local control have rendered the best efforts at school reform ineffective or a failure. Some scholars even argued that existing schools were so entrenched that change, even rather modest change, was next to impossible.

In the mid-1990s, a major shift in school reform occurred, and by the year 2000, the impact of this change was being felt throughout the country. In effect, the "bottom line" came to public education, and the single, overriding issue became, not if schools had been improved or restructured, but whether or not there was accurate, reliable evidence that students were learning effectively and achieving high academic standards. The focus changed from simply improving and/or restructuring schools to evaluating the effects of these efforts on student learning. As a result, teacher education, staff development programs, curriculum materials, the use of technology, instructional approaches, and whole-school improvement approaches, were suddenly being scrutinized regarding their impact on student achievement. The bottom line has become: Show me the evidence that all students are learning.

From School Improvement to Student Achievement

Since the early 1980s, there has been a proliferation of reports, monographs, books, articles, special journal issues, symposia, media and video productions, community forums, and scholarly debates on educational reform. Unfortunately, too many of the recommendations have proven to be wrong and may have actually inhibited or misdirected educational improvement. Some of the reform literature has been authored by the very people who support the practices of retention, tracking, expulsion, and continue to ignore the dropout problem. Many of these individuals presume to prescribe how public schools can be reformed and restructured.

The critical problem that continues to pervade the "how to do it" reform literature is that few of the authors have ever been involved in actually restructuring and improving schools. Far too many of these "reformers" appear to be unaware of schools that have been restructured, and to equate a reform "effort" with a single "success." Few report evaluative student assessment data. Check it out. In paper after paper, chapter after chapter, book after book of reform literature, look for even a name of a restructured school, let alone an address or phone number. The inverse is also true. If the reform literature has been written by someone who has been intimately involved in school restructuring, has a documented track record of success in school improvement, and who can identify schools, providing names and locations, then what you find might be of great value. Sadly, this informed group of educators and scholars represents a small minority of the vast array of educational reform literature available today.

The best and perhaps the only effective approach to school improvement may be to identify schools that have been reformed or restructured and that have demonstrated their success at educating all children and youth. This literature regarding schools that have been successfully restructured is impressive and growing. It is not only possible to identify projects and programs that have been successful in enhancing student achievement, research has also documented the elements in their programs that seem to make them so successful (see Chapter 5), as well as the strategies used in developing and implementing the programs. It is now possible to develop a composite of effective reform strategies by studying the improvement process used by such programs as Success for All, High Schools That Work, Alternative Schools, and Turnaround Schools. After carefully studying dozens of these schools' efforts and the accompanying long-term research and education data from their programs, and after carefully reviewing research reports from the Education Trust, the U.S. Office of Education, the Regional Educational Labs, various research centers and institutes from throughout the country as well as the works of concerned scholars, including Robert Slavin, James Comer, Hank Levin, Gary Wehlage, Michael Fullan, Joe Nathan, Phil Schlechty, Barbara Wasik, Wayne Jennings, Nancy Karweit, Ted Sizer, Mary Ann Raywid, Nancy Madden, John Goodlad, and others, three distinctive approaches to school reform have emerged. These approaches should serve to inform and guide communities and public educators in transforming schools from where they are to where they need to be.

Before exploring the approaches for effective school reform, it is important to first offer a word of caution about where to work, what to expect, and what not to do. The recent shift toward the use of student achievement as an accountability measure for evaluating the performance of schools must be acknowledged. Yet while student achievement has emerged as perhaps the single most essential criterion in school reform, there are ten caveats that must be considered and acknowledged throughout an improvement effort.

The Focus Must Be the School

Research has helped to define the limits of educational reform. The majority of effective reform efforts have focused not on teachers or individual classrooms but on the school. In an increasing number of states throughout the country, new academic standards and new high-stakes testing are being used to try and ensure the effectiveness of all schools. Nonetheless, the reform literature continues to focus on the individual school as ultimately responsible for improving student achievement. The best place to focus reform energies is on restructuring individual schools.

School Reform Must Be Comprehensive

School reform that focuses simply on one aspect of school life is not likely to be successful. In schools that have significantly improved their effectiveness with at-risk youth, reform efforts have focused on classroom instruction as well as school climate (Teddlie & Stringfield, 1993). Such a comprehensive approach is common to successful school reform efforts. It is found in Success For All Schools, High Schools That Work, alternative public schools, as well as most successful reform efforts. Levin has maintained that successful school restructuring must focus on the total school: "Essentially, we believe that successful efforts at restructuring must address all three legs of a triangle that encompasses the schools' organization, curriculum and instruction. Efforts that address only one or two of these legs will fall flat and fail" (Levin, 1993, p. 2). Similar conclusions have been drawn by Regional Educational Lab, the Education Trust, and research on charter schools. Research on school-reform efforts also recommends that to help at-risk youth, there must also be goals that encourage community and social services to join in efforts to improve schools.

Be Cautious of Imposing Educational Reform

It is essential to understand that educational reformers have long maintained that change cannot be imposed, mandated, or legislated, unless teachers, administrators, and community members agree with the reform effort. School reform has not often been accomplished by passing legislation, hiring a new superintendent or principal, establishing a new board policy, or requiring a new curriculum. As the noted architect Frank Lloyd Wright was once reported to have said, "From the ground up makes good sense for building. Beware of from the top down" (Wehlage et al., 1989, p. vii). But while efforts to improve school reform have a poor track record of success, the more recent approach of establishing high academic standards, assessing student achievement at the school level, publicly reporting school effectiveness, and implementing a variety of incentives and sanctions seems to be having a dramatic effect.

Reform Is a Complex, Long-Term Process

Educational reformers have often proceeded as if they were using the H. L. Mencken quote, "For every complex question there is a simple answer." Unfortunately, they ignore Mencken's conclusion that the simple answer is invariably wrong. There is nothing simple or easy about school reform. It must be understood that educational change is a complex, personally demanding, and long-term affair. Most comprehensive school reform programs estimate that it takes four to six years to implement their program. Michael Fullan asserts that an elementary school can be restructured in three years, a secondary school in six years, and a school district in eight years (Fullan, 2000). Creating alternative public schools may be somewhat faster, yet most scholars believe that it still takes at least three years to fully implement an effective new alternative program. Based on the Louisiana School Effectiveness Study, researchers concluded that "school improvement programs almost always take a minimum of three years to affect student achievement. Most school improvement programs should probably be conceived as a five-year process. . . . Moreover school improvement never ceases, since schools are always headed toward greater or lesser effectiveness" (Teddlie & Stringfield, 1993, p. 226). Teachers, administrators, and community members need to recognize from the outset that educational reform will not happen quickly. Success will require many years of personally challenging responsibility.

Large School Size Is a Fatal Flaw in School Restructuring Efforts

While there are many examples of elementary schools and some small middle schools and high schools that have been significantly restructured, it is very difficult to identify large comprehensive high schools in the United States or Canada that have been successfully restructured. Large school size appears to militate against significant educational reform. Considerable evidence supports this conclusion. The first five-year evaluation of the Coalition for Essential Schools reported little or no significant restructuring in the large, comprehensive high schools that made up this project (Muncey & McQuillan, 1993), and more recent evaluations have proven no more encouraging (Slavin & Fashola, 1998). It is interesting to note that, in the case studies of 14 schools with special at-risk programs, the only school that was dropped from the study was a large comprehensive high school in Atlanta: "this program was found to be indistinguishable from other conventional comprehensive high schools. The special program's impact on students was minimal or even negative" (Wehlage et al., 1989, p. 244). A high-school faculty of 80 teachers in Fairbanks, Alaska concluded two years of discussions and planning by voting down a proposal to modestly rearrange the daily schedule to create a weekly 90-minute planning and collaboration period. The school administrators and the teachers' union had agreed to implement the reform if 60 percent of the faculty voted approval. Only 58 percent supported the change, blocking the opportunity to jointly plan and collaborate toward improving the school. The good news is that significant change has occurred in some large comprehensive junior/middle schools and high schools, especially in the High Schools That Work Program. Nonetheless, school size represents a significant barrier to school reform.

Some Schools May Be All But Impossible to Improve

Research has documented that some schools stringently resist change. Teddlie and Stringfield stress that "an ineffective school did not get that way overnight—each has a unique history" (1993, p. 224). Such schools often have a long tradition of dysfunctional interpersonal relationships and an abnormal school culture. Some schools may be found in the midst of such negative community pressures that the only way to improve the school is to try to "create boundaries to buffer the school from negative influences" (1993, p. 37).

This is not to say that all schools cannot try to face change and improve. It is to say that some will face greater challenges. Some school reform efforts may demand the assignment of a new principal or reassignment of teachers, intensive team building by an external consultant, extensive work with community members, and long-term staff development (1993).

School Reform Requires Adequate Funding

School reform must have sufficient resources. Yet adequate finances for education continues to emerge as the most significant problem facing most communities. The Gallup Poll of the public attitudes about schools, cites inadequate funding as clearly the "single biggest problem for local schools" (Elam, Gallup & Rose, 1993, p. 138). 1993 was the first year Gallup polling found that inadequate funding was identified as the number one issue in U.S. education. This concern has continued throughout the decade. The process of improving a school will require short-term expenditures for staff development, research, and planning. Long-term improvements may well rest on the success of the school or district in abandoning ineffective practices in order to redistribute the available funding.

No School Is an Island

What goes on inside a school cannot be separated from what occurs in the community that surrounds it. Schools tend to be a reflection of their community. No one has helped to dramatize this interrelationship so well as James Comer. He has championed the idea that it is just as important to try to rejuvenate community pride and togetherness as it is to improve the local school. His work offers a vivid tribute to the effectiveness of establishing strong, supportive ties between the neighborhood school and the neighborhoods.

Plans for school improvement, reform, or significant restructuring must be concerned with the pressures beyond the classroom which exert powerful influences, both positive and negative, on the school. This may mean increasing school security by using metal detectors to keep weapons out of the school; it may mean rigid restrictions on school clothing to keep gang colors out of the hallways; it may mean school community planning and governance teams; it may mean local alliances with government, churches, and youth groups; and it may mean the coordination of social services.

Educators and others attempting to improve schools must also remember that any significant effort to reform or restructure or even improve schools usually results in vigorous protests from some segment of the community. Opposition may come from religious fundamentalists of the radical right or the American Civil Liberties Union on the liberal left or from anyone from the Catholic Church to university historians (Molnar, 1993). Unfortunately, school improvement plans to address the most urgent needs of at-risk youth seem to bring out the most vocal reactions, for they often include controversial responses: free condoms, planned parenthood, and safe sex versus abstinence; Just Say No versus careful use; traditional values versus alternative gay lifestyles. Community groups have often focused on censoring textbooks and library books, attacking values clarification and secular humanism. More recently, parent and community groups throughout the community have generated concern regarding outcome assessments as some type of subtle, evil means of undermining U.S. youth.

The only way to ensure successful school reform is to incorporate broad-based community involvement and support from the very beginning. More than any other institution, the school is a mirror of the community. To change the school is to change the community. Yet schools cannot be timid in their work of addressing the massive problems associated with at-risk youth. When schools and communities do work together, dramatic improvements can and will occur.

It May Be Easier to Start a New School

Given the long-term difficulty in transforming and restructuring existing schools, it may be more cost effective to start "new" schools. Certainly the success of alternative public schools, magnet schools, and charter schools documents the advantages of creating new schools. By creating new alternative schools that are staffed with teachers and administrators who choose to participate in a particular educational program, and are available to students and parents on a voluntary basis, dramatic restructuring can usually occur much faster than in existing schools.

Use Effective Characteristics as a Blueprint for School Reform

The essential elements of effective schools for at-risk youth that have been identified by research serve as a powerful model for school reform. No longer must a community "reinvent" the educational wheel. The essential elements can be used as a blueprint for strategic planning and long term school reform.

These ten caveats must be considered to effectively launch an improvement effort. Next, while there may be hundreds of clever strategies to improve some aspect of classroom instruction or successfully reform some portion of the entire school, too often these random acts fail to impact an entire school and are often very difficult to sustain. There are three specific comprehensive approaches to restructuring public education that have an impressive track record of success, particularly for youth at risk. Each of these approaches has been successfully replicated, and they provide a blueprint for any school district or community concerned with improving schools to better teach all youth. The first approach is using state standards and student achievement assessment to improve student performance. The second approach, restructuring existing schools, focuses on transforming K–12 schools and represents the greatest challenge to implement. The third approach focuses on school choice and involves a complex variety of activities involved in the creation and replication of diverse models of alternative, magnet, and charter schools. While one of the approaches, that of developing school choice, especially the development of alternative public schools, has been used successfully for more than 25 years, the other two have a much shorter but impressive record of success.

Each of these approaches can be unusually effective in significantly improving or restructuring schools, yet none is easy. Each of the approaches is complex, time-consuming, and fraught with pitfalls. Each has a number of common characteristics, including community involvement, coordinating social services, networking, and school-community consensus building, yet distinctive factors that also set them apart. Finally, all three approaches require years of effort to realize potential. Despite the challenges, these approaches work, and can be used to create or improve schools where all children and youth, particularly those at-risk, can learn and succeed.

The State Accountability Approach

The newest and perhaps the most widespread approach to school restructuring and improving student achievement involves state policy makers establishing demanding new standards for public education. Rather than trying to "improve" schools, state policy makers in many states are now focusing on student achievement. This bottom-line approach to education reform has proven unusually powerful. By the end of the 1990s, many states, including Alabama, Florida, Louisiana, New Mexico, North Carolina, South Carolina, Texas, Washington, and West Virginia, required all public schools to use state-mandated student-achievement assessments to determine whether elementary school children would be promoted. Over twenty states have or will soon have high-school graduation exams aligned with state standards (Education Commission of the States, 1998). And while each state has approached the issue somewhat differently, there are a number of characteristics that tend to define this approach:

- establishment of high academic standards for K–12 public education
- alignment of curriculum, instructional materials and strategies, assessments and teacher professional development with the standards
- restructuring of governance, accountability, and finance to help schools/school districts have the necessary capacity, incentives, and supports to help all students achieve the standards

Other features of this approach to school reform are far more controversial. Most states publish the student achievement-test scores for their schools. Texas and Kentucky assign each school a rating. Texas uses dropout rates, attendance rates, and the percentage of students in grades 3, 8, and 10 passing each of the reading, writing, and math portions of the Texas Assessment of Academic Skills (TAAS). Texas has discovered that publishing the ranking for each school (exemplary, recognized, acceptable, and low performing), seems to provide a powerful incentive for schools to improve their student performance. The number of schools that have improved their performance and thus their ranking has been described by the Education Commission of the States as "quite remarkable" (1998). Student achievement across the board and in all subgroups has increased substantially throughout the state of Texas.

Implementing new state standards and assessments provides schools and school districts with a dramatic wake-up call. When students first take the test and see their school's achievement reported for all the world to see, it is inevitably a shock for low-performing schools. When Virginia first began student assessment, fewer than 2 percent of the schools in the state passed the test. In almost every state, when the first test results were reported, school districts began scrambling to get policy makers to "factor" in their local demographics. Others pleaded to show "improvement" rather than how well their students did in obtaining specified achievement levels, and many alternative schools that had served as "rescue missions" to keep kids off the street and passing GED exams, now discovered that policy makers expected their students to perform up to state standards. Policy makers, increasingly better informed of educational research, have learned that all students can learn effectively and they expect all schools to perform, even high-risk students in schools in poor communities. In a growing number of states, bitter controversies have erupted, especially in minority communities where student achievement testing is viewed as a racist attempt to punish the most needy students.

Some states have also implemented a variety of other "get tough" regulations. In addition to publishing school test results and prohibiting social promotion and graduation, some states often close or reconstitute low-performing schools that are unable or unwilling to improve.

Because of the enormous complexity and cost of the standards-based approach to school reform, the efforts in the various states have been uneven and wracked with controversy. In 1995 the American Federation of Teachers (AFT) and later the Council for Basic Education (CBE, 1997) and the Fordham Foundation (1998), all conducted state-by-state evaluations of content standards. All three groups generally agreed that "A significant number of the states' content standards are models of clarity and rigor, but a large number of these states had established standards that were vague and of 'inadequate quality'" (Education Commission of the States, 1998a, p. 4).

The Mid-Continent Regional Education Lab and Archive, one of the nation's federally supported regional educational laboratories, serves as a national clearinghouse on standards, assessment, accountability, and technology and helps states to benchmark their standards.

Growing Concerns Regarding High-Stakes Testing

Student assessments have also been controversial. As explained earlier, many schools and school districts officially complained that standardized achievement tests could not properly assess student achievement, especially since the exams were being used as "high stakes" barriers to promotion and, in some cases, graduation. There were also incidents of lax test security in some school districts. State testing using a single standardized test led to a number of other problems and concerns during the last years of the 1990s.

- **Testing errors.** Testing companies made a number of serious mistakes, including losing student test results and having to retest students.
- **Teacher anxiety.** Many teachers felt humiliated by the public reporting of their students' achievement scores. So frustrating and anxiety producing was the state testing program in North Carolina that slightly more than 50 percent of the teachers in the state reported that they would consider changing jobs or changing schools if their school was designated as low performing. Most teachers in the state, 89 percent, reported that they felt labeled as a result of end-of-grade tests (Jones et al., 1999). The perceived threat to their feelings of competence has led to low morale among teachers.
- **Teaching to the test.** With teachers' emotions and anxieties running high, it is no wonder that many appear to abandon their existing curricula to pursue instructional programs that narrowly focus on raising test scores. And while most teachers would never consider "teaching for the test," in North Carolina, 80 percent of the teachers indicated that their students spent more than 20 percent of their instructional time practicing for the end-of-year test. More than 28 percent indicated that they spent more than 60 percent of instructional time having students practice for the test. More than 70 percent indicated that they and their students are spending more time practicing for end-of-year tests than in the past (Jones et al., 1999).
- **Disagreement over effectiveness.** Such an investment in preparing students for the test might be justified if the tests truly measured what educators and government leaders established as goals. Unfortunately, the nation's leading assessment experts have warned repeatedly that a single, standardized, multiple-choice test simply cannot measure what policy makers are hoping to achieve—the identification of students with greater knowledge and more sophisticated ways of using the knowledge. While there may be a new science of learning emerging, unfortunately, the science of testing and assessment lags far behind. As Anne C. Lewis, columnist for the *Kappan* has concluded, "The science of creating reliable assessments that get at students' genuine mastery of content isn't there yet, though researchers are scrambling to meet the demand" (1999a). Assessment expert Rich Stiggins concludes, "Despite the rush to standardized testing, there is a growing understanding and sophistication in utilizing a variety of assessments, including portfolios, performance competition, project learning, exhibitions, and other forms of authentic assessments (Stiggins, 1999).
- **Student anxiety.** If teachers experience high frustration, stress, and anxiety regarding end-of-year tests, students are affected even more seriously. Many teachers in North Carolina felt that more than 60 percent of their students felt more anxiety, and 24 percent felt that their students were now less confident. Almost 50 percent of the teachers studied worried that the testing program

would negatively impact students' love of learning, and many teachers reported fearing that their students would begin to suffer emotional effects like vomiting and crying, characteristics of high-stakes testing in Japan (Jones et al., 1999).

- **Lack of consistency/equity.** Some schools/school districts have been found to exclude large groups of poor and special education students from the tests in order to improve their schools' performances. And, unfortunately, social class continues to be the single most important variable in predicting scores on achievement tests. In North Carolina, 20 percent of the variance in a school's performance on end-of-year tests could be explained by the percentage of students in free and reduced lunch programs (Jones et al., 1999).

Accountability, by comparison, is an emotionally charged and controversial approach to school reform. Only time will tell whether or not more complex and authentic forms of assessment can be developed and successfully implemented.

The challenge of course, for state policy makers is not only to develop and implement standards and assessments, but to use these approaches as "tools" in achieving their described goals. These goals should include:

- documenting improved student learning
- improving teaching practices
- facilitating opportunities to learn from experiences with different types of schools
- establishing an understandable public accountability system
- increasing the efficiency of decision making with the effective use of learning across the educational system (Education Commission of the States, 1998)

Restructuring Existing Schools

It once was the accepted belief in the education profession that a school could not be changed. In Seymour Sarason's influential book *The Culture of School and the Problem of Change* (1971), he concluded that it was easier to start a new school than change an existing one. An even greater concern emerged from the Ford Foundation. After a multi-million-dollar model-school reform effort, the foundation concluded in a report entitled, *A Foundation Goes to School* (Nachigal, 1972) that their money and influence had little lasting effect on school effectiveness. And, in so many instances, the school reform goal was to "improve" schools through a wide variety of creative efforts, but until recently few ever seriously asked the salient question: Did students in fact learn more effectively?

The 1990s ushered in an entirely new approach to school reform. This effort included comprehensive schoolwide reform efforts that were designed to improve student achievement. Many of these efforts were well-organized projects that included curriculum materials, teacher training, consensus building and visioning, parental involvement, agreed-upon mission and goals, and agreements to monitor the impact of these efforts on students' achievement over time.

By the late 1990s the measure that had emerged in evaluating the success of school-reform efforts was not what structural changes had been made, how teachers had been retrained, or on what new instructional materials were being used. The new standard for school reform focused on evidence of student achievement. This new standard represented one of the most significant historical "sea changes" for public education and signaled a new age of school reform. (Sea Change, Fall, 1999). As a result, school reform efforts were immediately categorized into those successful in influencing student achievement, those that had promising effects, and those that had little or no evidence to document their effectiveness. And, for the states that had established new academic standards and high-stakes testing, the pressure suddenly escalated for *all* students to learn effectively, regardless of socioeconomic level. Those schools that were not successful were identified as low-performing schools, and a variety of incentives, supports, and punitive actions followed.

The good news is that the traditional conclusions regarding educational reform have been reversed. We now have thousands of schools that have demonstrated the ability to teach all students, including many who were previously enrolled in low-performing schools. By the year 2000, we know that existing public schools can be changed and student achievement can be remarkably increased.

The most difficult, most demanding, and most time-consuming approach to school reform is to attempt to change or improve an existing school. Yet, because it focuses on improving the existing schools of the nation, it must be considered as the most important challenge. So difficult is the process that many who have attempted this approach have concluded that it was impossible to change an existing school. Because of this, these educational reformers focused their energies on creating new alternative public schools. Today the idea that existing schools cannot be changed has been challenged by a growing number of schools that have demonstrated significant progress in student achievement. Yet evidence of just how hard it is to change existing schools continues to be reported.

Difficulty in Changing Existing Schools

A report from the University of Wisconsin Center on Organization and Restructuring of Schools reported that three separate studies recently provided rather discouraging results regarding school reform and restructuring. In one study, 6,000 individuals throughout the nation were solicited to identify schools that had been restructured. Two hundred and sixty-eight elementary schools, middle schools, and high schools were selected for the study. Each of the schools was investigated to determine the extent to which the schools had implemented 38 school restructuring concepts (heterogeneous grouping, students participating in small group work, integrated disciplines, differentiated staffs, collaborative relationships with parents and human services, etc.). Of the 38 factors studied, less than half were frequently reported being used via telephone interviews with principals and through written questionnaires. Even more discouraging, "subsequent site visits revealed that the frequency of fulfillment was only about half that concluded from in-depth interviews, i.e., in practice, many schools fell short of their principals' descriptors of restructuring" (Center on Organization and Restructuring of Schools, 1992, p. 2.) For example, 92 percent of the principals reported that their schools used heterogeneous grouping, but only 55 percent were found to use this approach during on-site visits. And remember, these were schools that had claimed to be outstanding examples of restructuring.

In a second study that explored the use of 16 characteristics of restructured schools in 1,037 middle-grade schools, the vast majority (44.6 percent) reported using only one to five of the 16 restructuring concepts. An additional 34.7 percent reported using only six to eight concepts (1992). The conclusion of these two studies, plus one other which reviewed over 100 proposals randomly selected from 16,000 proposals submitted to R. J. R. Nabisco Foundation for school reform projects, was that "the elements of school restructuring are not being widely accepted. . . . It is difficult to find schools in the nation that have been comprehensively restructured" (1992, p. 4). In fact, there seems to be a vast number of educators who are unable to conceptualize a restructured school. One explanation for the small number of schools funded by the New American Schools Development Corporation was the lack of creative proposals (Mecklenburger, 1992).

The most recent study, based on a survey of 3,380 high school principals, reported that school reform efforts were "spotty", with "few schools . . . attempting systemic reform" (Viadero, 1994, p. 1). Only 32 percent of the schools were involved in or planning comprehensive professional development programs to assist teachers in implementing curricular changes. Only seven of the 3,380 school principals surveyed reported comprehensive reform efforts were being used.

These findings are similar to the conclusions reported in the research and evaluation of one of the nation's premiere restructuring efforts, the Coalition of Essential Schools. The conclusion of the Essential Schools research was devastating: "although our research spent nearly five years, the structure, dominant pedagogy, and disciplinary divisions of American secondary schools have remained relatively unchanged for nearly a hundred years" (Muncey & McQuillan, 1993, p. 489). More recent evaluations have documented a similar conclusion (Slavin & Fashola, 1998).

A large number of schools, especially at the elementary level, have been able to document significant improvements in learning, but the actual number of schools that have been significantly restructured is relatively small. At the middle- and high-school levels, restructured schools are even more difficult to find. The good news is that recent research has documented a growing number of schools at all levels that have completed restructuring efforts and are successfully teaching all students effectively. Not only do we now know that existing schools can be restructured, there is consistent research evidence documenting how this challenging task can be accomplished.

Challenges to Restructuring Existing Schools

While success can be demonstrated in improving schools and to a lesser extent in restructuring existing schools, there are a number of factors that must first be recognized, understood, and overcome if the approach is to be successful. These factors relate directly to school size and the fact that most school faculties in existing schools have been assembled over the years with little regard to personal beliefs, commitment to educational philosophy, or preference for particular instructional approaches. The mix of different and often conflicting beliefs coupled with large school size and entrenched teaching staffs tends to paralyze and inhibit significant school reform.

Conflicting Beliefs Regarding School Reform

Many of the teachers in any existing school will not believe that school restructuring is necessary. Most teachers and administrators believe that they are being effective and that they enjoy a reputation for having a quality school. Researchers have been surprised to discover that "even in schools that are characterized by poor atten-dance, low scores on standardized tests, and high drop-out and failure rates—schools in which outsiders might assume that there would be consensus about the need for change, there was none." (Muncey & McQuillan, 1993, p. 489). Inevitably, the faculty of schools such as these blame conditions in society; the increasing num-bers of special education, at-risk, and minority students in their classes; and insuffi-cient resources for the school's shortcomings. Often, when school restructuring projects get under way, the efforts are supported by only a few teachers and admin-istrators. Even under the best of circumstances, there are always teachers who adamantly oppose restructuring efforts and who are offended by the implication that they are not doing an effective job. In almost every restructuring effort, one can hear teachers and administrators complain, "if only we could get rid of a few teachers, then we could be successful."

To address this problem, schools must be involved in long-term consensus building, and even then all of the teachers will most likely not be in complete agree-ment. School districts need to provide some type of nonpunitive, incentive-based transfer procedure that allows teachers to move to other school locations where their beliefs and practices are more congruent and compatible. More recently, school faculty who have been unwilling or unable to improve their effectiveness have been replaced through school reconstitution.

Conflicting Educational Beliefs

Faculty of any existing school will have very different philosophical and method-ological beliefs about teaching and learning. Until a school initiates a restructuring or improvement effort, teachers and principals rarely discuss different teaching and learning styles, instructional approaches, or educational philosophies. So often these issues are only discussed in university teacher education courses and too often are felt to represent little more than idealistic theory that has little to do with the day-to-day demands of the real world of schools and classrooms. When serious efforts at school improvement or restructuring get underway, significant and often diametri-cally opposed beliefs begin to emerge. As long as teaching is isolated, with individ-ual teachers doing their own thing behind their classroom doors, a school can function with dramatically diverse types of teachers. It is only when schoolwide goals and processes are discussed that fundamental disagreements often appear. The disagreements can often develop into serious divisions within a faculty. These conflicts are often exacerbated when those representing the emerging reform philosophy are felt to have more administrative support, added resources, and more recognition. Deep personal resentments can and often do emerge.

Once again, long-term consensus building coupled with intensive staff development is essential, but even then, incentive-based transfer policies may be necessary to assist schools and communities to develop schoolwide plans for restructuring.

Creating Smaller Schools

School size has been identified as one of the most significant factors in school effectiveness and school reform. Given the lack of success public education has experienced in attempting to restructure large schools, the focus of school reform of comprehensive middle and high schools must be on creating smaller schools (i.e., schools within schools, alternative public schools, or satellite programs). Large schools must be divided into small enough units so that teacher consensus can be developed.

Professional Development for Experienced Teachers

Most existing school staffs are composed of a majority of mature, experienced teachers. In most schools in the United States, the average teaching experience is approximately 15 years, which means that a school faculty is composed of significant numbers of teachers who are well established in their own particular instructional approach. Many have not actively participated in professional development courses or conferences for more than a decade and certainly long before the revolution in technology. As described in earlier chapters, the process of preparing these teachers to participate in distinctive new ways of teaching and learning is similar to that of deprogramming and can only occur through careful, long-term professional development.

Essential Strategies for Restructuring Existing Schools

In spite of the difficult problems facing school restructuring and improvement, there is sufficient research data available today to conclude without question that existing public schools can be changed and significantly improved. This conclusion is consistent with the major educational research that has been completed during the last decade. Studies have documented that the factors that make a difference between effective and ineffective schools are constant regardless of the type of student population they are serving or the socioeconomic and geographic setting of the school (Teddlie & Stringfield, 1993; The Education Trust, 1999).

There are a growing number of successful efforts at restructuring existing schools that are being used today, and most of these efforts employ a similar set of strategies. A careful look at the process that is used in the major whole-school reform projects and in schools that have been independently restructured offers a number of specific strategies that should prove useful. These strategies can be effective in schools at all levels.

Implementing an Accountability Model

The single most effective approach to restructuring existing schools and improving student achievement is to develop school-district or school-level academic standards, or use state standards to design aligned curriculum and instruction, assess student work, and evaluate the effectiveness of teachers. Effective schools must also use a comprehensive system to monitor individual student progress and provide extra, intensive support to any and every student who needs it. Eighty percent of all high-performing, high-poverty schools studied recently by The Education Trust reported using standards to design instruction, assess students, and evaluate teachers (The Education Trust, 1999, p. 3). Similarly, four out of five top-performing high-poverty schools had systematic ways of identifying and providing early support for students in danger of falling behind in their instruction. Accountability models are even more effective when there are state or school-district consequences for teachers and administrators in schools in which students fail to show measurable academic improvement.

Focus on Schools That Are Already Improving

A review of the problems that are faced in reforming or restructuring existing schools helps to dramatize the fact that it is nearly impossible to change a school unless a sufficient percentage of the stakeholders in the school are interested and willing to participate actively. For that reason, it is obvious that some schools will be more difficult to change than others, and some schools might be impossible to change. Research has helped to verify that most schools are in a process of constant change. They are either getting better or getting worse. In the 10 years of the Louisiana School Effectiveness Study, researchers were able to document that some schools were effective, remained effective for 8 to 10 years, and seemed to be constantly improving. Other ineffective schools remained ineffective and even seemed to decline over the same period (Teddlie & Stringfield, 1993).

To ensure maximum success in school reform or restructuring efforts, schools should be carefully reviewed (data regarding achievement, attendance, retention, reading scores, etc.). Efforts should be made to identify schools with naturally occurring improvements; that is, schools that are attempting to improve their effectiveness on their own and are ready for additional restructuring efforts. In addition, communities' interest, responsiveness, and support should be given careful attention. Just as there are community forces that stimulate one school to improve, other settings may inhibit school effectiveness.

School improvement, reform, or restructuring efforts will be much more successful in schools where evidence of school improvement is already emerging. School reform should focus first on those who are trying to help themselves.

It is important to remember that measuring school effectiveness is extremely complex; it is necessary that assessment and evaluation focus on more than achievement test results. Thorough assessments should include evidence on attitudes and behavior as well as cognitive indicators (Teddlie & Stringfield, 1993). A growing number of effective schools have established graduation competencies, senior projects, and a wide variety of authentic assessments of student achievement (Darling-Hammond et al., 1995). It is not only important to measure and evaluate the impact of a program, it is essential that this information be widely shared and communicated. As mentioned earlier the state of Texas has found that publishing statewide student achievement-test scores for each school provides a built-in incentive for schools to improve their performance. Parents, teachers, and administrators, as well as central administrators, school board members, and even state legislators need to be informed regarding hard, accurate evidence that school changes are providing desired results. This type of evidence might include:

- *Improvement in test scores*
- *Statistics about behavioral changes such as dropout rates, attendance rates, disciplinary actions, and so on*
- *Information about increased parental, business, and community involvement*
- *Anecdotal information for teachers, students, administrators, and parents*
- *Information about interagency agreements and projects (social agencies, libraries, recreational districts, higher education institutions)*
- *Survey results*
- *Reallocation of resources. (Ledell & Arnsparger, 1993, p. 21)*

Schools can also assess student attitudes toward schools, self-esteem, and even parent attitudes. They also need to investigate various aspects of their program to discover what is working or what is not working and why. In Success For All schools, regular assessment alerts teachers when students are not responding effectively to instruction, and the school then increases the amount of time and the frequency of one-to-one tutoring.

There is no more important means of validating a school restructuring effort than to demonstrate and document the positive impact on student learning. With the data at hand, teachers, communities, and schools can no longer blame poor student learning on external social conditions. Schools and their teachers must teach all children, assess their learning, and be held strictly responsible for their effectiveness or lack of effectiveness.

School and Community Involvement and Coordination

Every successful school restructuring effort involves parents, and most include community leaders, agencies, institutions, and students. It is interesting to note that every reform project connects with the community in its own unique way. The Accelerated School Project convenes a group of parents, teachers, and students in a process that is called "visioning." Visioning is designed to establish a unity of purpose. It leads to a discussion of commonly held values and beliefs and provides the foundation for all that follows in the restructuring project. The Accelerated School Project attempts to include parents in every aspect of the school.

Comer's School Development Program attempts to reestablish and strengthen ties between the home and the school and is equally interested in strengthening the African-American community as it is in restructuring its neighborhood schools. Parental involvement is a central focus of the program. Parents are encouraged to serve as teacher-aides, participate in the school planning and management team, and are expected to sponsor a wide variety of events (potluck suppers, fashion shows, book fairs, etc.) that bring the school and community together. Comer believes that children's relationships with their teachers cannot be improved without drawing parents into the circle. A planning and management team to involve parents and the community is also vital to the Comer School Development Program. The team consists of 12 to 15 parents, teachers, school staff members, and one or more mental health specialists and is coordinated by the principal. Another group that is organized is called a mental health team. Membership on this team varies from school to school but usually includes a social worker, a school psychologist, a counselor, a school nurse, a speech and hearing teacher, and the principal (Comer, 1999).

The Success For All Program, likewise, involves parents in a variety of ways. The program includes a family support team that helps parents understand how they can ensure their children will succeed in school, promotes good attendance, trains parent volunteers, and assists with student behavior. The family support team also coordinates services from social service agencies. Parents are encouraged to read to their children 20 minutes each evening at home, participate as volunteers in the school, and serve on the building advisory committee.

Successful restructuring projects must incorporate a significant program of community involvement that includes parents in school planning and governance and provides for parent education, volunteers, and the coordination of social services. In minority neighborhoods, the school may also need to offer ESL classes or English lessons to parents, assist families with social and legal problems, and generally serve as parent and community advocates. Each of these efforts to involve the community and to coordinate social services relates directly to the essential characteristics of effective schools for at-risk youth defined in Chapter 5.

School-Based Empowerment

It is not enough to involve parents, teachers, school administrators, students, and social service representatives in collaboration and planning. Success in restructuring efforts demands that these groups be delegated authority for school-based decision making. The school collaboration groups must be empowered with authority to plan, make decisions, and implement their program. Schools that are successful in restructuring efforts are always empowered to change the curriculum, the school organization, and the instructional practices in their school. This means that school boards and central administrators must be actively involved in decentralizing and delegating power and authority. Each school and its community must be authorized to govern their school and be held accountable for achieving their school district instructional goals and abiding by state and local rules and regulations. Empowerment, of course, must be coupled with responsibility, and this means holding schools accountable for student achievement.

Consensus Building

Another essential ingredient in the formula for success in school restructuring is school and community consensus building. Because of issues described earlier in this chapter regarding the conflicting beliefs of teachers and the different perceptions regarding school reform, consensus building is absolutely essential to any successful restructuring plan. Involving parents, community leaders, and social service representatives in the process also seems to have a powerful effect on helping teachers come to agreement. While there are differences in every school setting, consensus building tends to include the following steps:

- *Review school and community data.* The first step in the consensus building process is to collect, summarize, and present data about the school and community to a collaboration team. This might include reading scores; achievement test scores; absentee rates; drop-out rates; incidence of crime, violence, vandalism, and school disruption; incidence of teen pregnancies; incidence of drug and alcohol abuse; unemployment rates; child abuse rates; etc. Collaboration groups are encouraged to discuss the data, talk about how they feel about these data and express their ideas and concerns.
- *Identify problems and establish schoolwide goals.* From the review and discussion of the school and community data, the collaboration team attempts to identify and prioritize problems and then work toward agreement on a number of areas of needed action. These goals are then circulated within the school and community, among students, teachers, parents, community leaders, and social service agencies. The goal is to gain widespread consensus regarding specific goals for the school restructuring effort. It is important for schools and communities to understand that school restructuring must focus on every aspect of the school. It must consider the community settings, parents, and social services, as well as instruction, curriculum, school organization and governance. School goals must reflect a comprehensive effort at restructuring. To focus on any one area is not likely to result in success. Often it is far easier to gain consensus regarding the problems to be addressed and the goals of the school than it is to gain agreement on a particular plan of action.
- *Develop a plan of action.* The collaboration team then works to establish a plan of action to achieve their goals, and each plan will be unique to the local school. The great advantage of being associated with a well-established school-reform project program is that these programs provide a solid framework of tested approaches that can be highly predictable of success. While none of these programs provides a cookie cutter approach to school reform, each provides a process or framework for improving or restructuring. Yet schools do not need to be part of an external reform project to be successful at improving their effectiveness. Research has identified schools where naturally occurring improvements have been organized locally with little or no external restructuring stimulation.

Often these naturally occurring improvements have been more significant than those in schools that have been part of a school district restructuring plan. If a school is not part of an established restructuring program, school representatives may need to attend conferences or workshops; develop a reading and discussion program; use consultants; work with university professors, technical assistance centers, and educational laboratories; and visit other restructured schools.

- *Ensuring schoolwide participation and support.* It is important for collaborative teams to devise an approach to keep the entire school and community informed, involved, and supportive. The Accelerated School Project does this by establishing a number of small cadres to address the specific issues of curriculum, instruction, and organization. These cadres report their recommendations to a school-community steering committee that reviews and discusses the recommendations and then in turn seeks schoolwide discussion, input and approval. This process continues as a circular involvement between the cadre, the steering committee, and the school and community as a whole.

As described earlier, it is important that the collaborative team and the rest of the school not fall into "us-them" divisions. In the first five-year study of the Coalition of Essential Schools, it was reported that the recognition and support given to the coalition planning teams caused deep resentment among other teachers. The research also found that the coalition planning teams naively believed that the rest of the school would agree with whatever plans they developed and were surprised when this did not occur. Apparently, some planning teams did not invest sufficient time in convincing their colleagues of the importance and the effectiveness of their proposal and controversy and contentiousness developed (Muncey & McQuillan, 1993). Another area of concern related to participation was identified by the Coalition of Essential Schools researchers. Some coalition schools felt that, after a school faculty voted to participate in a reform, there was little need for further schoolwide training or discussion. In some schools, there seemed to be little discussion in the school as a whole after the initial vote, and in time the reform program became a source of divisiveness throughout the school (Muncey & McQuillan, 1993). Both the Accelerated School Project and the Success For All Program require a 90 percent approval through a faculty vote before inviting a school to join their programs, and each approach requires extensive, long-term planning and involvement in training. These factors appear to be critical to enable a school to maintain school and community-wide support.

School Reform Requires Staff Development

Few aspects of the educational establishment have such negative connotations and evoke such bad memories as that of professional staff development. Typically, this effort is held in school cafeterias at the end of the day or on release days and is referred to as teacher in-service. Research has repeatedly documented the futility of such efforts. Significant school reform demands long-term effective staff development which provides for the development of new personal skills and time for the slow and often difficult process of consensus building. Even more encouraging is the fact that teacher education and staff development has been identified as one of the key reasons for improved student achievement.

Staff development and training are absolutely essential to the success of any school restructuring effort, especially with the faculty of an existing school. The major comprehensive school-reform programs require professional development. The Accelerated School Project requires participation in a weeklong training program at Stanford University for each leadership team. This program includes representatives from the school, the school district, and often a local university professor. This training is followed by weeklong staff development and collaboration efforts at the school prior to the beginning of the school year and regular meetings convened throughout the year by the local accelerated team. Accelerated School Project personnel provide periodic onsite assistance and support. The cost for implementing the Accelerated School program is approximately $130 per child per year in addition to the standard per pupil district-level support. The Success For All Program costs, for a school of 400 students including staff training, reading tutors, and curriculum materials, is approximately $350 per child per year. The Comer School Development Program works with existing district personnel and involves initial training, follow up coaching, networking, and biannual implementation reviews. The costs are $15,000 per participating district.

For schools not affiliated with an established model or network, effective staff development becomes even more essential to success, especially for schools in high-poverty areas (Education Trust, 1999). In the Louisiana School Effectiveness Study, the researchers stressed the importance for each local school to carefully assess the needs of teachers and administrators and to develop and implement a carefully designed staff development program. Based on their study, the Louisiana researchers concluded that staff development programs needed to be highly individualized because different teachers have very different needs. The study further emphasized the importance of allowing teachers to move to different grade levels until they found their most effective niche. The same was true for principals. For those unwilling to participate, involuntary re-assignment of principals and some teachers may be necessary (Teddlie & Stringfield, 1993).

Finally, the use of technology is critical to improving schools, and the effective use of technology in the classroom demands extensive retraining. Efforts to retrain regular classroom teachers to use clusters of four to five computers in their classroom often include a 20-day staff development program during the first year, repeated again during the second year. Additional staff development and training is likely to continue for a period of five to seven years before a successful transition to the use of technology in teaching is accomplished.

Time for Collaboration

To improve a school, dedicated planning time is essential. Unlike business and industry, which are able to close down to retool, schools usually attempt to retrofit themselves while continuing the day-to-day stress-filled demands of educating children and youth. Some have used the analogy of changing a flat tire while the car is moving to characterize the challenges of school improvement. Teachers contend with a daily schedule that typically permits only one preparation period, a required supervision assignment on playground, hallway, or bus stop, and the remaining 80 to 90 percent of the day leading classroom instruction. Elementary teachers are also often required to be with their students during the lunch time. There is simply no time for schoolwide or even departmentwide collaborative planning in the typical school. Successful schools work hard to provide teachers with time to discuss students, compare instructional approaches, design materials, conduct team planning, and critique one another. Inevitably this is one of the most challenging aspects of school reform, since teacher contracts usually limit the time that teachers can be away from the direct supervision of students. There are, however, a number of innovative approaches which schools can employ to create the critical time necessary for collaboration. Most of these approaches are relatively inexpensive and each of them has been used with success by creative local schools:

- *In order for teachers to have planning days together many schools develop partnerships with colleges or universities so that professors may serve as "teachers for a day."*
- *Some schools . . . have student volunteer service programs where students do volunteer work in their community for one afternoon each week. This provides a rich learning experience for the students while simultaneously providing time for teacher collaboration.*
- *In some large schools and school districts, contracts have been negotiated that increase class size by one or two students. This can yield funds for additional substitute teachers to free up faculty for collaboration.*
- *In some elementary schools, groups of teachers are provided with the same lunch period and a following planning period so that they can work together.*
- *Some school districts permit schools to use professional leave in one- and two-hour blocks rather than using them as entire days. Even three to five professional leave days per year can be scheduled over many weeks in short one- to two-hour blocks of time.*
- *Some schools have lengthened the school day by 20 minutes four days a week in order to dismiss students at noon on Friday and allow teachers to work together for half a day each week.*
- *Some schools schedule hobby days or activity days one day or one half day a week or on alternate weeks and use community volunteers to work with students in their interest areas. (Raywid, 1993b, pp. 31–33)*

One of the most useful ways for school boards or state legislators to help encourage school reform is by providing funding for additional substitute teachers and extended contracts to free up teachers for planning and collaboration.

Beyond the use of state accountability and the restructuring of existing schools approaches, one other approach has demonstrated unusual success in reforming public education. This approach requires the development of new models of public schools which become available to families and children by choice. Replicating alternative public schools will be described first, followed by creating and replicating charter schools.

These strategies do not attempt to change existing schools. Rather, they attempt to attract students, teachers, administrators, and parents who have shared beliefs about education to work together to create new public schools. All of the various stakeholders in these two approaches to restructuring voluntarily choose to partici-pate, and as a result, these schools begin with a spirit of consensus and collabora-tion. Because of this, planning time can be drastically reduced, at least in terms of disagreements that require conflict resolution. Collaboration time can thus focus on the actual design of the task of improving the school. In study after study over the past 20 years, the concept of choice has been identified as paramount to successful school restructuring efforts. The success of this approach in effectively educating all students, particularly those at risk, warrants immediate attention from any group or organization concerned with improving schools.

Reforming Public Education through School Choice

In the late 1960s and early 1970s Mario Fantini began calling for open enrollment and optional public schools. Since that time, public school choice has established a thirty-year track record of improving student achievement, improving attitudes, and helping high-risk students find success in public school and graduate. Over the years, the con-cept of school choice has evolved and expanded from a few small alternative schools for at-risk youth to include the widest possible variety of educational opportunities:

- Alternative or Optional Schools: A wide variety of established alternative schools that serve all types of students.
- Contract Schools: School districts "contract" with an organization or group to offer public education services. This includes everything from contracting with a Sylvan Learning Center to teach reading to arranging with a private organization to teach disruptive and/or suspended students.
- Career Theme or Technical Magnet Schools: Parents and students may achieve all high school graduation requirements by participating in a career-theme school that includes real work and service experiences.
- Open Enrollment Programs: Parents and their children may choose to attend another public school in their district, or a school in another district.
- Area Learning Centers: Established first in Minnesota, these learning centers are open during the day and the evening, are open year-round, serve K–12 stu-dents, provide for GED and child care, and are available to students on a full- or part-time basis.
- Charter Schools: Now available in thirty-six states and Washington, D.C., charter schools exchange many of the rules and regulations of public education for documenting student achievement.
- Voucher Programs: Currently three states have established voucher programs to provide scholarships to private schools for poor students "trapped" in low-performing schools.
- Home Schools: During the past 15 years, there has been a dramatic growth in home schooling and, more recently, combinations of home schooling and pub-lic schools. Most states require public schools to offer a variety of services, courses, and programs to home-schooled students.

- Internet Courses and Programs: During the past 10 years, there have been a growing number of courses, programs, and high school graduation programs available through the internet. These learning opportunities are offered by public schools, community colleges, universities, and private organizations.
- Blending High School with College: A number of states encourage high school students to begin taking college courses during the 11th and 12th grades. A number of states permit students to double-list the courses so that they meet high school graduation requirements as well as college requirements.

The goal of these various choice options has been to better serve the needs and interests of students and their parents, increase the range of educational opportunities available, and force public schools to compete for students.

In October 1999 a number of the nation's big-city mayors attended a meeting on charter schools, vouchers, and accountability conducted by the Manhattan Institute. John O. Norquist, mayor of Milwaukee, argued that in order to stem further middle-class flight to the suburbs and private schools, public education in large cities must provide parents with as much choice as they have in food and entertainment. "Choice is what cities are all about," he said. "Whatever you want, you're going to find more choice in cities" (White, 1999). Anthony A. Williams, mayor of Washington, D.C., praised charter schools because they had helped city school systems, "ramp up competition and decrease costs" (White 1999). Over 10 percent of the students in the D.C. public schools are currently enrolled in charter schools.

While most public schools in the United States may have only a few alternative schools for at-risk youth, the school-choice movement is gaining momentum. At least 29 states have established some type of open enrollment laws, 37 have established charter schools, four have established some type of tax credit or deduction, and three have created voucher programs all within the last decade (Ziebarth, 1999). The state of Minnesota, long one of the revolutionary leaders in public education, has established the widest possible set of school options. *The Choice Program Handbook,* 1998, published by the Minnesota Department of Children, Families, and Learning, is a comprehensive catalog of public-school choice programs available for parents and students. These choices include postsecondary enrollment programs; open enrollment; graduation incentives; diploma opportunities for adults over twenty-one; pregnant minors and minor parents programs; area learning centers; and charter schools. Many urban districts (Chicago, Louisville, Houston, Los Angeles, Portland, Seattle, Cleveland, and Milwaukee) offer a remarkable array of choice: alternative and optional programs, magnet programs, and schools within schools. Many now include charter schools, and some school districts offer some type of scholarship or voucher programs. These programs involve as many as 25 percent of the student body in these districts. A recent national study quoted in other places in this book, reported that nationwide as many as 25 percent of public-education students are currently involved in some type of optional program (Hardy, 2000). Charter schools alone are now serving as many as 1 to 2 percent of all public school students in a few states (Manno et al., 1999).

Unfortunately, even in school districts like Cleveland and Milwaukee, where many choice options are available, parents are unfamiliar with concepts like vouchers and charters. As one report stated, "While leadership debates on [school choice options] are thriving, most citizens have only the vaguest notion what terms like voucher and charter mean, much less how these ideas might affect their lives." For most people, even parents of school-age children, these terms are little more than, "something they saw something about in the newspaper" (Raspberry, 1999).

Choice in public education appears to be here to stay and is growing at a remarkable pace. For states, schools, and communities interested in establishing legislation to approve and fund charter schools, establish and fund at-risk alternative schools, and create alternative schools and career-theme schools, there is a growing "catalog" of effective optional educational models. Each of these models reflects the essential characteristics of effective schools, offers a national network of support, and provides a wide variety of established opportunities for authentic assessment (Barr & Parrett, 1997a). Most important, the creation of public-school options can effect an almost immediate restructuring of educational programs.

Starting and Replicating Alternative Schools

The most effective approach to school restructuring that has ever been developed is alternative public schools. Unfortunately, in too many school districts, despite decades of documented success, alternative schools are often viewed with suspicion by both professional educators as well as the general public (Wehlage et al., 1989; Barr & Parrett, 1997a). Yet the record of alternative school success is impressive.

Starting in the mid to late 1960s, a number of schools and communities in various parts of the country began to design new approaches to education, make them available by choice to parents and students, and implement programs such as alternative public schools within existing school districts. The first such schools tended to be dropout centers or dropout prevention schools, yet a few early alternative schools were so unique, so truly restructured, that they captured the attention of educators and the national media.

One of the first such schools was the Philadelphia Parkway School, where learning was planned to occur not in the school but in the banks, businesses, and museums up and down the Philadelphia Parkway. The school served all types of students and was described as a "school without walls." Another such creative school was the K–12 St. Paul Open School in Minnesota, which replaced course graduation requirements with learning competencies and developed a highly individualized approach to education. In Berkeley, California, a cluster of alternative schools were developed and implemented that attracted national attention. Other schools like Harlem Prep in New York, the Metropolitan Learning Center and Vocational Village in Portland, Oregon, and the Chicago Metro School were also soon in operation and attracting national attention. By the early 1970s, a wide variety of completely restructured schools were in operation in communities throughout the nation. At the time there was no state or federal program requiring, supporting, or even recognizing alternative public schools. There was not a single book on the topic. And, with the exception of a few isolated articles, these alternative schools were largely unrecognized.

Isolated and alone, these first alternative public schools quickly became the models for a movement to improve schools throughout the nation.

Indiana University became the first institution of higher education to identify and study these schools. They conducted the first descriptive research on these schools; created and published a newsletter entitled *Changing Schools*; published the first national directories of alternative public schools; developed a teacher education program designed to prepare teachers and administrators for the new roles that were emerging in alternative schools; and founded a national professional association, the National Consortium for Options in Public Education. Many of the early evaluations of alternative school effectiveness were conducted by researchers at Indiana University. The professors and their graduate students then began to collect evaluative studies from alternative schools throughout the country and publish research about these schools. Within a few short years, every major journal in America had published special issues on alternative schools. Even *Good Housekeeping* and other popular magazines had focused on this startling new development in public education.

While only a dozen or so alternative schools were in operation during the mid to late 1960s, by the mid 1980s there were over 15,000 of these schools in the United States, and today there are over twenty thousand of these schools serving 15 percent of all public school students (Hardy, February, 2000). The early scholars of alternative schools discovered that while alternative public schools represented a considerable range of diversity, and were being developed in communities largely isolated from one another, all of the schools shared a remarkably common set of characteristics:

- They were all small public schools with less than 500 students.
- They were usually designed to address the needs of a particular group of students (dropouts, potential dropouts, talented and gifted) or to reflect a particular educational philosophy (open schools, continuous progress schools, Montessori education, community based learning, etc.).
- They were available to parents, students, teachers, and administrators on the basis of voluntary choice.
- They attempted to match teaching and learning styles.
- Because of their experimental status, these schools were evaluated not only on student achievement but on other factors, including self-esteem, attitudes towards schools, and attendance rates. (Barr, 1972)

Early studies reported that these schools were among the first in America to establish agreed upon, schoolwide goals, and routinely measure the effectiveness of programs in achieving their goals (Raywid, 1983). For schools that were started primarily on the faith and confidence of small groups of teachers, administrators, and parents, the school evaluation and student assessment data that was reported was remarkably positive (see Chapter 8).

Building on a Track Record of Success
It is not surprising that the vast majority of these early alternative schools are still in operation today and the number of these schools continue to grow. In much the

same way that the High Schools That Work Program, Accelerated Schools, Success For All Schools, and the School Development Program have created effective models for replicating other schools, many alternative schools have likewise been models for the creation of other schools (Education Commission of the States, 1991). The Philadelphia Parkway School became the model for the Chicago Metro School and dozens of other schools without walls. Montessori alternative public schools were first tried in Cincinnati and Indianapolis in the 1970s and today can be found throughout the United States. The walkabout concept of the Learning Unlimited School in Indianapolis led Phi Delta Kappa to create a *Walkabout Newsletter* and training program that ultimately contributed to the development of dozens of similar schools nationwide. The Foxfire program which started in Rabun Gap, Georgia, in 1966 has now spread to over 1,000 urban, suburban, and rural schools across the country.

Dropout prevention programs using behavior contracts and individualized learning were replicated throughout the country. Teen parent schools have also developed strong, supportive organizations and now exist in school districts throughout the nation. The St. Paul Open School that pioneered graduation competencies later influenced the development of Minnesota's Community Learning Centers Network and other schools throughout the country. The out-of-school learning experiences used by schools without walls, Learning Unlimited, and the St. Paul Open School likewise led directly to documenting the power and effectiveness of action learning and contributed to the expansion of the concept into the Executive High School Internship Program, volunteer service programs, youth-tutoring-youth programs, and others. The success of the School for the Performance Arts in Cincinnati quickly led to the creation of similar magnet schools in many major cities in the United States. Alternative schools, operating under the umbrella concept of magnet schools, have been the focus of national conferences and training sessions and have provided a rich body of research which has helped expand this concept throughout the nation's major cities (Estes et al., 1990; Waldrip et al., 1993; Barr & Parrett, 1997a). Today there are more than two dozen established models being used for alternative and magnet schools. Models include open schools, Montessori schools, career academies, multiple-intelligence schools, and adventure-based programs.

Recent summaries of research continue to document the strength of the alternative public school concept as an approach to significant restructuring. Tim Young, in *Public Alternative Education: Options and Choice For Today's Schools,* has identified eight characteristics of alternative schools which should be considered in any school restructuring effort.

1. *Public schools of choice typically demonstrate a willingness to innovate and experiment. They are frequently on the cutting edge of educational issues and change.*
2. *Alternative schools are close to their clients (parents and students), attending to a variety of academic and nonacademic needs through the stated concern for the whole student.*
3. *Their smallness allows greater program autonomy and decision making than is the case in most conventional schools.*

4. *Treating students with respect, emphasizing group cooperation rather than individual competition, and extending appropriate reward structures are hallmarks of public schools of choice. Student success is not dependent on the failure of others.*

5. *The smallness of schools of choice facilitates a common set of shared values and goals among students and staff.*

6. *By not attempting to be all things to all people, schools of choice can specialize in and concentrate on what they do well. The student clientele served and curriculum offered are frequently limited, narrowly defining the school to focus on the most important and immediate needs of students.*

7. *Most public schools of choice are small. They operate with a simple organization and lean staff.*

8. *Although they operate within the guidelines of the central school district, they are able to exercise considerable individual autonomy. Sometimes that autonomy is the result of neglect by the central administration. More often, however, it is the recognition of expertise and effectiveness. (Young, 1990, p. 51)*

Alternative and Magnet Schools Today

Today alternative public schools continue to grow and expand. A number of state associations have been developed that support alternative schools, and they exert growing pressure on school boards, state departments of education, and state legislatures to support and expand the concept. Nationally, there is no single professional association responsible for representing the alternative school movement. The primary strength of alternative public schools resides today in strong state associations. There does exist a national network of alternative school educators who support one another and meet annually for an international conference hosted each year by a different state association for alternative schools.

Some of the nation's strongest state organizations are the Washington Alternative Learning Association, the Oregon Association of Alternatives in Education, the Colorado Options in Education, the Iowa Alternative Education Association, and the Minnesota Association of Alternative Programs. Other state organizations can be found in Connecticut, Illinois, Kansas, Michigan, Ohio, and Pennsylvania, each of which holds annual state conferences. Many of these states have influenced state legislation to require alternatives to suspension and dropping out. A number of states have passed enabling legislation that officially recognizes alternative schools and establishes policies to govern their development. Other states such as Oregon have required every school district to establish alternative schools for at-risk youth.

The success and growth of the alternative public schools concept can be seen in the number of school districts throughout the country that now use this concept to address the needs of at-risk youth. Almost every conceivable type of program philosophy and student can be found in the many alternative public schools that exist today. Virtually every medium to large city in the United States offers a variety of alternative public schools to students and their parents. Most have large waiting lists of parents and students who would like to participate. It has also become evident that the success of alternative public schools coupled with the large numbers of parents and students unable to participate in the alternatives has fueled the growing national interest in providing all parents with educational options.

Challenges in Starting and Replicating Alternative and Magnet Public Schools

While the strategy of replicating alternative public schools is a proven concept in school reform, it is not without difficulties and challenges. And while the alternative school concept alleviates many of the problems associated with changing existing schools, there are five complex issues which must be addressed:

Perceptions of suspicion and illegitimacy. In spite of the fact that alternative public schools are almost universally considered an essential part in any districtwide effort at reducing dropouts and serving at-risk youth, they are often viewed with suspicion. In a study of 14 at-risk programs, Wehlage and his colleagues concluded that "in some communities . . . alternative schools still are considered illegitimate by the profession and the public. This perception of illegitimacy can make it difficult, if not impossible, for these programs to carry out the important function of offering high quality programs to students and providing leadership and innovation" (Wehlage et al., 1989). Part of this suspicion and lack of respect may originate from the fact that many alternative schools enroll at-risk youth and thus attract the negative connotations that so many people hold for these students. Many alternative schools have been so successful at educating at-risk youth that traditional educators sometimes assume that these schools must be watering down their instruction. Too often principals, counselors, and teachers in conventional schools have believed that no one could effectively teach these youth. And since alternatives often employ instructional methods that differ substantially from conventional schools, have different rules and student policies, and offer different daily schedules, educators from conventional schools often view the success of alternative schools to be an implicit criticism of their own work (Barr & Parrett, 1997).

Alternative schools tend to be highly visible and vulnerable. Because of their innovative programs and their effectiveness, alternative schools usually attract considerable interest. Often, alternative schools attract greater interest and recognition from outside their school district than they do from within. Schools often host large numbers of visitors to their community and school and serve as a subject of news stories, research reports, and media coverage. This often creates exactly the type of "us-them" problem within a school or district that was found to hamper efforts within schools in the Coalition of Essential Schools study. This type of divisiveness can create difficulties and continuing problems for alternative schools. It can lead to conflicts over resources, demands for stricter enforcement of districtwide policies, and negative publicity that can keep students and parents from choosing to leave a conventional school to attend an alternative school. And whenever a school district faces any type of financial difficulty, there are often pressures to eliminate those "extra" programs serving special student needs. As a result, alternative educators in many school districts tend to spend an inordinate amount of time defending their programs, students, and themselves and in rallying community and district support to maintain their programs.

Using alternative schools as dumping grounds.   Closely related to other problems, public school teachers, counselors, and principals often use the option of alternative public schools to try and purge their classrooms and schools of the most difficult, disruptive, and emotionally disturbed students. Some school districts may have approved the creation of quasi-alternative schools simply to serve as another, more sophisticated tracking system.

It is for this reason that most alternative schools, even though they plan to address the needs of at-risk youth, tend to focus on approaches to learning rather than on certain types of students and work to attract a cross-section of the student population.

Confusion regarding the concept.   One of the consequences of starting new alternative schools is that many of the teachers, parents, and students who choose to participate in the school may not have an adequate understanding of the school concept. Many teachers believe that they hold a particular philosophical commitment only to discover that they have difficulties operationalizing their beliefs. Teachers may often feel that they would love to teach in a continuous progress program using individualized learning contracts and outcome assessments, only to discover that they miss their role in the traditional classroom. Students may also have difficulties moving from traditional classrooms to some types of alternatives, especially those that expect students to take a major responsibility for their own learning. Some students will lack the self-discipline to work effectively in this new type of situation, and almost all students will need some form of assistance in making the transition from traditional classrooms to alternative schools. Often, it will take these students several months to make the adjustment. During this time parents tend to get very uneasy about what is occurring with their child and their learning. For these reasons, teachers who choose to teach in an alternative school must have an opportunity to transfer out if they are unhappy. Students, too, must be able to readily opt in and opt out. Because of this, most alternative public schools tend to have rather liberal transfer policies for both teachers and students.

Conflicts between school district policies and alternative programs.   Inevitably, there will be difficulties in trying to accommodate highly innovative alternative schools and their nontraditional instructional approaches in curriculum with state and local policies. One of the most difficult problems is attempting to relate highly individualized, interdisciplinary learning activities to state graduation requirements and college entrance requirements. This causes frustration for alternative school students and teachers alike. And since many state education policies focus on issues involving time (i.e. number of instructional days, number of hours in courses, and even the number of minutes assigned daily to required courses at the elementary level), individualized, continuous progress, and mastery learning concepts create havoc when applied to the traditional requirements.

There are also a multitude of state and local regulations, policies, transportation schedules, health and safety requirements, building and fire codes, and other things that pose continuing problems for alternative schools. Many alternative school educators report that continually trying to accommodate the policies and prepare required reports for the state and local district is like being "nibbled to death by a duck." Unfortunately, over time such external policies and requirements can consume a considerable amount of time, detracting from a program's effectiveness.

How to Start Alternative and Magnet Public Schools

Starting an alternative or magnet public school has become far easier during recent years. Originally, these schools were started by small groups of true believer activists who organized political campaigns to force school boards to allow them to create a new school that reflected their particular interest or philosophy. As more and more alternative schools have been developed, evaluated, and researched and the concept better understood, this approach has become more acceptable and easier to implement. This is largely due to the work of the professional associations of alternative schools mentioned earlier, who have lobbied successfully with legislators, state departments of education, and local school boards to support the concept. School districts are increasingly being required by states to develop alternative schools and programs as a last ditch safety net for dropouts, and many states even provide special funding formulas to support the development and maintenance of alternative schools. Many school districts (Grand Rapids, Michigan, Toronto, Ontario, and Eugene, Oregon) have developed enabling policies that provide an established process for groups to propose new alternative public schools, so that over time these communities will have more different learning opportunities for parents and students.

While almost every alternative public school is started in a rather distinctive way, there are a number of steps that are almost always present in the process. Sometimes parents are the motivating force for starting a new school; other times, it has been teachers, school administrators and occasionally even students. Alternative public schools have been started by a single school district, by a consortium of several school districts, by a county school district to serve a large area, by a community college, or by other groups or individuals. Regardless of who the initiating group may be, the following steps have been identified as essential (Barr & Parrett, 1997).

Consensus Building   The process of consensus building in creating an alternative school is dramatically different from the process needed to restructure an existing school. Teachers, parents, and even students who share particular beliefs or particular concerns discover or seek out one another and usually create some type of school or community organization, planning committee, or action group and attempt to create a particular kind of school. Parents can be extremely forceful in these groups, especially when they are helping to develop a school that can serve their own children. These groups will often conduct extensive readings, attend alternative schools conferences or workshops, and usually visit alternative schools in other cities and states. Educators from existing alternative schools are often sought by local groups to assist their planning effort. Inevitably, the local planning group reflects consensus toward developing an alternative school that would serve a particular type of student or provide for a particular type of educational program.

Developing a Preliminary Proposal Out of the consensus-building phase, a preliminary proposal should be developed that includes: a rationale, philosophy, the problem(s) to be addressed, overall school goals and objectives; a general statement regarding the teaching and learning approach; curriculum to be emphasized; the type of students to be served; a timeline; and a general budget. The task of developing the preliminary proposal is in itself part of the consensus-building process, for it requires a group to assemble their ideas and beliefs into a written statement.

Seeking Authorization and Approval In approaching the central administration of a school district or the school board, experience has taught that a group seeking to develop an alternative public school should usually not seek board approval at their initial presentation. Rather the board should be approached on at least two or three different occasions. The first time provides a briefing and information session for the board that informs the board of the group's rationale and purpose. Next the group might present a preliminary proposal or concept paper and seek board approval for an official planning process to study the issue and make recommendations. Often at the first or second board appearance, the group may solicit educational consultants, teachers, administrators, or parents from an existing alternative school to help provide information to the board and answer questions. Only after a school board has developed a positive attitude toward the alternative school and agreed to or encouraged a study group to explore the concept should the board be presented with a full proposal and asked to approve the establishment of an alternative school.

Selecting Teachers and Administrators It is essential that the teachers and administrators who plan and develop the alternative school are also the majority of faculty who will be teaching in the new program. For this reason, the preliminary planning team must be expanded to include other teachers and administrators from the school district. This involves informing potential teachers and administrators and encouraging those interested to learn about the alternative school concept and the development of the school. Often many teachers will be identified in the process who have had extensive training or experience in exactly the type of alternative that is being developed. Some years ago when the Indianapolis School District was planning a new Montessori Alternative Elementary School, the board worried that the time and cost of training public school teachers in the Montessori approach might be prohibitive. A districtwide survey discovered that there were over 20 elementary teachers in the Indianapolis public schools who were already certified Montessori teachers and quite excited about joining the planning group and having an opportunity to teach in the new Montessori alternative. Furthermore, it is absolutely essential that the preliminary planning group has the authority to participate in the final selection of teachers and administrators for the school.

Planning and Development The approved planning process is extremely important to the creation of an alternative school. It is a time when the new school is conceptualized and designed. For many parents, teachers, administrators, and students this is an exciting opportunity to design the school of their dreams.

While it is important that there is adequate time for planning, there can be a danger of having too much time for planning. More than one school district has approved a study group and then required a two-year planning schedule in hopes that the group will plan the program to death. Successful alternative schools should not take over a year to plan. There is only so much that can be accomplished before the school is open, and a shorter planning and implementation schedule leads to maximum participation, enthusiasm, and commitment.

Once the school has opened its doors, continued planning should include visits to other schools, not to simply replicate what is found but for the teachers, administrators, and parents of the new school to learn from experienced veterans of alternative schools. During the following summer, the alternative school faculty should have sufficient time to revise curriculum, participate in further staff development and training, and to reevaluate the school's effectiveness.

Funding the planning and development process will require modest support to provide for summer contracts, travel to other schools, consultants for staff development, and equipping the facility.

Successful Implementation   Once the alternative school is approved, there are a large number of decisions to be made on a variety of topics:

- *Selecting a facility.* Often alternative schools are located in small, abandoned school facilities, in an isolated corridor of an existing school, or located away from schools in leased facilities in the community. Alternative schools have been started in churches, warehouses, former bank buildings, hotels, gas stations, and almost anywhere an empty retail or office building is available. Magnet schools, which are usually housed in a facility that relates to a particular curriculum focus, can be found in hospitals, aircraft hangers, shopping malls, theaters, and even at the city zoo. For at-risk youth, who often possess negative attitudes toward school, an off-campus location has many advantages. One superb location for an at-risk alternative high school is a community college. A community college campus provides a positive adult environment for the students to attend school. Care needs to be taken in advance to ensure that any facility meets state and local building, fire, and health codes for schools.
- *Selecting students.* After the number and types of students have been determined, a careful process of information, recruitment, and selection must occur. This usually includes school district communication, newspaper articles, and media announcements. It often begins with information and orientation sessions for all building principals and counselors, open community meetings, evening meetings with students and parents, and many informal contacts. Following an application period, personal interviews are held with students and their parents. It is essential that the faculty of the alternative school have responsibility for selecting students based on the approved criteria and procedure. Often alternative schools will demand a written commitment or contract from the parent to agree to become active in some form of volunteer participation in the alternative

school. While available on the basis of personal choice, alternative schools can ensure a diversified student body by establishing internal quotas. Many schools establish a lottery process due to the high number of applicants and make an effort to enroll a student population that reflects their community. Thus a school can provide for ethnic, economic, and gender balance and avoid the negative connotation of serving only at-risk students.

- *Decision making.* A component as essential to effective alternative programs as school choice is shared decision making. The school decision-making process should grow out of the planning process and include a carefully planned school management team which involves parents, students, and teachers in some significant sense.

Following these steps, most successful alternative schools have accomplished their initial goal of starting their program. From that point a number of other factors are critical to their success.

Ensuring Success in an Alternative or Magnet Public School

After almost 30 years of experience, a number of issues have been identified that are crucial to the success of a new alternative or magnet school.

Address a Real Need   To ensure a favorable reaction from school district officials, school boards, and communities, alternative schools should address a pressing need in the schools or the community. The need might be to reduce the dropout rate, deal more effectively with the large numbers of teen parents, or help the achieving students be more intellectually challenged. Alternative and magnet schools should focus squarely on addressing a particular problem or need. There is no better reason to start an alternative school than to initiate a program to address the growing needs of at-risk youth.

Use Existing School District Funds   To be successful, alternative and magnet schools should be funded by the local school district in the same way as all other schools. The alternative school should function within the existing per pupil cost based on the established pupil-teacher ratio in a school district. This means each alternative school will obtain teachers on the basis of the number of students they attract and admit to the school. Alternative schools funded solely by external grants often do not survive once the grant expires.

Start Small but Not Too Small   Compared to other public schools, alternative and magnet schools are always relatively small. This is clearly one of the reasons that they have been so successful. Unfortunately, decisions are often made to start an alternative school as a pilot project or in some other small way and then plan to expand later. To be successful, alternative schools should begin with a sufficient number of students to justify at least four teachers. With a careful selection of the four teachers, most of the major content areas can be addressed. With fewer teachers, the school program will place unreasonable demands on the faculty and often will force students to rely on other schools to meet graduation requirements. This in fact can reduce the alternative school to only a part-time program. For maximum success with at-risk youth, alternative schools should provide as much of a total education program as possible.

Another approach to starting an alternative or magnet school is adding a grade per year (for example, a school could start with the ninth grade and each year add the next grade) until an entire high-school program is in place.

Using Existing Teachers in the School District   To be successful, alternative and magnet schools should be a home-grown product. While it might be good to recruit a few teachers with unique experience from outside the community, the school should be planned, developed, and operated by teachers and administrators from within the district. In fact, alternative schools often recruit some of the most respected teachers in a school district for their expertise and to instantly create credibility. It is also vital that teachers who will teach in the alternative schools be involved in the team that plans the program.

Be As Autonomous As Possible   Alternative and magnet public schools should be as independent and autonomous as possible. Administratively, this means the alternative school should have a principal or head teacher who reports in exactly the same manner as any other building principal in the school district. Educationally, this means that the alternative school should work to have as much freedom as possible from rules and regulations and be evaluated on the performance outcomes of the students. Most states have policies that permit schools to apply for a waiver to the existing administrative rules governing public education and to replace them with an alternate plan.

Be Able to Document Effectiveness   Because of the innovative or experimental basis of alternative and magnet schools, they must be able to document their effectiveness. Each successful school must develop a program evaluation plan as well as a student assessment plan to monitor their effectiveness, identify problems and needs, and provide a basis for making necessary adjustments. Alternative public schools pioneered the use of performance outcomes by requiring graduation competencies rather than required courses and likewise were among the first public schools to routinely assess and report student attendance rates, student attitudes, behavioral problems, as well as achievement scores. Many schools also regularly conduct long-term, follow-up evaluations of their former students.

Seek Long-Term Commitments   Boards of education should provide a three-to-five-year commitment to any alternative school plan that is approved. As noted earlier, it takes three years to document improved achievement and as many as five to seven years to truly establish any new educational program. While these schools should achieve a positive impact on student achievement much sooner than existing schools who are involved in a restructuring or improvement effort, it is unreasonable for school districts or school boards to evaluate an alternative program too soon. Some evaluations have been required at the end of the first semester or the first year, which is far too early to effectively assess program success. It is essential that these schools have sufficient time to make an adequate impact on students.

Don't Expand Too Rapidly   Often large urban school districts will establish large numbers of alternative or magnet programs. Recently, New York approved over 30 "New Vision" schools that were started almost immediately with little or no opportunity for the teachers in the new schools to have time to plan and develop together. In fact, the teachers in the new schools had little time to even meet one another. When students arrived, some of the schools were in chaos.

Alternative and Magnet Schools as a Strategy for Reform

As a strategy for significant school reform, alternative and magnet public schools have a track record of success that is unequaled. The reason is simple. Rather than trying to force teachers, students, and parents to accept a particular approach to education, as is so often the case with restructuring existing public schools, alternative schools provide people with the opportunity to choose to participate. While choice is a rather simple, truly democratic idea, it has proven revolutionary in public education, where there has been a long tradition of assignment rather than choice. Students have almost always been assigned to a school on the basis of where they live. Teacher and principals are also usually assigned. Yet, the rapid diversification of teaching and learning, the growing acceptance of very different approaches to instruction, and the growing conviction that different teachers teach in different ways and that different students learn best in very different ways have created great strain on the public school tradition of assignment.

It is this idea of assignment that has created such problems and resistance to school reform. Any time an existing school has been restructured, it forces all of the parents and students in that particular school assignment area to attend that particular school, whether or not they support the particular approach to education that is being used or whether in fact it is the most effective approach for their child. The same is true for teachers and administrators. By attempting a forced fit of teachers to a particular educational philosophy or approach, deep personal conflicts are unavoidable and consensus building becomes a challenge. If a neighborhood elementary school becomes a year-round school, a highly individualized, continuous progress school, a Montessori school, a traditional back to basics school, or even an open school, many parents would undoubtedly be very unhappy and some students would experience difficulties adjusting to the particular approach that is being implemented. A classic example of this phenomenon today is the year-round school. Because the year-round school demands a very different kind of schedule for family vacations, child care, and transportation, some parents are absolutely, adamantly opposed to the idea; others feel it is a godsend. The difference in assigning parents to year-round schools or letting them voluntarily choose to participate in year-round schools reflects the same principle of choice that characterizes the success of alternative schools. Unlike universities and community colleges where students are provided with a wide range of choices in educational programs and approaches, public schools have maintained a rather rigid and usually arbitrary approach of assigning students, teachers, and parents to particular schools and to specific kinds of programs.

Alternative and magnet public schools solve this type of problem by providing a group of teachers, students, parents, and administrators with an opportunity to develop an educational program that they have all agreed upon and supported. This group then implements the educational program and invites others who might be interested in participating. This means that alternative public schools must be very clear about their philosophy, goals, curriculum, and educational approach and must sell their approach to the community. Parents and students then have the opportunity to choose an approach to education that they support and are comfortable with.

Research has documented repeatedly during the past 25 years that students, parents, teachers, and administrators who choose to participate in a particular program tend to be happier and more content than others in public education; they are more invested in the school and in learning. In a small way, this simple idea has revolutionized public education and has given rise to wholesale calls for choice in public education. As a reform strategy for transforming schools, alternative schools have had no equal, at least until very recently.

Creating and Replicating Charter Schools

A truly revolutionary development in public education was started in 1991 in Minnesota and has brought about dramatic change in public education, at least in some states. For at-risk youth, it offers great promise. The revolution is occurring in thousands of schools nationwide, and the surprising political and public interest that is occurring around these schools suggests a growing acceptance of a completely new concept of public education. The revolution is occurring as states and school districts begin to establish new policies that permit contract or charter public schools. Often referred to as boundary-breaking schools or break-the-mold schools, education outside the box, or educational "unbundling," these schools represent a significant paradigm shift in public education in the United States. These charter schools also represent a significant shift in public policy. Where this new policy has been established, it permits school districts or states to transfer responsibility for public education to groups of teachers and parents. With the exception of a few first amendment guarantees, charter schools provide a process that allows for most state and local regulations that govern public education to be relaxed or waived. These schools then gain the freedom to redesign or reinvent public education. In return, the state establishes accountability standards that focus on student achievement.

School districts have always had the authority to negotiate contracts and, in fact, they have negotiated contracts for almost everything from food services to janitorial services to security services to collective bargaining agreement with teachers. Large school districts may regularly maintain as many as 150 contracts for a complete range of services. School districts also have the authority to contract for educational and instructional services. Often schools will contract for special education services, media services, even for athletic coaches; often they contract for alternative schools. It is not unusual for a number of small school districts to work together collectively to contract with a single school district or a county school district to support an alternative public school that would serve students from each of the member districts. Recently, some school districts have been willing to negotiate contracts that permit greater flexibility in using financial resources and waiving some rules and regulations in exchange for assessing learning outcomes. Charter schools were the next logical step.

Charter schools differ from contract schools and require state legislation to permit their development. Once a state establishes charter legislation, it provides a small group of teachers and parents the opportunity to become the legal equivalent of a mini school district. "Statutes for charter schools greatly reduce the number of regulations, policies and laws governing a school, thereby freeing participants to try innovative approaches. Charters require learning results or the charter is terminated—the ultimate accountability" (Designs For Learning, 1993, p. 4). Some new charter schools are likewise attempting to gain waivers from state rules, local policies, and even freedom from the local bargaining unit—once again in exchange for accountability for student achievement.

The first charter schools in the United States were started in Minnesota in 1991 and in California in 1992. By the end of 1999, charters had been approved in 37 states, plus Puerto Rico and Washington, D.C. Charters have grown from 1,200 schools in 1998, to 1,700 schools in 1999, enrolling approximately 350,000 students. Arizona alone has 359 charter schools serving 45,000, or 5.6 percent of the state's 800,000 students. Roy Romer, former governor of Colorado, has described the importance of charter school legislation. He believes that it provides:

> *The opportunity to completely rethink and redesign a public school—from its overall vision for students, to its educational program, to the relationship between the school and its teachers, to assessment, to administrative practices and governance. It requires that a charter school, as a public school meet public imperatives of accountability and equity, but does not require that it be all things to all people. Charter school activity has the potential to create a more vibrant and diverse range of public school programs available for parents and students who want and need alternatives to the conventional approach. (Romer, 1993, p. 1)*

Gary Hart, the state senator who wrote the California charter legislation, has referred to the charter concept as "a license to dream" (Riley, 1993, p. 15). In Georgia, charter school legislation has established the following concept:

> *In effect, charter schools will be self-regulated like a chartered business. The "charter" will be a binding performance contract between the charter school, its local board of education and the State Board of Education. This charter, when approved by the local board of education and the State Board of Education, will substitute for state education statutes as well as state and local rules, policies, regulations and standards as a governance structure for the charter school. With the freedom provided under the Charter Schools Act, schools will be able to rethink and redesign "from the ground up," including, but not limited to, what students learn, how it is packaged and*

how it is delivered; how school instructional staff are deployed, how students are placed, grouped and scheduled; how school decisions are made; how funds are allocated and used; and how the community is involved in supporting the school; as well as defining the rules, roles, and responsibilities of all involved in schooling. (Wilt, 1993, p. 10)

Why Charter Schools?

The charter school movement has been a logical outgrowth of a number of developments: the widespread success of alternative public schools, the growing fear of educational vouchers, the growing demand for restructuring public education, and a number of developments in the state of Minnesota, including the creation of Community Learning Centers and the legislation that established public school choice for the citizens of the state. Many of the new charter schools were formerly existing alternative schools. Charter schools have been developed for a number of reasons:

The Inertia of Large Educational Bureaucracies   Just as growing frustration generated growing pressure on the federal government to reinvent itself and the shocking realization that the once huge, bureaucratic corporations like General Motors and IBM seemed unable to respond rapidly and decisively to the changing developments in the international marketplace, so too have public school districts come under attack for the size, inertia, escalating costs, and administrative gridlock of their bureaucracies. Trying to provide high-quality public education with scarce and diminishing dollars has led a number of large city school districts to slash their administrative costs and prompted a growing number of states to pass legislation establishing charter schools. As New Jersey Governor Jim Florio has said, "the difference between school-as-usual and charter schools is like the difference between the old G.M. assembly line and the new Saturn team assembly" (Riley, 1993, p. 17). Public education via charter schools is like creating mom and pop vegetable stands, gourmet wine and cheese shops, and small independent neighborhood groceries to compete with large supermarket chains. Charter or contract schools bring cottage industry to education in much the same way that has occurred so dramatically in the high-tech industry.

Relief from Stifling Rules, Regulations, and Policies   Almost every aspect of public education is regulated by specific administrative rules, local policies, state laws, and collective bargaining agreements. In most states, these regulations assign students and their families to a particular school, establish the number of school days in year, regulate the minutes of the school day, and prescribe the kind of building that can be used to house a school, the kinds of people who can and cannot work with children and youth, formulas for defining average daily attendance, salary schedules, and even rates of salary increases. The regulations governing public education also define what can be considered a textbook and provide an approved list of acceptable instructional materials. These regulations make school innovations difficult if not impossible. Attempts to improve instruction and restructure schools have encountered the following problems:

- Some schools have attempted to develop creative approaches to student evaluations, only to discover that the state requires letter grades.
- Some schools have attempted to use the university model of having large class instruction in certain subject areas coupled with very small classes in other areas, only to discover that the state or school district has an established maximum class size.
- Schools attempting to employ outstanding professionals from the arts and business community have discovered that only state certified teachers can be hired.
- Schools that have tried to develop shared decision making have discovered that local school boards arc only willing to provide partial autonomy at the school or community level.
- Schools that have attempted to develop extensive use of individualized, independent learning, using learning contracts and out of school practica, have found that average daily attendance rules prescribe seat time inside a school classroom.
- Schools that have established graduation competencies have found it virtually impossible to relate student learning to the required course graduation requirements.

It is these and many other rules, regulations, and policies that have frustrated schools, especially innovative and alternative schools, and made almost any proposed educational change either impossible or, almost as bad, possible only within a very limited set of prescribed guidelines that tend to cripple the innovation.

Flat-Line Funding for Education   Given the economic and political realities of the day, it is evident that local, state, and federal funding for public education is not likely to improve during the rest of this decade. With taxpayer revolts, an economy that is growing sluggishly, and escalating costs in health, welfare, judiciary, and prisons, many fear that school funding may not even keep up with inflation. Yet most calls for reform these days carry big-ticket price tags. The cost of adding one additional day to the school year or one hour to the school day or to reduce the per-pupil ratio by one child in a state or school district is staggering. Likewise, the cost for providing computers for every three to five children seems far beyond our means. There seems no reason to believe that this situation will change significantly in the near future, and it may get worse. There is a growing conviction that new ways of utilizing existing resources must be found. Charter or contract schools provide just the sort of flexibility for using existing resources in new and creative ways.

Support from Diverse Interests   In spite of the opposition of the educational establishment, especially teachers' unions and central administrators, the concept of charter or contract schools has gained strong support from the business community. In California, the Business Round Table loved the concept and wanted the legislature to establish 500 charter schools. The California Teachers Association wanted no charter schools (Riley, 1993). Charter legislation has been supported by school boards, businesses, and by innovative and alternative school educators who see the concept as a way of gaining freedom from stifling regulation and gaining ownership of their local school. In some states, particularly California, the growth of interest in some type of statewide voucher plan tended to consolidate support for the controversial charter legislation. Out of fear that California citizens would approve a voucher plan that would see tax dollars channeled to private schools, a strange group of professional and private bedfellows emerged to support the charter legislation (Wilt, 1993).

The National Educational Association and the American Federation of Teachers initially were slow to support charter schools and often even campaigned against them. However, when legislation began providing charters that did not require certified teachers, the teacher unions quickly switched ground, lobbying for charters that required certified teachers.

The charter and contract school concept has emerged from the decades of alternative public school innovations and the movement to provide choice in public education. The roots of the charter and contract school concept can be found in Minnesota. Minneapolis-St. Paul has always been one of the country's most creative areas for public education. Minneapolis and St. Paul public schools were among the first to develop alternative public schools and some of the nation's most unique programs. The Minneapolis Southeast District pioneered the creation of clusters of elementary alternative schools, while neighboring St. Paul created its famed Open School. Minnesota also became the first state to approve voluntary choice for parents in public education, providing families with the opportunity to choose preferred programs within any public school district. Recently, a group in Minneapolis was funded by the New American Schools Development Corporation to develop the first break-the-mold Community Learning Centers Network, and, as has been mentioned, Minnesota was the first state to pass charter school legislation.

Two of the individuals in Minnesota who have been instrumental in the development of these concepts are Wayne Jennings and Joe Nathan. Jennings was the first principal of the St. Paul Open School and Nathan was the school's first curriculum director. Nathan's work with the governor of Minnesota and with the Education Commission of the States was instrumental in helping to legitimize the concept of choice in public education. Today, Nathan is the director of the Center for School Change at the University of Minnesota's Hubert Humphrey Institute for Public Affairs, and Jennings is the director of a private consulting firm, Designs for Learning, as well as director of a charter school.

Characteristics of Charter Schools

As more charter school legislation is passed and new charter schools are started, it is possible to identify a number of defining characteristics.

Waiver of Existing State and Local Educational Requirements   Almost every state has developed a process to waive the education requirements at the state and local levels for various types of experimental schools. Proposals to waive requirements usually provide for different, though educationally sound, approaches to accomplish the educational goals of the state and local school districts in exchange for solid evidence that these goals are being obtained. Given what is known about systemic pressures and school cultures, attempting to change the basic rules and regulations of schooling at the state, local, and union levels seems to hold great promise for liberating public education for experimentation and innovation. Examples of waived policies include:

- *Certified teachers not required.* Perhaps most remarkable, many of the new charter schools that are under way are not requiring the exclusive hiring of certified teachers. Some charter school statutes require only that certified teachers or administrators be responsible for the hiring of all other instructional personnel.
- *Maintaining public school status.* Charter schools continue to be public schools and must follow the basic legal principles of public education:

> *It [the charter school] may not teach religion. It may not charge tuition. It must be open to the public: no picking and choosing "nice kids"; no elite academies. It may not discriminate. It must follow health and safety requirements. It is accountable to its public sponsor for meeting the objectives that it and its sponsor agree on. (Kolderie, 1993, p. 2)*

Creative Funding and the Reallocation of Resources   State and local tax dollars are used to fund charter schools and provide the resources to support instructional services to a specified group of students. The charter schools usually include:

- *Funding by existing per-pupil cost.* Funding for charter schools is based on the existing per-pupil cost of the local school district or the state. Most states specify some percentage of the regular per-pupil cost, some states provide 100 percent funding. In Colorado, charter schools receive 80 percent of the per-pupil cost of the local school district (Wilt, 1993, p. 10).
- *Lump sum funding.* A charter school will be funded in a lump-sum amount without line-item restrictions. This provides available funds to be used in the most flexible, creative, and useful manner. This type of funding is not a revolutionary or even a new idea; it is similar to how colleges and universities have traditionally been funded.
- *Internal reallocation of existing funds.* Rather than invest the majority of existing funds in professional staff, charter schools have the freedom to invest in fewer certified teachers and administrators, or as many charter schools are doing, hiring no administrators and using these savings to hire larger numbers of aides, paraprofessionals, and to purchase or lease educational technology.

Creative Staffing   In addition to waivers for state regulations and new ways of allocating resources, charter schools are able to use new approaches to staffing and develop new concepts for the roles of teachers and administrators.

- *New roles for teachers and administrators.* Teachers become planners, managers, and coordinators of learning. In addition to the traditional responsibilities of instruction, each professional teacher supervises and coordinates a number of instructional aides and paraprofessionals who assist in some aspect of student instruction. Techniques of shared decision making seem to reduce the need to invest in school administrators.

- *Extensive use of paraprofessionals.* Using fewer professional staff, charter schools are able to dramatically reduce the per pupil ratio by employing paraprofessionals and aides, all under the supervision of certified teachers.
- *Extensive use of parents, volunteers, and part-time teachers.* Charter and contract schools use large numbers of volunteers and part-time teachers from business, industry, the arts, and from nearby colleges and universities to supplement the curriculum, mentor students, and provide tutorial services.
- *Extensive use of cross-age tutoring.* Often older students are used to tutor and mentor younger students in reading in the academic areas (Designs for Learning, 1993).

Accountability through Competency-Based Performance Outcomes   Rather than using required courses built around class seat-time, many charter school students are monitored and assessed on their performance in accomplishing specified learning goals and competencies, as well as by statewide achievement tests. For example, rather than grading a person with a letter grade for a required course and using standardized tests to exclusively determine achievement, students are developing portfolios of actual work used to document and evaluate their learning. With charter and contract schools, control of public education shifts from process to performance. In order to stay open, charter schools must achieve the student performance objectives that are agreed to by the sponsor and must continue to attract sufficient parents and students to maintain established enrollment levels. In California, charters for new schools must contain:

> *descriptions of student outcomes which are clearly stated, that reflect student engagement in a rich and challenging curriculum, and which are measurable. All charter schools will be required to administer the new statewide assessments and to meet the performance standards which are developed in conjunction with these standards. In addition to these required assessments, charter school petitioners and local governing boards should agree on a comprehensive set of measures which will, together with the required statewide tests, give both the school and the district a clear picture of how the school and its students are doing. (Wilt, 1993, p. 11)*

Teachers as Owners   For the first time, public school teachers could become the owners of their schools. While a number of possible models exist, teachers could form a cooperative or a partnership and become small-business entrepreneurs. Teachers could also choose to join the local bargaining unit, form their own bargaining unit, or as owners, decide they no longer need a bargaining unit. As Stephanie Moore, an authority on California's charter school movement, has said, "it's like becoming an employee business" (Riley, 1993, p. 15).

Local Autonomy Each charter school becomes almost completely autonomous. They are in fact a mini school district, and as such, provide for the first time in the United States the opportunity for more than one organization to offer public education in a community.

Voluntary Choice Charter schools are available to families and students on the basis of choice. Teachers and all other staff also choose to participate in a charter. Some states have even permitted public school teachers the freedom to take leaves of absence to work in a charter school with the opportunity to return to their former employer if they choose.

Research on Charter Schools
After almost ten years, a number of research efforts have helped to identify four characteristics that seem to typify charter schools:

- Demand for charter schools continues to grow, but new schools face sobering obstacles regarding facilities costs and start-up costs.
- Most charters have shown rather remarkable staying power. Fewer than one in 20 have closed voluntarily, merged with others, or been closed down by authorities.
- Most charters are similar to their districts in the racial and economic backgrounds of their students, about one-third are more likely to serve poor and minority students (Education Commission of the States, 1998).
- Charter schools prompted a number of new battles in a number of states. One issue continues to be whether a state board or some other type of authorizing agency can overrule a decision by a local school board. In Colorado, where in 1999 there were 18,000 students attending 69 charter schools, the Colorado supreme court ruled that the "state has the power to overrule local school boards." This decision (which is the first in the nation) has cheered charter proponents and may set the stage for similar court challenges in other states. (Pipho, 1999, p. 181)

A team of researchers from Michigan State University recently completed a study of charter schools and interdistrict choice policies in their state. Since charter school legislation is significantly different in every state, it is difficult to make any national generalizations. But, this study of charter school policies in a single state provides insights that may prove helpful elsewhere. The Michigan charter school policies seem to have benefited the students who attend charter schools, especially those from poor families, by providing them with options and opportunities they would not otherwise have. The policies also resulted in the creation of schools that were more responsive to parent preferences. Unfortunately, the researchers also expressed a concern about charter schools. They concluded that students who did not take advantage of the new charter schools or were unable to gain admission were being left far behind in declining districts that seemed to be ill equipped or unable to compete in the education marketplace. As one of the researchers stated, "Choice may impose a cost on students who do not choose." Overall, researchers feared that student departure to charter schools, or switching to other school districts, seemed to "accelerate the decline of school quality," rather than making these school districts more competitive. The Michigan study found that most charter schools were at the elementary level and the charters provided fewer and less expensive special education services than neighboring school districts. The charters that were studied were far more innovative in governance and management than they were in teaching and learning. Michigan charters were also different from public school systems because they used extensive outsourcing for services with for-profit educational management organizations.

The report suggested that policy makers should consider the following recommendations:

- More information should be available to parents on all public schools.
- Responsibility for turning around failing schools must be explicitly assigned, as well as assigning responsibility for educating students in the event that a school district fails.
- Charter schools should be granted more financial support to put them on a more equal footing with school districts.
- Responsibility for monitoring charter schools should be clarified. (Schnaiberg, 1999)

By the end of the 1990s, there was little systematic research that focused on the ability of charter schools to foster improved student achievement. A recent study by the University of Minnesota Center for School Change and the Center for Education Reform documented improvements in student achievement in a significant number of charter schools in twelve states (Education Commission of the States, 1998a). Some of the schools showed gains of more than a year of academic growth.

Starting a Charter School
Starting a charter school tends to involve far more legal and technical issues than other school restructuring approaches. There is also a considerable difference between charter schools and contract schools. While state legislation is a prerequisite to the creation of charter schools, any school could develop some type of contract school. And depending on the state policies governing experimental public schools, some contract schools have obtained the same type of waivers of state regulations that charter schools have achieved.

Groups who have started charter schools have described how much they have gained from research literature that has documented how to start an alternative public school (Sweeney, 1993; Barr & Parrett, 1997; Nathan, 1997). In addition to effective strategies for starting alternative schools, some groups that have successfully started charter schools offer the lessons they have learned from satisfactorily completing the process:

1. *Spend adequate time talking about the shared vision: every word counts.*
2. *Involve key players early on in developing the vision and reaching consensus.*

3. *Coalesce with other parents and teachers in your district or area planning schools of choice or charter schools regardless of their philosophical bent.*
4. *Solicit the expert assistance of district personnel early on in planning.*
5. *Seek district flexibility and be clear about what waivers you will be asking for.*
6. *Include union participation where appropriate and when worthwhile.*
7. *Keep the programs or schools small and cohesive.*
8. *After students and teachers choose the program, continue to offer choices within the program.*
9. *Clearly define the roles of students, parents, teachers, and community members.*
10. *Experiment with the administrative hierarchy: flatten it wherever possible.*
11. *Have a distinct, themed program.*
12. *Develop curricula that is particular to your program. Programs may not be cloned.*
13. *Commit to continually renew the program and make it better. (Sweeney, 1993, p. 9)*

At-Risk Youth and Charter Schools

The concept of charter and contract schools has the potential to liberate alternative school programs that serve dropouts and to stimulate the development of more K–12 community learning centers such as have been developed in Minnesota to serve all ages and ethnic groups and to help integrate education with jobs. However, there are also nagging concerns regarding the charters. In California, both the good and bad can be found for at-risk youth. Some at-risk alternative schools and contract schools have achieved a charter status; but, "disappointingly, very few of California's charter schools have been generated by and for low income or minority communities in . . . urban inner cities" (Riley, 1993, p. 16). Unfortunately, the majority of at-risk youth are found in the nation's largest cities, and to create charter or contract schools in these urban areas confronts formidable obstacles: big-city politics, big labor unions, and local school board rivalries. The very individuals who need improved education often live in impoverished communities which may lack the sophistication and the legal assistance to develop and manage a charter school. Equally troubling, since charter schools must demonstrate high student achievement in order to stay open, there may be a tendency for groups to propose charters primarily for communities where there is already a strong track record of student success. Only time will tell.

Guaranteeing Success: The Blueprint Completed

The three approaches that have been described in this chapter, restructuring existing schools, replicating alternative schools, and creating and replicating charter schools, have demonstrated dramatic success in restructuring schools to ensure that at-risk children and youth learn effectively and stay in school. The descriptions of effective restructuring approaches provide the final component of a complete blueprint for guaranteeing that the needs of at-risk children and youth are effectively addressed. The blueprint has included:

- Assistance in identifying those who are the at-risk.
- Documentation of school myths and programs that are ineffective or, even worse, destructive to the at risk.
- An analysis of why schools have proven so difficult to change.
- A summary of essential components of effective at-risk programs based upon significant long-term research.
- A comprehensive review of effective school and community programs for at-risk students from infancy through the high-school years.
- A description of allies in restructuring schools as well as problems to be avoided.
- Three detailed descriptions of successful approaches to restructuring schools to meet the needs of at-risk youth.

There has also been an effort to identify real schools and programs that continue to be effective in improving the learning of at-risk youth. These schools include conventional public schools in rural and urban communities and schools in a variety of poverty settings. They include comprehensive reform models such as Accelerated Schools, Success For All schools, school development programs and a wide variety of alternative and magnet public schools. They also include community learning centers and the new charter schools.

These schools are transforming the lives of children and youth and are providing the last best hope for our nation's social and economic future. These efforts stand as a striking challenge to communities throughout the nation to step forward and take action to do what must be done, to follow the blueprint that research has provided, to fulfill the American promise of equal education for all.

$Chapter$ 10

Creating the Will
to Educate All Students

*Hope is definitely not the same thing as optimism. It is not the
conviction that something will turn out well, but the certainty
that something makes sense, regardless of how it turns out. It is
hope, above all, that gives us strength to live and to continually
try new things, even in conditions that seem hopeless.*
—*VACLAV HAVEL*

Almost two decades after *A Nation At Risk* was published, sending shock waves throughout the United States, it is difficult to capture exactly where we are today, even to determine if schools are getting better or worse, or if much of anything in schools has actually improved at all. Yet one thing is increasingly clear: By the end of the twentieth century dramatic educational changes had captured the political attention of the country and promised to dominate education policy and schooling well into the next decade.

The gathering storm of change is characterized by a confusion of competing ideas, pressure groups, and political activists. It includes religious zealots, business entrepreneurs, techno-reformers, child advocates, state legislators, governors, chambers of commerce, minority groups, and churches. It involves right-wing religious groups hammered together into a loose conservative coalition seeking to replace the teaching of evolution with the teaching of creationism, whole language with phonics, bilingual education, and "return prayer to the schoolgrounds and classrooms of the country." It involves other religious factions which have simply abandoned the classrooms of the nation's schools for the sanctity of church-based religious schools. It involves a determined array of business leaders and politicians committed to raising the achievement level of all American youth in order to keep abreast of the accelerating demands of the technological marketplace and to measure up to international levels of competitive achievement. It includes a growing number of home-schooling parents who place the safety and well-being of their children over the chaos of the democratic melting pot of violence-prone public education. It involves educational reformers who seek to diversify public education through the creation of new schools and new educational approaches. It includes the expansion and evolution of alternative public schools, schools of choice, magnet schools, career-theme schools, technical schools, charter schools, and even private schools available in some states through public voucher programs. It is joined by a growing wave of educators who are developing statewide, results-driven school-improvement projects and staff-development training programs, all designed to restructure public schools through documenting improvement in student achievement. It features dramatic increases in private, for-profit business ventures moving vigorously to the economic opportunities available in public education, to start private schools, to improve instruction, and to manage the failed and frustrated schools and school districts of the nation's cities. And last, but in the long run, perhaps most potent of all, it embraces the technological revolution that has swept into the public school with private television broadcasts; educational programming of public and cable television, computer-based instruction, internet and distance schools, courses and programs; and the vast implications of the information age.

Public education today is confronted by a patchwork of dozens and dozens of local, state, and national pressure groups; political parties, education, and business groups; researchers and technocrats, all competing with one another as well as with the battered educational institution of the nation's public schools. By the year 2000, confrontations have erupted almost everywhere, and educational wars are being waged in local school boards, state legislatures, textbook publishing houses, churches, homes, community centers, and the United States Congress.

Remarkably, in small, secure community pockets throughout the country that are protected by the concept of local control, many school districts continue to function unchanged and largely uncriticized in the midst of a twilight complacency. These school districts continue to practice the age-old, failed traditions of public education while the confrontation rages around them.

It is unclear whether the nation's public schools will be torn apart into an apartheid of the new haves and have-nots, or perhaps, emerge into a new type of public school capable of educating all students, ensuring that they learn effectively and attain new high levels of achievement regardless of their background, socioeconomic level, and personal needs and abilities. Unfortunately, in the year 2000, it remains to be seen whether public education will become an abandoned educational ghetto, serving only the poor and high-risk students of the "other America," or if it will be transformed into a competitive, new, effective institution serving all students.

Of course, experts on every side claim victory and point to defeats. The discussions surrounding school reform have become increasingly political and often reflect little more than widespread confusion. Simultaneously, there seems to be a surprising optimism that coincides with a gathering despondency; a smug confidence contrasted with utter hopelessness. Part of the problem is that almost every point of view tends to be accurate, at least for some geographic area, type of community, segment of the population, educator, or parent perspective. Public education in the United States continues to represent a cluttered mosaic of hope and pain, of technological advancement and shocking human tragedy, of violence and humility, of educational breakthroughs, and of stunning personal heartbreak. Public education is a snapshot of who we are, a gestalt of our national character.

From the beginning, many have argued that our schools simply could not be as bad as they had been depicted in *A Nation At Risk*. And as our improving economy coincided with recent signs that the Japanese economic machine might be faltering, it is easier to be sensitive to this point of view. From this perspective, the schools do not need to be reformed or restructured; if it ain't broke, it is often heard, don't try to fix it. That is not to say that these educators do not believe that schools need to be continually, incrementally improved; it does mean that they have resisted comprehensive overhaul. Public schools seem to resist even modest restructuring efforts. Rather than schools failing, proponents of maintaining the current system argue that it is the diverse U.S. student population who now take the SAT and those international math and science exams that have so tarnished the U.S. reputation. It is not that our schools are failing, but that they are so successful. It is that so many poor, minority, and marginal students are now taking these exams, and the scores from this U.S. composite are then compared with the monocultural student populations of the national public school systems of Japan, Korea, and Germany. How can public schools be so bad if the United States leads the technological revolution in the world? Look at NASA, the advancements in communications and the innovations in the field of medicine, the resurgence of U.S. business, and the emerging information highways. Look at the reported declining dropout rate. Look at American universities, where the students of the world come to complete study. Look at the fall of Communism and the continued international leadership of the United States. Now really, can our schools be all that bad?

There are school districts and individual schools throughout America where public education exists in something of a 1950s time warp of changelessness; where teachers still talk 90 percent of the time and the role of the student learner is to listen, memorize, and complete work sheets; where bells still ring every 50 minutes and even in this age of the computer and the Internet, the primary technology is an overhead projector, a VCR, or a chalkboard. These schools and indeed a majority of public schools in America continue to employ retention and tracking, and large numbers of children still fail to learn and later drop out of school. In spite of the widespread educational experimentation and innovation that is occurring today, a number of credible surveys report that the vast majority of schools have changed little, if at all in our lifetime (Berends, 1992; Lee & Smith, 1992; Kohn, 1999). To so many people, our schools are working and working well.

To others, just the opposite is true. Public education, they believe, is not only moribund and failing, but literally falling apart. They say the schools mirror the disintegration of the American family, the crumbling of U.S. social values, the hopelessness of so many urban communities, random and mindless violence, and a nation ripped apart between the haves and have-nots, between those who enjoy the good life and the growing underclass of the other America. There is hard, tangible evidence to support this view. One need only to look at the escalating cost of health and welfare, aid to families with dependent children, the judicial quagmire, and the dramatic growth in new prisons. Look at the 1.8 million people in prison today, the one and a half million teen parents in the United States, the increasing birthrate of drug babies, the drug and alcohol abuse by school children. Look at the 20 percent of the U.S. student population who live in poverty, the five million children of immigrant parents who entered the public schools during the 1990s, bringing over 150 languages other than English into the nation's classrooms, and the 40 percent of U.S. children being reared by a single parent. Look at the increase in the number of murders and violent crimes on our city streets; look at the violence in our schools. Look at state-by-state comparisons of percentage increases in the cost of crime, corrections, and health and social services and then compare these to the stagnant budgets for K–12 and higher education. The United States today is building prisons, not schools and universities.

Add to these grim harbingers of the future a widespread taxpayers' revolt— property tax limitation bills, defeated school bond elections, crumbling buildings, school closures, and the growing number of school districts that have simply declared bankruptcy and closed their doors—and a dismal picture of U.S. education begins to turn tragic. Prompted by hopelessness and despair, some urban school districts are giving up and turning over public education to outsiders. Others, in a desperate effort to salvage public education in America, are searching out an unprecedented complex of inventive solutions (Jennings, 1993a).

A Decade of Change

During the 1990s almost every conceivable approach to school reform was used by state legislators, state boards of education, school districts, and even judges to try to make schools more effective. In Chelsea, Massachusetts, the school district was turned over to Boston University to manage. In New Jersey, using a pioneer "academic bankruptcy" law, the state seized control of the Jersey City school district and managed the school district for ten years until student achievement scores began to improve. The Chicago public schools, taken over by the mayor, turned over 600 public schools to local parents to manage. The Kentucky supreme court declared that public education was in violation of the Constitution and directed legislators to create a new system of public education. In Texas, the state legislature equalized school funding and began requiring wealthy school districts to subsidize their less fortunate neighboring school districts, and Michigan abolished the property tax as the primary method of funding schools. A growing number of states, including Kentucky, Connecticut and South Carolina began requiring school districts to establish alternative schools. Voucher plans were approved in Ohio, Wisconsin, and Florida, and charter-school legislation was passed in more than 37 states. Over 20 states overruled the local control of public schools by establishing comprehensive statewide school-reform legislation that included new academic standards and "high stakes" student-assessment exams. Some states prohibited promotion or graduation unless students successfully passed the state achievement tests. And throughout the country, low-performing schools unable or unwilling to improve were closed or reconstituted with new faculty and administrators. During the 1990s, after decades of talking about school reform and making recommendations, dramatic changes occurred.

On one hand, this seems to be a time of chaos and utter confusion. On the other, it is a time of rich experimentation and development; for some, it is a time of business as it has always been. What can be learned from all of these developments? What direction and insight can be discerned from the current tangle of public education? What can we learn from the confrontative and fragmented educational scene? Emerging from all of this are several conclusions that cannot be ignored.

Social Disintegration

There are areas of social disintegration in the United States that threaten our society and our culture. These include critical changes in the family structure, crime and violence in our cities, the escalating number of children who are being born to single teenage women, and the breathtaking increases in the cost of social services for the poor and criminal. The increasing abuse of drugs and alcohol among our children and youth, growing illiteracy, and the failure of significant percentages of U.S. youth to succeed in school is pervasive and frightening.

International Competition

The international marketplace now demands a literate, educated, technologically fluent workforce. The world of work has given way to the age of the mind. There is only one way to succeed economically today, and that is through a solid, sound education and continuous lifelong learning. By the year 2000, there was a growing shortage in U.S. technology companies of well-educated engineers and scientists.

The Importance of Education

The only possible answer to the problems and the needs of the contemporary marketplace is better education for all, education that provides for meaningful employment. Public education must educate all children and educate them very well. The local school is the last great hope, perhaps the only hope for so many of our nation's children.

Growing Numbers of At-Risk Youth

Unfortunately, a large percentage of U.S. youth arrive at school unprepared to learn, fail to succeed in school, ultimately drop out of school, and often spend their life unemployed or underemployed, many becoming wards of the state or even criminals. Equally frightening is the documentation of the increasingly risky and dangerous behaviors that are being practiced by large percentages of the nation's children and youth.

Schools Make a Difference

Based on recent conclusions from longitudinal research that has followed and assessed developments in schools for five to ten years, we now know that schools can make a positive, significant impact on children and youth, even those from the most economically depressed and socially dysfunctional backgrounds.

All Children Can Learn

We now know how to provide high quality, effective education for all. There are thousands of schools throughout the nation that are doing this well. There are schools that are teaching all children to read, ensuring that all children succeed in school and graduate, and documenting the fact that they are successful, even carefully identifying the reasons for their success. They are also documenting effective ways to transform public education into schools that are effective for all.

Identifying School Failure

If some schools and communities are providing effective education for all students in significant restructured settings, then it is a savage indictment of all of the rest. It means that large numbers of schools and communities are short-changing and failing large numbers of U.S. children and youth who could, with appropriate educational programs, succeed in school and become productive members of our society.

Schools Can Be Changed and Improved

Last of all, we now understand how to restructure schools and change educational programs so that they can be effective for all. At last, there is a chance to improve public education and provide high quality education for all.

As our nation enters the millennium, it is clearly a time for action in communities throughout the country. Any less reflects a conscious intellectual separatism, no less destructive than the racial separatism found in the Balkan States, a separatism that will continue to divide our nation between those who are educated and the growing underclass of Americans who have few skills and even less hope. It is time to end this destructive pattern of educational apartheid in the United States.

Imperatives for the Future of Public Education

Public education remains the last and only place left in the United States in which students from all walks of life come together to form a cultural mosaic. Public education is truly the nation's common ground. Nowhere in the world does an educational institution bring together such a diverse group of people. What is increasingly clear is that for public education to survive it must become more competitive. Like American businesses of two decades ago, public education must become more effective, more consumer conscious, and more cost effective. Public education must step out-side the traditional box of failed programs and practices, must selectively abandon failed approaches, and streamline, downsize, and diversify. Public schools must step into a new age of educational competition. Unfortunately, there are a growing num-ber of indications that some school districts seem to be unwilling or, even worse, unable to shrug off the bureaucratic complacency that tends to characterize any monopoly and become more competitive. One study in Michigan quoted earlier in this book (Schnaiberg, 1999), indicated that only 25 percent of the school districts operating in conjunction with charter schools had made any significant response as a result of the new charters. These researchers concluded that rather than charter schools leading to better, more diverse school districts, the charters only added to the decline of school districts as more and more students and parents participated in some type of school choice. The sad truth may well be that some districts, especially those serving poor and minority communities in our nation's cities, may be all but impossible to improve. Unfortunately, it is difficult to imagine an entire school district being "reconstituted" like a failing school, but there are, in fact, examples wherein state agencies and the courts have "taken over schools" and managed them until stu-dent achievement improved. What is becoming more and more evident is that too many public school districts seem unable to improve student performance and ill prepared to compete in the education marketplace. By the year 2000, it is evident that a set of urgent imperatives have emerged that will make public education more com-petitive and, in fact, are defining the future of public schools in the United States.

Ensure That All Children Arrive at School Ready to Learn

It is essential that all public schools recognize the importance of prenatal and infant care and development, early childhood care, and preschool education. Every public school in the nation must develop vigorous parent-education programs, work to establish strong community child care opportunities, support preschool programs like Head Start, and work with social service agencies to ensure that all children are inoculated and cared for. Research has documented in the most powerful manner, that educational success is determined to a large degree by how infants and children are cared for during the early years of their lives, long before they arrive at school. To achieve educational excellence, every child, especially the children of poverty and dysfunctional families, needs sufficient health care, high-quality child care, effective preschool, and all-day kindergarten programs.

Offer Choices to Students, Parents, Educators, and Patrons

School districts must provide educational choices for parents, students, and teachers through the development of a diversified system of optional schools and programs. More and more parents are leaving traditional classrooms to participate in a wide variety of public-school programs available by choice. With an increasingly diversified student body and a rapidly changing world, no one educational program can well serve all students. Furthermore, research has documented the powerful impact of school choice on parent commitment as well as student motivation, attitudes, and achievement. And these options can be made available with the widest possible diversity of students. It is absolutely clear that many parents will seek out educational alternatives and choices that meet their needs, whether or not public education provides those choices.

Provide a Safe Learning Environment

Schools must ensure a safe learning environment. The murderous acts of school violence in recent years have shocked the nation and elevated school safety to the number-one educational concern of parents, teachers, and students. Fortunately, research has provided a variety of predictive profiles and early-warning signs that can assist schools in the early identification of violent and violence-prone children and youth. Research has also documented effective intervention programs and ways to "bully-proof" a school. Schools must do everything possible to ensure a safe, secure school building, to have policies to identify and assist troubled youth, and to offer a curriculum that promotes social and emotional growth with high behavioral standards. But many parents expect far more than a safe school; a growing number want a positive educational environment, free from vulgar language, litter, graffiti, bullying, and disruptive behavior. Clearly those parents who are assigned to a school that does not conform to their expectations are increasingly moving their children to other environments.

Address the Needs of All Students

With the growing diversity of students and the problems associated with disrupted and dysfunctional families, schools must endeavor to address the needs of all students. Schools must serve as the front line to protect students from their parents, feed poor students, and do everything possible to address the needs of students so that they will be ready to learn. This may demand drug, alcohol and health programs and services, and the coordination of a wide variety of other social services. Many public schools today are moving toward a "full service" approach that takes schooling and education far beyond academic learning.

Guarantee That All Children Learn to Read

During the 1990s the importance of reading was documented in the most significant manner. Since school learning and success in life depends on the ability to read, it is absolutely essential that *all* children learn to read effectively. As the recognition of the importance of reading became widespread, reading was transformed from "just another school subject" to a skill that is a guaranteed birthright of all children. Reading effectiveness is being increasingly mandated by state policy as a requirement for all students.

Keep All Children in School

The long-term impact of dropping out of school has been thoroughly documented over and over again. The lifetime earnings of every dropout is significantly diminished, as is the increased probability of a dropout becoming unemployed, a teenage parent, abusive with drugs and alcohol, and in trouble with the law. In order to ensure that all school-age youth stay in school, some states have established policies to deny driver's licenses to school dropouts. Research has also documented that it is essential that schools provide a safe learning environment, with effective interventions regarding the disruptive, violent, and bullying students. It is also evident that these students should not be expelled, unsupervised, into the community. Violent and disruptive students must be kept in a school program but a school with significant security.

Progress from Equal Opportunity to High Achievement for All

Schools must ensure that all students pursue a rigorous academic program, that the academic curriculum be enriched with career education and out-of-school learning opportunities so that all students achieve high standards of achievement. Research has documented that all children and youth can and will learn and that a school can overcome the effects of poverty and dysfunctional families. So powerful is this research, that the concept of "equal opportunity" is being replaced by "equal achievement." Many schools in low-economic settings throughout the country have demonstrated significant success at raising the achievement levels of the most poor and/or at-risk students.

These schools have documented the essential characteristics that make them so effective, beginning with a rigorous curriculum. If students are denied a rigorous core curriculum, their performance is diminished. If students complete a rigorous academic curriculum, their achievement increases. These gains have been documented repeatedly in a number of states (see Chapters 5, 7, and 8).

Research has also documented that students learn effectively both in school and out of school. To be most effective, schools need to enrich the academic curriculum with career themes, educational expeditions which focus on applied learning, and opportunities for internships, practice, and service learning in business, social agencies, hospitals, and other community locations. Learning in the real world, applying academic learning to relevant situations, and learning in programs with career themes serve to motivate and engage students. Academic learning can be broadened and enriched by life experiences out of school and in the surrounding communities.

Staff Schools and Programs with Caring, Demanding, and Well-Trained Teachers

Schools must employ highly qualified, caring, and demanding teachers and support their work to teach all students. Well-prepared teachers who care for and hold high expectations for their students have a powerful influence on the students' behavior, attitudes, and achievement. Increasingly, teachers are being evaluated not only on their ability to plan excellent lessons, motivate students, ask probing questions, or maintain an orderly classroom, teachers today are being expected to document and demonstrate their ability to foster effective learning with all students. The National Board for Professional Teaching Standards includes as part of its assessment of teacher applicants not only the ability to plan and teach a lesson, but to collect students' work samples as the students progress through the lesson. The state of Oregon has established a requirement of documenting the ability to foster effective student learning as part of initial and continuing teacher certification. More recently, a number of school districts including Denver, have established pilot merit-pay plans based on teachers' success in teaching children to read.

Select Results-Based Curriculum and Programs

Schools must select curriculum materials, instructional programs, and staff development programs based on evidence. A new age has dawned in the world of textbooks, instructional materials, programs, and staff development. No longer can schools select materials and instructional programs based on the fact that "it is a best-seller in California or Texas," or because of marketing and advertising campaigns. The day has arrived when schools must expect and demand evidence of the effectiveness of instructional materials and programs on student achievement.

Promote Social and Emotional Growth

There is a growing research base that documents the effectiveness of promoting the social and emotional growth of students. In a time of so many family problems, the school must help students learn respect and responsibility, manage their anger, and mediate their conflicts in appropriate ways. Social and emotional growth must become reorganized as essential components of the schools' curriculum and instructional programs.

Carefully Monitor Student Achievement and Accelerate Learning

Schools must collect and report documented evidence of student achievement and evaluate achievement against rigorous objective standards. Schools must also provide for intensive programs to help students who do not achieve the standards to accelerate their learning and catch up. It is no longer enough to simply advise parents that their children have completed the 1st, 5th, or 11th grade or that they have graduated from high school. What matters today is that there is evidence to document what students have learned, to document what they know and are able to do, and to measure this evidence against objective standards. Schools must document the ability of all students to read, master the basics, and achieve academic standards. Students who fall below expected levels of achievement must receive intensive assistance. A successful approach that dramatizes this imperative is the Reading Recovery Program, which takes the lowest-skilled readers in a school and through intensive one-to-one tutoring is able to document dramatic gains in often only a few weeks.

Downsize and Personalize Schools

Public schools must be downsized and personalized through the development of small educational environments to ensure safety, improve behavior, and engage all students in effective learning. School size has been identified in a number of significant studies as directly related to school violence. Columbine High School in Littleton, Colorado, seemed to demonstrate this relationship in the saddest possible way. Conversely, there is almost a total lack of violence in small, alternative schools, including those that serve high-risk youth. Research has thoroughly documented that when schools are small and learning is personalized, student behavior improves, learning increases, and positive attitudes toward school are enhanced.

Streamline Administrative Structure and Service

Schools must streamline the administrative structure and welcome parents and community leaders as full partners in public education. Decades of controversy over administrative costs, coupled with recent developments in charter schools, have provided cogent evidence that there are different and perhaps more cost-effective approaches to school administration. Many small, quasi-independent charter public schools have demonstrated effective management by teams of teachers rather than an administrator. Charter schools have demonstrated that administrative costs can be sufficiently reduced and that parents and community volunteers can provide a wide variety of low-cost or no-cost services to the schools. As with the administrative restructuring of companies like IBM, Motorola, and the American automotive industry, districts and schools need to reinvent their organization and structure, delegate more authority to local schools and classroom teachers, and seek a wide variety of outsourcing for such needs as transportation, food service, and security.

Increase Stakeholder Involvement and Satisfaction

The populace of the United States has become far less tolerant of an authoritative, top-down approach to governing schools and interacting with parents. One by one, district by district, the antiquated cold-war-style leadership in districts and schools is vanishing, giving way to leadership structures that better relate to and serve all constituents, families, and other stakeholder groups. The advent of educational choices in public education has contributed greatly to, and will continue to fuel, this improvement.

From Hope at Last to Hope Fulfilled

The central focus of improving American schools, either directly or indirectly, has been on the children of the growing underclass of the "other America." Improving the schools of our nation is really about increasing the successes of our at-risk and violence-prone children and youth. The state legislatures of our nation are waging a political assault focused on demanding that all children not just have equal access to quality education but in fact demonstrate achievement. Most public schools in America have only demonstrated isolated, marginal success with children of poverty and immigration. For America's youth at risk, the continued use of the interventive approaches of tracking, retention, suspension, expulsion, and classifying immense numbers of students as learning disabled has not and will not improve efforts to successfully educate at-risk youth.

Hope in the new millennium for students at risk is characterized by a new age of research that has documented without a doubt that all youth can and will learn. Schools throughout the country are, indeed, successfully teaching the vast majority of their students to high levels of achievement. New educational efforts are meeting new, high academic standards, prohibiting social promotion, creating and expanding alternative and magnet schools, passing charter-school legislation, creating voucher programs for underserved students, and where necessary, even closing or reconstituting failing schools.

In the year 2000, it is unfortunate that other groups are working just as hard to escape from the very students that are finally being successfully served in many districts. The goal of these groups is to flee the disruptive, violent, and challenged learners of America. Simply put, these groups want to escape the abused children, the teenage parents, other less advantaged students and affluent teenage terrorists. They seek to avoid students who are victims of drug and alcohol abuse, the illiterate, and often, the minorities. These groups seek to escape the mentally impaired, the hyperactive, the bully, and the violent student. Representatives from this point of view are moving to the gated communities and private schools of the suburbs. They seek the security and sanctity of home schooling, private academies, and religious schools. These are the groups who are abandoning public education and, by their actions, generating a growing educational apartheid in America.

As the new millennium arrived, the confrontation continued, not just for the hearts and minds of the nation's at-risk youth, but in a very real sense, for the future of public education in the United States and, perhaps, our very democracy. A dominant question continues to frame America's challenge: Can public education in the United States change quickly and dramatically enough to effectively address the needs of at-risk children and youth, raise the achievement level of these students to new levels, and ensure parents of all students the safety and security of the public school environment?

Five years ago, when the first edition of this book was published, research had clearly documented a "new hope" for at-risk youth. At that time isolated cases throughout the country were demonstrating dramatic success. Five years later, as a result of widespread political, social, and educational efforts, quite a remarkable change is occurring in the public schools of the United States. Far from the "hope" that all students could achieve through the growing promise of new insight, research, and programs, it is now possible to declare that all students, even the most significantly at risk are, in fact, achieving high levels of academic performance in a growing number of schools in every section of the country. America's public schools have indeed moved from "hope at last" to "hope fulfilled" for a growing number of public-school children. The challenge facing our communities is to determine whether we have the will to learn from and incorporate these achievements from "many" of the nation's public schools to every public school . . . and in the process educate, for the first time in our nation's history, all of America's youth.

Works Cited

The achievers (22 December 1998). *The Washington Post,* D4.

Abercrombie, Karen L. (23 June 1999). Programs that promote summer learning gain popularity. *Education Week, 18*(41), 13.

Adler, J. (30 March 1998). The tutor age. *Newsweek,* 47–57.

Adler, M. A. (1982). *The Paideia Proposal.* New York: Macmillan.

Alexander, Karl, & Entwistle, Doris. (5 May 1999). Children, schools, and inequality. *Education Weekly.*

Alexander, William M., & McEwin, D. Kenneth. (1989). *Earmarks of schools in the middle: A research report.* (ERIC Document Reproduction Service No. ED 312 312).

American Academy of Child & Adolescent Psychiatry. (November 1995). *Facts for families: Children & TV violence.* [On-line]. Available: <http://www.aacap.org/web/aacap/factsFam/violence.htm>.

American Association of School Administrators. (1991). *101 Ways parents can help students achieve.* Washington, DC: Author.

American Psychological Association. (1993). *Violence and youth: Psychology's response.* Los Angeles: Center for Media Literacy.

American Psychological Association. (1996). *Violent versus nonviolent kids.* Published in Peaceful Schools, October 1998, NWREL Information Services.

Another take on violence: School size and location, are they factors? (June 1999). Newsletter of the Rural School and Community Action, Randolph, VT.

Arkansas Department of Education. (1992). Multicultural Reading and Thinking (McRat). Proposal submitted to the Program Effectiveness Panel of the National Diffusion Network. Washington, DC: U.S. Department of Education.

Arsen, David, Plank, David N., & Sykes, Gary. (1999). *School choice policies in Michigan: The rules matter.* Michigan State University: School Choice and Educational Change.

Ascher, Carol. (1993). *Changing schools for urban students: The school development program, accelerated schools, and success for all.* (Trends and Issues No. 18). New York: ERIC Clearinghouse on Urban Education, Columbia University.

Banks, Ron. (1997). *Bullying in schools.* ERIC Digest. (ERIC Document Reproduction Service ED 407 154).

Barnett, W. S. (1996). Lives in the balance: Age-27 benefit cost-analysis of the High/Scope Perry Preschool Program. *(Monographs of the High/Scope Educational Research Foundation, 11)*. Ypsilanti, MI: High/Scope Press.

Barr, Robert D. (1972). The age of alternatives: A developing trend in education reform. *Changing Schools, 1*(1), 1–3.

Barr, Robert D. (1981). Alternatives for the eighties: A second of development. *Phi Delta Kappan, 62*(8), 570–73.

Barr, Robert D. (1982). Magnet schools: An attractive alternative. *The Elementary Principal, 28*(2), 37–40.

Barr, Robert D., & Parrett, William H. (1997a). *How to create alternative, magnet, and charter schools that work*. Bloomington, IN: National Educational Service.

Barr, Robert D., & Parrett, William H. (1997b, Spring). Reading/alternative schools keys to safer communities. *School Safety,* 20–24.

Barr, Robert D., Parrett, William, & Colston, B. (1977). An analysis of six school evaluations: The effectiveness of alternative public schools. *Viewpoints, 53*(4), 1–30.

Barr, Robert D., & Ross, Barbara. (1989). *Teenage parent programs: The problems and possibilities*. Corvallis, OR: Oregon State University.

Barr, Robert D., & Smith, Vernon H. (1976). Where should learning take place? In William Van Til (Ed.), *Issues in secondary education: The seventy-fifth yearbook of the National Society for the Study of Education* (pp. 153–77). Chicago, IL: University of Chicago Press.

Bauwens, Jeanne & Hourcade, Jack J. (1994). *Cooperative teaching: Rebuilding the schoolhouse for all students*. Austin, TX: Pro-Ed.

Beane, Allan L., & Espeland, Pamela. (1999). *The bully-free classroom: Over one hundred tips and strategies for teachers K–8*. Minneapolis, MN: Free Spirit Publishing.

Beane, J. A. (1997). *Curriculum integration*. New York: Teachers College Press, Columbia University.

Bell, Terrel H., & Elmquist, Donna L. (1991). *How to shape up our nation's schools*. Salt Lake City, UT: Bell & Associates

Bempechat, Janine. (1999). Learning from poor and minority students who succeed in school: Children's views on success and failure have a big impact on their learning. *Harvard Education Letter, 15*(3), 1–3.

Benard, Bonnie. (1991). *Fostering resiliency in kids: Protective factors in the family, school, and community*. Portland, OR: Northwest Regional Educational Laboratory.

Bennett, Hal. (1972). *No more public school*. Berkeley, CA: The Bookworks.

Benson, P. L., Galbraith, J., & Espeland, P. (1998). *What kids need to succeed*. Minneapolis, MN: Free Spirit Publications.

Berends, M. (1992). *A description of restructuring in nationally nominated schools*. Madison, WI: University of Wisconsin, Center for Organization and Restructuring of Schools.

Berla, Nancy. (1991). Parents and schooling in the 1990s. Parent involvement at the middle level school. *The ERIC Review, 1*(3), (ERIC Document Reproduction Service ED 340 387).

Bernard, Bonnie. (1991). *Fostering resiliency in kids: Protective factors in the family, school, and community*. Portland, OR: Northwest Regional Educational Laboratory.

Berndt, Thomas, & Ladd, Gary (Eds.). (1989). *Peer relationships in child development*. New York: John Wiley and Sons.

Big kids teach little kids: What we know about cross-age tutoring. (1987). *Harvard Education Letter, 3*(2) 1–4.

Bottoms, Gene, & Mikos, Pat (1995). *Seven most-improved High Schools That Work*. High Schools That Work: A Report on Improving Student Learning. Atlanta, GA: Southern Regional Education Board.

Bracey, Gerald W. (1989). Moving around and dropping out. *Phi Delta Kappan, 70*(5), 407–410.

Braddock, Jomills H., II (1990). *Tracking of Black, Hispanic, Asian, Native American and White students: National patterns and trends.* Baltimore, MD: The Johns Hopkins University, Center for Research on Effective Schooling for Disadvantaged Students.

Bransford, John D., Brown, Amy L., & Cocking, Rodney R. (Eds.). (1999). *How people learn: Brain, mind, experience, and school.* Washington, DC: National Academy Press.

Burke, Fred. (1998). An anatomy of education reform. The Phelps-Stokes fund, New York. *Dialogue: An Essay on Opinion and Policy, 7.*

Burke, Nancy. (1998). *Teachers are special: A tribute to those who educate, encourage, and inspire.* New York: Random House Value Publishing.

Camp competition builds middle-school confidence. (1997). *What Works in Teaching and Learning, 29*(18), 1–2.

Campbell, Linda & Campbell, Bruce. (1999). *Multiple intelligences and student achievement: Success stories from six schools.* Alexandria, VA: Association for Supervision and Curriculum Development.

Carnegie Corporation. (1993). Turning points revisited: A new deal for adolescents. *Carnegie Quarterly, 38*(2), 1–6.

Carnegie Council on Adolescent Development. (1989). *Turning points: Preparing American youth for the 21st century: Report of the Task Force on Education of Young Adolescents.* Washington, DC: Author.

Carnegie Council on Adolescent Development. (1992). *A matter of time: Risk and opportunity in the non-school hours. Report of the Task Force on Youth Development and Community Programs.* Washington, DC: Author.

Center for Research on Effective Schooling for Disadvantaged Students. (November 1990). *One-to-one tutoring: Procedures for early reading success.* Baltimore, MD: The Johns Hopkins University.

Center for the Study of Reading. (1989). *10 ways to help your children become better readers.* Champaign, IL: University of Illinois.

Center on Organization and Restructuring of Schools. (1992). *Estimating the extent of school restructuring. Brief to Policymakers.* (No. 4).

Chandler, Kathryn A. (13 April 1998). Gangs, violent crime in schools rose since 1989. *The Idaho Statesman,* 4A.

Charlesworth, Rosalind. (1989). "Behind" before they start? Deciding how to deal with the risk of kindergarten "failure." *Young Children, 44*(3), 5–13.

Children's Defense Fund. (1998). *The state of America's children: Yearbook 1998.* Washington, DC: Children's Defense Fund.

The Choice Program Handbook. (1998). Minneapolis, MN: Minnesota Department of Children, Families and Learning. Author.

Christensen, Linda. (Fall 1998). Reconstituting Jefferson. *Rethinking Schools, 13*(1), 1–3.

Christians plot course to vacate public schools. (24 August 1998). *Education USA, 40*(17), 1, 3.

Clay, M. M. (1991). *Becoming literate: The construction of inner control.* Portsmouth, NH: Heinemann.

Coalition of Essential Schools. (1999). *A response to an educators' guide to schoolwide reform.* Providence, RI: Fall Forum Publications.

Coleman, James. (1991). *Policy perspectives: Parental involvement in education.* Washington, DC: U.S. Department of Education, Office of Educational Research and Improvement.

Coles, Adrienne D. (2 June 1999). More teachers and students say violence in schools is declining. *Education Week, 18*(30), 8.

Colorado Foundation for Families and Children. (December 1995). *School expulsions: A cross-system problem.* Denver, CO: Author.

Colorado Foundation for Families and Children. (1999). *Colorado fatherhood connection.* Denver, CO: Author.

Comer, James P. (1988). Educating poor minority children. *Scientific American, 259*(5), 42–48.

Comer, James P. (1993). *School power: Implications of an intervention project.* New York: Free Press.

Comer, James P. (1999). *Child by child: The Comer process for change in education.* New York: Teachers College Press.

Combs, Arthur W., Miser, Ann B., & Whitaker, Kathryn S. (1999). *On becoming a school leader: A person-centered challenge.* Alexandria, VA: Association for Supervision and Curriculum Development.

Cushman, Kathleen. (June 1999). Essential school structure and design: Boldest moves get the best results. *Horace, 15*(5), 1–7.

Dallea, Georgia. (9 February 1987). For the conflicts of youth, help from a peer. *New York Times,* p. 1.

Dalton, David W. (1986). How effective is interactive video in improving performance and attitudes? *Educational Technology, 26*(1).

Darling-Hammond, Linda, Ancess, Jacqueline, & Falk, Beverly. (1995). *Authentic assessment in action: Studies of schools and students at work.* New York: Teachers College Press.

Darling-Hammond, Linda, & Falk, Beverly. (Summer 1996). *Alternatives to grade retention, reasons for restructuring.* National Center for Restructuring Education, Schools, and Teaching, p. 1.

Davis, William E. (1995). The full-service-schools movement: Emerging opportunities—emerging threats. Paper presented at the Annual Meeting of the American Psychological Association (New York: August 1995).

Davis, William E., & McCaul, Edward J. (1991). *The emerging crisis: Current and projected status of children in the United States.* Orono, ME: University of Maine, Institute for the Study of At-Risk Students.

Demos, Virginia. (1989). Resiliency in infancy. In Timothy Dugan and Robert Coles (Eds.), *The children in our time* (pp. 3–22). New York: Bruner/Mazel.

Deshler, Donald D., Schumaker, J. B., Alley, G. R., Warner, M. M., & Clark, F. L. (1982). Learning disabilities in adolescent and young adult populations: Research implications. *Focus on Exceptional Children, 15*(1), 1–12.

Designs for Learning. (1992). *Community learning centers: Design* (Draft). St. Paul, MN: Author.

Designs for Learning. (October 1993). *Community learning centers,* 1–2. St. Paul, MN: Author.

Development of accelerated middle schools. (1993). *Accelerated Schools, 3*(1), 10–15.

Dill, V.S. (1998). *A peaceable school.* Bloomington, IN: Phi Delta Kappa Educational Foundation.

Diller, Lawrence H. (Fall 1998). Running on Ritalin. *Teacher Magazine, 10*(2), 50–53.

Dryfoos, Joy G. (1998). *Full-service schools: A revolution in health and social services for children, youth, and families.* San Francisco, CA: Jossey-Bass.

Duttweiler, Patricia Cloud. (1992). Engaging at-risk students with technology. *Media and Methods, 29*(2), 6–8.

Edelman, Marian Wright. (1993). Foreword. In James P. Comer, *School power* (2nd ed. 1993) (pp. vii–viii).

Education Commission of the States. (1991). *Restructuring the education system: A consumer's guide.* Vol. 1, Denver, CO: Author.

Education Commission of the States. (1998a). *The progress of education reform 1998.* Denver, CO: Author.

Education Commission of the States. (1998b). *Selecting school-reform models: a reference guide for states.* Denver, CO: Author.

The Education Trust. (1999). *Dispelling the myth: High-poverty schools exceeding expectations.* Washington, DC: Author.

Eisenberg, Michael B., & Ely, Donald P. (Winter 1993). Plugging into the "Net." *The ERIC Review, 2*(3), 2–3.

Elam, Stanley M., Rose, Lowell C., & Gallup, Alec M. (1993). The 25th Annual Phi Delta Kappa/Gallup Poll of the Public's Attitudes Toward Public Education. *Phi Delta Kappan, 75*(2), 137–57.

Elias, Marilyn. (15 April 1999). Quality care prepares kids for school, life. *USA Today,* D-1.

Elias, Maurice J., Zins, Joseph E., Weissberg, Roger P., Frey, Karen S., Greenberg, Mark T., Haynes, Norris M., Kessler, Rachael, Schwab-Stone, Mary E., & Shriver, Timothy P. (1997). *Promoting social and emotional learning. Guidelines for educators.* Alexandria, VA: Association for Supervision and Curriculum Development.

Epstein, Joyce L. (1985). After the bus arrives: Resegregation in desegregation schools. *Journal of Social Issues, 41,* 23–43.

ERIC Clearinghouse on Elementary and Early Childhood Education. (1990). *Guidelines in family television viewing.* (ERIC Document Reproduction Service ED 320 662).

ERIC Clearinghouse on Elementary and Early Childhood Education. (1993). *What should be learned from kindergarten?* Urbana, IL: Author.

Erickson, Donald A. (December 1981). A new strategy for school improvement. *Momentum, 12*(4), 48.

Erickson, John W. (1988). *The next step.* Newport, OR: Lincoln County School District.

Ernst, D., & Amis, B. (November 1999). A growing movement. *INFOBRIEF, 19,* 1–8.

Estes, Nolan, Levin, Daniel, & Waldrip, Donald R. (1990). *Magnet Schools: Recent developments and perspectives.* Austin, TX: Morgan Printing and Publishing.

Evans, Dennis L. (26 May 1999). Evil, Unexplained. *Education Week, 18*(37), 34.

Fager, Jennifer. (February 1997). *Scheduling alternatives: Options for student success.* Portland, OR: Northwest Regional Education Laboratory.

Fager, Jennifer. (1998). *All students learning: Making it happen in your school.* Portland, OR: Northwest Regional Educational Laboratory.

Fager, J. & Boss, S. (1998). *Peaceful Schools.* Portland, OR: Northwest Regional Educational Laboratory.

Federal Interagency Forum on Child & Family Statistics. (1997). *America's children: Key national indicators of well-being.* [On-line]. Available: <http://www.cdc.gov/nchswww/about/otheract/children/child.htm>.

Froschl, Merle, Sprung, Barbara, Mullin-Rindler, Nancy, Stein, Nan, & Gropper, Nancy. (1999). *Quit it! A teacher's guide on teasing and bullying for use with students in grades K–3.* New York: Educational Equity Concepts.

Frymier, Jack. (1992). Children who hurt, children who fail. *Phi Delta Kappan, 73(12),* 257–59.

Frymier, Jack, Barber, L., Carriedo, R., Denton, W., Gansneder, B., Johnson-Lewis, S., & Robertson, N. (1992). *Growing up is risky business, and schools are not to blame.* Final report, Phi Delta Kappa study of students at risk, vol. 1. Bloomington, IN: Phi Delta Kappa.

Frymier, Jack, & Gansneder, Bruce. (1989). The Phi Delta Kappa study of students at risk. *Phi Delta Kappan, 71*(2), 142–146.

Fullan, M. (2000). The return of large scale school reform. *Journal of Education Change, 1.*

Gamoran, Adam. (October 1996). Do magnet schools boost achievement? *Educational Leadership, 54*(2).

Gathercoal, Forrest. (1992). *Judicious parenting.* San Francisco, CA: Caddo Gap Press.

Gathercoal, Forrest. (1999). *Judicious discipline,* 4th Ed. Ann Arbor, MI: Caddo Gap Press.

Gegax, T. Trent, & Bai, Matt. (10 May 1999). Searching for answers. *Newsweek, 31.*

Glasser, William. (1975). *Reality therapy: A new approach to psychiatry.* New York: HarperCollins Publishers.

Glasser, William. (1998). *Choice theory: a new psychology of personal freedom.* New York: HarperCollins Publishers.

Glickman, Carl. (1991). Pretending not to know what we know. *Educational Leadership, 48*(8), 4–10.

Goleman, Daniel. (1995). *Emotional Intelligence.* New York: Teachers College Press.

Goleman, Daniel. (1996). Emotional intelligence: Why it can matter more than IQ. *Learning 24*(6), 49–50.

Goodlad, John. (1984). *A place called school: Prospects for the future.* New York: McGraw-Hill.

Gottfredson, Gary D. (April 1988). *You get what you measure, you get what you don't: Higher standards, higher test scores, more retention in grade.* Paper presented at the annual meeting of the American Educational Research Association, New Orleans, LA.

Gregoire, C. (2000). *Bruised inside—What our children say about youth violence, what causes it, and what we need to do about it.* Washington, DC: National Association of Attorneys General.

Gregory, Thomas. (1993). *Making high school work: Lessons from the Open School.* New York: Teachers College Press.

Gross, Steven J. (1998). *Staying centered: curriculum leadership in a turbulent era.* Alexandria, VA: Association for Supervision and Curriculum Development.

Haberman, Martin, & Dill, Vicky. (1993). The knowledge base on retention vs. teacher ideology. Implications for teacher preparation. *Journal of Teacher Education, 44*(5), 352–60.

Hardy, Lawrence. (February 1999). Building blocks of reform. *The American School Board Journal, 186*(2), 16–21.

Hardy, Lawrence. (February 2000). Public School Choice. *The American School Board Journal, 187*(2), 22–26.

Hawkins, D. (1999). *Violence in America.* Cambridge, England: Cambridge University Press.

Hawthorne school. (1991). Unpublished evaluation report. Seattle, WA.

Heckinger, Fred M. (1992). *Fateful choices: Healthy youth for the 21st century.* New York: Carnegie Council on Adolescent Development.

Herman, Rebecca. (1999). *An educator's guide to schoolwide reform.* Washington, DC: American Institutes for Research.

Herndon, Ron (Director). (1990). *Partners for success* [video]. Portland, OR: Western Productions.

Herrmann, Beth Ann. (Ed). (1994). *The volunteer tutor's toolbox.* Newark, DE: International Reading Association.

Heubert, Jay P., & Hauser, Robert J. (Eds). (1999). *High stakes: Testing for tracking, promotion, and graduation.* Washington, DC: National Academy Press.

Hill, David. (1999). Everyone gets to play at Indiana middle school. *Education Week, 18*(34), 6–7.

Hillard, A. (1991). Do we have the will to educate all children? *Educational Leadership, 49*(1), 31–36.

Hobbs, Beverly. (1993). *School-community collaboration as a strategy for meeting the needs of at-risk youth*. Unpublished doctoral dissertation. Corvallis, OR: Oregon State University.

Hodgkinson, Harold L. (1985). *All one system: Demographics of education, kindergarten through graduate school*. Washington, DC: Institute for Educational Leadership.

Hodgkinson, Harold. (1993). American education: The good, the bad, and the task. In Stanley Elam (Ed.), *The state of the nation's public schools*. Bloomington, IN: Phi Delta Kappa.

Holmes, C. Thomas. (1990). Grade level retention effects; A meta-analysis of research studies. In Lorrie A. Shepard & Mary Lee Smith (Eds.), *Flunking grades: Research and policies on retention*. New York: Falmer Press.

Hopfenberg, Wendy S., & Levin, Henry M. (1993). *The accelerated schools resource guide*. San Francisco, CA: Jossey-Bass.

Howe, Harold II. (November 1991). America 2000: A bumpy ride on four trains. *Phi Delta Kappan, 73*(3), 192–203.

Hyman, I. A., & Snook, P. A. (March 2000). Dangerous schools and what you can do about them. *Phi Delta Kappan, 81*(7), 489–501.

Illich, Ivan. (1971). *De-schooling society*. New York: Harper and Row.

Illig, David. (1997). *Reducing class size: A review of the literature and options for consideration*. ERIC Digest. [ERIC Document Reproduction Service ED 407 699].

Institute for At-Risk Infants, Children, and Youth and Their Families. (1991). *Toward the development of models for evaluating teachers and educational personnel who work with at-risk students and their families: Identification of effective teaching strategies and practices for working with at-risk children and their families: A status report*. Tampa, FL: Author.

Institute for Educational Leadership. (1986). *Dropouts in America: Enough is known for action*. Washington, DC: Author.

Ivins, M. (16 November 1999). Media must deal with real issues. *The Idaho Statesman,* 7B.

Jacobson, Linda. (11 November 1998). Report highlights traits of ten top early childhood programs. *Education Week, 18*(11), 5.

Jenson, Eric. (1998). *Teaching with the brain in mind*. Alexandria, VA: Association for Supervision and Curriculum Development.

Johnson, D. W., & Johnson, R. T. (1994). *Learning together and alone: Cooperative, competitive, and individualistic learning* (4th ed.). Boston, MA: Allyn & Bacon.

Johnston, Robert C. (9 September 1998). California targets K–12 social promotions. *Education Week, 18*(1).

Jones, M. Gail, Jones, Brett D., Hardin, Belinda, Chapman, Lisa, Yarbrough, Tracie, & Davis, Marcia. (November 1999). The impact of high-stakes testing on teachers and students in North Carolina. *Phi Delta Kappan, 81*(3), 199–203.

Jones, V. F., & Jones, L. S. (1995). *Comprehensive classroom management: Creating positive learning environments for all students* (4th ed.). Boston, MA: Allyn & Bacon.

Josephson, Wendy. (1996). *Television violence: A review of the effects on children of different ages*. Ottawa, Ontario: National Clearinghouse on Family Violence.

Joyce, Bruce. (1986). *Improving America's schools*. New York: Longman, Greenman and Co.

A jump-start on school (January 1998). *Governing*(11), 4, 33.

Kann, L., Kinchen, S. A., Williams, B. I., Ross, J. G., Lowry, R., Hill, C. V., Grunbaum, J. A., Blumson, P. S., Colins, J. L., & Kolbe, L. J. (1998). Youth risk behavior surveillance—United States, 1997. *CDC Surveillance Summaries*. MMWR (No. SS-3). Washington, DC: U.S. Government Printing Office.

Kantrowitz, Barbara, & Wingert, Pat. (10 May 1999). How well do you know your kid? *Newsweek,* 36.

Karoly, Lynn A., Greenwood, Peter W., Everingham, Susan S., Hoube, Jill, Kilburn, M. Rebecca, Rydell, C. Peter, Sanders, Matthew, & Chiesa, James. (1998). *Investing in our children: What we know and don't know about the costs and benefits of early childhood interventions.* Santa Monica, CA: RAND.

Katz, L. G., & Chad, S. D. (1989). *Engaging children's minds: The project approach.* Norwood, NJ: Ablex Publishing.

Kelly, Karen. (January/February 1999). Retention versus social promotion: Schools search for alternatives. *Harvard Education Letter, 15*(1), 1–3.

Kennedy Manzo, Kathleen. (9 June 1999). Group to launch new international assessment. *Education Week, 23*(39), 5.

Keough, Robert. (28 April 1999). What's up, doc? *Education Week, 18*(33), 26–31.

Killion, Joellen. (1999). *What works in the middle: Results-based staff development.* Oxford, OH: National Staff Development Council.

Kirst, Michael W. (1993). Strengths and weaknesses of American education. Stanley Elam (Ed.), *The state of the nation's public schools.* Bloomington, IN: Phi Delta Kappa.

Klonsky, Susan, & Klonsky, Michael. (September 1999). In Chicago: Countering anonymity through small schools. *Educational Leadership, 57*(1), 38–41.

Kohl, Herbert. (1991). *I won't learn from you.* Minneapolis, MN: Milkweed Editions, Thistle Series.

Kohn, A. (1999). *The schools our children deserve.* New York: Houghton Mifflin Company.

Kolderie, Ted. (1993). The states begin to withdraw the "exclusive." *Changing Schools, 21*(3), 1–8.

Kotulak, R. (1996). *Inside the brain.* Kansas City, MO: Andrews and McMeel.

Kozol, Jonathan. (1991). *Savage inequalities: Children in America's schools.* New York, NY: Harper Perennial Publishers.

Krovetz, Martin L. (1999). *Fostering resiliency: Expecting all students to use their minds and hearts well.* Thousand Oaks, CA: Corwin Press, Inc.

Kuykendall, Crystal. (1992). *From rage to hope.* Bloomington, IN: National Educational Service.

Lambert, Linda. (1998). *Building leadership capacity in schools.* Alexandria, VA: Association for Supervision and Curriculum Development.

Lang, C. (1992). *Head Start: New challenges, new chances.* Newton, MA: Education Development Center.

Ledell, Marjorie, & Arnsparger, Arleen. (1993). *How to deal with community criticism of school change.* Alexandria, VA: Association for Supervision and Curriculum Development.

Lee, V., & Smith, J. B. (1992). *Effects of school restructuring on the achievement and engagement of middle grade students.* Madison, WI: University of Wisconsin, Center on Organization and Restructuring of Schools.

Leinhardt, Gaea, & Pallas, Allan. (1982). Restrictive educational settings: Exile or haven? *Review of Educational Research, 52,* 557–78.

LeTendre, Mary Jean. (1991). Improving Chapter 1 programs: We can do better. *Phi Delta Kappan, 72*(8), 576–80.

Levin, Henry M. (1989). *Accelerated schools: A new strategy for at-risk students.* Policy Bulletin no. 6, pp. 1–6. Bloomington, IN: Consortium on Educational Policy Studies.

Levin, Henry M. (1993). Accelerated visions. *Accelerated Schools, 3*(1), 1–2.

Levin, Henry M. (1991). What are accelerated schools? *Accelerated Schools, 1*(1), 1.

Lewis, Anne C. (October 1999). Time for schools to perform. *Phi Delta Kappan, 81*(2), 99, 100.

Lewis, Anne C. (November 1999). Standards and testing. *Phi Delta Kappan, 81*(3), 179–80.

Lieberman, David. (9–11 July 1999). Internet gap widening. *USA Today,* 1A.

Lohman, G. (31 March 2000). Diploma on-line. *The Herald.* Miami, FL.

MacIver, Douglas J., & Epstein, Joyce L. (1990). *How equal are opportunities for learning in disadvantaged and advantaged middle grade schools?* (Report No. 7). Baltimore, MD: The Johns Hopkins University, Center for Research on Effective Schools for Disadvantaged Students.

Madden, Nancy A., Slavin, R. E., Karweit, N. L., Dolan, L., & Wasik, B. A. (1991). Success for all. *Phi Delta Kappan, 72*(8), 593–599.

Magi Educational Services. (1985). *New York State magnet school research study.* Larchmont, NY: Author.

Maneuvers with Mathematics. (1995). Proposal submitted to the Program Effectiveness Panel of the National Diffusion Network. Washington, DC: U.S. Department of Education.

Mann, Dale. (1986). Can we help dropouts: Thinking about the undoable. *Teachers College Record, 87*(3), 307–323.

Manno, Bruno V., Finn Jr., Chester E., Bierlein, Louann A., & Varouek, Gregg. (March 1999). How charter schools are different: Lessons and implications from a national study. *Phi Delta Kappan, 79*(7), 48–98.

Mark of Cain. (15 January 1990). *Newsweek,* p. 6.

Marano, Hara Estroff. (1998). *Why doesn't anybody like me? A guide to raising socially confident kids.* New York: Morrow, William, and Company.

Mason Elementary School: Helping children beat the odds. (1993). *Accelerated Schools, 3*(1), 4–9.

Massachusetts Advocacy Center. (1988). *Before it's too late: Dropout prevention for the middle schools.* Carrboro, NC: Author.

McCafferty, Dennis. (19–21 November 1999). The best little school in Texas—and maybe America? *USA Weekend,* 16.

McCartney, Kathleen (April, 1999) Effect sizes from the NICHD study of early child care: NICHD early child care research network. Paper presented at the Biennial Meeting of the Society for Research in Child Development. Albuquerque, NM.

McGraw, Dan. (18 January 1999). Inspired students. *U.S. News & World Report, 126*(2), 66–71.

McGuillie, Strike. (8 November 1993). When fundamentalists run the schools. *Newsweek,* p. 45.

McPartland, James M., & Slavin, Robert E. (1990). *Policy perspectives: Increasing achievement of at-risk students at each grade level.* Washington, DC: U.S. Department of Education.

Mecklenburger, James A. (1992). The beginning of the "break-the-mold" express. *Phi Delta Kappan, 74*(4), 280–289.

Middle school model builds on common theme. (1997). *What Works in Teaching and Learning, 29*(18), 1–3.

Middle schools reflect essential school ideas. (1999). *Horace, 15*(3), 2.

Miller, William H. (1988, July 4). Employers wrestle with "dumb" kids. *Industry Week,* p. 48.

Molnar, Alex. (1993). Fundamental differences? *Educational Leadership, 51*(4), 4–5.

Muncey, Donna E. (1994). A response. *Teachers College Record, 96*(2), 167–73.

Muncey, Donna E., & McQuillan, Patrick J. (1993). Preliminary findings from a five-year study of the Coalition of Essential Schools. *Phi Delta Kappan, 74*(6), 486–89.

Nachtigal, Paul. (1972). *A foundation goes to school.* New York: The Ford Foundation.

Nash, M. A. (1990). *Improving their chances: A handbook for designing and implementing programs for at-risk youth.* Madison, WI: University of Wisconsin—Madison, Vocational Studies Center, School of Education.

Narvaez, Jr., Albert. (September, 1995). A gem of a choice. *Educational Leadership, 52*(1), 9–11.

Nathan, Joe (Ed.). (1989). *Public schools of choice.* St. Paul, MN: The Institute for Learning and Teaching.

Nathan, Joe. (1996). *Charter schools: Creating hope and opportunity for American education.* San Francisco: Jossey-Bass Publishers.

A nation at risk. (1983). A report by the National Commission on Excellence in Education, Washington, DC: U.S. Department of Education.

National Association of Secondary School Principals. (1996). Breaking ranks: Changing an American institution. A Report of the National Association of Secondary School Principals on the High School of the Twenty-first Century. *NASSP Bulletin, 80*(578), 55–66.

National Center for Early Development & Learning. (June 1999). *Executive Summary.* [On-line]. Available: <http://www.fpg.unc.edu/~ncedl/PAGES/cqes.html>.

National Center for Educational Statistics. (1991). *Dropout rates decline over decade.* Washington, DC: U.S. Department of Education, Office of Educational Research and Improvement.

The National Commission on Teaching & America's Future. (September 1996). *What matters most: Teaching for America's future.* (Summary Report). New York: Author.

National PTA. (1998). *National Standards for parent/family programs.* Chicago, IL: Author.

National School Boards Association. (1989). *An equal chance: Educating at-risk children to succeed.* Alexandria, VA: Author.

National School Safety Center. (1999). Checklist of characteristics of youth who have caused school-associated violent deaths. [On-line]. Available: <http://www.webmaster@nssc1.org>.

Natriello, Gary. (1988). *An examination of the assumptions and evidence for alternative dropout prevention programs in high school.* Report No. 365. Baltimore, MD: The Johns Hopkins University, Center for Social Organization of Schools.

Nevada toughens middle school. (1998). *Education Week, 17*(43), 4.

New initiatives can help students prepare for college early. (January 1999). *Community Update, 63.* U.S. Department of Education.

Newman, Fred. (1987). *Conference proceedings: Meeting the needs of youth at risk.* Portland, OR: Northwest Regional Educational Laboratory.

NICHD Exhibit. (17 April 1999). The NICHD study of early child care. [On-line]. Available: <http://www.apa.org/ppo/nichd/study.html>.

Nichols, J. (1990). R.I.P. The deadly art of team-teaching with a talking head. Paper presented at the Rural Education Symposium of the American Council on Rural Special Education and the National Rural and Small Schools Consortium (Tucson, AZ: 18–22 March 1990).

Northwest Regional Education Laboratory. (1990a). *Annual Report to Members* [ERIC Document Reproduction Service, No. ED 331 627].

Northwest Regional Education Laboratory. (1990b). *Effective schooling practices: A research synthesis 1990 update.* Portland, OR: Author.

Northwest Regional Education Laboratory. (1993a). *Community as classrooms.* (Northwest Report, pp. 6–7). Portland, OR: Author.

Northwest Regional Education Laboratory. (1993b). *Schools, agencies team up for health.* (Northwest Report, pp. 1–4.) Portland, OR: Author.

Northwest Regional Education Laboratory. (1998). *Catalog of School Reform Models.* Portland, OR: Author.

Northwest Regional Education Laboratory. (Spring 1999a). Learning in peace: Schools look toward a safe future. *Northwest Education, 4*(3), 10.

Northwest Regional Education Laboratory. (1999b). *Research you can use to improve results.* Alexandria, VA: Author.

Oakes, Jeannie. (1993). *Last chance high: How girls and boys drop in and out of alternative schools.* New Haven, CT: Yale University Press.

Office of Educational Research and Improvement (1992). *New reports focus on eighth graders and their parents.* Washington, DC: U.S. Department of Education, National Center For Educational Strategies.

O'Neil, J., & Willis, S. (1998). Revitalizing the disciplines. *The best of ASCD's Curriculum Update.* Alexandria, VA: Association for Supervision and Curriculum Development.

O'Neill, Patrick. (25 May 1998). Experts: Inner chaos fuels kids who kill. *The Oregonian,* A13.

Our mission and goals. (15 October 1997). *Success by 6, 1*(1). Author.

Palinscar, A. S., & Brown, A. L. (1984). Reciprocal teaching of comprehension-fostering and comprehension-monitoring activities. *Cognition and Instruction, 2,* 117–75.

Pallas, A. M., Natriello, G., & McDill, E. L. (1989). The changing nature of 9 disadvantaged population: Current dimensions and future trends. *Educational Researcher, 18*(5), 4 and 16–22.

Parnell, Dale. (1982). *The neglected majority.* Washington, DC: Community College Press.

Parrett, William. (1979). *An investigation of teachers' and students' perceptions of instructional practices in alternative schools.* Unpublished doctoral dissertation, Indiana University, Bloomington, IN.

Perry, Bruce. (3 May 1999). Why the young kill. *Newsweek (Special Report),* 32–35.

Phi Delta Kappa International. (12 August 1998). The 30th annual Phil Delta Kappa/Gallup Poll of the public's attitudes toward the public schools. [On-line]. Available: <http://www/pdkintl.org/kappan/kp9809-3.htm>.

Pinnell, Gay Su. (1990). Success for low achievers through Reading Recovery. *Educational Leadership, 48*(1), 17–21.

Pinnell, G. S., Lyons, C. A., DeFord, D. E., Bryk, A.S., & Seltzer, M. (1994). Comparing instructional models for the literacy education of high-risk first graders. *Reading Research Quarterly, 29,* 9–38.

Pipho, Chris. (November 1999). The evolutions of standards, charters, and finance. *Phi Delta Kappan, 81*(3), 181–82.

Profile Approach to Writing. (1995). Profile Approach to Writing: Submission to the Program Effectiveness Panel of the U.S. Department of Education. Washington, DC: U.S. Department of Education.

Project SEED, Inc. (1995). Project SEED: Submission to the program effectiveness panel of the U.S. Department of Education. Berkeley, CA, & Dallas, TX: Author.

Raasch, Chuck. (28 December 1997). Adults see world of peril for today's kids. *Idaho Statesman,* 5A.

Ramey, Craig T., & Ramey, Sharon L. (1999). *Right from birth: Building your child's foundation for life.* New York: Goddard Press, Inc.

Rasmussen, John. (March 1998). Looping—discovering the benefits of multiyear teaching. *Education Update, 40*(2), 1, 3.

Raspberry, William. (30 November 1999). Polls on school options don't mean much. *Idaho Statesman,* 7B.

Ray, Brian D. (1997). *Strengths of their own—home schoolers across America: Academic achievement, family characteristics, and longitudinal traits.* Salem, OR: National Home Education.

Raywid, Mary Ann. (1983). Schools of choice: Their current nature and prospects. *Phi Delta Kappan, 64*(10), 684–688.

Raywid, Mary Ann. (1993a). Community: An alternative school accomplishment. In G. Smith (ed.), *Public schools that work* (pp. 23–44). New York: Routledge.

Raywid, Mary Ann. (1993b). Finding time for collaboration. *Educational Leadership, 51*(2), 30–34.

Raywid, Mary Anne. (1994). Alternative schools: The state of the art. *Education Leadership 52*(1), 26–31.

Raywid, Mary Anne. (1999). Central Park East Secondary School: The anatomy of success. *Journal of Education for Students Placed at Risk, 4*(2), 131–51.

Reid, E. M. (1989). Exemplary Center for Reading Instruction: Submission to the Program Effectiveness Panel of the U.S. Department of Education. Washington, DC: U.S. Department of Education.

Resnick, M. D., Bearman, P. S., Blum, R. W., Bauman, K. E., Harris, K. M., Jones, J., Tabor, T., Beuhring, T., Sieving, R. E., Shew, M., Ireland, M., Bearinger, L. H., & Udry, J. R. (10 September 1997). Protecting adolescents from harm: Findings from the national longitudinal study on adolescent health. *Journal of American Medical Association 287*(10), 823–32.

Rich, Dorothy. (19 May 1999). Competing for our clients: Winning the hearts and minds of parents. *Education Week, 18*(36), 46, 49.

Ridenour, Amy. (1999). *This Father's Day, think about the vital role of dads in family life.* Washington, DC: National Policy Analysis, The National Center for Public Policy Research.

Riley outlines sobering facts on crime (2 August 1993). *Education USA, 6.*

Riley, Pamela. (1993). California's charter schools. *Changing Schools, 21*(3), 14–18.

Riley, Richard W. (1999). The American high school in the 21st century. Speech given at the National Press Club in Washington, D.C.

The Ritalin wrangle. (May/June 1999). *Teacher Magazine on the WEB.* [On-line]. Available: <http://www.edweek.org/tm/current/08health.h10>

Roderick, Melissa. (December 1995). Grade retention and school dropout: Policy debate and research questions. *Phi Delta Kappan (Research Bulletin, 15).*

Rogers, Marie. (June 1994). Resolving conflict through mediation. *Solutions and Strategies.* Clemson, SC: National Drop Out Center, 9, 1–12.

Rogien, Lawrence R. (1999). *School Safety Statistics, May 1999.* Unpublished manuscript, Boise State University.

Romer, Roy. (1993). Charter schools: A tool for reinventing public education. *Changing Schools, 21*(3), 1–9.

Safe Schools and Communities Coalition. (1998). *Alternative education: A force for the future.* Connecticut Office of Policy and Management.

Safe schools: Safe students: A guide to violence-prevention strategies. (1998). Minneapolis: Johnson Institute. Author.

Sarason, Seymour. (1971). *The culture of school and the problem of change.* Boston, MA: Allyn and Bacon.

Schnaiberg, Lynn. (9 June 1999). Home schooling queries spike after shootings. *Education Week 18*(39), 3.

Schnaiberg, Lynn. (27 October 1999). Mixed results seen for public-school choice in Michigan. *Education Week, 5.*

Schnaiberg, Lynn. (22 September 1999). More students taking advantage of school choice, report says. *Education Week, 19*(3), 6.

Schorr, Lisbeth. (1992). *Service integration and beyond: The challenge in integrating education and human services: Strategies to strengthen Northwest families.* Forum Proceeding, Northwest Regional Educational Laboratory.

Schorr, Lisbeth B., & Schorr, Daniel. (1989). *Within our reach: Breaking the cycle of disadvantage.* New York: Anchor Books/Doubleday.

Schweinhart, L. J., Barnes, H. V., & Weikart, D. P. (1993). *Significant benefits: The High/Scope Perry Preschool study through age 27* (Monographs of the High/Scope Educational Research Foundation, 10). Ypsilanti, MI: High/Scope Press.

Sea change: Meeting the challenge of school wide reform. (Fall 1999). *NW Education, 5*(1). Portland, OR: Northwest Regional Education Laboratories.

The secret life of teens. (10 May 1999). *Newsweek,* p. 45.

Shaywitz, Bennett A., & Shaywitz, Sally E. (1990). Prevalence of reading disability in boys and girls: Results of the Connecticut longitudinal study. *Journal of American Medical Association, 264*(8), 998–1002.

Shepard, Lorrie A., & Smith, Mary Lee. (1989). *Flunking grades: Research and policies on retention.* London: Falmer Press.

Shore, Rima. (1997). *Rethinking the brain: New insights into early development.* New York, NY: Families and Work Institute.

Sinclair, R. L., & Ghory, W. J. (1987). *Marginal students: A primary concern for school renewal.* Berkeley, CA: McCutchan.

Skills Reinforcement Project. (1992). Proposal submitted to the Program Effectiveness Panel of the National Diffusion Network. Washington, DC: U.S. Department of Education.

Slavin, Robert E. (1991a). Chapter 1: A vision for the next quarter century. *Phi Delta Kappan, 72*(8), 586–89, 591–92.

Slavin, Robert E. (1991b). Synthesis of research of cooperative learning. *Educational Leadership, 48*(5), 71–82.

Slavin, Robert E. (1994). *Using student team learning* (4th ed.). Baltimore: Johns Hopkins University, Center for Social Organization of Schools.

Slavin, Robert E., & Fashola, Olatokunbo S. (1998). *Show me the evidence! Proven and promising programs for America's schools.* Thousand Oaks, CA: Corwin Press.

Slavin, Robert E., Karweit, Nancy L., & Wasik, Barbara A. (December 1992). Preventing early school failure. *Educational Leadership, 50*(4), 10–18.

Slavin, Robert E., & Madden, Nancy A. (1989). What works for students at risk: A research synthesis. *Educational Leadership, 46*(5), 4–20.

Smith, Gerald R., Gregory, Thomas, B., & Pugh, Richard C. (1981). Meeting students' needs: Evidence for the superiority of alternative schools. *Phi Delta Kappan, 62*(8), 561–64.

Smith, Gregory A. (Ed.) (1993). *Public schools that work.* New York: Routledge. 254 pp.

Smith, R. C., & Lincoln, C. A. (1988). *America's shame, America's hope: Twelve million youth at risk.* Flint, MI: Charles Stewart Mott Foundation.

Smith, Vernon, Barr, Robert, & Burke, Daniel. (1976). *Alternatives in education: Freedom to choose.* Bloomington, Indiana: Phi Delta Kappa.

Spear-Swerling, Louise, & Sternberg, Robert J. (January 1998). Curing our "epidemic" of learning disabilities. *Phi Delta Kappan, 79*(5), 397–401.

Special Early Childhood Report 1997. (October 1997) Washington, DC: The National Education Goals Panel. Author.

St. Paul Open School. (1993). Program guidelines. [Brochure.] St. Paul, MN: Author.

State of New York. (1993). *Executive budget.* Albany, NY: Author.

State Policy Research, Inc. (January 1993). State Policy Reports. Vol. 11(2). Birmingham, AL: Author.

Steinberg, Lawrence. (1996). *Beyond the classroom: Why school reform has failed and what parents need to do.* New York: Simon & Schuster.

Steins, Nancy, Sjostrom, Lisa, & Gaberman, Emily. (1996). *Bullyproof: A teacher's guide on teasing and bullying for use with fourth and fifth grade students.* Westhaven, CT: National Education Association.

Stern, Marilyn, & VanSlych, Michael R. (1986). *Enhancing adolescent's self-image: implementation of a peer mediation program.* Paper presented at the meeting of the American Psychological Association, Washington, DC.

Stevens, R. J., Jadden, N. A., Slavin, R. E., & Farnish, A. M. (1987). Cooperative integrated reading and composition: Two field experiments. *Reading Research Quarterly, 22,* 433–54.

Stevenson, David, & Schneider, Barbara L. (1999). *The ambitious generation: America's teenagers, motivated but directionless.* New Haven, CT: Yale University Press.

Stichter, Charlotte. (1986). When tempers flare, let trained student mediators put out the flames. *American School Board Journal, 173*(3), 41–42.

Stiggins, Richard J. (November 1999). Assessment, student confidence, and school success. *Phi Delta Kappan, 81*(3), 191–98.

Study: High-quality child care pays off. (28 April 1999). *Education Week, 18*(33), 9.

Sweeney, Mary Ellen. (1993). Successful strategies for charter schools. A checklist. *Changing Schools, 21*(3), 9.

Taylor, Kate (24 May 1998). Experts seek reasons for epidemic of youth violence. *Oregonian,* A11.

Teaching for America's future. (September 1966). *What Matters Most.* New York: National Commission on Teaching and America's Future.

Teddlie, Charles, & Stringfield, Sam. (1993). *Schools make a difference: Lessons learned from a ten-year study of school effects.* New York: Teachers College Press.

Texas school ties promotion solely to state test scores. (3 June 1998). *What Works in Teaching and Learning,* 1, 3.

Tomlinson, Janis (May 1999). A changing panorama. *Infobrief: An information Brief of the Association for Supervision and Curriculum Development, 17.*

Trends in the well-being of American youth. (September 1996). National Centers for Education Statistics.

Trotter, A. (3 June 1998). $80 million gift to boost technology in Idaho schools. *Education Week.* [On-line]. Available: <http://www.edweek.org>.

Tucker, Adam. (1999). A response to an educator's guide to schoolwide reform. *Coalition of Essential Schools* (Addendum to an Educators' Guide to Schoolwide Reform).

Tucker, Mare S., & Codding, Judy. (1998). *Standards for our schools: How to set them, measure them, and track them.* San Francisco: Jossey-Bass.

U.S. Department of Commerce. (1999). *Statistical Abstract of the United States 1998.* Pittsburgh, PA: U.S. Census Bureau.

U.S. Department of Education. (1987a). *What works: Research about teaching and learning* (2nd ed.). Washington, DC: Author.

U.S. Department of Education. (1987b). *What works: Schools that work.* Washington, DC: Author.

U.S. Department of Education. (1998a). *Early warning, timely response: A guide to safe schools.* Washington, DC: Author.

U.S. Department of Education. (1998b). *Turning around low-performing schools: A guide for state and local leaders.* Washington, DC: Author.

U.S. Department of Education. (1999). Taking responsibility for ending social promotion: A guide for educators, state and local leaders. [On-line]. Available: <http://www.ed.gov/pubs/socialpromotion.html>.

Ventura, Stephanie J., Mathews, T. J., & Curtin, Sally C. (1999). Declines in teenage birth rates, 1991–98: Update of National and State Trends. *Centers for Disease Control and Prevention, 47*(25).

Viadero, Debra. (9 February 1994). "Impact of reform said to be spotty and not systemic." *Education Week, 13*(20), 1, 12.

Viadero, Debra. (18 January 1999). Higher standards. *U.S. News & World Report, 126*(2), 52–54.

Viteritti, J. P. (February 23, 2000). School choice: Beyond the numbers. *Education Week, 19*(24), 38–44.

Waldrip, Donald R., Marks, Walter L., & Estes, Nolan. (1993). *Magnet school policy studies and evaluations.* Austin, TX: Morgan Printing.

Walser, Nancy. (January/February 1998). Multi-age classrooms: An age-old grouping method is still evolving. *Harvard Education Letter, 14*(1), 1–3.

Walsh, Mark. (26 April 1995). Sylvan makes quiet inroads into public schools. Education Week on the Web. [On-line]. Available: <http://www.edweek.org>.

Walsh, Mark. (7 May 1997). Court strengthens protections for districts from civil rights suits. *Education Week* (16), 7.

Walsh, Mark. (4 August 1999). Edison project plans expansion as new investors provide $71 million boost. *Education Week, 18*(43), 10.

Wasik, Barbara, & Slavin, Robert E. (1993). Preventing early reading failure with one to one tutoring. A review of five programs. *Reading Research Quarterly, 28*(2), 179–200.

Waterman, Alan S. (Ed.). (1979). *Service learning: Application from the research.* Mahwah, NJ: Lawrence Erlbaum Associates.

Wehlage, Gary G., Rutter, Robert A., Smith, Gregory A., Lesko, Nancy, & Fernandez, Ricardo R. (1989). *Reducing the risk: Schools as communities of support.* Philadelphia, PA: The Falmer Press.

Wells, Amy Stuart. (1991). *Middle school education—The critical link, striving for excellence: The national goals.* Washington, DC: U.S. Department of Education, Office of Educational Research and Improvement, Educational Resource Information Center.

Werner, Emmy, & Smith, Ruth. (1982). *Vulnerable but invincible: A longitudinal study of resilient children and youth.* New York: Adams, Bannister & Cox.

West, Pete. (19 June 1996). Career academies appear to benefit students and teachers. *Education Week,* p. 15.

What are accelerated schools? (1991). *The Accelerated Schools Newsletter, 1*(1), 1–16.

Wheaton, C., & Kay, S. (October 1999). Every child will read—we guarantee it. *Education Leadership, 57*(2), 1–7.

Wheelock, A. (1998). *Safe to be smart: Building a culture for standards-based reform in the middle grades.* Columbus, OH: National Middle School Association.

Wheelock, C. (1986). Dropping out: What the research says. *Equity and Choice, 3*(1), 7–10.

White, Kerry A. (3 November 1999). Gathering of mayors focuses on vouchers, charter schools. *Education Week.*

White, Kerry A. (1999). High-poverty schools score big on Kentucky assessment. *Education Week, 18*(34), 18, 20.

Whitmire, Richard. (23 April 1997). Kids who are read to usually learn better: Students make strides in short, long term. *Idaho Statesman,* 10A.

Wigtil, James V., & Wigtil, Joanne M. (1993). Counseling with at-risk students. In Ann Vernon (Ed.) *Counseling children and adolescents* (pp. 160–179). Denver, CO: Love Publishing.

Wilson, James Q. (4 December 1997). *Two Nations.* Paper presented at the Annual Dinner of the American Enterprise Institute, Washington, DC.

Wilt, Joan. (1993). Charter schools: An entrepreneurial approach to public schools. *Changing Schools, 21*(3), 10–12.

Winter, Sam. (1986). Peers as paired reading tutors. *British Journal of Special Education, 13*(3), 103–106.

Wolfe, Pat, & Brandt, Ron. (November 1998). What do we know from brain research? *Education Leadership, 56*(3), 8–13.

Young, Timothy. (1990). *Public alternative education: Options and choice for today's schools.* New York: Teachers College Press.

Young, Timothy, & Clinchy, Evans. (1993). *Choice in public education.* New York: Teachers College Press.

Ziebarth, Todd. (Winter 1999). Choice: New trend in education governance. Education Commission of the States: *State Education Leader, 17*(1), 11–14.

Zimmerman, Jack, Norris, Dia, Kirkpatrick, Jerry, Mann, Augusta, & Herndon, Ron. (1989). *Partners for success: Business and education.* Portland, OR: National Association for Schools of Excellence.

Appendix *A*

Where to Find Help

As the crisis of educating all youth continues to focus the nation's attention on improving schools and expanding community interventions, resources such as these can assist individuals and organizations with their critical efforts toward seeking solutions to this continuing peril.

Organizations, Institutes, and Centers

Alliance for Parental Involvement in Education (ALLPIE), PO Box 59, East Chatham, NY 12060-0059. Phone: (518) 392-6900. E-mail: <allpie@taconic.net>.

Alternative Education Resource Organization (AERO), 417 Roslyn Road, Roslyn Heights, NY 11577. Phone: (800) 769-4171. Web site: <http://www.edrev.org>.

American Council on Rural Special Education, Miller Hall 359, Western Washington University, Bellingham, WA 98225.

Antioch New England Graduate School, 40 Avon Street, Keene, NH 03431. Phone: (603) 357-3122. Web site: <http://www.antiochne.edu>.

Association for Experiential Education, 2305 Canyon Blvd., Suite 100, Boulder, CO 80302. Phone: (303) 440-8844.

Association of Waldorf Schools of North America, 3911 Bannister Road, Fair Oaks, CA 95628. Phone: (916) 961-0927. Web site: <http://www.waldorfeducation.org>.

Center for Applied Research and Educational Improvement. Web site: <http://carei. coled.umn.edu/charter.html>.

Center for Community Education, State University of New Jersey-Rutgers, School of Social Work, 73 Easton Avenue, New Brunswick, NJ 08903.

Center for Dropout Prevention, University of Miami, School of Education, Box 248065, Coral Gables, FL 33124.

Center for Early Adolescence, University of North Carolina at Chapel Hill, Suite 211, Carr Mill Mall, Carrboro, NC 27510.

Center for Education Reform, 1001 Connecticut Avenue, NW, Suite 204, Washington, DC 20036. Phone: (800) 521-2118. Web site: <http://edreform.com>.

Center for Education Reform. Web site: <http://edreform.com/charters.htm>.

Center for Inspired Learning. Web site: <http://www.inspiredinside.com/learning>.

Center for Research on Effective Schooling for Disadvantaged Students, Johns Hopkins University, 3505 North Charles Street, Baltimore, MD 21218.

Center for Research on Elementary and Middle Schools (formerly Center for Social Organization of Schools, Johns Hopkins University, 3505 North Charles Street, Baltimore, MD 21218.

Center for the Prevention of School Violence, 20 Enterprise Street, Suite 2, Raleigh, NC 27607-7375. Phone: (919) 515-9397. Fax: (919) 515-9561. E-mail: <pamela_riley@ncsu.edu>. Web site: <www.ncsu.edu/cpsv/>. Director: Dr. Pamela Riley.

Center for Safe and Drug Free Schools, 3782 Jackson Avenue, Memphis, TN 38108. Phone: (901) 385-4240. Fax: (901) 385-4221. Supervising Psychologist: Mr. Ken Strong.

Center for Safe Schools, 1300 Market Street, Suite 301, Lemoyne, PA 17043. Phone: (717) 763-1661. Director: Mr. Charles Spanno.

Center for School Improvement, Boise State University, 1910 University Drive, Boise, ID 83725. Email: <CSI@BoiseState.edu>.

Center for School Safety, Eastern Kentucky University, 300 Stratton Building, 521 Lancaster Avenue, Richmond KY 40475-3102. Codirector: Bruce Wolford.

Center for Social Organization of Schools, The Johns Hopkins University, 3003 North Charles Street, Suite 200, Baltimore, MD 21218. Phone: (410) 516-8800. Fax: (410) 516-8890. Web site: <http://scov.csos.jhu.edu/indes.html>.

Center for the Study and Teaching of At-Risk Students, Institute for the Study of Educational Policy, University of Washington, Miller Hall, Seattle, WA 98195.

Chapter 37, 1701 North Congress Avenue, Austin, TX 78701-1494. Phone: (512) 463-9073. Fax: (512) 475-3665. Secretary: (512) 463-9982. Program Director for Safe Schools: Mr. Billy G. Jacobs.

Charter School Research Site. Web site: <http://csr.syr.edu>.

Children's Defense Fund, 122 C Street, NW, Washington, DC 20001.

Cities in Schools, Inc., 1023 15th Street, NW, Suite 600, Washington, DC 20005.

Down to Earth Books, PO Box 163, Goshen, MA 01032. Web site: <http://www.crocker.com/~maryl/index.html>.

Drug-Free Schools & Communities Programs (OSPI), Washington State School Safety Center, PO Box 47200, Olympia, WA 98504-7200. Phone: (360) 753-5595. Fax: (360) 664-3028.

Drugs Don't Work, Connecticut Safe Schools Coalition, 30 Arbor Street, Hartford CT 06106. Phone: (860) 231-8311. Fax: (860) 236-9412. Ms. Cate Boone.

Education Commission of the States, 1860 Lincoln Street, Suite 300, Denver, CO 80295.

EnCompass, 11011 Tyler Foote Road, Nevada City, CA 95960. Phone: (530) 292-1000.

Family Resource Coalition, 230 N. Michigan Avenue, Room 1625, Chicago, IL 60601.

Genius Tribe, PO Box 1014, Eugene, OR 97440-1014. Phone: (541) 686-2315.

Goddard College, Plainfield, VT 05667. Phone: (802) 454-8311. Web site: <http://www.goddard.edu>.

Great Ideas in Education/Holistic Education Press, PO Box 328, Brandon, VT 05733-0328. Phone: (800) 639-4122. Web site: <http://www.great-ideas.org>.

Growing Without Schooling, Holt Associates, 2380 Massachusetts Avenue, Suite 104, Cambridge, MA 02140. Phone: (617) 864-3100. Web site: <http://www.holt-gws.com>.

Heinemann, 361 Hanover Street, Portsmouth, NH 03801-3912. Phone: (800) 793-2154. Web site: <http://www.heinemann.com>.

Home Education Magazine, PO Box 1083, Tonasket, WA 98855. Phone: (800) 236-3278.

Hubert Humphrey Institute, Center for School Change, 301 Nineteenth Avenue South, Minneapolis, MN 55455.

Independent Sector, 1828 L Street Northwest, Washington, DC 20036.

Institute for At-Risk Infants, Children and Youth and Their Families, University of South Florida, 4202 Fowler Avenue, Tampa, FL 33620.

Institute for Children At Risk, Continuing Professional Education, Lewis and Clark College, Campus Box 85, Portland, OR 97219.

Institute for Education Reform. Web site: <http://www.csus.edu/ier/charter.html>.

Institute for Educational Renewal (INFER), Jackson State University, PO Box 17088, Jackson, MS 39217.

Institute for Responsive Education, 605 Commonwealth Avenue, Boston, MA 02215.

Institute for the Study of At-Risk Students, College of Education, 306 Shibles Hall, University of Maine, Orono, ME 04469.

International Quality Leadership Institute, Solving violence in our communities: A common sense approach. Contact: David Banner. E-mail: <dbanner@wmt.net>.

International Renewal Institute, Inc., 2626 South Clearbrook Drive, Arlington Heights, IL 60005-5310, Phone: (800) 348-4474. Fax: (847) 290-6609.

John Dewey Project on Progressive Education, 535 Waterman Building, University of Vermont, Burlington, VT 05405. Phone: (802) 656-1355.

Jola Publications, 2933 North Second Street, Minneapolis, MN 55411. Phone: (612) 529-5001.

Missouri Center for Safe Schools. University of Missouri–Kansas City, School of Education, 319 Education Building, 5100 Rockhill Road, Kansas City, MO 64110. Phone: (816) 235-5657. Fax: (816) 235-5270. Director: Dr. Pat Henley.

National Association for Core Curriculum, 1650 Franklin Avenue, Suite 104, Kent, OH 44240. Phone: (330) 677-5008.

National Association of Partners in Education, Inc., 601 Wythe Street, Suite 200, Alexandria, VA 22314.

National Association of State Boards of Education, 1012 Cameron Street, Alexandria, VA 22314.

National Center on Effective Secondary Schools, School of Education, University of Wisconsin-Madison, 1025 West Johnson Street, Madison, WI 53706.

National Center for Parents in Dropout Prevention, National Committee for Citizens in Education, Suite 301, 10840 Little Patuxent Parkway, Columbia, MD 21044.

National Center for Social Work and Education Collaboration, Fordham University, 113 West Sixtieth Street, Suite 704, New York, NY 10023. Phone: (212) 636-6699. Fax: (212) 636-6033. Director: Carolyn Denham, Ph.D.

National Coalition of Alternative Community Schools, 1266 Rosewood #1, Ann Arbor, MI 48104. Phone: (734) 668-9171. Web site: <http://www.geocities.com/Athens/8187/ncacs.htm>.

National Coalition of Education Activists, PO Box 679, Rhinebeck, NY 12572. Email address: <ncea@aol.com>.

National Committee for Citizens in Education, 10840 Little Patuxent Parkway, Suite 301, Columbia, MD 21044.

National Community Education Association, 119 North Payne Street, Alexandria, VA 22314.

National Community Education Association, 3929 Old Lee Highway, #91A, Fairfax, VA 22042. Phone: (703) 359-8973. Web site: <http://www.ncea.com>.

National Crime Prevention Council, 733 15th Street North West, Suite 540, Washington, DC 20005.

National Dropout Prevention Center, Clemson University, 393 College Avenue, Clemson, SC 29634.

National Dropout Prevention Network, Ohio State University, 1960 Kenny Road, Columbus, OH 43210.

National Dropout Prevention Network, P.O. Box 4067, Napa, CA 94558.

National Dropout Prevention Network, 1517 L Street, Sacramento, CA 95814.

National Resource Center for Children in Poverty, School of Public Health, Columbia University, New York, NY 10032.

National Rural and Small Schools Consortium, Miller Hall 359, Western Washington University, Bellingham, WA 98225.

National School Conference Institute, P.O. Box 941, Rimrock, AZ 86335.

National School Safety Center, Northwest Regional Educational Laboratory, 101 SW Main Street, Suite 500, Portland, OR 97204. Phone: (503) 275-9500. Fax: (503) 275-0458. E-mail: <info@nwrel.org>. Web site: <http://www.nwrel.org>.

National School Safety Center, Westlake Village, CA.

New Horizons for Learning, PO Box 15329, Seattle, WA 98115. Phone: (206) 547-7936. Web site: <http://www.newhorizons.org>.

New York Charter Schools Resource Center, 41 Robbins Avenue, Amityville, NY 11701. Phone: (516) 598-4426. Fax: (516) 598-4436. E-mail: <nycharters@yahoo.com> Internet: <www.nycharterschools.org>.

New York State School Safety Center, New York State Education Department, Comprehensive Health and Pupil Services, 318 EB, Albany, NY 12234. Phone (518) 486-6090. Ms. Arlene Sheffield.

Northeast Foundation for Children, 71 Montague City Road, Greenfield, MA 01301. Phone: (800) 360-6332. Web site: <http://responsiveclassroom.org>.

Office of School Safety, State Department of Education, State Office Park South, 101 Pleasant Street, Concord, NH 03301. Phone: (603) 271-3828. Fax: (603) 271-3830. Assistant to the Commissioner: Mr. Gerald P. Bourgeois.

Rethinking Schools, 1001 East Keefe Avenue, Milwaukee, WI 53212. Phone: (800) 669-4192. Web site: <http://www.rethinkingschools.org>.

Safe and Drug-Free Schools, South Carolina State Department of Education, Room 1114, 1429 Senate Street, Columbia, SC 29201. Phone: (803) 734-8101. Fax: (803) 734-4387. Education Associate: Mr. Wayne Cole.

Safe Schools and Violence Prevention Office. California Department of Education, 560 J Street, Suite 260, Sacramento, CA 95814. Phone: (916) 343-2183. Fax: (916) 323-6061. Program Administrator: Ms. Mary Weaver.

Stanford Accelerated School Project, c/o Henry M. Levin, CERAS 402, Stanford University, Stanford, CA 94305.

State Department of Education, Commonwealth of Virginia, PO Box 2120, Richmond, VA 23218-2120. Phone: (804) 225-2928. Fax: (804) 371-8796. Safe School, Ms. Marsha Hubbard.

U.S. Charter Schools. Web site: <http://www.uscharterschools.org>.

Vocational Studies Center, University of Wisconsin-Madison, School of Education, 964 Educational Sciences Bldg., 1025 West Johnson Street, Madison, WI 53706.

WestEd's Choice and Charter Schools Page. Web site: <http://www.wested.org/policy/charter>.

Youth Service America, 1319 F Street North West, Suite 900, Washington, DC 20004.

Zephyr Press, PO Box 66006, Tucson, AZ 85728-6006. Phone: (800) 232-2187. Web site: <http://www.zephyrpress.com>.

Resource Directories

Center on Organization and Restructuring of Schools. (1993). *1993 bibliography on school restructuring.* Madison, WI: Author. 35 pp.

Directory of Public, Magnet, and Theme-Based Schools, 1996. Magnet Schools of America, 2111 Holly Hall, Suite 704, Houston, TX 77054. Phone: (713) 796-9536.

Far West Laboratory for Educational Research and Improvement. (1989). *Papers, programs, and technical assistance services for educators of at-risk students.* San Francisco: Author. 102 pp.

International Consulting Associates. (1990). *Quick reference guide to school dropouts.* Stockton, CA: Author. 52 pp.

Mastny, A. Y. (1989). *Linking schools and community services: Resource directory.* New Brunswick, NJ: Center for Community Education, School of Social Work, Rutgers, State University of New Jersey. 80 pp.

Oregon Department of Education. (1989). *Oregon's innovative approaches for students who are seriously emotionally disturbed or otherwise at risk.* OR: Author. 101 pp.

Patterns: A Directory of State Alternative Education Associations, Published annually, 1201 NW 109th Street, Vancouver, WA 98685. Phone: (306) 574-4017, $6 plus $3 postage/handling.

Simons, J. (1989). *Where to find data about adolescents and young adults: A guide to sources.* Washington, DC: Children's Defense Fund, 31 pp.

Trent, S. C. (1992). School choice for African-American children who live in poverty: A commitment to equity or more of the same? *Urban Education, 27*(3), 291-307.

Newsletters and Journals

The following newsletters and journals cover a broad range of topics concerning at-risk youth and those who work in this area. These publications also list upcoming conferences, grants, organizations, current research, publications and resource materials, new programs, and summaries of research—all relating to at-risk youth.

Accelerated Schools. A quarterly publication and official newsletter of the Accelerated Schools Project, Center for Educational Research at Stanford School of Education, Stanford University, Stanford, CA 94305-3084. Phone: (415) 725-1676. Free.

CDS: The Johns Hopkins University. Published by the Center For Research on Effective Schooling for Disadvantaged Students, 3505 N. Charles St., Baltimore, MD 21218. (301) 338-7570.

Changing Schools. The Journal of Alternative Education. Published three times a year. Colorado Options in Education, 98 N. Wadsworth Blvd., #127, Box 191, Lakewood, CO 80226. $15 a year.

Community Learning Centers. Published monthly by Public School Incentives, 2550 University Ave., W., Suite 347N, St. Paul, MN 55114-1052. Telephone: (612) 645-0200. Free.

Educating At-Risk Youth. A publication of the National Professional Resources, Inc., P.O. Box 1479, Port Chester, NY 10573. Telephone: (914) 937-8879. Fax: (914) 937-9327. Published September-June (10 issues), $68 a year.

Educational Directions: Reaching Excellence With Alternatives. Annual publication of the Florida Association of Alternative School Educators, Inc., 7608 Royal Palm Way, Boca Raton, FL 33432. (407) 395-3063. Individual copies cost $2.00.

Educational Leadership. Published monthly by Association for Supervision and Curriculum Development, 1250 North Pitt Street, Alexandria, VA 22314.

Education Literature Review. Published monthly by Management Development Associates, 421 Second Street NW, Winter Haven, FL 33881. Phone: (941) 293-4882. $135 a year.

Fine Print. A periodic publication of the Center for School Change. Hubert H. Humphrey Institute of Public Affairs, 301 19th Avenue South, University of Minnesota, Minneapolis, MN 55455. $5 a year.

The Harvard Education Letter. Bi-monthly publication of the Harvard Graduate School of Education, Longfellow Hall, Apian Way, Cambridge, MA 02138-3752. Subscription is $24.00 a year.

Horace. Published monthly by Coalition of Essential Schools, Box 1969, Brown University, Providence, RI 02903. Phone: (401) 351-2525. Fax: (401) 351-0882. Internet: <http://www.essentialschools.org>.

Issues in Restructuring Schools. Published quarterly by Center on Organization and Restructuring of Schools, School of Education, University of Wisconsin–Madison, 1025 W. Johnson Street, Madison, WI 53706. Phone: (608) 263-7575. Free.

The Journal of At-Risk Issues. Published biannually by the National Dropout Prevention Center/Network, 209 Martin Street, Clemson, SC 29634-0726. Phone: (864) 656-2599. $25 a year.

The Journal of Education for Students Placed at Risk. Published quarterly by Lawrence Erlbaum Associates, Inc., 10 Industrial Avenue, Mahwah, NJ, 07430. Phone: (201) 236-0072. Internet: <http://www.erlbaum.com>.

The National Dropout Prevention Newsletter. A quarterly publication of the National Dropout Prevention Network and the National Dropout Prevention Center, Clemson University, Clemson, SC 29634-5111. Phone: (803) 656-2599. $25 a year.

Northwest Education. Published quarterly by the Northwest Regional laboratory, 101 SW Maine Street, Suite 500, Portland, OR 97204. Phone: (503) 275-9515.

Media

America's schools: Who gives a damn? (1991). New York: Columbia University, School of Journalism; Public Broadcasting System. 120 minutes.

Breaking the cycle: Parent and early childhood education: The Kenan model. (1990). Louisville, KY: National Center for Family Literacy. 15 minutes.

Can schools really help all children learn? (1999). Arlington Heights, IL: Skylight. 85 minutes.

Charter school idea. (1995). South Carolina: South Carolina ETV. 120 minutes.

Common good: Social welfare and the American future. (1990). New York: The Ford Foundation. 20 minutes.

Crafting of America's schools: The power of localism. (1997). Port Chester, NY: National Professional Resources. 40 minutes.

Diversities in mentoring: Profiles from programs serving minority and at-risk youth. (1990). Pittsburgh, PA: Project Literacy. 56 minutes.

Effective schools for children at risk. (1991). Alexandria, VA: Association for School and Curriculum Development. 8 minutes.

"Every child can succeed." (1992). Bloomington, IN: Agency for Instructional Technology. (900) 451-4509. "Every child can succeed" is an educational package containing print material and 17 twenty-to-thirty minute video programs profiling elementary schools that have succeeded in effectively teaching children at risk of school failure. The material, developed as part of a systematic effort to study and document school success, can be used separately or as a series to provide a complete professional development program for parents, teachers, and administrators.

Failing grades: Canadian schooling in a global economy. (1993). Canada: Society for Advancing Educational Research, VICOM. 76 minutes.

Getting back on track: Video solutions to reaching America's at-risk youth. South Carolina Educational Television, P.O. Box 11000, Columbia, SC 29211. Telephone: (800) 553-7752.

Growing up at risk. (1988). Dayton, OH: Kettering Foundation. 12 minutes.

Has anyone seen Phil? (1989). Dallas, TX: Plays for Living Production in association with J.C. Penney Company, Inc. 45 minutes.

How are kids smart? Multiple intelligences in the classroom. (1995). Port Chester, NY: National Professional Resources, Inc. 31 minutes.

Judicious discipline: Students as citizens in the classroom. (no date). Communication Media Center. 30 minutes.

Learn and live. (1997). George Lucas Educational Foundation. 60 minutes.

Learning to change: Schools of excellence for at-risk students. (1990). Atlanta, GA: Southern Regional Council, Inc. 29 minutes.

Masters of disaster. (1985). Bloomington, IN: Indiana University. 29 minutes.

Milestones in mentoring. (1990). Pittsburgh, PA: Project Literacy. 120 minutes.

Multicultural prism: Voices from the field. (no date). Illinois: Expanding Cultural Diversity Project, Western Illinois University. 38 minutes.

New American schools: A preview. (1996). Denver, CO: Education Commission of the States, New American Schools Development Corporation. 8 minutes.

Off track: Classroom privilege for all. (1998). New York: Columbia University, Teachers College Press. 30 minutes.

One plus one. (1989). Pittsburgh, PA: Plus Project Literacy. 60 minutes.

Partners for success. (1990). Portland, OR: Westcom Productions, Inc. 31 minutes.

Partners in education. (1989). Northbrook, IL: Mindscape, Inc. 17 minutes.

Polished stones: Mathematics achievement among Chinese and Japanese elementary school students. (1989). Michigan: University of Michigan. 35 minutes.

Project second chance: Dropouts in America. (n.d.) Arkansas Educational Television Network Foundation. 60 minutes.

Restructuring America's schools: Special preview. (1991). Alexandria, VA: Association for School and Curriculum Development. 6 minutes.

Schools that work: Learning in America. (1990). Arlington, VA: McNeil/Lehrer and WETA-TV. 120 minutes.

Stand and deliver. (1988). Warner Brothers, Inc. 103 minutes.

Will school reform ever work? (1999). Arlington Heights, IL: Skylight. 80 minutes.

Why do these kids love school? (1990). Menlo Park, CA: Concentric Media. 60 minutes.

Sources for Funding

The following private and public agencies, corporations, and foundations have identified improving the lives of at-risk youth as a funding priority. For up-to-date information, funding guidelines, and applications, contact the foundation or agency directly, as funding priorities are subject to change on a yearly basis.

Each of the following sources has, in the past, funded at-risk projects. The majority of them accept proposals on an open cycle basis without yearly deadlines. Most of these funding agencies have yearly grant amounts which are based on their own investment earnings; thus, amounts available for funding vary. This list represents a limited selection of funding sources.

When contacting a funding source, it is recommended that a careful review of guidelines and application procedures be completed prior to proposal development and submission. Those listings without telephone numbers prefer to be contacted by mail. These resources serve as an appropriate initial step toward the determination and location of appropriate external funding agencies which individuals, agencies, schools, and programs may consider for projects related to at-risk youth.

Two recommended resources, in addition to the list below, are the *National Guide to Funding for Elementary and Secondary Education*. The Foundation Center, 79 Fifth Avenue, Dept. TY, New York, NY 10003-3050 (also available in major libraries) and *Grants for At-Risk Youth,* second edition, Aspen Publishers Inc., 200 Orchard Ridge Drive, Gaithersburg, MD, 20878. Phone 1-800-638-8437. <www.aspenpublishers.com>.

Aetna Life and Casualty Foundation, National Grants Program, Youth Employment, 151 Farmington Avenue, Hartford, CT 06156, (203) 273-3340

Alcoa Foundation Grants—Education, Alcoa Foundation, 1501 Alcoa Building, Pittsburgh, PA 15219, (412) 553-4696

Allstate Foundation Grants, Allstate Foundation, Allstate Plaza, F-3, Northbrook, IL 60062

American Express Foundation Grants, American Express Foundation, American Express Plaza, 19th, New York, NY 10004

AMR Corporation Grants Program, AMR Corporation, P.O. Box 61616, Dallas/Fort Worth Airport, TX 75361

Apple Computer Corporation, 4000 Kruse Way Place, Building 1 Suite 100, Lake Oswego, OR 97035, (503) 635-7711

Apple Corporate Grants, Apple Computer Corporation, 20525 Mariana Avenue, Cupertino, CA 95014, (408) 996-1010

Arco Foundation Education Grants, Arco Foundation, 515 S. Flower Street, Los Angeles, CA 90071, (213) 486-3334

Boeing Company Charitable Trust Grants, Boeing Company Charitable Trusts, 7755 E. Marginal Way S., Seattle, WA 98124, (206) 655-1131

Carnegie Corporation of New York, 437 Madison Avenue, New York, NY 10022, (212) 371-3200

Chevron Contributions Program, Chevron Corporation, P.O. Box 7753, San Francisco, CA 94120-7753, (415) 894-5464

Coca-Cola Foundation, P.O. Drawer 1734, Atlanta, GA 30301, (404) 676-2121

Danforth Foundation, Gene Schwilck, 231 S. Bemiston Avenue, St. Louis, MO 63105, (314) 862-6200

Davis (Edwin W. & Catherine M.) Foundation, 2100 First National Bank Building, St. Paul, MN 55101, (612) 228-0935

Dayton Hudson Corporation Foundation Grants, 77 Nicollet Mall, Minneapolis, MN 55402, (612) 370-6948

Dresser Foundation Grants, Dresser Foundation, P.O. Box 718, Dallas, TX 75221

Exxon Education Foundation Grants, Exxon Education Foundation, P.O. Box 101, Florham Park, NJ 07932, (214) 444-1104

FMC Foundation Grants, 200 East Randolph Drive, Chicago, IL 60601, (312) 861-6135

Ford Foundation, 320 East 43rd Street, New York, NY 10017, (212) 573-5000

General Mills Foundation Grants, General Mills Foundation, P.O. Box 1113, Minneapolis, MN 55440, (612) 540-3338

Grant (William T.) Foundation, Faculty Scholars Program, 515 Madison Avenue, New York, NY 10022-5403, (212) 752-0071

Green (Allen P. & Josephine B.) Foundation, Box 523, Mexico, MO 65265

Hazen (Edward W.) Foundation, 505 Eighth Avenue, 23rd Floor, New York, NY 10018, (212) 967-5920

Hearst Foundation, 888 Seventh Avenue, 27th floor, New York, NY 10106, (415) 543-0400

IBM Corporation, IBM Education Systems, 4111 Northside Parkway, Atlanta, GA 30327, (404) 238-3981

Johnson (Robert Wood) Foundation, College Road, P.O. Box 2316, Princeton, NJ 08543-2316, (609) 452-8701

Joyce Foundation, Discretionary Fund, 135 South LaSalle Street, Suite 4010, Chicago, IL 60603-4886, (312) 782-2464

Kellogg (W.K.) Foundation, Executive Assistant-Programming, 400 North Avenue, Battle Creek, MI 49017-3398, (616) 968-1611

MacArthur (John D. & Catherine T.) Foundation, Education Programs, 140 South Dearborn Street, Chicago, IL 60603, (312) 726-8000

Meyer (Fred) Charitable Trust, 1515 Southwest Fifth Avenue, Suite 500, Portland, OR 97201 (503) 228-5512

Moody Foundation Grants, 704 Moody National Bank Building, Galveston, TX 77550

Mott (Charles Stewart) Foundation, 1200 Mott Foundation Bldg., Flint, MI 48502-1851, (313) 238-5651

Oregon Community Foundation, 1110 Yeon Building, 522 Southwest Fifth Avenue, Portland, OR 97204, (503) 227-6846

Pew Charitable Trust, Health and Human Services, Three Parkway, Suite 501, Philadelphia, PA 19102-1305, (215) 587-4054

Phillips Petroleum Foundation Grants, 16th Floor, Phillips Building, Bartlesville, OK 74004, (918) 661-9072

Polaroid Foundation, 750 Main Street, Cambridge, MA 02139, (617) 577-4035

Prudential Foundation Grants, Prudential Plaza, Newark, NJ 07101, (201) 802-7354

Richardson (Smith) Foundation, Children and Families At Risk Program, 266 Post East, Westport, CT 06880, (212) 861-8181

RJR Nabisco Foundation, RJR Nabisco, Inc., Roger Semerad, 1456 Pennsylvania Ave., NW, Suite 525, Washington, DC 20004, (202) 626-3200

Rockefeller Foundation Grant Program, Hugh B. Price, 1133 Avenue of the Americas, New York, NY 10036, (212) 869-8500

Scripps Howard Foundation, Albert J. Schottelkotte, P.O. Box 5380, Cincinnati, OH 45201, (513) 977-3825

Spencer Foundation, 900 North Michigan Avenue, Suite 2800, Chicago, IL 60611, (312) 337-7000

Templeton (Herbert A.) Foundation, 1717 S.W. Park Avenue, Portland, OR 97201, (503) 223-0036

Toyota USA Foundation, 19001 South Western Avenue, Torrance, CA 90509, (213) 618-6766

Tucker (Rose E.) Charitable Trust, 900 Southwest Fifth Avenue, 24th Floor, Portland, OR 97204, (503) 224-3380

UPS Foundation Grants, UPS Foundation, 51 Weaver Street, Greenwich Office Park 5, Greenwich, CT 06836-3160, (203) 862-6287

Xerox Corporation Educational and Career Opportunities for Young People, Xerox Corporation, P.O. Box 1600, Stamford, CT 06904, (203) 968-3306

Appendix B

School Self-Evaluation Checklists for Serving Students At Risk

In order to provide schools and communities with assistance in ensuring that all students at risk can be adequately served, five self-evaluation checklists have been included. These self-evaluation checklists include:

- Staff Self-Evaluation Checklist: Beliefs/Baseline Assessments
- Evaluation Profile: Preschool and Elementary School
- Evaluation Profile: Middle Level School
- Evaluation Profile: High School
- Student Self-Evaluation Checklist

These self-evaluation instruments have been developed and field tested in order to stimulate discussions in schools and communities and serve as evaluation tools. The checklists relate statements of fact, perceptions, and beliefs to the best available research on students at risk and provide a basis for school/community consensus building. They also provide a way for schools and communities to monitor baseline data and to evaluate their effectiveness in meeting the needs of at-risk youth. Each statement in the five checklists relates directly to research findings and experienced-based practice that have been discussed.

The first checklist focuses on beliefs and is presented in an agree—disagree format. It also includes a baseline assessment profile. The following three checklists provide a way to inventory and evaluate the degree to which a specific school is addressing the needs of students at risk.

Staff Self-Evaluation Checklist

Beliefs

The following self-evaluation was created based on a comprehensive review of research and evaluation of schools that document success with all children. This checklist should provide a strong indicator of whether or not the teachers, administration, and parents associated with a school have the beliefs and dispositions necessary to guarantee success for students at risk. For personal, schoolwide, or school/community assessment, please answer the following questions. Following the completion of the self-evaluation, small groups should discuss their responses and attempt to develop consensus points of view.

Alternative Program: Staff Survey

Program:_____   Host School:_____

Circle one: **Building Administrator   Team/Program Leader   Teacher   Other**

Circle the most appropriate answers to the questions in this survey.

1. **Do students volunteer to participate in the program?**

   Always   Sometimes   Seldom   Never   Uncertain

2. **Are there established criteria for admitting students to the program?**

   Yes   No   Uncertain

3. **Do teachers participate in the student admission process?**

   Always   Sometimes   Seldom   Never   Uncertain

4. **Are students ever denied admission?**

   Often   Sometimes   Seldom   Never   Uncertain

5. **Are students ever assigned to the program?**

   Often   Sometimes   Seldom   Never   Uncertain

6. **Do you believe the teachers in the program care about their students?**

   All   Most   Some   None

7. **Do you believe that teachers in the program hold high expectations for all students?**

   All   Most   Some   None

8. **Did you choose to work in this program?**

   Yes   No   N/A

9. **Do the teachers and students form a positive learning community?**

   Yes   Somewhat   Seldom   No

10. **Do you have a specific background or training that prepared you for work with this program?**

    Substantial   Some   Little   None

11. **May teachers easily transfer to another school or program if they are dissatisfied?**

    Yes   No

12. **Are noncertified teachers employed in this program?**

    Often   Seldom   Never

13. **Are there specific criteria for hiring/placing teachers in the program?**

    Yes   No

14. **Are parents or others involved in the hiring of the program's faculty?**

    Yes   Somewhat   Minimally   No

15. **Is the program's curriculum designed to meet the needs of all enrolled?**

    Yes   Somewhat   Minimally   No

16. **Does the program provide individualized instruction?**

    Always   Often   Seldom   Never

17. **Does the program provide competency-based learning?**

    Yes   No

18. **Does the program utilize learning contracts?**

    Always   Often   Seldom   Never

19. **Does the program emphasize the development of self-concept and self-esteem?**

    Always   Often   Seldom   Never

20. **Does the program provide opportunities to "catch up" or "accelerate" learning?**

    Yes   No

21. **Do students have a choice in program classes and curriculum?**

    Yes   No

22. **Does the program complement classroom teaching and learning with out-of-school opportunities?**

    Yes   No

23. **Does the program use incentives to motivate students?**

    Yes   No

24. **If the students lack basic skills (e.g., reading), does the program provide interventions?**

    Yes   No

25. **Does the program provide one-to-one tutoring?**

    Yes   No

26. **Does the program offer a vocational, technical, or career emphasis?**

    Yes   No

27. **Does the program involve the students in community internships?**

    Yes   No

28. **Does the program involve the students in community service activities?**

    Often   Seldom   Never

29. **Does the program conduct follow-up study/monitoring of exiting/ graduating students?**

    Yes   No

30. **Does the staff use technology in their teaching?**

    Often   Seldom   Never

31. **Might the program be more successful if located in a separate facility?**

    Yes   No   Uncertain

32. **May students attend the program on a part-time basis?**

    Yes   No

33. **Does the program operate beyond the regular host school hours?**

    Yes   No

34. **Does the program provide short-term granting of academic credit (as opposed to quarterly/semester)?**

    Yes   No

35. **Does the program operate in the summer?**

    Yes   No

36. **Does the program have a partnership(s) with local business or industry?**

    Yes   No

37. **Does the program utilize volunteers as a resource?**

    Yes   No

38. **Does the program assist students with accessing social services (food stamps, housing, transportation, counseling, etc.)?**

    Yes   No

39. **Does the program assist students with accessing health/medical services?**

    Yes   No

40. **Does the program offer any of the following?**

    - Drug and Alcohol Prevention Programs   Yes   No
    - Parenting Education   Yes   No
    - Pre/Post-Natal Programs/Services   Yes   No
    - Child Care Programs   Yes   No
    - Counseling Programs   Yes   No
    - Self-Esteem-Building Activities   Yes   No
    - Peer Tutoring   Yes   No
    - Cross-Age Tutoring   Yes   No
    - Self-Help Groups   Yes   No
    - Athletics/Sports   Yes   No
    - Music   Yes   No
    - Arts   Yes   No
    - Physical Education   Yes   No
    - Outdoor Education   Yes   No

- Entrepreneurial Opportunities   Yes   No
- Special Education Services   Yes   No
- Mentor Program   Yes   No
- Job Services   Yes   No

41. Overall, how would you rate the success of the program?

Very successful   Somewhat successful   Not very successful   Not successful

42. Please provide additional comments on program strengths or needed improvements.

Baseline Assessment Profile

Schools should establish baseline data to effectively monitor progress toward identifying and serving the at-risk student population. Data should be updated and reviewed on a regular basis by the school staff and community.

1. What percentage of students score at or above national averages on standardized achievement tests? _____

2. What percentage of students qualify for free lunch programs? _____

3. What percentage of students qualify for Chapter I services? _____

4. What is the school's average weekly absentee rate? _____

5. What percentage of the students qualify for special education services? _____

6. What percentage of the students are identified as learning disabled? _____

7. What percentage of the students qualify for bilingual services? _____

8. What percentage of the students have received counseling or other social services for crisis intervention? _____

9. What percentage of the students have been adjudicated? _____

10. What is the school's weekly average number of incidents of violence or vandalism? _____

11. What is the school's weekly average number of classroom disruptions that are referred to the principal? _____

12. What is the dropout rate for the school? _____

13. What is the percentage of teenage mothers in the school? _____

14. Does the school maintain an intervention team to support at-risk youth? _____

15. Does the school provide a diverse array of intervention services for at-risk youth? _____

Evaluation Profile: Preschool and Elementary School

Please check each statement that reflects an accurate description of your school or school district. This checklist can be used individually or by groups of teachers, parents, and administrators. Discussions should then be conducted to compare individual responses and work for schoolwide consensus on as many items as possible. Once completed, the checklist should serve as a profile of the school's effectiveness in addressing the needs of students at risk. The profile can also be used to compare the effectiveness of different schools in serving students at risk.

Shared Vision/Goals

1. Does the school have a shared vision and/or agreed-upon schoolwide goals? _____

2. Is the school involved in a schoolwide improvement or restructuring program that is supported by the majority of teachers and parents, (i.e., programs like Success For All, Accelerated Schools, or some local independent plan)? _____

3. Do teachers, parents, and the principal share the responsibility for planning, governing, and managing the school? _____

4. Does the school district encourage local control or have a policy providing site-based management? _____

5. Does the school have a planning or governance council consisting of parents, teachers, and administrators? _____

6. Does the school regularly utilize parents and other adults as classroom volunteers? _____

7. Does the school district provide alternative schools that focus on different approaches to teaching and learning (e.g., Montessori schools, nongraded schools, open schools, continuous progress schools)? _____

8. Does the school serve less than 500 students? _____

9. Do parents, teachers, and administrators hold high expectations for all students? _____

Parents

10. Does your school have a parenting skills program? _____

11. Does your school offer opportunities for parents to help children prepare for school? _____

12. Are parents encouraged to assist in the school's instructional programs? _____

13. If parents are unable or unwilling to assist in the school's instructional programs, are supplemental arrangements provided for these children? _____

14. Are parents encouraged to volunteer in the school? _____

15. Are parents provided an opportunity to participate in school planning and governance? _____

Early Childhood and Preschool

16. Does the school have a child care program? _____

17. Does the school have a preschool program? _____

18. Does the school have a kindergarten program? _____

19. Does the school provide all-day kindergarten? _____

20. Does the school participate in a Head Start or similar preschool enrichment program? _____

Curriculum and Instruction

21. Does the school qualify for Chapter I? _____

22. Does the school qualify for a schoolwide Chapter I program? _____

23. Does the school participate in the Reading Recovery program? _____

24. Does the school use a one-to-one tutorial program:
    - using the Reading Recovery program? _____
    - using trained, certified teachers? _____
    - using trained volunteers? _____
    - using peer tutors? _____

25. Does the school curriculum emphasize reading, writing, story telling and communicating? _____

26. Does the school utilize a non-graded or multi-age grouping in the early elementary grades?   _____

27. Does the school encourage cooperative learning?   _____

28. Does the school cluster computers in each elementary classroom? _____

29. Does the school provide enriched resources for the preschool through third grade?   _____

30. Does the school have a program of frequent, continuous, and planned student assessment of reading, writing, and mathematics? _____

31. Do all third graders in the school read at or above grade level? _____

32. Does the school refuse to retain students in grades K–3?   _____

33. Does the school teach all children as if they were gifted and talented?   _____

34. Does the school place primary emphasis on ensuring a strong foundation in the subjects of reading, writing, and math?   _____

35. Do students tutor one another?   _____

Social Services

36. Does the school have a free breakfast program for qualifying students?   _____

37. Does the school have a free lunch program for qualifying students? _____

38. Does the school have some type of youth services council or committee, comprised of school and social service agencies, that addresses the needs of at-risk youth and their families using a case management approach?   _____

39. Does the school have a free meal program during the summer?   _____

40. Does the school coordinate the resources and services of social service agencies?   _____

41. Does the school participate in community partnerships?   _____

42. Does the school have a morning or afternoon extended day program for latchkey, at-risk, and other students?   _____

43. Does the school provide counselors or social workers to assist students and their families?   _____

After individual teachers, administrators, and parents have completed the checklist and through discussions have developed schoolwide consensus on as many items as possible, the profile should serve as an indicator of effectiveness in meeting the needs of students at risk. Since each item on the Evaluation Profile reflects the best available research regarding the components of school effectiveness for students at risk, the greater the number of items that accurately describe a school, the greater the likelihood that the school is effectively serving students at risk.

Evaluation Profile: Middle-Level School

Please check each statement that reflects an adequate description of your school or school district. This checklist can be used individually or by groups of teachers, parents, and administrators. Once consensus items are identified, the checklist should serve as a profile of the school's effectiveness in addressing the needs of students at risk. The profile can also be used to compare the effectiveness of different schools in serving students at risk.

Shared Vision/Goals

1. Have teachers, administrator, and parents conducted a consensus-building process that has culminated in a shared vision and/or schoolwide goals? _____

2. Is the school organization modeled more on elementary schools than senior high schools? _____

3. Are students involved in the planning and governance of the school through some type of student council or student government? _____

4. Does the school have a planning and/or governance committee or council that includes teachers, administrators, parents and students? _____

Curriculum and Instruction

5. Has the school been organized into a number of small learning groups where a cohort of students and teachers work together for most of the school day? _____

6. Does the school curriculum include a focus on the developmental needs of young adolescents (e.g., healthy lifestyles, sexual and social development, communication, critical thinking, recreation)? _____

7. Does the school curriculum include an interdisciplinary core? _____

8. Does the school use flexible scheduling to provide longer blocks of time for core subjects and interdisciplinary study? _____

9. Does the school offer a number of elective courses that focus on career education and exploration, recreation, and interest areas? _____

10. Does the school emphasize cooperative learning in the classroom? _____

11. Are students grouped into heterogeneous classes? _____

12. Does the school have a mentor program for students at risk? _____

13. Does the school have a counselor or social worker who assists students and their families? _____

14. Does the school have a computer technology laboratory? _____

15. Does the school have clusters of computers in each classroom? _____

16. Do teachers serve as classroom counselors and advisors during a prescribed time during the day? _____

17. Does the school involve students in out-of-school activities?
    - Field trips _____
    - Career exploration _____
    - Service activities _____
    - Cross-age tutoring _____
    - Intramural sports/recreation _____
    - Other _____

18. Does the school provide drug and alcohol programs for students who need them? _____

19. Is the school involved in a schoolwide restructuring or improvement effort that is supported by the majority of the teachers? _____

20. Do students in the school have opportunities to participate in alternative programs? _____

21. Are there high expectations for student learning? _____

22. Are these high expectations held for all students? _____

23. Does the school have opportunities for students to participate in clubs and extra-curricular activities? _____

24. Does the school have a transition program to help elementary students successfully matriculate to the middle-level school? _____

25. Does the school have a transition program to help students matriculate to high school? _____

26. Do students have opportunities to participate in after-school community youth clubs? _____

27. Are opportunities provided to learn the skills of conflict resolution? _____

Parents

28. Are parents involved in establishing school and community rules and regulations? _____

29. Are parents encouraged to be involved in the school? _____

30. Do parents participate as volunteers in the schools? _____

31. Are parents encouraged to assist students with homework? _____

After individual teachers, administrators and parents have completed the checklist and through discussions have developed schoolwide consensus on as many items as possible, the profile should serve as an indicator of effectiveness in meeting the needs of students at risk. Since each item on the Evaluation Profile reflects the best available research regarding the components of school effectiveness for students at risk, the greater the number of items that accurately describe a school, the greater the likelihood that the school is effectively serving students at risk.

Evaluation Profile: High School

Please check each statement that reflects an adequate description of your school and/or school district. This checklist can be used individually or by groups of teachers, parents, and administrators. Once consensus items are identified, the checklist should serve as a profile of the school's effectiveness in addressing the needs of students at-risk. The profile can also be used to compare the effectiveness of different schools in serving students at risk.

Shared Vision/Goals

1. Does the school have a shared vision and/or agreed upon schoolwide goals? _____

2. Is the school involved in a schoolwide improvement or restructuring program that is supported by the majority of teachers and parents (i.e., programs like Coalition of Essential Schools)? _____

3. Do teachers, parents, and the principal share the responsibility for planning, governing, and managing the school? _____

4. Does the school district encourage local control or have a policy providing site-based management? _____

5. Does the school have a planning or governance council consisting of parents, teachers, and administrators? _____

6. Does the school regularly utilize parents and other adults as classroom volunteers? _____

7. Does the school offer a school-within-a-school or alternative programs? _____

8. Do parents, teachers, and administrators hold high expectations for all students? _____

Parents

9. If parents are unable or unwilling to assist in the school's instructional programs, are supplemental arrangements provided for these children? _____

10. Are parents encouraged to volunteer in the school? _____

11. Are parents provided an opportunity to participate in school planning and governance? _____

Curriculum and Instruction

12. Does the public school offer alternative or magnet programs specifically designed to meet the needs of at-risk youth? _____

13. Are all students, regardless of academic levels, offered the opportunities to participate in district alternative/magnet schools? _____

14. Does the district offer some type of teen parent program or young parent program? _____

15. Is the teen parent program designed to provide an educational program for all teen parents in the community? _____

16. Does the school district offer a comprehensive vocational training program? _____

17. Does the school district or school have a 2 + 2 program in cooperation with a local community college? _____

18. Does the school district or school participate in a partnership with local business and industry or a Private Industry Council? _____

19. Does the school district or school participate in apprenticeship programs? _____

20. Does the school district or school offer any program similar to the Foxfire Experience? _____

21. Does the school district or school provide for real life, out of school programs? _____

22. Does the school district or school have a mentoring program? _____

23. Does the school district or school have a career education program? _____

24. Do students in the school district or school have access to a U.S. Job Corp program? _____

25. Does the school district or school offer students a summer catch-up program or evening program? _____

26. Does the school district or school offer students a high school equivalency program? _____

27. Does the school district or school offer students the opportunity to leave high school and pursue coursework at a community college or university? _____

28. Does the school district or school provide students with the opportunity to use computers, in conjunction with classroom instruction? _____

29. Does the school district or school provide for drug and alcohol prevention programs and drug and alcohol support groups? _____

30. Does the school district or school have a health clinic available for high school students? _____

31. Does the school district or school participate in a self-esteem building program? _____

32. Does the school have an outdoor education program? _____

Social Services

33. Does the school have a free breakfast program for qualifying students? _____

34. Does the school have a free lunch program for qualifying students? _____

35. Does the school have some type of Youth Services Council or committee, comprised of school and social services agencies that addresses the needs of at-risk youth and their families using a case management approach? _____

36. Does the school have a free meal program during the summer? _____

37. Does the school coordinate the resources and services of social service agencies? _____

38. Does the school participate in community partnerships? _____

39. Does the school have a morning and/or afternoon extended day program for latchkey, at-risk and other students? _____

40. Does the school provide counselors or social workers to assist students and their families? _____

After individual teachers, administrators, and parents have completed the checklist and through discussions have developed schoolwide consensus on as many items as possible, the profile should serve as an indicator of effectiveness in meeting the needs of students at risk. Since each item on the Evaluation Profile reflects the best available research regarding the components of school effectiveness for students at risk, the greater the number of items that accurately describe a school, the greater the likelihood that the school is effectively serving students at risk.

Alternative Program: Student Survey

Program:_____   High School:_____

Circle the most appropriate answers to the questions in this survey.

1. **Do you believe the teachers in the program care about their students?**

   All   Most   Some   None

2. **Do you believe that teachers in the program hold high expectations for all students?**

   All   Most   Some   None

3. **Did you participate in an orientation prior to beginning in the program?**

   Yes   No

4. **Did your parents participate in an orientation prior to your enrolling in the program?**

   Yes   No

5. **Were you assigned to the program?**

   Yes   No

6. **Did you and/or your parents sign a contract prior to admission to the program?**

   Yes   No

7. **Would the program be more successful if operated in a separate facility?**

   Yes   No   Uncertain

8. **Do you feel safe in the program?**

   Yes   No

9. **Does the program involve the students in community-based learning?**

   Yes   No

10. **Does the program involve the students in community service activities?**

    Often   Seldom   Never

11. **Do students use technology in their classes at school?**

    Often   Seldom   Never

12. **Do the teachers and students form a positive learning community?**

    Yes   Somewhat   No

13. **Could you succeed if you transferred back to the traditional school?**

    Yes   No

14. **Is this program meeting your educational needs?**

    Yes   No

15. **What are the best aspects of the program?**

16. **What needs to be improved in the program?**

17. **Overall, how would you rate the success of the program?**

    Very successful   Somewhat successful   Not very successful   Not successful

Index